# Beginning C# 7 Hands-On – The Core Language

Learn the C# language by coding it element by element

**Tom Owsiak**

BIRMINGHAM - MUMBAI

# Beginning C# 7 Hands-On – The Core Language

First published: August 2017

Production reference: 2121017

Published by Packt Publishing Ltd.
Livery Place
35 Livery Street
Birmingham
B3 2PB, UK.

ISBN 978-1-78829-654-0

www.packtpub.com

# Credits

**Author**
Tom Owsiak

**Acquisition Editor**
Dominic Shakeshaft

**Content Development Editor**
Gary Schwartz

**Technical Editor**
Joel D'Souza

**Copy Editors**
Tom Jacob
Gladson Monteiro

**Project Coordinator**
Suzanne Coutinho

**Proofreader**
Safis Editing

**Indexer**
Rekha Nair

**Graphics**
Kirk D'Penha

**Production Coordinator**
Arvindkumar Gupta

# About the Author

**Tom Owsiak** has eight years of experience as a teacher in Mathematics, Physics, Statistics, and Programming. He has worked for five years as a database programmer using various technologies such as .NET, Clipper, SQL, SQL Server, SAS, and Excel, and many related technologies.

Tom is the publisher of one of the most successful courses on Udemy, called *Learn C# With Visual Studio 2013*. Currently, Tom works as a Mathematics and Computer Science teacher at Mercy College in Dobbs Ferry, NY.

# www.PacktPub.com

For support files and downloads related to your book, please visit www.PacktPub.com. Did you know that Packt offers eBook versions of every book published, with PDF and ePub files available? You can upgrade to the eBook version at www.PacktPub.com and as a print book customer, you are entitled to a discount on the eBook copy. Get in touch with us at service@packtpub.com for more details. At www.PacktPub.com, you can also read a collection of free technical articles, sign up for a range of free newsletters and receive exclusive discounts and offers on Packt books and eBooks.

https://www.packtpub.com

Get the most in-demand software skills with Mapt. Mapt gives you full access to all Packt books and video courses, as well as industry-leading tools to help you plan your personal development and advance your career.

# Why subscribe?

- Fully searchable across every book published by Packt
- Copy and paste, print, and bookmark content
- On demand and accessible via a web browser

# Customer Feedback

Thanks for purchasing this Packt book. At Packt, quality is at the heart of our editorial process. To help us improve, please leave us an honest review on this book's Amazon page at `https://www.amazon.com/dp/1788296540`.

If you'd like to join our team of regular reviewers, you can email us at `customerreviews@packtpub.com`. We award our regular reviewers with free eBooks and videos in exchange for their valuable feedback. Help us be relentless in improving our products!

# Table of Contents

# Preface

*Beginning C# Hands-On - The Core Language* teaches you the core C# language and syntax in a working Visual Studio environment. This book covers everything from the core language through to more advanced features, such as object-oriented programming techniques. This book is for C# beginners who need a practical reference to the core C# language features. You'll also gain a view of C# through web programming with web forms, so you'll learn HTML, basic CSS, and how to use a variety of controls, such as buttons and drop-down lists. You'll start with the fundamentals of C# and Visual Studio, including defining variables, interacting with users, and understanding data types, data conversions, and constants.

You'll move on to checking conditions using `if...else` blocks, and how to use loops to do things such as repeat blocks of code. After covering various operators to evaluate and assign control structures, you'll see how to use arrays to store collections of data. By the time you've finished the book, you'll know how to program the vital elements of the core C# language. These are the building blocks that you can then combine to build complex C# programs.

## What you need for this book

Visual Studio 2017 will install and run on Windows 7 or above, and 2 GB or 4 GB of RAM is recommended. Minimum 1 GB hard disk space is essential too.

## Who this book is for

This book will appeal to anyone who is interested in learning how to program in C#. Previous programming experience will help you get through the initial sections with ease, although it's not mandatory to possess any experience at all.

# Conventions

In this book, you will find a number of text styles that distinguish between different kinds of information. Here are some examples of these styles and an explanation of their meaning. Code words in text, database table names, folder names, filenames, file extensions, path names, dummy URLs, user input, and Twitter handles are shown as follows: "Specifically, `Default.aspx` is a file that contains the markup of the elements on the web page."

A block of code is set as follows:

```
<asp:DropDownList ID="DropDownList1" runat="server" AutoPostBack="True">
    <asp:ListItem>Monday</asp:ListItem>
    <asp:ListItem>Tuesday</asp:ListItem>
    <asp:ListItem>Wednesday</asp:ListItem>
</asp:DropDownList>
```

When we wish to draw your attention to a particular part of a code block, the relevant lines or items are set in bold:

```
<asp:DropDownList ID="DropDownList1" runat="server" AutoPostBack="True">
    <asp:ListItem>Monday</asp:ListItem>
    <asp:ListItem>Tuesday</asp:ListItem>
    <asp:ListItem>Wednesday</asp:ListItem>
</asp:DropDownList>
```

**New terms** and **important words** are shown in bold. Words that you see on the screen, for example, in menus or dialog boxes, appear in the text like this: "If you wish, click on **Browse** and save the file to a location you choose and click on **OK**."

Warnings or important notes appear like this.

Tips and tricks appear like this.

# Reader feedback

Feedback from our readers is always welcome. Let us know what you think about this book-what you liked or disliked. Reader feedback is important for us as it helps us develop titles that you will really get the most out of. To send us general feedback, simply email `feedback@packtpub.com`, and mention the book's title in the subject of your message. If there is a topic that you have expertise in and you are interested in either writing or contributing to a book, see our author guide at `www.packtpub.com/authors`.

# Customer support

Now that you are the proud owner of a Packt book, we have a number of things to help you to get the most from your purchase.

# Downloading the example code

You can download the example code files for this book from your account at `http://www.packtpub.com`. If you purchased this book elsewhere, you can visit `http://www.packtpub.com/support` and register to have the files emailed directly to you. You can download the code files by following these steps:

1. Log in or register to our website using your email address and password.
2. Hover the mouse pointer on the **SUPPORT** tab at the top.
3. Click on **Code Downloads & Errata**.
4. Enter the name of the book in the **Search** box.
5. Select the book for which you're looking to download the code files.
6. Choose from the drop-down menu where you purchased this book from.
7. Click on **Code Download**.

Once the file is downloaded, please make sure that you unzip or extract the folder using the latest version of:

- WinRAR / 7-Zip for Windows
- Zipeg / iZip / UnRarX for Mac
- 7-Zip / PeaZip for Linux

The code bundle for the book is also hosted on GitHub at
`https://github.com/PacktPublishing/Beginning-CSharp-Hands-On-The-Core-Language`.
We also have other code bundles from our rich catalog of books and videos available at
`https://github.com/PacktPublishing/`. Check them out!

# Downloading the color images of this book

We also provide you with a PDF file that has color images of the screenshots/diagrams used
in this book. The color images will help you better understand the changes in the output.
You can download this file from
`https://www.packtpub.com/sites/default/files/downloads/BeginningCSharpHandsOnTh`
`eCoreLanguage_ColorImages.pdf`.

# Errata

Although we have taken every care to ensure the accuracy of our content, mistakes do
happen. If you find a mistake in one of our books-maybe a mistake in the text or the code-
we would be grateful if you could report this to us. By doing so, you can save other readers
from frustration and help us improve subsequent versions of this book. If you find any
errata, please report them by visiting `http://www.packtpub.com/submit-errata`, selecting
your book, clicking on the **Errata Submission Form** link, and entering the details of your
errata. Once your errata are verified, your submission will be accepted and the errata will
be uploaded to our website or added to any list of existing errata under the Errata section of
that title. To view the previously submitted errata, go to
`https://www.packtpub.com/books/content/support` and enter the name of the book in the
search field. The required information will appear under the **Errata** section.

# Piracy

Piracy of copyrighted material on the internet is an ongoing problem across all media. At
Packt, we take the protection of our copyright and licenses very seriously. If you come
across any illegal copies of our works in any form on the internet, please provide us with
the location address or website name immediately so that we can pursue a remedy. Please
contact us at `copyright@packtpub.com` with a link to the suspected pirated material. We
appreciate your help in protecting our authors and our ability to bring you valuable
content.

# Questions

If you have a problem with any aspect of this book, you can contact us at
questions@packtpub.com, and we will do our best to address the problem.

# 1

# Why C# and How to Download and Install the Visual Studio Community Edition

If you visit a page like indeed.com and enter C# in the **what** box, you'll get results that show that there are many jobs in this field, as shown in *Figure 1.1.1*. This shows that C# is a very valuable skill to master. Perhaps you just like to tinker, and C# is great for that as well:

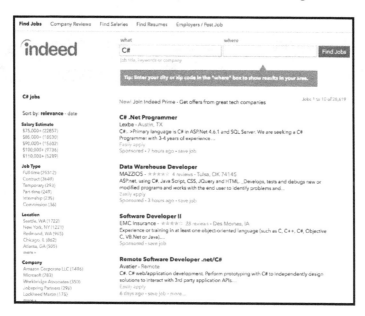

Figure 1.1.1: The many job listings for C# programmers

# Locating and downloading the Visual Studio Community edition

In this chapter, we're going to take a look at how to get Visual Studio 2017. You can either go directly to `www.visualstudio.com/downloads` or just do a search for Visual Studio 2017 download. This should bring you to a page similar to this one:

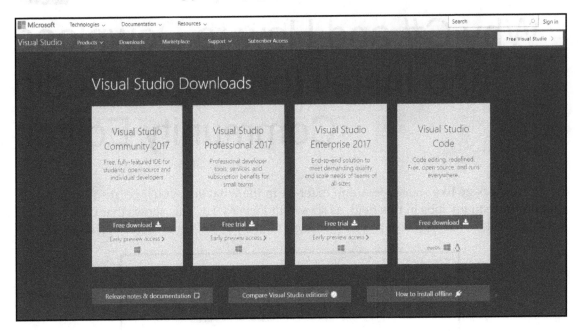

Figure 2.1:

Keep in mind that these pages are updated regularly. In the preceding screenshot, you will see that there are several versions. The one that interests us, of course, is Visual Studio Community 2017, the free version.

Click on **Free download**. This should automatically download a small installer. Depending on how your system is set up, it will either download it directly to the `Downloads` folder, or prompt you for where you want to save it. I've created a `VS_Community` folder inside `My Downloads` folder and saved it there. Of course, you can save it wherever you want to. Once this is done--it won't take long as it's just a small file--locate the downloaded `VS_Community.EXE` file and open it up.

Once you open it, you should see this screen.

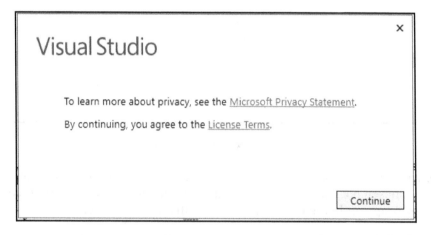

Figure 2.2: The License screen

Click on **Continue**, which should take you through to the next screen:

Figure 2.3: Choosing download components

From here, you can select the set of features you want to install on your system. For our purposes, I've chosen **.NET desktop development** at the top. If you click on it, you should see a check mark appear in the top corner to show that it's been selected:

Figure 2.4: Selecting .NET desktop development

Down at the bottom of the window, there's a location bar. If you click on the three little dots, you can select where you want the Visual Studio program to be installed on your system. On the right-hand side, you have a summary field:

Figure 2.5: Selecting the following frameworks

This tells you what's going to be installed; also, down at the bottom, it says **Total install size, 3.06 GB**, so that's how much minimum free space you need wherever you're going to install this. Then, of course, click on the **Install** button in the lower right-hand corner. This should bring you to a page similar to this one:

Figure 2.6: Installation in progress

Now, it's just a matter of waiting for everything to be downloaded and then applied to your system. One thing that I recommend you do at this point is temporarily disable your antivirus software while this is being installed because it could interfere with the installation process. I got to about 90 percent and my system hung when I installed it. I went back and disabled my anti-virus software and it installed fine. You may have to do the same.

Once it's downloaded and installed, you should see a screen similar to this one:

Figure 2.7: The Welcome screen

From here on, of course, you can either look at the release notes if you want, or just click on the **Launch** button. Go ahead and click on the **Launch** button. This should bring you to a screen similar to this one:

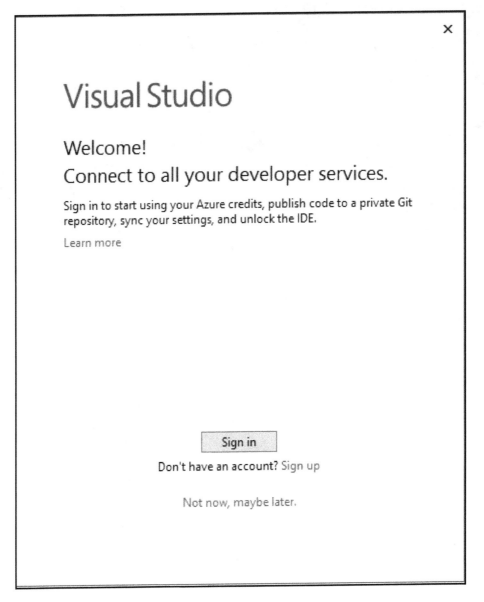

Figure 2.8: The Sign in screen

If you want, you can sign in with your Microsoft account,if you remember. I chose **Not now, maybe later**. The next step is to choose the interface:

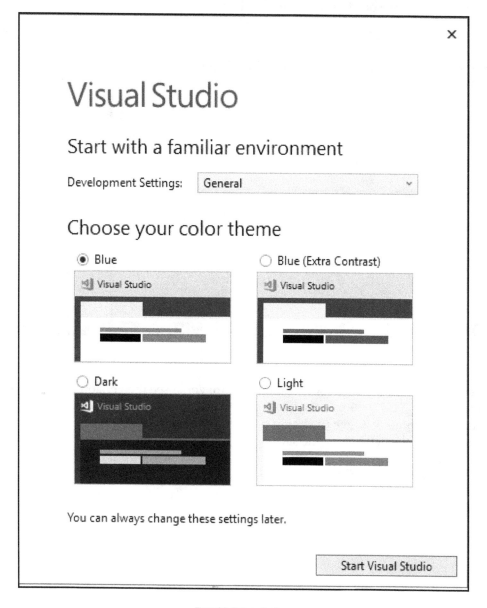

Figure 2.9: Choose color theme

I like the standard **Blue** one. Of course, you can use the **Dark** one or the **Light** one, whichever one you like, and then click on **Start Visual Studio**. Once it's loaded, it should look very similar to the one that you see right here:

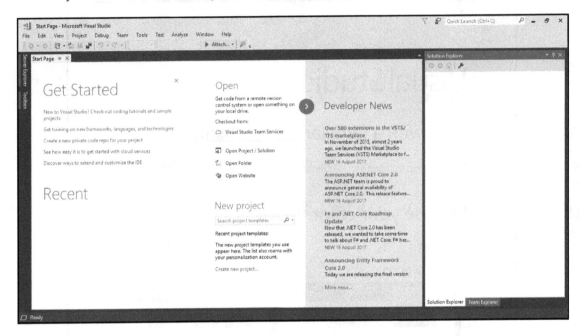

Figure 2.10: Getting Started

Now Go to **Help > About Microsoft Visual Studio**; you'll see the version that you have installed. Mine is 15.3.0, which is the latest version at the time of this writing. Make sure that yours is the same or above (it should be, as you just downloaded the latest version from Microsoft); otherwise, the code samples that we create will not work because they rely on the features of C# available in this version. Okay, close the **About** box. That's it! You're now ready to start learning C# 7.

# Summary

In this chapter, you learned how to locate, download, install, and launch Visual Studio Community.

In the next chapter, we'll take greater control of Visual Studio and configure it to some extent.

# 2

# Customizing Visual Studio to Make it Feel More Personal

In this chapter, we will configure the appearance of Visual Studio a little further.

## Customizing Visual Studio

To get started with customizing Visual Studio, click in the **Quick Launch** box in the upper right-hand corner, as shown in the following screenshot. Then, enter a word, such as font, and select the first item:

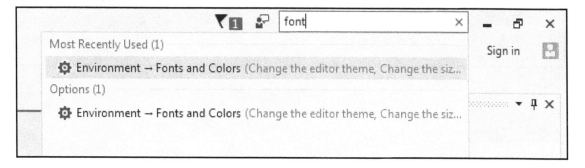

Figure 1.2.1: Searching for font settings options

# Selecting the text editor font and size

From here, you can configure many different settings. For example, you can select a **Text Editor**, which controls the size of the code in the window so that it's easy to read. The font size should be something big, such as 20—it makes a real difference; that is, when you are learning, how big things are makes a difference. They're easier to understand simply because they're bigger. Refer to the following screenshot to see how this is done:

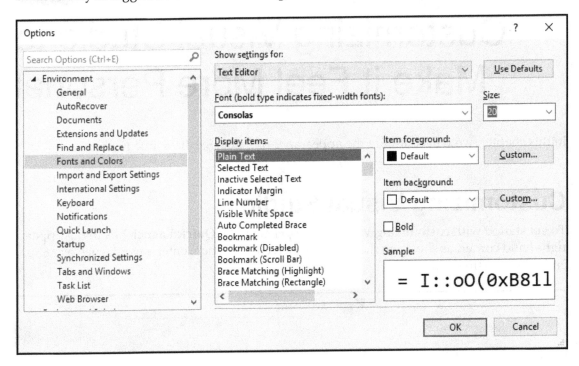

Figure 1.2.2: Selecting the text editor font and size

# Selecting the Statement Completion font and size

In the next stage, we will customize the **Statement Completion** settings, as shown in the following screenshot. This is a very useful feature that makes coding more efficient. Again, set it to something big:

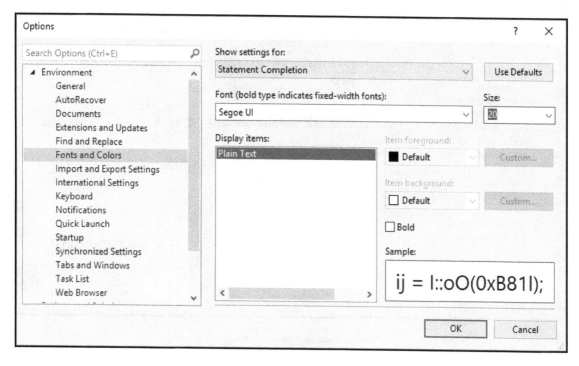

Figure 1.2.3: Selecting the Statement Completion font and size

# Selecting the Environment font and size

Next, let's configure the **Environment** fonts. Again, there are many possible options. One that I use very commonly is **Segoe UI**. Once more, set it to something big, for example,18; that is, something easy to read in any case, as shown in the following screenshot:

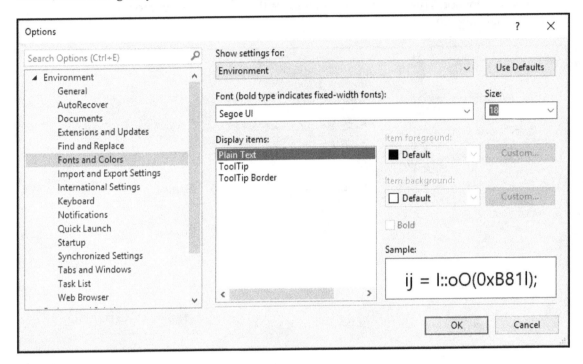

Figure 1.2.4: Selecting the Environment font and size

Click on **OK** when you're finished. Some of these changes take effect immediately and some don't. For example, as you will see with **Environment** fonts, the text enlarges immediately.

# Positioning Visual Studio panels

Now, one thing that's useful is being able to position some of the panels. What do I mean by this? Try the following.

Click on **View** and then select **Solution Explorer**—that's a window or a panel. You can position this panel in many places. If you click where it says **Solution Explorer** and drag it, you can liberate this panel and then place it where you like. You are also given a really nice preview of what to expect once it drops. So, if you drag the **Solution Explorer** and hover your mouse at the top box located on the cross, a transparent blue area appears. The blue area tells you that it's going to go across the top. Again, if you click and drag it to the left-hand side of the screen and drop it, the **Solution Explorer** will be positioned on the left-hand side.

Figure 1.2.5: Positioning the Solutions Explorer window

This is how you can control the layout of the panels—just drag them around the screen. Sometimes, you'll get a cross like the one shown in the preceding screenshot. This simply tells you that if you hover your mouse over the middle of the cross, the document that you're holding with your mouse will be tabbed together with other open windows, like the **Start Page** in this example. Now they are basically tabbed as a unit—the **Start Page** and the **Solution Explorer** panel. If you drag it once more and then drop it on the right-hand side, for instance, it will appear where it is commonly positioned:

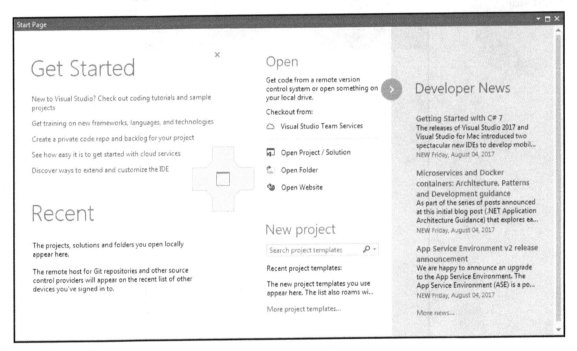

Figure 1.2.6: Positioning the Start Page panel

One more useful thing that you can do is enable **Auto Hide** of panels such as **Solutions Explorer**. This means that when you're not using a panel, it hides from view, giving you access to more space.

If you click on the pin at the top right-hand corner of the panel, as shown in the following screenshot, you can enable **Auto Hide**. On the other hand, if you want it back, you click on the words **Solution Explorer** that appear vertically below the right-hand side of the screen, and then it reappears. If you want to pin the panel back to the position you had selected, just click on the pin again. Now it is back to where you had positioned it, and it will stay there even if you mouse away from it:

Figure 1.2.7: Click on the pin at the top right-hand side of the Solutions Explorer window to enable Auto Hide

# Summary

In this chapter, we reviewed some of the things that you can do to make working in Visual Studio easier.

In the next chapter, we will create a simple C# program and run it.

# 3

# Creating and Running Your First Page

In this chapter, you will create and run a simple first web page. It will contain the minimum that you need to be able to do work with C# later.

## Starting a new project in Visual C#

To begin, crank up Visual C# and do the following:

1. In the **File** menu, select **New**, and then select **Web Site**.
2. Press *Shift + Alt + N*.

3. From the **New Web Site** box, select **Visual C#** for the language, as shown in the following screenshot:

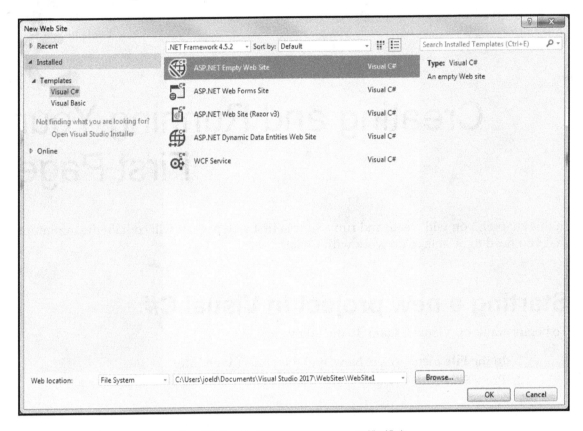

Figure 2.1.1: Be sure to select Visual C# as the language, not Visual Basic

4. To keep things as simple as possible, select **ASP.Net Empty Web Site**.

At the bottom of the dialog box, in the **Web location** field, the default value `File System` is sufficient.

If you wish, click on **Browse** and save the file to a location you choose and click on **OK**.

# Working with Solutions Explorer

After you click on **OK**, you'll see the **Solutions Explorer** window on the right-hand side of the screen, as shown in the following code. The **Solutions Explorer** shows the *structure* of how things are designed in Visual C#. You'll notice that there is a *Solution*; within the Solution, there is a website, and within the website there are different files that make up the site.

Specifically, Web.config is a file that stores basic website configuration settings. We can see the following code after we click on the Web.config file:

```xml
<?xml version="1.0"?>

<!--
    For more information on how to configure your ASP.NET
    application, please visit https://go.microsoft.com/
    fwlink/?LinkId=169433
    -->
<configuration>
    <system.web>
      <compilation debug="true" targetFramework="4.5.2" />
      <httpRuntime targetFramework="4.5.2" />
    </system.web>
</configuration>
```

# Adding a document to your browser

In the next stage, you need to add a document that can be shown in a browser. To accomplish this, do the following:

1. Right-click on the name of the website and select **Add**.
2. Select **Web Form**, and leave the name as Default.
3. This will generate a very simple template. You can close **Solutions Explorer** so that it's out of the way, if you wish.

# Working with HTML code in Visual Studio

The code across the top of the screen is highly specific to Microsoft. You wouldn't see this, for example, in HTML pages generated by hand or otherwise, unless you were working with a Microsoft product.

```
<%@ Page Language="C#" AutoEventWireup="true" CodeFile="Default.aspx.cs"
Inherits="_Default" %>
```

The following code shows an HTML document. Essentially, HTML gives structure to web pages. Visual Studio is a very powerful system:

```
<%@ Page Language="C#" AutoEventWireup="true" CodeFile="Default.aspx.cs"
Inherits="_Default" %>

<!DOCTYPE html>

<html xmlns="http://www.w3.org/1999/xhtml">
<head runat="server">
    <title></title>
</head>
<body>
    <form id="form1" runat="server">
        <asp:TextBox ID="TextBox1" runat="server"
        OnTextChanged="TextBox1_TextChanged"></asp:TextBox><br />
        <asp:Label ID="Label1" runat="server" ></asp:Label>
    </form>
</body>
</html>
```

Note the following on the screen:

- The HTML code within the screen is collapsible.Select the text you want to treat as a collapsible region.When collapsed, you'll see an ellipsis ( . . . ) between two <html> tags.

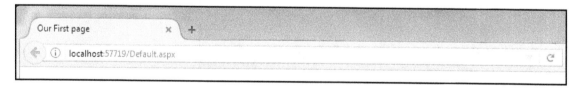

Figure 2.1.2: Preview code with the mouse hover

- If you hover your mouse over the ellipsis, you'll see that the code which has been collapsed appears in a preview box.

If you click on the left-hand side to expand the <html> tag, you have the <head> section. This is where you can store additional information, for example, the <title> tags of a web page. I entered Our First page as the title. The title is what is visible when a page is launched on the tab of a browser, for example, Microsoft Edge and Google Chrome:

Our First page        ×    +

ⓘ  localhost:57719/Default.aspx

Figure 2.1.3: The tab of a browser

After that, you have the <body> tag. Within the body, again you have a <form> tag. The <form> tags are useful for submitting information to web servers for processing. Within the form, you have a <div>tag, or logical division of a page:

```
<body>
    <form id="form1" runat="server">
    <div>

    </div>
    </form>
</body>
```

These elements are individually collapsible; so there is a logical structure to the document. Note the `<html>` opening and closing tags. It's good to have structured things; so you insert them as pairs—one opening and one closing.

Note where the code says `runat`. This is what's known as an *attribute*, which is a property that something possesses. In this case, the `<form>` tag has the `runat` attribute and it is called `server`. This means that the form can be dynamic—it can submit information, process it, and return it processed with some output when returned. We will discuss this in greater detail as you progress throughout the book.

```
<form id="form1" runat="server">
```

# Launching the HTML code

Now we'll launch this HTML code using the following steps:

1. Begin by putting some text within the `<div>` tags. Enter `Our First Web Page`.
2. Next, click on the drop-down menu of the run button, select whichever browser you are using, and launch the code in that browser:

Figure 2.1.4: Select a browser

3. After a few seconds, `Our First Web Page` appears, as shown in the following screenshot:

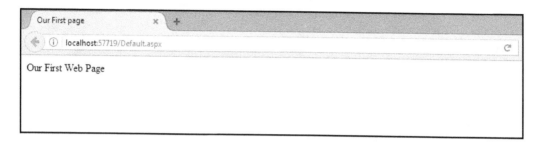

3. Figure 2.1.5: Source code generated and sent to the browser

In Microsoft Edge, when you click the ellipsis at the top right-hand side of the screen and click on**Zoom** on the drop-down menu, it will zoom in and the text will appear larger.

If you want to see what has actually been generated and sent to the browser, right-click and select **View Source**. As you can see in *Figure 2.3.5*, much has been generated.

In Microsoft Edge, for example, there are many different ways that you can view this information. You can very simply turn on `Pretty Print`, *Ctrl+Shift+P*, and now it is nicely formatted.

For our purposes, what you need to know is that the code you type and the code that ends up on the browser side are a little different. The code on the browser side is somewhat enhanced behind the scenes automatically—you don't really have to worry about it at all. However, you should be aware of what's going on.

To unload or close the document, click on **Stop Debugging** in the toolbar, or press *Shift + F5*.

# Summary

In this chapter, you learned how to create a very simple HTML document and how to run it in a browser. With this knowledge in place, you can now go on to learn how to connect it in C#.

# 4

# Creating and Running a Page That Incorporates C#

In this chapter, we will improve our HTML page by adding C# code. You will use the template that you set up in the previous chapter.

## Improving your first program

To continue the development of your first C# program, do the following:

1. If you wish, you can place something like `Our First C# Page` between the `<title>` tags.
2. Make sure that the **Solution Explorer** window is displayed. If it isn't shown, go to **View|Solution Explorer**. (*Ctrl+Alt+L* is the key combination, if you prefer using those.)

3. In **Solution Explorer**, expand the node that says `Default.aspx`.

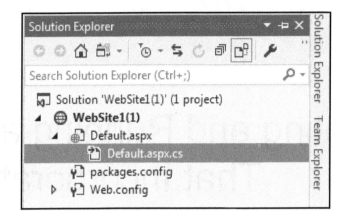

Figure 2.2.1: Default.aspx.cs in Solution Explorer

4. Open `Default.aspx.cs`, as shown in the following screenshot. This is where you place your C# code:

```
1  using System;
2  using System.Collections.Generic;
3  using System.Linq;
4  using System.Web;
5  using System.Web.UI;
6  using System.Web.UI.WebControls;
7
8  public partial class _Default : System.Web.UI.Page
9  {
10     protected void Page_Load(object sender, EventArgs e)
11     {
12
13     }
14 }
```

Figure 2.4.2: Default.aspx.cs is where you place C# code

Notice that by default, at this stage, the code gets grayed out, as shown in the following screenshot. This means that you can remove it. You can just delete it—it's not necessary for our purposes:

```
1  using System;
2  using System.Collections.Generic;
3  using System.Linq;
4  using System.Web;
5  using System.Web.UI;
6  using System.Web.UI.WebControls;
7
8  public partial class _Default : System.Web.UI.Page
9  {
10     protected void Page_Load(object sender, EventArgs e)
11     {
12
13     }
14 }
```

Figure 2.2.3: Select and delete the grayed-out code

# Working in the Design view

Before we talk more about C#, let's go back to `Default.aspx` and switch to the**Design** view, as shown in the following screenshot:

Figure 2.2.4: Change to the Design view

Now we'll add one visual item to the page—a label for displaying text in web pages. To do this, follow these steps:

1. In the menu bar, click on **View** and then on **Toolbox** (*Ctrl+ Alt + X*).
2. In the **Search** box at the top left-hand side, type `Label`.
3. Once it finds `Label`, click on it and drag it inside the `<div>` tag, as shown in the following screenshot. You can then close the toolbox:

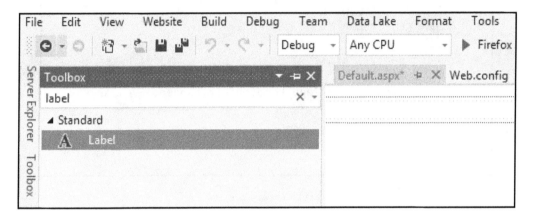

Figure 2.2.5: Use Toolbox to search for a visual element

# Working in the Source view

In the next stage, switch back to the **Source** view. Here, you will see the code or markup generated for that item:

```
Team Explorer - Connect    Default.aspx.cs    Default.aspx*  H  X  Web.config
   1  <%@ Page Language="C#" AutoEventWireup="true" CodeFile="Default.aspx.cs" Inherits="_Default" %>
   2
   3  <!DOCTYPE html>
   4
   5  <html xmlns="http://www.w3.org/1999/xhtml">
   6  <head runat="server">
   7      <title>Our First page</title>
   8  </head>
   9  <body>
  10      <form id="form1" runat="server">
  11      <div>
  12          <asp:Label ID="Label2" runat="server" Text="Label"></asp:Label>
  13      </div>
  14      </form>
  15  </body>
  16  </html>
  17
91 %
Design    Split    Source    <html> <body> <form#form1> <div> <asp:Label#Label2>
```

Figure 2.2.6: The code or markup generated for an item is selected here

Keep in mind that this is specific to Microsoft, but you can still recognize it. You basically have an `ID` and `Label1` attribute, which is an attribute. This is how you refer to the item in your C# code. You can change it to something more meaningful, say `sampLabel`, for sample label.

Here, `runat="server"` means that the content that the label displays can be generated automatically and dynamically, for example, over the course of your connection to a web page or server.

The `Text` control is what you see. Thus, if you remove the word `Label` and then switch back to the **Design** view, it will just say `sampLabel`, which is the `ID`:

```
<asp:Label ID="sampLabel" runat="server" Text="label"></asp:Label>
```

# Adding comments

Now let's go back to `Default.aspx.cs` and add the following comments under `using System`. These are notations for yourself—they are not executable code:

```
//1. using is a keyword, so it's blue
//2. System is a name space that stores already created code
//3. using System brings in existing code
```

The benefit of using existing code is that you'll have less code to create. Now go down to the next level, and insert the comments, as shown in the following screenshot:

```
File  Edit  View  Website  Build  Debug  Team  Tools  Test  Analyze  Window  Help
                            Debu   Any CPU      Microsoft Edge
Default.aspx.cs        Default.aspx

//1. using is a keyword, it's blue
//2. System is a name space that stores already created code
//3. using System brings in existing code
using System;

//4. class is a required container for creating our own code samples

public partial class _Default : System.Web.UI.Page
{
    //5. Code below is where we place our own code
    //6. Page_Load is code that runs when a page loads from a server
    protected void Page_Load(object sender, EventArgs e)
    {

    }
}
```

Figure 2.2.7: Adding comments to your code

```
//4. a class is a required container for creating our own code samples
```

Later, we will create a class. For now, because of the design of C#, it has to be there as a scaffolding into which you place your own code.

At the next stage, also as shown in the above screenshot, enter the following comments above the block of code that begins with `protected void Page_Load`:

```
//5. Code below is where we place our own code
//6. Page_Load is code that runs when a page loads from a server
```

# Adding attribute properties

Remember that the connection between what you see in the markup, which appears in the selected code in *Figure 2.2.6*, is the `sampLabelID`. This is how you refer to it in your C# code.

Next, on the `Default.aspx.cs` screen, enter `sampLabel`, which is a visible object (as might appear on a web page), and the things that can be used with a label, such as its properties, among other things. For now, grab the `Text` property—the text feature of a label. You do that by typing the name of the object, dot (`.`), and then `Text`. You set that equal to the text that you want to display, for example, `Hello World!;`, as shown in the following screenshot:

```
13  using System.Web.UT·
14  using System.Web.U  ⚡ AppRelativeTemplateSourceDirectory
15                      ⚡ TemplateControl
16  public partial cla                                               I
17  {                   ⚡ TemplateSourceDirectory
18      protected void ⚡ Text                          string Label.Text { get; set; }
19      {               ⚡ ⚡ ⚙                          Gets or sets the text content of the Label control.
20          sampLabel.Te|
21      }
22  }
```

Figure 2.2.8: Adding a property to an attribute

Now let's add some comments above `sampLabel.Txt = "Hello World!";`:

```
//7. A label is an object
//8. Objects possess features like a text property
//9. = is called the assignment operator
```

The assignment operator takes the value on the right-hand side, which is `"Hello World!";`, and assigns it to the `Text` property of the label. When you put something between double-quotes, it's called a string. A string is a sequence of characters between double-quotes. When this code runs, `Hello World` will show on the web page that you view.

Now add the following comment, which too appears in *Figure 2.2.9*:

```
//10. Hello World will show in the web page
```

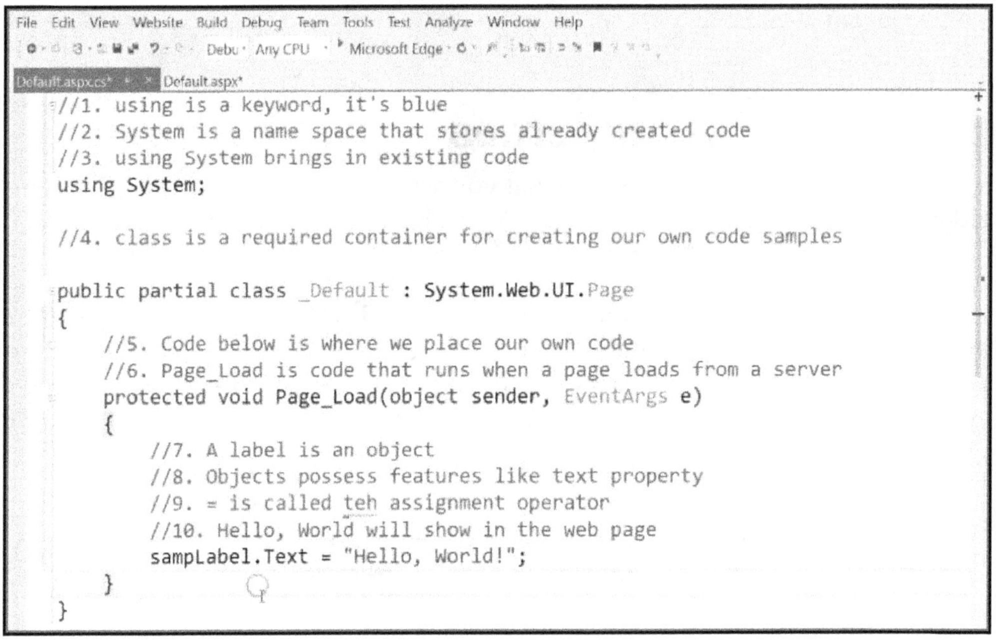

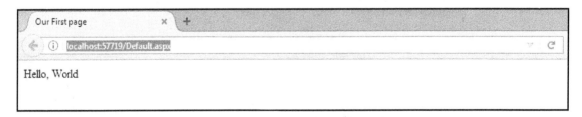

Figure 2.2.9: Completing your comments

# Viewing the code in your browser

That's a lot of preliminary work! Now let's take a look at the action. The following screenshot shows the code when opened in Microsoft Edge:

Figure 2.2.10: Your code opened in Microsoft Edge

The code produces `Hello, World!` on the page. Thus, we have generated some very basic C# powered content. You can enlarge the type to your liking by clicking the ellipsis ( . . . ) in the upper-right corner of the screen and selecting **Zoom**. Also note that the screen is entitled `Our First Page` in the upper-left corner.

One thing to observe at the top left-hand side of *Figure 2.2.10* is a localhost identifier, which is your local computer. The number is the logical software port `57719`. Where it says `Default.aspx`, `Default` is the name of a page and `.aspx` is the extension on the page.

To close, click on the brown square button in the toolbar to stop debugging. Close the window. The code is shown in the following screenshot:

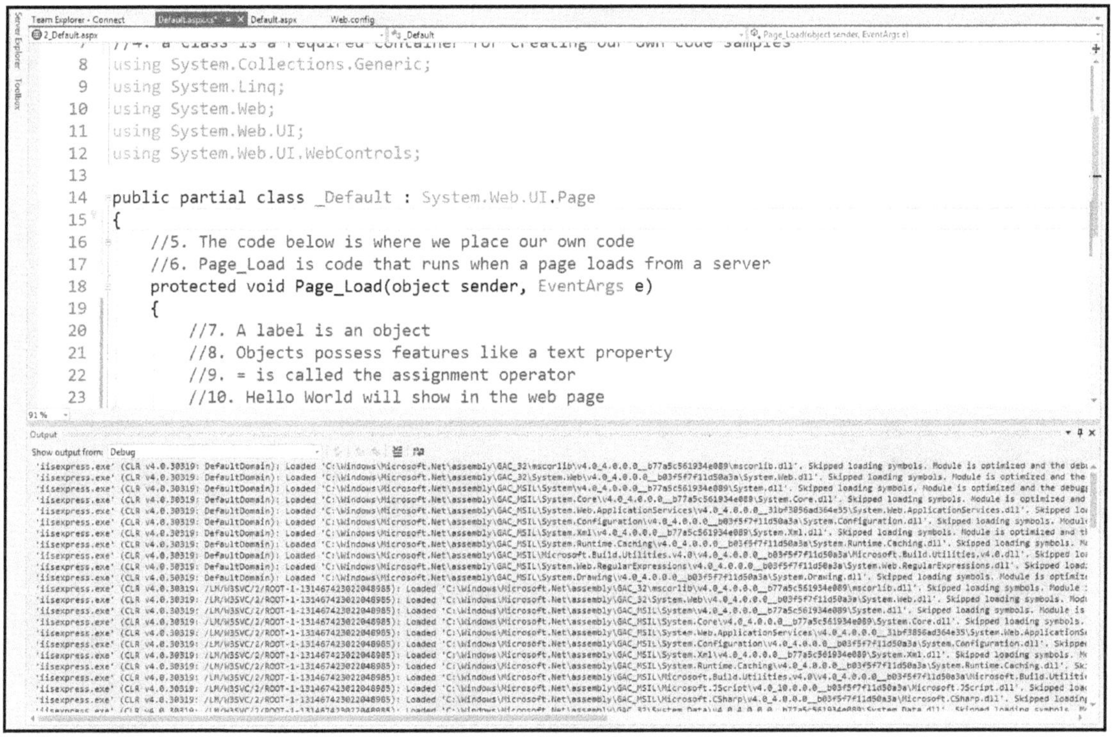

Figure 2.2.11: Click on the brown button in the toolbar to stop debugging

# Summary

In this chapter, you learned some of the basics of running a simple web page powered by C#. In the next chapter, we'll talk about variables.

# 5

# Creating and Using a Single Variable

In this chapter, you will learn about variables. We will begin with a simple project already in place to save time.

## Setting up Visual C# to deal with a variable

Remember from the previous chapter that there's a `Label` control involved; be sure that you have that up. Start by doing the following:

1.  Switch to the **Design** view, by clicking the button in the lower-left corner. Your screen should look like the one shown in the following screenshot:

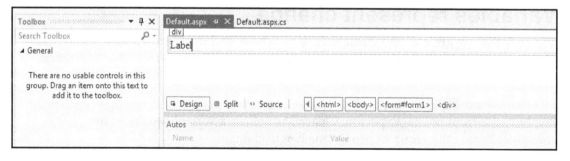

Figure 2.3.1: Visual C# Design view

If you are missing **Toolbox**, remember to click on **View** and then on **Toolbox** (press *Ctrl + Alt + X* if you prefer to use key combinations), and then drag and drop **Label** into the **Design** view.

2.  In the next stage, go back to the **Source** view.
3.  Name it `sampLabel` as before.
4.  Go into `Default.aspx.cs` on the right-hand side, as shown in the following screenshot:

```
13
14   public partial class _Default : System.Web.UI.Page
15   {
16       //5. The code below is where we place our own code
17       //6. Page_Load is code that runs when a page loads from a server
18       protected void Page_Load(object sender, EventArgs e)
19       {
20
21
22
23       }
24   }
```

Figure 2.3.2: Our Default.aspx.cs view

# Variables represent change

The code that we are going to create will be very basic and deal with variables. The first question is, ultimately, why introduce a variable in the first place? This is an important aspect. It is usually based on an observation that something is changing.

Imagine something as simple as this. You see a group of people, and you observe that their height varies from person to person. Clearly, `height` is a variable quantity; that is, it's changing. Within the group of people, the height changes.

So, let's start by adding this comment to our code:

```
//7. You see a group of people and the height changes
```

In code like C#, for example, we introduce a variable to represent this change. C# is *strongly typed*, which means that every single variable has a definite data type.

Imagine a variable in a simplified sense as a little box. If a box is designed to hold numerical values, you cannot put a non-numerical value into that box—you cannot put a word into a box that is designed to hold numbers. It doesn't work.

# Declaring a variable

Double is a data type in C#. It is good for representing measured values of things that you can make that have decimal points, such as 65.75. Then you usually give a variable a very easy-to-understand and purposeful name. So, consider this example:height.

Now imagine that you pick out one value, say 65.00, and close it with a semicolon (;), as shown in the following code:

```
//1. using is a keyword, so it's blue
//2. System is a name space that stores already created code
//3. using System brings in existing code

using System;

//4. a class is a required container for creating our own code samples

public partial class _Default : System.Web.UI.Page
{
    //5. The code below is where we place our own code
    //6. Page_Load is code that runs when a page loads
    from a server
    protected void Page_Load(object sender, EventArgs e)
    {

        //7. You see a group of people and the height
        changes
        double height = 65.00; //8. Declares and set a
        variable value
        sampLabel.Text = "John's height is " + height;
    }
}
```

# Matching variable types

The line we just added declares and sets up a variable based on an observation of something in the world. Hover your mouse over this line, and it says Double. This is an absolutely important thing to understand. The data type on both sides *match*, as shown in the following screenshot. If you don't have harmony between the two, many times this leads to errors, especially when you're learning for the first time—it's really crucial.

```
//7. You see a group of people and the height changes
double height = 65.00; //8. Declares and set a variable value
```
    ■ struct System.Double
    Represents a double-precision floating-point number.

Figure 2.3.3: The data type on both sides must match

Now I will add the following simple comment. This is the language that you would use to describe that line. Note that it is a statement: it ends with a semicolon, so it completes a definite action—the declaration and setting of a variable.

```
//8. Declares and sets a variable value
```

To display this, as usual, type `sampLabel`, dot (`.`), and `Text`. Then assign it to be displayed. This means putting in an equal sign and building up a string on the right-hand side between the quotes. For example, type `John's height is`, and to add his height, type the plus sign (+) and then the height variable.

> Understand that here + does not mean add two numbers; it means combine two strings.

Hover your mouse over the plus sign (+). It's an *operator*—it operates on things. Specifically, string left refers to `John's height is` and object right refers to the quantity on the right-hand side, that is, the `height` variable, as shown in the following screenshot:

```
sampLabel.Text = "John;s height is" + height;
```
                        ⚙ string string.operator +(string left, object right)
```
}
```

Figure 2.3.4: String left refers to "John's height is " and object right refers to the quantity on the right side—the height variable

After it runs, it generates another string. The first word, **string,** indicates that when you add two strings, a string and an object in this particular case, the object that you get back is another string. This means that `John's height is + height;` is a string; `Text` also stores strings, so the two data types are matched.

As you can see in the following screenshot, the popup starts with a string. If you don't have the two data types matched, many times this results in errors when you're learning for the first time:

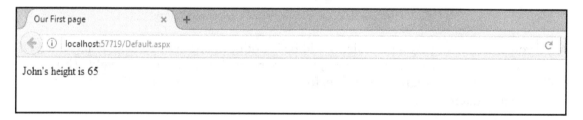

Figure 2.3.5: The two data types must match, or else errors will be the result

# Running the code

Now let's run the code. Crank it up in Google Chrome, for example, and you'll see the image shown in the following screenshot:

Figure 2.3.6: Your code opened in Google Chrome

If you right-click and select **View page source**, the only thing that's been generated is the highlighted text shown in *Figure 2.3.7*. The label has been converted into basic HTML behind the scenes. All of the other stuff has been added by default—don't worry about it. It has to be present because of the way this stuff has been designed by the people who created ASP.NET:

```
1
2
3   <!DOCTYPE html>
4
5   <html xmlns="http://www.w3.org/1999/xhtml">
6   <head><title>
7
8   </title></head>
9   <body>
10      <form method="post" action="./Default.aspx" id="form1">
11  <div class="aspNetHidden">
12  <input type="hidden" name="__VIEWSTATE" id="__VIEWSTATE"
    value="Pn58eK0EXfbDOMnjb9Qf/Epfc1jZyQknPgkjH9RviLNFtk1eJqyT6v06ucE6y4PQmD2I2fDEQe6/pZKFoPkqjfZqMDn8x
    2+Gi3ZmQpk6niXEgR/nfS1qkq247zYpF1A2NUev6GSGp1/E2aXPUvaktA==" />
13  </div>
14
15      <div>
16
17          <span id="sampLabel">John's height is 65</span>
18
19      </div>
20
21  <div class="aspNetHidden">
```

Figure 2.3.7: The generated text is highlighted, and the label is converted into basic HTML

Now you understand why a variable should be introduced and how to display its value. Of course, when you look at another person, they are normally of a different height. Thus, we will enter height and assign a new value, for example, 55.5, and close with a semicolon to complete the statement, as shown here:

```
height=55.5;
```

Next, we will add a comment as follows:

```
height=55.5; //9. Assigns a new value usually based on some observation
```

To display this updated value, enter the following:

```
sampleLabel.Text+=
```

# Appending new text

Enter the following comment:

```
//10. += appends new text to existing text
```

If you only put =, the previous text will be overwritten. It will vanish. The+=operator appends new text to the existing text.

Now imagine that we enter `Mary's height is " + height;`.

Next, we will run the following code in the next section:

```
//1. using is a keyword, so it's blue
//2. System is a name space that stores already created code
//3. using System brings in existing code
using System;
//4. a class is a required container for creating our own code samples
public partial class _Default : System.Web.UI.Page
{
    //5. The code below is where we place our own code
    //6. Page_Load is code that runs when a page loads
    from a server
    protected void Page_Load(object sender, EventArgs e)
    {
        //7. You see a group of people and the height
        changes
        double height = 65.00;
        //8. Declares and set a variable value
        sampLabel.Text = "John's height is " + height;
        height = 55.5;
        //9. Assign new value usually based on some
        observation
        //10. += appends new text to the existing text
        sampLabel.Text += "Mary's height " + height;
    }
}
```

# Running the code with the appended text

Look very carefully at what happens when we run this code using Google Chrome, as shown in *Figure 2.3.8*. It's almost where we want it to be, except that `John's height` and `Mary's height` need to be separated into two lines:

Figure 2.3.8: John's and Mary's heights need to be separated into two lines

# Embedding a line break

To fix this, you can embed a line break. To do this, you enter the`<br>`tag right in front of Mary's. When you run the code now, you will observe the screen shown in the following screenshot:

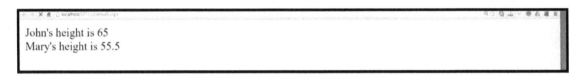

Figure 2.3.9: A line break <br> has been inserted to separate the text into two lines

Now we have the output that we want. First `John's height` and then `Mary's height` on separate lines. The values shown are coming from C#. The fact that `Mary's height` is on its own line is because we embedded the `<br>` tag into the string, so it produces a new line in HTML.

# Summary

In this chapter, you learned the basics of introducing and using variables. In the next chapter, we'll work with a new feature called string interpolation, which allows embedding variable names directly into strings. This makes coding much more streamlined.

# 6
# String Interpolation and Updating Visual Studio

In this chapter, we'll use a new feature that was introduced in C# 6.0 called string interpolation. This feature allows embedding variable names directly into strings, which makes coding much more streamlined.

The latest version of Visual Studio has the string interpolation feature built into it. You will only need to follow the first instructions here if you have an older version of Visual Studio, or if you are having problems with string interpolation. If you are using the latest version of Visual Studio, then you can jump to the "Printing a variable" heading to see string interpolation in action.

## Selecting a NuGet package

Open our project, right-click on the name of the website in **Solution Explorer**, and then select **Manage NuGet Packages...**, as shown in the following screenshot:

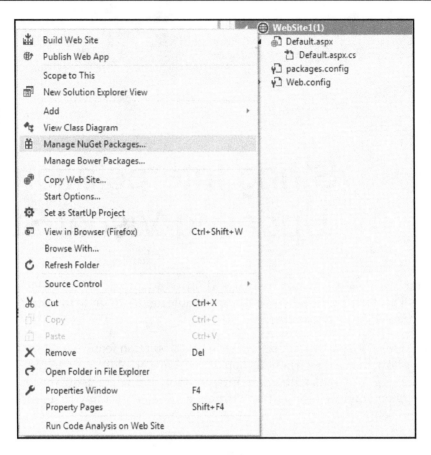

Figure 2.4.1: Selecting Manage NuGet Packages

Next, click on **Browse** in the **NuGet Package Manager** screen that appears. Packages that you can add to Visual Studio to extend its features are shown in the window on the left-hand side. Enter `codeDom` in the **Search** box at the upper-left corner and press *Enter*:

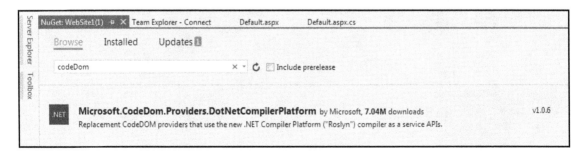

Figure 2.4.2: The CodeDom package

# Installing a NuGet package

From the items that appear, select the following and install it into your project by clicking on the **Install** button on the right-hand side, as shown in following screenshot:

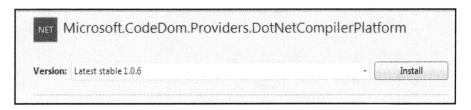

Figure 2.4.3. Installing the selected NuGet package

As this is an official product from Microsoft, click on the **I Accept** button:

Figure 2.4.4: Accepting the Microsoft.CodeDom.Providers.DotNetCompilerPlatform license

After a moment, you'll see a message that says **======Finished=====** at the bottom of the screen:

```
Successfully installed 'Microsoft.CodeDom.Providers.DotNetCompilerPlatform 1.0.6' to WebSite1(1)
Executing nuget actions took 3.21 sec
Time Elapsed: 00:00:03.8366970
========== Finished ==========
```

Figure 2.4.5: The Finished output after installation

Now click on the **NuGet Package Manager** tab to close the panel. This takes you back to `Default.aspx`. Click on the `Default.aspx.cs` tab.

# Printing a variable

Now I will show you how to use this new feature. As in the previous chapter, I will enter the following, keeping things very simple:

```
double height = 65; //7. Creates and assigns a variable
```

In the next stage, let's say that you want to print a variable. To do so, enter the following command. Note that I have placed a dollar sign ($) on the right-hand side. In the context of string interpolation, the dollar sign has nothing to do with money. It is a symbol that is required to allow you to embed variable names directly into strings:

```
sampLabel.Text=$
```

Next, type double quotes and enter the following:

```
sampLabel.Text=$"Height is "
```

Unlike before when we had to type a plus sign (+) and the name of the variable, we can now just embed the variable directly. So, type an open curly brace ({), and the name of the variable, and close the curly brace, as shown here:

```
sampLabel.Text=$"Height is {height}";
```

This is string interpolation. Let's add the following comments above this line:

```
//8. $ makes string interpolation work
//9. string interpolation allows us to put variable names directly into
strings
```

Note that when you run this code, it's the same as before. Take a look at it.

Launch the code in Google Chrome, as shown in the following screenshot:

Figure 2.4.6: Launching the code with string interpolation in Google Chrome

If you right-click on the screen and select **View page source**, you will see the screen that appears in the following screenshot. You will observe that the output is the same as before. Nothing has changed, except that now it's easier to code—it's more streamlined:

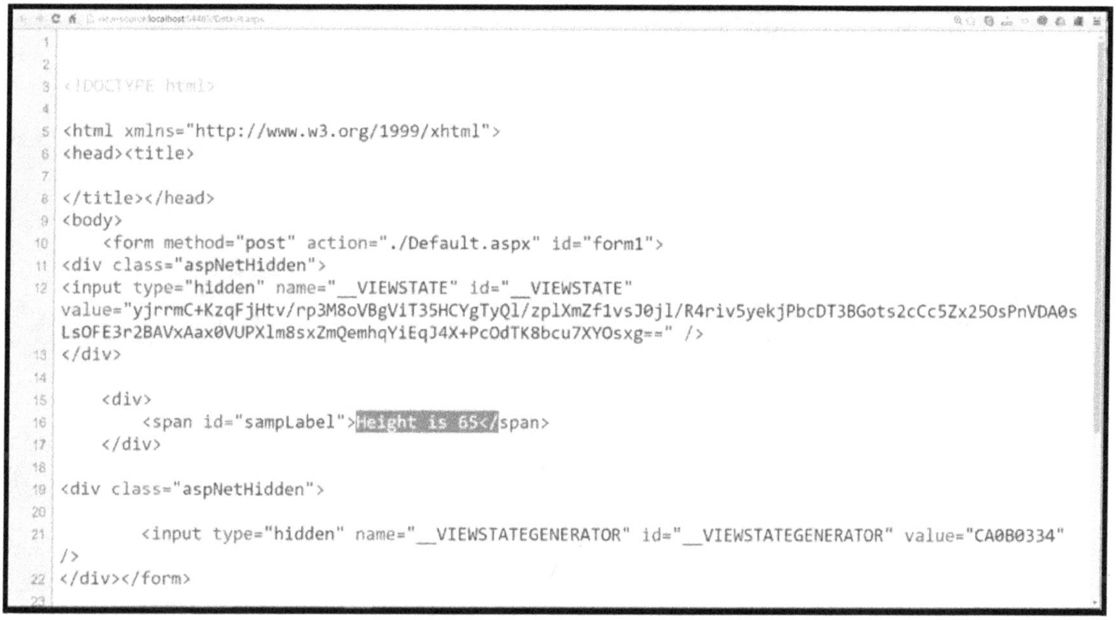

Figure 2.4.7: The source code

# Summary

In this chapter, you learned about a new feature called string interpolation. This feature helps streamline coding.

In the next chapter, we will work with string interpolation again. We will create strings and then format them to look more professional, so that they can display currency symbols, for example.

# Formatting Output Strings for More Professional Results

In this chapter, you'll learn how to format output so that it looks more professional. I'll begin as usual with a very simple template in HTML, and then switch over to `Default.aspx.cs`.

## Setting a value and formatting it as currency

The following screenshot shows how `Default.aspx.cs` looks now:

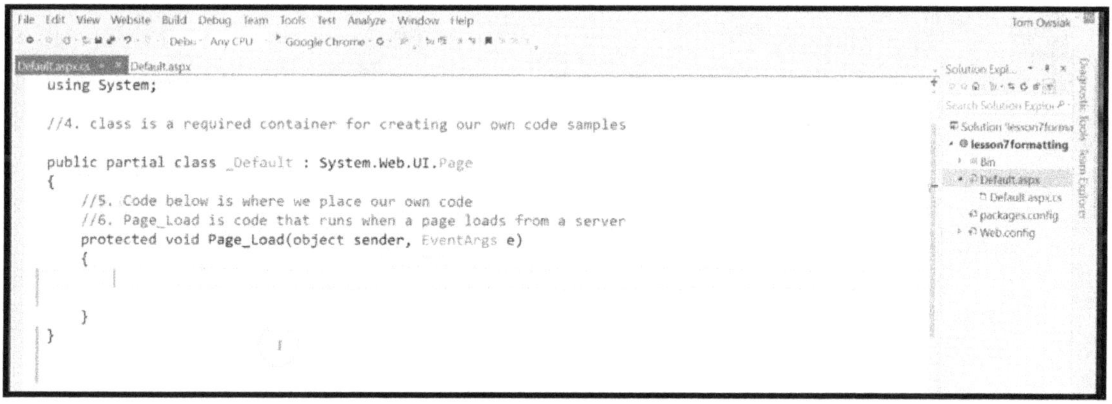

```
File  Edit  View  Website  Build  Debug  Team  Tools  Test  Analyze  Window  Help                    Tom Owsiak
                          Debu  Any CPU      Google Chrome

Default.aspx.cs    Default.aspx
    using System;

    //4. class is a required container for creating our own code samples

    public partial class _Default : System.Web.UI.Page
    {
        //5. Code below is where we place our own code
        //6. Page_Load is code that runs when a page loads from a server
        protected void Page_Load(object sender, EventArgs e)
        {

        }
    }
```

Figure 2.5.1: The current state of Default.aspx.cs

We'll now add some code so that it looks like this:

```
double x = 25.098114;//7. Value is needed so we have something to format
```

The value we set doesn't matter much, of course. We also added the preceding comment after the value.

Obviously, formatting is a big issue. You want the output that you generate on a web page, depending on your needs (for example, currency), to appear properly formatted.

Next, let's add the following comment:

```
//8. {x:C} prints the value of x formatted as currency
```

Now let's add the following statement below the comment:

```
sampLabel.Text = $"{x} formatted as currency is {x:C}";
```

Note that the $ symbol is there for string interpolation—it's not related to the fact that you want to print as money at all. Also, the C character applies the currency symbol. Always remember to close statements with a semicolon. Now this should show us some money on the screen. The following code block shows the code we entered up to this point in bold:

```
using System;

//4. a class is a required container for creating our own code samples

public partial class _Default : System.Web.UI.Page
{
    //5. The code below is where we place our own code
    //6. Page_Load is code that runs when a page loads from a server
    protected void Page_Load(object sender, EventArgs e)
    {
        double x = 25.098114;//7. Value is needed so we have something
        //to format
        //8. {x:C} prints the value of x formatted as currency
        sampLabel.Text = $"{x} formatted as currency is {x:C}";
    }
}
```

# Rounding the output

Now let's open the code in Google Chrome. Take a look at the action, as shown in the following screenshot:

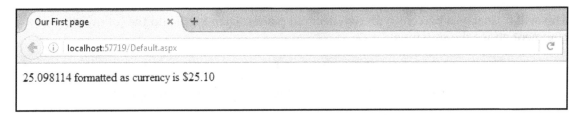

Figure 2.5.2: Code to show currency as output opened in Google Chrome

So, there you go:$25.10. And it's got a $ symbol.

One thing to observe about this output is that it rounds up. So, for example, if you put in 25.098114, as I did, it's going to show you two decimal places. This means that here, 8 is checked because it's greater than 5. The number before it is rounded, so keep that in mind. Though it has the dollar symbol, it rounds up using basic school rules that you perhaps learned years ago (or maybe not). My modest effort at applying these rules is shown in the following screenshot:

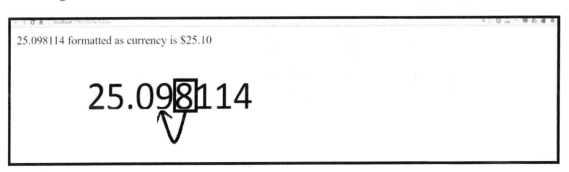

Figure 2.5.3: Rounding the output

So, that's one kind of format specification. Let's take a look at another one here. For example, we can format values as a percent. To do that, I'm going to change the value of x and insert the comment that follows:

```
x = 0.3459;//9. Saving a decimal so the percent P2 specifier is easier to
see in action
```

I picked the value at random—it doesn't matter. I'm assigning a decimal—that's the reason.

# Formatting a value as a percent

Next, we will enter the following:

```
sampLabel.Text = $"{x} formatted as a percent is {x:P2}";
```

This will format as a percent with two decimal places. Then I will add the following comment above the statement:

```
//10. The action shows the value of x formatted as a percent
```

The highlighted portion in the following code block displays the addition of this code:

```
//1. using is a keyword, so it's blue
//2. System is a name space that stores already created code
//3. using System brings in existing code
using System;
//4. a class is a required container for creating our own code samples
public partial class _Default : System.Web.UI.Page
{
    //5. The code below is where we place our own code
    //6. Page_Load is code that runs when a page loads from a server
    protected void Page_Load(object sender, EventArgs e)
    {
        double x = 25.098114;//7. Value is needed so we have something
        to format
        //8. {x:C} prints the value of x formatted as currency
        sampLabel.Text = $"{x} formatted as currency is {x:C}";
        x = 0.3459;//9. Saving a decimal so the percent P2 specifier
        is easier to see in action
        sampLabel.Text = $"{x} formatted as a percent is {x:P2}";
        //10. The action of shows the value of x formatted as a
        percent
    }
}
```

Now let's take a look at the output in Google Chrome, as shown in the following screenshot:

0.349533 formatted as a percent is 34.95 %

Figure 2.5.4: Value displayed as a percent in your browser

So, `34.95%` is displayed. Note that this output doesn't show the previous output.

To fix that, we're going to take the following actions regarding this line:

```
sampLabel.Text += $"<br>{x} formatted as a percent is {x:P2}";
```

1. You want to append, so change the = sign to a +=sign to append.
2. You also want to make sure that the line starting with the open curly brace is on its own line in the web page; so insert a <br> tag, which generates a break in the HTML.

Now let's take a look at this in Google Chrome, as shown in the following screenshot:

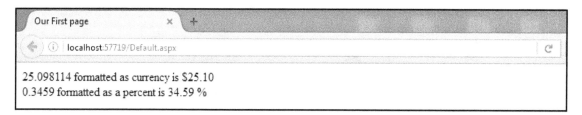

Figure 2.5.5: Output broken over two lines in the browser

There you go! Chrome added `formatted as currency` and `formatted as a percent`.

Let's do one more kind of formatting. As you can imagine, there are additional ones, but they all function in a manner very similar to these.

# Formatting a value as a date

Next we'll show a date, To show a date, you use `DateTime.Now` and then extract the date. First, let's enter the following comment:

```
//11. To show a date, use DateTime.Now
```

To actually extract the date, you'll have to enter something like the following:

```
//12. To actually get the date, {DateTime.Now:d}, which gets the date.
```

The dcharacter gets the date. If you want to get the time, you can add t, and so on. But we'll only get the date for now.

Now we'll enter the following statement below the two comments:

```
sampLabel.Text += $"<br> Today's date is {DateTime.Now:d}";
```

In the preceding statement, we add += to append, the $ symbol for string interpolation, double quotes to make a string, and <br> to push down to the next line in HTML. Then we say Today's date is and then insert curly braces for string interpolation again, and say DateTime.Now. Obviously, DateTime.Now is something that already has been designed and created by other people and is available to us. We then add :d to get the date out and close with a semicolon.

Your code should look as follows:

```
//1. using is a keyword, so it's blue
//2. System is a name space that stores already created code
//3. using System brings in existing code

using System;

//4. a class is a required container for creating our own code samples
public partial class _Default : System.Web.UI.Page
{
    //5. The code below is where we place our own code
    //6. Page_Load is code that runs when a page loads from a server
    protected void Page_Load(object sender, EventArgs e)
    {
        double x = 25.098114;//7. Value is needed so we have something
        to format
        //8. {x:C} prints the value of x formatted as currency
        sampLabel.Text = $"{x} formatted as currency is {x:C}";
        x = 0.3459;//9. Saving a decimal so the percent P2 specifier is
        easier to see in action
        //10. The action of shows the value of x formatted as a percent
        sampLabel.Text += $"<br>{x} formatted as a percent is {x:P2}";
        //11. To show a date, use DateTime.Now
        //12. To actually get the date, {DateTime.Now:d}, which gets
        the date.
        sampLabel.Text += $"<br> Today's date is {DateTime.Now:d}";
    }
}
```

Now let's open the code again in Google Chrome. Let's refresh the page, rebuild it, and reload it. We can click on the arrow in the toolbar, rebuild it, and reload it to confirm that the date is seen. This program was run on 8/10/2017, as shown in the following screenshot:

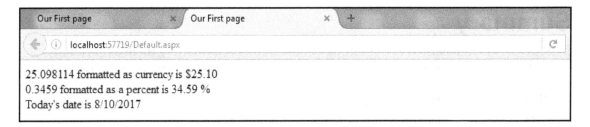

Figure 2.5.6: The date on which this program was run is 8/10/2017

If you right-click and **View page source**, it looks like the following screenshot. The <br> tag, as you can see, is present in the HTML. Visually speaking, you have the output on several lines, and that is it:

```
<!DOCTYPE html>

<html xmlns="http://www.w3.org/1999/xhtml">
<head><title>
    Our First page
</title></head>
<body>
    <form method="post" action="./Default.aspx" id="form1">
<div class="aspNetHidden">
<input type="hidden" name="__VIEWSTATE" id="__VIEWSTATE"
value="AxPUNIFadHWyRZkHab6ecobCN/O9BJRLu6DTCbrTSeARWCPtsbG+9R2NyJzzOD45tKtb4PpRV7qF3hrQNr+dHayvPeLjgeSItpWZDbRI
FagFdzXonOMQQ6/9TIE41hAWVp/Nn7g6XszCVPhuYKH2WeUe3WN1lnxQ36RnguRBXfioD9uoaZTCqDX+dYqHVUqUtMYY6Q2rIgR+mGjj+OvF
/GkG11hputMD3hk4jOb5J6dhnNt8xEhUpI5FxKirlkcomzObyT7D/UTe6fBhcNIc5g==" />
</div>

    <div>
        <span id="sampLabel">25.098114 formatted as currency is $25.10<br>0.3459 formatted as a percent is
34.59 %<br> Today's date is 8/10/2017</span>
    </div>

<div class="aspNetHidden">

    <input type="hidden" name="__VIEWSTATEGENERATOR" id="__VIEWSTATEGENERATOR" value="CA0B0334" />
</div></form>

<!-- Visual Studio Browser Link -->
<script type="application/json" id="__browserLink_initializationData">
    {"appName":"Firefox","requestId":"e03b730b7b0043c196d084a391cfa962"}
</script>
<script type="text/javascript" src="http://localhost:58205/36282184db494324a3020cfb7b1bc0fd/browserLink"
async="async"></script>
<!-- End Browser Link -->

</body>
</html>
```

Figure 2.5.7: The code for formatting values as currency, percentages, and dates

# Summary

In this chapter, you learned about setting values and then formatting them as currency, percentages, and dates. You also learned about how the output of a value is rounded.

In the next chapter, you'll learn how to use different data types to build up a description of an object.

# 8

# Using Variables and Data Types

In this chapter, we will learn how to describe an object using several different data types.

## Setting a page title automatically

So, we have our little HTML page `Default.aspx` as always, but what we will do is, we'll go into `Default.aspx.cs`, and, inside `Page_Load`, we will create a description of an object that we can visualize easily, for example, a table:

```
Default.aspx.cs                    ×
No selection
1 //1. using is a keyword, it's blue
2 //2. System is a name space that stores already created code
3 //3. using System brings in existing code
4 using System;
5
6 //4. class is a required container for creating our own code samples
7
8 public partial class _Default : System.Web.UI.Page
9 {
10     //5. Code below is where we place our own code
11     //6. Page_Load is code that runs when a page loads from a server
12     protected void Page_Load(object sender, EventArgs e)
13     {
```

Figure 2.6.1: Your starting HTML page

But first, to show how you can do this, we'll figure out how to set a page title automatically. You can do this by typing `Page.Title` and then setting that equal to `"Table Catalog";`, like this:

```
Page.Title = "Table Catalog";
```

Remember to terminate the statement with a semicolon.

Before we do anything else, let's see what this produces on the screen when we launch the page. So far, `Default.aspx` looks as shown in the following code block. Notice that the `<title>` tags are empty:

```
<%@ Page Language="C#" AutoEventWireup="true" CodeFile="Default.aspx.cs"
Inherits="_Default" %>

<!DOCTYPE html>

<html xmlns="http://www.w3.org/1999/xhtml">
<head runat="server">
    <title></title>
</head>
<body>
    <form id="form1" runat="server">
    <div>
        <asp:Label ID="sampLabel" runat="server" Text="Label"></asp:Label>
    </div>
    </form>
</body>
</html>
```

Start Google Chrome. You can see that it says **Table Catalog** in the upper-left corner, as shown in the following screenshot:

Figure 2.6.2: The page title, Table Catalog, in Google Chrome

If you right-click and go to **View page source**, it's also visible there. This time, it has been generated from C#, as shown in the following screenshot. It's a nice little feature. Now close this screen:

```html
<!DOCTYPE html>

<html xmlns="http://www.w3.org/1999/xhtml">
<head><title>
    Table Catalog
</title></head>
<body>
        <form method="post" action="./Default.aspx" id="form1">
<div class="aspNetHidden">
<input type="hidden" name="__VIEWSTATE" id="__VIEWSTATE"
value="Uq24IbEAVun5Tdc7R1YqNb9dsndjfxqGFUMsWVDP7VCFdmxFdVhYyqaL+bEJatjTdnzALoe/PYCg9Fq1FcpvXbS8fY2X8Gmy3CPD2xIdnOA=" />
</div>

    <div>
    </div>

<div class="aspNetHidden">

        <input type="hidden" name="__VIEWSTATEGENERATOR" id="__VIEWSTATEGENERATOR" value="CA0B0334" />
</div></form>

<!-- Visual Studio Browser Link -->
<script type="application/json" id="__browserLink_initializationData">
    {"appName":"Firefox","requestId":"92497e0086ac417ba62aa53f8912cfb9"}
</script>
<script type="text/javascript" src="http://localhost:58205/36282184db494324a3020cfb7b1bc0fd/browserLink"
async="async"></script>
<!-- End Browser Link -->

</body>
</html>
```

Figure 2.6.3: The page title, Table Catalog, has been set automatically

# Setting a page title so that it can be controlled dynamically

In the next stage, we will insert a comment inside `Page_Load`, as shown here. It sets the value of the page title so that it can essentially be controlled dynamically. You can imagine it changing depending on which page you load, and so on.

```csharp
//7. Sets value of page title so it can be controlled dynamically
Page.Title = "Table Catalog";
```

In the next step, knowing that a table is basically an object, and therefore has a description, we'll type `string`, that is, a data type, which is as follows:

```
string desc = "This is a fancy table from France";
sampLabel.Text = desc;
```

When we type `string`, which is a data type, this stores sequences of characters between double quotes. Then, we'll give it a variable here called `desc`, which is short for description. On the right-hand side, we will put the value that it stores.

Strings are a little more sophisticated. For our purposes and at this simple level of explanation, however, it's a variable, and that's it. We enter, `"This is a fancy table from France,"` and close it with a semicolon. To make this display, simply type `sampLabel.Text` and set it equal on the right-hand side to desc, and that's it.

Data type consistency between the two sides of an assignment operator matters. So, on the left-hand side, we have a string, and on the right-hand side, when you hover your mouse over it, we also have a string, as you can see in the following screenshot. So, the two data types are consistent:

Figure 2.6.4: The string output

The `Text` property can also store a string, as shown in the following screenshot; and `desc` is also a `string`, as seen in *Figure 2.6.6*, once again achieving data type consistency between the two sides of the assignment operator:

```
sampLabel.Text = desc;
```
🔧 string System.Web.UI.WebControls.Label.Text { get; set; }
Gets or sets the text content of the System.Web.UI.WebControls.Label control.

Figure 2.6.5: The Text property stores a string

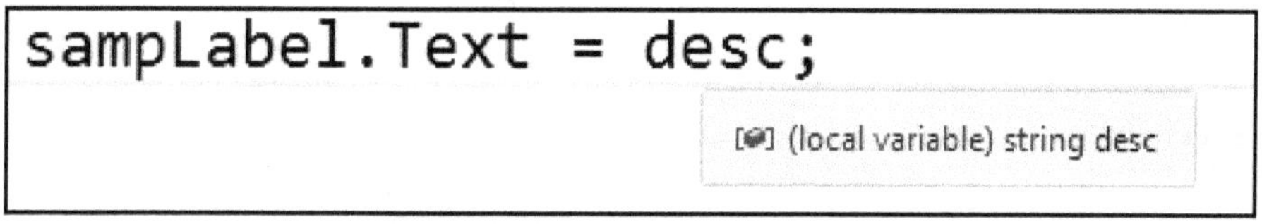

```
sampLabel.Text = desc;
```
[⊜] (local variable) string desc

Figure 2.6.6: Desc is also a string

Next I'll describe this variable briefly so that you understand its purpose. I'll enter comment 8 as we build up a little catalog using data types:

```
string desc = "This is a fancy table from France"; //8. Stores desc. of
table
```

Comment 9 simply assigns `desc` to the `Text` property of labels so that it can be displayed:

```
sampLabel.Text = desc; //9. Assigns desc to text property of label for
displays purposes
```

Run the code at this point in Google Chrome (which I use most of the time because it's easy), go into **View source**, and view it big, as you can see in the following screenshot. That's simple enough:

If you have too much code, remember that code is collapsible. You can click on the little minus boxes, and it will collapse that code into single lines so that you have more room to work with on the page.

```html
<!DOCTYPE html>

<html xmlns="http://www.w3.org/1999/xhtml">
<head><title>
    Table Catalog
</title></head>
<body>
    <form method="post" action="./Default.aspx" id="form1">
<div class="aspNetHidden">
<input type="hidden" name="__VIEWSTATE" id="__VIEWSTATE"
value="CHnhiR7QuwV7vvVmo1d3Uxvo6NfgMveHXRfet+U5dcGUdSwvVMIXN2XC31/kJPqjZdtfh9ILpwVTksVG3zOscJBmLxb+sy+IGFzstDmQ
WoToksB2xOL1YZvs/dUa6gzsR+SlOksYWCkBBadLbYLDG6kZHqTzVrLunSpu0Xb7HKA=" />
</div>

    <div>
        <span id="sampLabel">This is a fancy table from France</span>
    </div>

<div class="aspNetHidden">

    <input type="hidden" name="__VIEWSTATEGENERATOR" id="__VIEWSTATEGENERATOR" value="CA0B0334" />
</div></form>

<!-- Visual Studio Browser Link -->
<script type="application/json" id="__browserLink_initializationData">
    {"appName":"Firefox","requestId":"41d4f2dbd8c94c4ab827431708ade5d6"}
</script>
<script type="text/javascript" src="http://localhost:58205/36282184db494324a3020cfb7b1bc0fd/browserLink"
async="async"></script>
<!-- End Browser Link -->

</body>
</html>
```

Figure 2.6.7: Viewing the source in Google Chrome

# Working with a Boolean data type

In the next stage of the process, we will work with `bool`. This is the Boolean data type. It is good for storing the `true`/`false` values. Tables, as you might know, have a little piece that you can put in the middle to make the table bigger, or you can display it at its normal size. So we'll capture this in code as a `true` or `false` value; either a table has that feature or it doesn't, we will say `extendable`. By entering `bool extendable`, what we're asking is, can the table be made longer—yes or no? If we say the table is `true`, the code is as follows:

```
bool extendable = true;
```

Again, on the left-hand side, if you hover your mouse over `bool`, you'll notice that it's a Boolean, as shown in *Figure 2.6.8*. On the right-hand side, as shown in *Figure 2.6.9*, the word `true` is reserved—it's a keyword. It's a Boolean value type as well. The two data types are matched between the two sides. Alright, excellent!

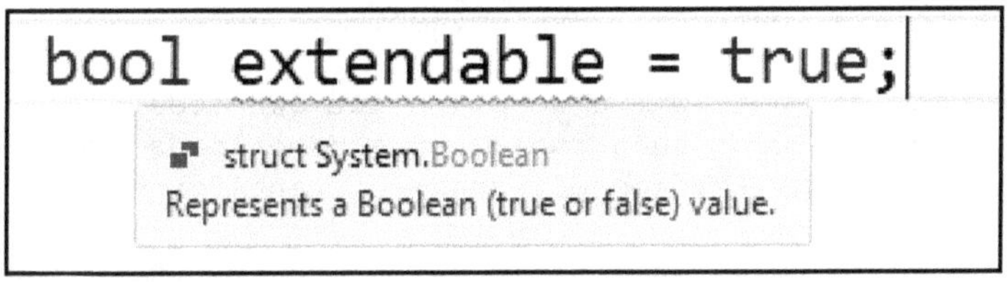

Figure 2.6.8: bool is a Boolean operator

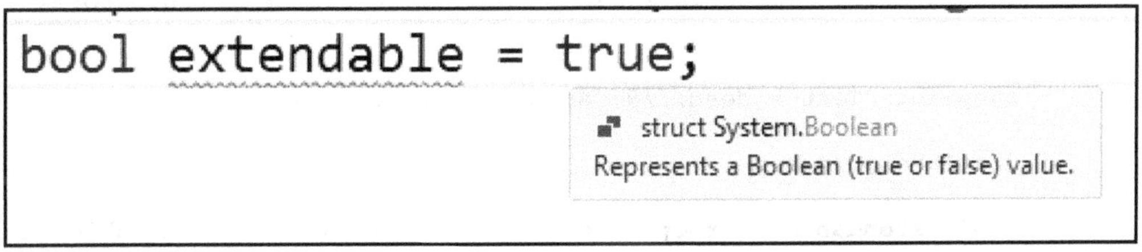

Figure 2.6.9: The word true is reserved—it's a keyword

Let's take a look. Comment 10 would essentially be that this one variable simply determines whether a table can be made longer—a true or false kind of question:

```
bool extendable = true; //10. Variable tells whether a table can be made
longer
```

To print this, we will start with `sampLabel.Text`. Now, remember, you want to append the current stuff to the previous one, so enter +=, the$ symbol for string interpolation, double quotes to make a string, and <br> to push down to the next line so that the content is stacked and not all on a single line.

Now you'll enter"<br>Extendable:" and then the value of the variable itself, so extendable. Finally, close with a semicolon, and this is what you have:

```
sampLabel.Text += $"<br>Extendable:{extendable}";
```

The following is the code we have written so far:

```
//1. using is a keyword, so it's blue
//2. System is a name space that stores already created code
//3. using System brings in existing code
using System;
//4. a class is a required container for creating our own code samples
public partial class _Default : System.Web.UI.Page
{
    //5. The code below is where we place our own code
    //6. Page_Load is code that runs when a page loads from a server
    protected void Page_Load(object sender, EventArgs e)
    {
        //7. Sets value of page title so it can be controlled dynamically
        Page.Title = "Table Catalog";

        string desc = "This is a fancy table from France"; //8. Stores
desc. of
        table
        sampLabel.Text = desc;//9. Assigns desc to text property of label
    for
        displays purposes

        bool extendable = true; //10. Variable tells whether a table can be
made
        longer
        sampLabel.Text += $"<br>Extendable:{extendable}";
    }
}
```

This will, of course, simply print it. Let's observe that in action. Close this and open it in Google Chrome. There you go! It is Extendable: True and This is a fancy table from France:

Figure 2.6.10: The result of a true/false value output to Google Chrome

One thing to be observed here is that when you generate output, even though sometimes you might put a lowercase t in true, it comes up as an uppercase T in the output because of the way C# has been designed. It's not anything wrong that you've done.

# Using the decimal data type to set monetary values

In the next stage, we will add a decimal data type, which is good for presenting monetary values because of the way it has been designed. Enter price followed by an equals sign. On the right-hand side, you'll type 399.99 and then close with a semicolon. However, this doesn't work:

```
decimal price = 399.99;
```

On the left-hand side, you have a decimal data type, and on the right-hand side, you have a double data type and you cannot convert between them. So, to make 399.99 be recognized as a decimal type, put an M character after it. This helps to ensure data type consistency—decimal on the left and decimal on the right—now there's no data clash. Great!

```
decimal price = 399.99M;
```

So, let's follow this with a comment here:

```
decimal price = 399.99M; //11. Stores price of table
```

That's it with using the `decimal` data type.

To display it, you can proceed as before. Enter `sampLabel.Text, +=` to append, a $ symbol for string interpolation, double quotes to make a string, and <br> to push it down to the next line in HTML. Then you will enter `Price:`, and in curly braces for string interpolation again, place the value, or rather the name of the variable whose value you want to print, and then terminate with a semicolon and that's it.

Follow this, of course, with a simple comment like the one shown here. Because it is a monetary value, obviously, I recommend that you format it as currency, so that it looks professional:

```
sampLabel.Text += $"<br>Price:{price:C}"; //12. Prints price of table
```

The following code block shows the complete code for all that you've done in this chapter:

```
//1. using is a keyword, so it's blue
//2. System is a name space that stores already created code
//3. using System brings in existing code

using System;

//4. a class is a required container for creating our own code samples
public partial class _Default : System.Web.UI.Page
{
    //5. The code below is where we place our own code
    //6. Page_Load is code that runs when a page loads from a server
    protected void Page_Load(object sender, EventArgs e)
    {
        //7. Sets value of page title so it can be controlled
        dynamically

        Page.Title = "Table Catalog";
        string desc = "This is a fancy table from France"; //8. Stores
        desc. of table
        sampLabel.Text = desc;//9. Assigns desc to text property of
        label for displays purposes

        bool extendable = true; //10. Variable tells whether a table
        can be made longer
        sampLabel.Text += $"<br>Extendable:{extendable}";
        decimal price = 399.99M;//11. Stores price of table
        sampLabel.Text += $"<br>Price:{price:C}"; //12. Prints price of
        table
    }
}
```

Now let's look at this again in Google Chrome, as shown in the following screenshot. As you can see, it's looking pretty good:

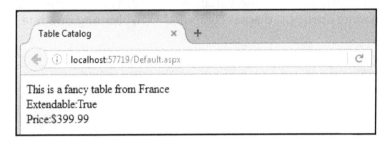

Figure 2.6.11: Using the decimal data type to display a monetary value in Google Chrome

Right-click on this screen and **View page source**. Regardless of how fancy it seems to be, it's sent out to basic HTML. Also notice that **Table Catalog**, which is dynamically generated, is now within the `<title>` tags. This is the way you would do it if you did it by hand. So, there's nothing deeply mysterious happening here. Unload the page and that is it. Refer to the following screenshot:

```
<!DOCTYPE html>

<html xmlns="http://www.w3.org/1999/xhtml">
<head><title>
    Table Catalog
</title></head>
<body>
    <form method="post" action="./Default.aspx" id="form1">
<div class="aspNetHidden">
<input type="hidden" name="__VIEWSTATE" id="__VIEWSTATE"
value="OdXbCzH2By3tawD+jUUglhfTG0uElrUOBN1iPRej1LOaglrkM21KlngykXcPAEcBZSHryU8AvqHr6MpJDQbbAedbWMNu8MmLAltCNdET
nD8pqsIFYrUP5pWgrm5zn4ARTO1mBv8M5tnJJO17HyJNpaYVB4C+fooWr4EzNOOF161OPFVHPByz7Upj3dGH8Xd71Dn4d5y1Vjs7RXOkJqYM7g=
=" />
</div>

    <div>
        <span id="sampLabel">This is a fancy table from France<br>Extendable:True<br>Price:$399.99</span>
    </div>

<div class="aspNetHidden">

    <input type="hidden" name="__VIEWSTATEGENERATOR" id="__VIEWSTATEGENERATOR" value="CA0B0334" />
</div></form>

<!-- Visual Studio Browser Link -->
<script type="application/json" id="__browserLink_initializationData">
    {"appName":"Firefox","requestId":"2e112e9d12c74d92bfe8a2b275af7ed7"}
</script>
<script type="text/javascript" src="http://localhost:58205/36282184db494324a3020cfb7b1bc0fd/browserLink"
async="async"></script>
<!-- End Browser Link -->

</body>
</html>
```

Figure 2.6.12: The source code for this chapter on using variables and data types

# Summary

In this chapter, you learned how to use variables and data types. In the next chapter, you'll continue to learn more about C#, discuss computed variables, and do some very simple mathematics.

# Computed Variables and Basic Math

# 9

In this chapter, we are going to talk about some math operations—really basic stuff. So, imagine a simple situation: two people who have individual salaries. Our starting point in `Default.aspx.cs` is shown in the following screenshot:

```csharp
//1. using is a keyword, so it's blue
//2. System is a name space that stores already created code
//3. using System brings in existing code

using System;

//4. a class is a required container for creating our own code samples

public partial class _Default : System.Web.UI.Page
{
    //5. The code below is where we place our own code
    //6. Page_Load is code that runs when a page loads from a server
    protected void Page_Load(object sender, EventArgs e)
    {

    }
}
```

Figure 2.7.1: Our starting point for this chapter

# Declaring and setting two variables to signify two different salaries

I'll begin by inserting comment 7 on the line below the open curly brace:

```
//7. line declares and sets two variables to represent two different
salaries
```

Now, in C#, when the data type of a variable is the same as the data type of another variable, you can put them on the same line, as shown here:

```
//7. line declares and sets two variables to represent two different
salaries
  decimal salaryOne = 25000, salaryTwo = 65000;
```

Now type `decimal`, which is a good data type for storing monetary values. Then you can enter `salaryOne`, which is equal to some value, say `25000`. Put a comma and then you don't have to type `decimal` again: you can simply enter `salaryTwo` and set that equal to `65000`. So, when the data type is the same, you write it once and then make a list of variable assignments on the rest of the line.

## Adding the two salaries

When you type `salaryOne + salaryTwo`, the addition (plus) sign here is an operator. Operators, as you know, operate on things. *Figure 2.7.2* shows a *tooltip*; it displays useful information. When you hover your mouse over the + sign in the statement, do you see where it says `decimal left` in the tooltip? That refers to the value of `salaryOne`. Where it says `decimal right`, that refers to the value of `salaryTwo`. Further, the + operator is simply a symbol, like the addition symbol in the statement itself—that's the operator. When it operates, it produces a new value and the data type of the value is a `decimal`. That is, what the `decimal` term means:

```
decimal totalSalary = salaryOne + salaryTwo;
                            ⓥ  decimal decimal.operator +(decimal left, decimal right)
```

Figure 2.7.2: Tooltip for the statement adding the two salaries

So, this means that you're going to revise the statement and type the following:

```
decimal totalSalary = salaryOne + salaryTwo;
```

The result of adding two decimals is another `decimal` data type value. Now let's add a few comments above the statement, as follows:

```
//8. Values are added on the right side, and the result is another decimal
type
//9. The result is saved to the variable named totalSalary
```

The addition happens first, and after that the result is saved to the variable named `totalSalary`.

Now that we have the preceding statements available, it's been created and set, and we can print it to the screen. So, we will say the following:

```
sampLabel.Text = $"Total salary is {totalSalary:C}";
```

Again, the $ symbol is for string interpolation and double quotes are inserted to make a string. After `"Total salary is,` put the `totalSalary` variable name within the curly braces. Then end quote and type a semicolon to close the statement. Because we are dealing with monetary values, let's put `:C` after `totalSalary` to format the output as currency. That's our code!

Note that as you type the variable name, it will show an IntelliSense popup, as seen in the following screenshot. In this case, IntelliSense shows a list of items for quick access:

```
{
    //7. line declares and sets two variables to represet two different salaries
    decimal salaryOne = 25000, salaryTwo⊙ GetUniqueIDRelativeTo

                                        ⊙. SavePageStateToPersistenceMedium              ecimal type
    //8. Values are added on the right s
    //9. The result is saved to the vari⊙ ToString
    decimal ↕(local variable) decimal totalSalary ⊙ totalSalary
    sampLabel.Text = $"Total salary is {to|"
```

Figure 2.7.3: IntelliSense allows you to speed up your coding and reduce errors by providing context-sensitive assistance

Our code up to this point is shown in the following code block:

```
//1. using is a keyword, so it's blue
//2. System is a name space that stores already created code
//3. using System brings in existing code

using System;
```

```
//4. a class is a required container for creating our own code samples
public partial class _Default : System.Web.UI.Page
{
    //5. The code below is where we place our own code
    //6. Page_Load is code that runs when a page loads from a server
    protected void Page_Load(object sender, EventArgs e)
    {
        //7. line declares and sets two variables to represent two
different salaries
        decimal salaryOne = 25000, salaryTwo = 65000;
        //8. Values are added on the right side, and the result is another
decimal type
        //9. The result is saved to the variable named totalSalary
        //10. Total salary is computed variable or calculated variable
        decimal totalSalary = salaryOne + salaryTwo;
        sampLabel.Text = $"Total salary is {totalSalary:C}";
    }
}
```

Now let's run this in Google Chrome, as shown in the following screenshot. The `Total salary` is nicely formatted as `$90,000.00`; perfect!

Figure 2.7.4: Total salary result as it appears in Google Chrome

# Averaging the two salaries

Another common mathematical operation would be to find the average of the two salaries. Let's start by adding comment 10 as follows:

```
//10. totalSalary is a computed variable or calculated variable
```

What this means is that the value of `totalSalary` is the result of a calculation on the right side of the equals, so it's called a computed or calculated variable.

Next, we'll find an average. So, because `totalSalary` has already been created and its value has been set, we can use it in code that comes below that line:

```
decimal averageSalary = totalSalary / 2;
```

We start with `decimal averageSalary =`. To find an average of two quantities, you normally add them together and divide by two. However, it's a good idea to avoid using repeated operations that have already been done to do that. In other words, you type `totalSalary` divided by 2 instead—there's no need for you to type `salaryOne + salaryTwo` again because `totalSalary` is the sum, which has already been found. So, let's do that and make a meaningful comment right above it:

```
//11. totalSalary/2 is the average salary
```

Comment 11 essentially is that `totalSalary/2 is the average salary`, or the salary per person. If you hover your mouse over the division symbol (/), as shown in *Figure 2.7.5*, again it's an operator and you'll see that it says **decimal left** and then **decimal right**. This means that after it runs, it produces another decimal data type, and we know that because this popup and the statement starts with a `decimal` data type. The data types match:

```
//11. totalSalary/2 is the average salary
decimal averageSalary = totalSalary / 2;
                                    decimal decimal.operator /(decimal left, decimal right)
```

Figure 2.7.5: The decimal data types match

Same principle as earlier: when you hover your mouse over the + sign, there is a `decimal` data type. Again, the popup starts with a `decimal` data type, as does the statement, so they're matched, as shown in the following screenshot:

```
decimal totalSalary = salaryOne + salaryTwo;
                                    decimal decimal.operator +(decimal left, decimal right)
```

Figure 2.7.6: Again, the data types match

Let's display it now by adding the following line:

```
sampLabel.Text += $"<br>The average salary is {averageSalary:C}";
```

Remember, we want to append, so insert +=; add double quotes to make a string and the $ symbol for string interpolation. Next, we say "The average salary is". Within the curly braces, we write the name of your variable, or averageSalary:C, to format it as currency, and close with a semicolon. Don't forget the <br> tag, so that this line will appear on its own line in the page.

Your final coding for this chapter is shown in the following code block:

```
//1. using is a keyword, so it's blue
//2. System is a name space that stores already created code
//3. using System brings in existing code

using System;

//4. a class is a required container for creating our own code samples

public partial class _Default : System.Web.UI.Page
{
    //5. The code below is where we place our own code
    //6. Page_Load is code that runs when a page loads from a server
    protected void Page_Load(object sender, EventArgs e)
    {
        //7. line declares and sets two variables to represent two
        different salaries
        decimal salaryOne = 25000;
        decimal salaryTwo = 65000;
        //8. Values are added on the right side, and the result is
        another decimal type
        //9. The result is saved to the variable named totalSalary
        //10. Total salary is computed variable or calculated variable
        decimal totalSalary = salaryOne + salaryTwo;
        sampLabel.Text = $"Total salary is {totalSalary:C}";
        //11. totalSalary/2 is the average salary
        decimal averageSalary = totalSalary / 2;
        sampLabel.Text += $"<br>The average salary is
        {averageSalary:C}";
    }
}
```

Now let's observe the action. Open Google Chrome and run the program, as shown in the following screenshot, to view the output:

Figure 2.7.8: The output showing average salary in Google Chrome

Notice that the total salary is nicely formatted as $90,000.00, and the average salary is nicely formatted as $45,000.00. Perfect!

Remember to right-click and select **View page source**. All you can see behind the scenes is simple text—nothing fancy. That's it. And of course, there is the supporting HTML. Remember, the purpose of HTML is to give structure to web pages, as shown in the following screenshot:

```
<!DOCTYPE html>

<html xmlns="http://www.w3.org/1999/xhtml">
<head><title>

</title></head>
<body>
    <form method="post" action="./Default.aspx" id="form1">
<div class="aspNetHidden">
<input type="hidden" name="__VIEWSTATE" id="__VIEWSTATE"
value="ZKf7it1S64XdKHLONWZUDVeiMxYGQRjbtLsOBhiFHsPmDS2idEy1wjvnNJs1XaclqlwgRh+Xy3OEDm+Zspk9LanRGq+PjjNUO1OVZInP
jtGWbdkDrXau29i1+N6Xtvm0gJBjT5MOzTS7xTE204yMEvQ363D3vZTn6rCaVyrZFdgHbIOuH3Qumh2oXXDyLtxwQjJRzRbDVMwfv17fND5H/g=
=" />
</div>

    <div>
        <span id="sampLabel">Total salary is $90,000.00<br>The average salary is $45,000.00</span>
    </div>

<div class="aspNetHidden">

    <input type="hidden" name="__VIEWSTATEGENERATOR" id="__VIEWSTATEGENERATOR" value="CA0B0334" />
</div></form>
<!-- Visual Studio Browser Link -->
<script type="application/json" id="__browserLink_initializationData">
    {"appName":"Firefox","requestId":"62d678a3adef450d96fac04c672c6404"}
</script>
<script type="text/javascript" src="http://localhost:58205/36282184db494324a3020cfb7b1bc0fd/browserLink"
async="async"></script>
<!-- End Browser Link -->

</body>
</html>
```

Figure 2.7.9: The page source for this chapter

# Summary

In this chapter, you learned how to use some simple math operations to add and average two salaries. In the next chapter, you will learn how to interact with users by collecting information from a text box in the web page.

# 10

# Interacting with Users Through the Web Page

In this chapter, you will learn how to read input, convert that input, and then produce output. So, let's take a look.

## Using Toolbox to search for a command

Open up the simple project. Go to **View** and then **Toolbox**, and drag **Toolbox** to position it on the left-hand side, as shown in the following screenshot:

```
6  <head><title>
7         Table Catalog
8  </title></head>
9  <body>
10     <form method="post" action="./Default.aspx" id="form1">
11  <div class="aspNetHidden">
12  <input type="hidden" name="__VIEWSTATE" id="__VIEWSTATE"
    value="T9+fgAPir2+06n2Xae7LlyBaGlC2ndTjF3/KIiv9PmLixh3QJF6VA4dBxcOsMYc36JhL9htMBE2uKI+30weQ3pH868Dnn
    JwpJukQDW9k/rVQ7bi9F7FrG5KS77q1X5BTHk00enz3EytE3lWLD/dHC+xRK7gJpGG5NdpV5eRhEoE5+3djoTl83A1tOVId3ALWk
    VjpGxCSx9V0cBCuu4jZeg==" />
13  </div>
14
15     <div>
16         <span id="sampLabel">This is a fancy table from
    France<br>Extendable:True<br>Price:$399.99</span>
17     </div>
18
19  <div class="aspNetHidden">
20
21         <input type="hidden" name="__VIEWSTATEGENERATOR" id="__VIEWSTATEGENERATOR" value="CA0B0334"
    />
22  </div></form>
```

Figure 2.8.1: Our starting project for this chapter

Next,type `tex` into the **Search** box,which searches for items containing `tex`. Then drag and drop a text box control into the markup:

```
<asp:TextBox ID="TextBox1" runat="server"></asp:TextBox><br />
```

To ensure that the text box and a label are stacked vertically, on the right end of the statement type `<br>`, and that's it.

Now, when you look at it in the **Design** view, you have the box, and it's on top of **Label**, as shown in the following screenshot:

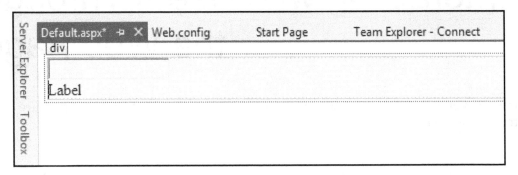

Figure 2.8.2: In the Design view, the box is on top of Label

# Adding an Event Handler

In the next stage, we will add an Event Handler. The purpose of doing this is so that after somebody inputs something into a box and hits *Enter*, you are able to process that value.

So, go into the **Design** view, and double-click on the box. This brings up Event Handler. The Event Handler is basically the code that runs when some event, like pressing a key, has occurred.

In our case, I'll add the following comment:

```
//7. Code below runs when the text is changed inside our little box
```

# Working with string input

In the next stage, you have to divide the sequence of steps that will do something useful. So, imagine that somebody inputs a value, you grab the value, and then you show that same value. However, it's been increased, for example, by 10 percent. To accomplish that, we'll do the following, starting with inserting comment 8:

```
//8. First read the value from the text property of the box
```

For A box that is called a `TextBox` to have a `Text` property is very sensible. Alright, let's do that by typing the following:

```
string input = TextBox1.Text;
```

If you go back to `Default.aspx` in **Source** View, when you drag an item in, it is automatically given the name `TextBox1`, as shown in the following screenshot, and that is what you also see being used in *Figure 2.8.4*:

```
<div>
    <asp:TextBox ID="TextBox1" runat="server" OnTextChanged="TextBox1_TextChanged"></asp:TextBox>
    <asp:Label ID="sampLabel" runat="server" Text="Label"></asp:Label>
</div>
```

Figure 2.8.3: When you drag an item in, it is automatically given the name TextBox1

```
//8. First read the value from the text property of the box
string input = TextBox1.Text;
```

Figure 2.8.4: You also see the name TextBox1 in Default.aspx.cs

Now further, if you hover your mouse over `Text` (in `TextBox1.Text`), as shown in the following screenshot, you see that it's got a **string** at the start which it can store, for example, and the same thing at the beginning of the statement; it's also a **string**, so the two data types are matched:

```
//8. First read the value from the text property of the box
string input = TextBox1.Text;
```

string System.Web.UI.WebControls.TextBox.Text { get; set; }
Gets or sets the text content of the System.Web.UI.WebControls.TextBox control.

Figure 2.8.5: The two data types, string, are matched

# Converting string input to a numerical value

Now that we have a `string` input, it means the following: imagine that somebody inputs the number 10, which will go between double quotes. We need to strip away the double quotes and produce a numerical version of the input. Keep in mind that when you type 10, it's not the way you see it that matters; it's how the computer sees it that matters. So, the computer will see the input as a string. You need to strip away the double quotes, as you need a numerical value. To do that you can convert it as follows:

```
double x = Convert.ToDouble(input);
```

# Working with methods

This is a way of making a method act on a variable. Let's express that in the comment for our purposes, with this simple level of explanation:

```
//9. Convert is a class that stores the ToDouble method
```

In a class, again at this level of explanation, you should think of it as a container; one of those things is a method, and a method is essentially the following:

```
//10. A method is a block of code that accepts input, operates on the input
and produces output
```

A method is a block of code that basically gets loaded into memory: it operates and produces output. So, in other words, this is what happens: a method is a block of code that accepts input, operates on input, and produces output. That's it. It's a little machine, just the way a program, if you think about it, is a little machine.

Now this is very important: hover your mouse over `ToDouble`, and notice that after it runs it produces a `double`, which is the same as the data type at the beginning of the statement. So, the data types match. Obviously, that's a big theme in C#. Furthermore, do you see where it's a `string` value? Well, in our case, that simply refers to the input that's also a `string` value, and we know that because it's from earlier where it says `string` input—it's a `string` data type. So, `string` in `string` input goes into `ToDouble`, and we know that this is OK because according to the definition of `ToDouble`, the value that it accepts is a `string` return type and the value that it produces after it runs is a `double`; that is then emphasized right at the beginning of the statement. Same `double`, as shown in the following screenshot:

Figure 2.8.6: All the data types match—a big theme in C#!

# Working with the converted numerical value

In the next stage, imagine that you've produced a numerical version that's acceptable; that is, you can make use of it. And what we are going to do is simply say the following:

```
sampLabel.Text = $"{x} increased by 10% is {x * 1.1}";
```

Again, we use the $ symbol for string interpolation and double quotes for a string. Now we want to say this in code: your value increased by 10%, or 110% percent of your value is a new number. In other words, increased by 10% is (and the only math that we are doing here is really very basic math). If you have a number, for example, 10, and you want 110% percent of it, multiply it by 1.1 and that will give you 110% of the number.

We do the same thing in our code. We take x, multiply it by 1.1, and close with a semicolon. That's it.

So, in the following line, there's a couple of different things on which we'll comment:

```
//11. x*1.1 produces 110% of the value of x and this value is then printed
on the screen
```

Remember, at runtime, x will be replaced by its actual value. The calculation will be done, and then we'll go into the string to be printed on the screen. Let's observe the action here. Open Google Chrome.

Alright, so we have a big box, as shown in the following screenshot. Again, it might be smaller on your screen when you launch it. You can use **Zoom** to increase or decrease it. I like a big one when you're learning; I think it helps.

Figure 2.8.7: When you open the code in Google Chrome, you see a big box

Now we'll input the number 100, for example, and then hit *Enter*. It now says 100 increased by 10% is 110, as shown in the following screenshot. That is correct:

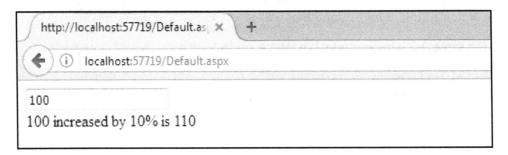

Figure 2.8.8: When 100 is entered into the box, it says 100 increased by 10% is 110

There's a flaw in the design of the program, and eventually we'll get to it. For now, just be aware of it. If you input a word such as ten, you can recognize it in your mind as a number 10. Programs, however, are not so smart. Everything always has to be spelled out very clearly. So, if you input the word ten and hit *Enter*, it generates an error message, like the one shown in *Figure 2.8.9*. It doesn't work; it doesn't allow that. It generates a format exception that the input was not in a format the current code can handle. It can handle 10, but it cannot handle the word ten. OK? So keep that in mind.

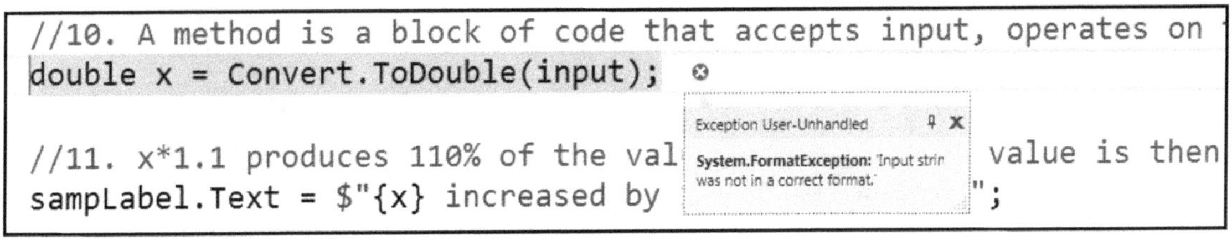

```
//10. A method is a block of code that accepts input, operates on
double x = Convert.ToDouble(input);  ⊗

//11. x*1.1 produces 110% of the val                              value is then
sampLabel.Text = $"{x} increased by                             ";
```

Exception User-Unhandled    ⊹ ✗

**System.FormatException:** 'Input strin
was not in a correct format.'

Figure 2.8.9: Error message generated when the word "ten" is the input instead of the number 10

# Summary

In this chapter, you learned how to read input from a text box using an Event Handler. You then converted that input into a form that your program could use by means of a method of a built-in class. Finally, you performed a calculation on your input and produced the output on the screen.

In the next chapter, we'll examine the use of something called *Method Chaining* to write more compact code.

# 11

# Using Method Chaining to Write More Compact Code

In this chapter, you will learn how to read input and then process it using *method chaining*. This is the ability to call multiple methods from left to right. In other words, the benefit is that you write less code.

## Inserting a text box into the markup

Let's begin with `Default.aspx`, as shown in the following screenshot, and then we will drag in a text box:

Figure 2.9.1: Our Default.aspx starting point for this chapter

To open the toolbox, go to **View** | **Toolbox** (*Ctrl+Alt+X*). Then, type `tex` into the **Search** box, and drag **TextBox** into the markup, as shown in the following screenshot:

```
<div>
    <asp:TextBox ID="TextBox1" runat="server" OnTextChanged="TextBox1_TextChanged"></asp:TextBox><br />
    <asp:Label ID="sampLabel" runat="server" Text=""></asp:Label>
</div>
```

Figure 2.9.2: TextBox is inserted into the markup

Remember, all that appears in `Default.aspx` is called *markup*.

# Entering your C# code

In the next stage, we'll switch to the **Design** View, and see that there's a box and it's a label, as shown in the following screenshot:

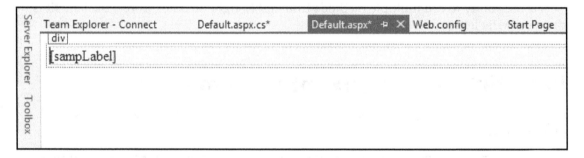

Figure 2.9.3: In the Design view, you see the box here and the label

Double-click on the box and that brings up a stub, as shown in the following code block. This is where we put our C#:

```
protected void TextBox1_TextChanged(object sender, EventArgs e)
{
}
```

Now, if you go back to the **Source** View for a second, it says `OnTextChanged` = and then the name of the `TextBox1_TextChanged` Event Handler, as shown here:

```
<asp:TextBox ID="TextBox1" runat="server"
OnTextChanged="TextBox1_TextChanged"></asp:TextBox>
```

The Event Handler is this block of code that you saw in the stub above. That's why the name `TextBox1_TextChanged` in the Event Handler and that name in the `Default.aspx` statement is the same. This is the connection between the markup in C#.

# Introducing method chaining

Now I'll write the following code in the stub. You can follow along by viewing the following line of code. First, we'll say `bool`, which is short for Boolean and a true or false type of quantity, and then enter `isLetterPresent`. What we will do is create a program that collects input and checks whether it contains a certain letter or not, as an example. Of course, the example that I'm showing you is completely made up, just to illustrate some concepts.

```
bool isLetterPresent = (TextBox1.Text).ToLower().Contains("e");
```

Now we'll say, insert `TextBox1.Text`. So, first we get the `Text` value from the `TextBox` by writing that line. Then after that, we type `.` (dot) and then we can apply methods. Remember, a method is prepackaged bit of functionality that we can use in our programs at this level of explanation.

Next, we will simply say `ToLower()`, and that will convert our value from the box to lowercase. Then type `.` (dot) again, and then we can perform another action, such as checking whether our box value contains the letter e:

```
bool isLetterPresent = (TextBox1.Text).ToLower().Contains("e");
```

Figure 2.9.4: Method chaining

We can say, for example, `Contains`, and then between double quotes put e. First, we read the value from the box, then we convert it to lowercase, and finally, we check whether it contains the letter e. This is method chaining.

Because the last method to be run is `Contains("e")`, we have to ensure that the result produced by the last method gives a data type that is compatible with `bool`. To do that, hover your mouse over `Contains`, as an example, and when you look at the popup, as seen in the following screenshot, you see it says `bool`, and that is compatible; that is, you see the same data types:

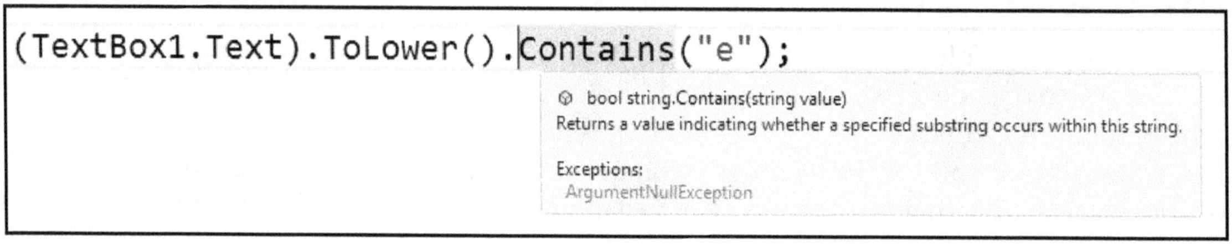

```
(TextBox1.Text).ToLower().Contains("e");
```

> ⊘ bool string.Contains(string value)
> Returns a value indicating whether a specified substring occurs within this string.
>
> Exceptions:
>  ArgumentNullException

Figure 2.9.5: The last data type is compatible with bool

This will work as expected. Now let's add some comments as follows.

We'll start with comment 7, assuming that we're numbering all the way from the top. So, first you get the value from the box, and by that I mean a `Text` value:

```
//7. First get text from text box
```

The second stage (comment 8) would then essentially be: run `ToLower` to convert the input to lowercase. The benefit of this is that if you want to make a case *insensitive* search, you convert everything to lowercase—don't mix the casing because then you might not find something that you want to find:

```
//8. Run ToLower to convert the input to lower case
```

For comment 9, we'll say: check for the presence of the letter e in the input. You do this using the `Contains` method. So, in comment 10, we note that the Contains method gives a `true` or `false` result, which means that `Contains` and `bool` are matched:

```
//9. Check for presence of letter e in the input
//10. Contains method gives a true or false kind of result
```

Now, in the next stage, imagine that we've gone through this whole process and we simply want to display some output to the users to confirm what we've done. So, enter the following code:

```
sampLabel.Text = $"It's {isLetterPresent} that your input contains the
letter e.";
```

There are, of course, a variety of messages that you can display, but enter the $ symbol for `string` interpolation, double quotes to make a string, and then say `"It's "`. Now you have to think a bit abstractly, the way you would think in English. It's either true or false, so your input contains the letter e.

Once more, it's true or maybe it's false that your input contains the letter e. That bit, that is, true or false, means that you put a placeholder with a variable name. So, our variable specifically is `isLetterPresent`.

We continue by entering it's true or false that your input contains the letter e. `";`. Remember to close with a semicolon.

# Testing your code

Now let's observe the action when we run the program; we'll launch it in Google Chrome. As shown in *Figure 2.9.6*, we have a box. Type the word `Hello`, for example, and hit *Enter*. It says that `It's True that your input contains the letter e`, and that is right. Now, for the sake of variety, enter a different word, such as fly, and then hit *Enter*. Now it says that it's *False* that your input contains the letter e, as seen in *Figure 2.9.7*:

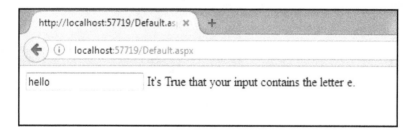

Figure 2.9.6: Message that is displayed when your input is True

Figure 2.9.7: Message that is displayed when your input is False

Remember, if you right-click and select **View page source**, behind the scenes, the box that we created in the markup is converted to a standard HTML box, as shown in *Figure 2.9.8*. The code highlighted in the screenshot is for a standard HTML box—that's all it is. Below that, in the screenshot, you'll observe that a label becomes a span in HTML; that's a development in HTML. You see it? But the `<div>` tag, a logical division of the page, stays the same as you see it:

```
<div>
    <input name="TextBox1" type="text" value="fly" id="TextBox1" />
    <span id="sampLabel">It's False that your input contains the letter e.</span>
</div>
```

Figure 2.9.8: The box that you created in the markup is converted to a standard HTML box

Let me close the **Page Source** window, hit the brown button in the `Default.aspx.cs` windows to unload, and close the output window.

Here, for clarity, the final `Default.aspx.cs` code for this chapter is as per the following code block:

```
//1. using is a keyword, so it's blue
//2. System is a name space that stores already created code
//3. using System brings in existing code

using System;

//4. a class is a required container for creating our own code samples
public partial class _Default : System.Web.UI.Page
{
    //5. The code below is where we place our own code
    //6. Page_Load is code that runs when a page loads from a server
    protected void Page_Load(object sender, EventArgs e)
    {

    }
    protected void TextBox1_TextChanged(object sender, EventArgs e)
    {
        //7. First get text from text box
        //8. Run ToLower to convert the input to lower case
        //9. Check for presence of letter e in the input
        //10. Contains method gives a true or false kind of result
        bool isLetterPresent = (TextBox1.Text).ToLower().
        Contains("e");
        sampLabel.Text = $"It's {isLetterPresent} that your input
        contains the letter e.";
    }
}
```

# Summary

These are the basics of method chaining. Specifically, `ToLower.Contains` is the bit that expresses method chaining.

In the next chapter, we'll take a look at making very simple decisions.

# 12
# Reacting to a Single Condition with If/Else Blocks

In this chapter, you'll learn how to use `if/else` blocks to make decisions.

## Adding checkbox to your code

Start by opening up **Toolbox** by going to **View** | **Toolbox** (*Ctrl+Alt+X*). Then type `Ch` and drag **CheckBox** into the markup, as shown here in the following screenshot:

```
 1  <%@ Page Language="C#" AutoEventWireup="true" CodeFile="Default.aspx.cs" Inherits="_Default" %>
 2
 3  <!DOCTYPE html>
 4
 5  <html xmlns="http://www.w3.org/1999/xhtml">
 6  <head runat="server">
 7      <title></title>
 8  </head>
 9  <body>
10      <form id="form1" runat="server">
11          <asp:CheckBox ID="CheckBox1" runat="server" />
12          <asp:Label ID="sampLabel1" runat="server" Text="Label">
13          </asp:Label>
14      <div>
15
16      </div>
17      </form>
18  </body>
19  </html>
20
```

Figure 3.1.1: CheckBox has been dragged into the markup

**CheckBox** is just a box—it either has a check mark or it doesn't. That's it. Then under CheckBox, wrap the Label within a panel by typing panel into the **Search Toolbox** field. Drag and drop a **panel** control into the page, as shown in the following screenshot:

# Adding a panel statement

Figure 3.1.2: A panel line has been inserted into the markup

Close **Toolbox**—we don't need it anymore. Now, space it out a little (by hitting the *Enter* key few times<asp:Label>) and then drag the **Label** into the space between the tags that define the panel markup. That's it.

In the**Design**view, we have just [CheckBox1] with [sampLabel] beneath it. Look at it.

# Testing the checkbox

Now crank it up in Google Chrome. You will see a simple checkbox. When you click on it, it gets checked or unchecked because this is a true or false type of quantity:

Figure 3.1.3: CheckBox appearing in the Chrome browser

So, `checked = "true"`, not `checked = "false"`. There are only two possible values, and this is a good candidate for working with `if/else` blocks in C# for that very reason.

# Working with the AutoPostBack property

Now go back to the `Default.aspx` source code. One more thing that I want to do on `CheckBox` is to add a property or attribute called `AutoPostBack` and set that equal to `true`, as shown in the following code block:

```
<asp:CheckBox ID="CheckBox1" runat="server" AutoPostBack="true" />
```

This will retrieve a fresh copy of the page from the server basically every time you either check or uncheck the box.

In the next stage, if you want a default value in the box when it first loads to be checked, type `Checked="true" "/>`, so you get the following:

```
<asp:CheckBox ID="CheckBox1" runat="server" AutoPostBack="true"
Checked="true"/>
```

Even here, when you type =, notice that only two options pop up, either `false` or `true`. These are used to control `if/else` blocks, so keep that in mind.

Now run the code in Google Chrome. Give it a second to do its magic, and voila! See? Notice that when you uncheck it, the icon spins to indicate that it's getting a copy from the server, and then when you check it again, the same thing happens. Now we have a page that is dynamic, and that is accomplished by enabling `AutoPostBack` in this simple case:

Figure 3.1.4: The checkbox appearing as checked in the Google Chrome browser

Go to the **Design** view, and then double-click on `[CheckBox1]`. This generates an event handling stub. The code that we have to write goes below the open curly brace. If you go back to `Default.aspx` in the **Source** View, notice that the following has been added at the right-hand side of the `CheckBox` line:

```
OnCheckedChanged="CheckBox1_CheckedChanged"/>
```

The name of the `CheckBox1` item is the same as the name of the item in the stub in `Default.aspx.cs` shown in the following and preceding code blocks. That's how you establish the connections in C# so that actions are taken and handled properly.

```
protected void CheckBox1_CheckedChanged(object sender, EventArgs e)
```

# Constructing an if statement

So, now we'll enter the following between the curly braces in the `Default.aspx.cs` stub:

```
if (CheckBox1.Checked)
```

We saw previously that checked means either `true` or `false`. That is why we can use it with an `if` statement, as you see in the preceding line of code. If you hover your mouse over `if`, as shown in the following screenshot, it says `bool`, which is short for Boolean. In other words, this is a true or false kind of quantity, which means that you can use it with an `if` statement to make a decision:

```
if (CheckBox1.Checked //7. Checks to see wheter a check box is checked
{
         bool CheckBox.Checked { get; set; }
      Gets or sets a value indicating whether the CheckBox control is checked.
```

Figure 3.1.3: Using bool and if to make a decision

If the box has been checked, then we can show the panel. To do that, we will enter the following between the curly braces beneath our `if` statement:

```
Panel1.Visible = true;
```

Now, as you can see in *Figure 3.1.6*, `true` is a Boolean value, a `true` or `false` value. It's a keyword and it's shown in color. It's not a word as we think of it; that is, it has a specific reserved meaning in C#:

```
Panel1.Visible = true;// 8. Code runs when a user wants to see the panel.
          struct System.Boolean
          Represents a Boolean (true or false) value.
```

Figure 3.1.6: true is a Boolean, a true or false value

When you hover your mouse over `Visible`, you observe that it's also `bool`, a Boolean. So, in other words, the two data types are matched on the two sides:

```
Panel1.Visible = true;// 8. Code runs when a user wants to see the panel.
          bool System.Web.UI.Control.Visible { get; set; }
          Gets or sets a value that indicates whether a server control is rendered as UI on the page.
```

Figure 3.1.5: The two data types are matched

Here we'll add comment 7 to continue from the top. This statement checks to see whether `CheckBox` is checked. So many checks, huh?

```
if(CheckBox1.Checked) //7. Checks to see whether a check box is checked
```

Now the following code runs essentially when a user wants to see panel, so add comment 8:

```
Panel1.Visible = true; //8. Code runs when a user wants to see panel
```

# Constructing an else statement

Remember, within the `panel` markup is a `label` markup that contains text. On the other hand, if the box is not checked—we've unchecked the box. We'll add an `else` statement, and run some other code simply to hide the **panel**:

Now enter the following code:

```
else
 {
 Panel1.Visible = false;
 }
```

We'll enter `else` and run some other code simply to hide the `panel` control. Again, we will start with `Panel1.Visible` and set that equal to `false`, which is another Boolean, as you can see in the following screenshot. It's still a `true` or `false` value; it's a reserved keyword and is in color, that's how you know.

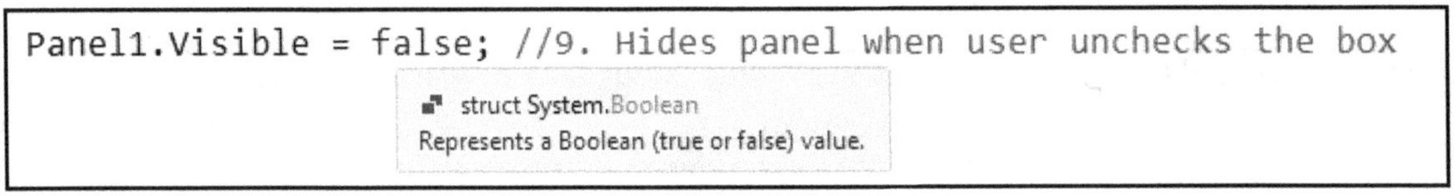

```
Panel1.Visible = false; //9. Hides panel when user unchecks the box
            struct System.Boolean
            Represents a Boolean (true or false) value.
```

Figure 3.1.6: false is a Boolean, a true or false value

The `false` keyword is a Boolean data type on the right-hand side, and on the left-hand side, `Visible` is also designed to store `true` or `false` values, which means that the two data types are matched. Now we can set comment 9 here, essentially saying that this line hides the `panel` control when the user unchecks the box. That's the objective there.

```
else
{
    Panel1.Visible = false; //9. Hides panel when user unchecks box
}
```

That's our simple code—that's all the C# we need.

# Testing your code

Now crank up the project in Google Chrome. You'll notice first that the box is checked. OK? If you click on it, it will be unchecked.

Figure 3.1.9: Checked and unchecked

There's one more thing that we have to do with this. Close the window and close Chrome. Now go back to `Default.aspx`, and add the `Hello World` text, as shown here:

```
<asp:Label ID="sampLabel" runat="server" Text="">Hello, World</asp:Label>
```

Now run it again one last time. Alright, `Hello World` is displayed when you check the box, as seen in the following screenshot; uncheck the box, it goes away, and so on. Behind the scenes, this is all powered by C#:

Figure 3.1.10: Check the box and Hello World is displayed

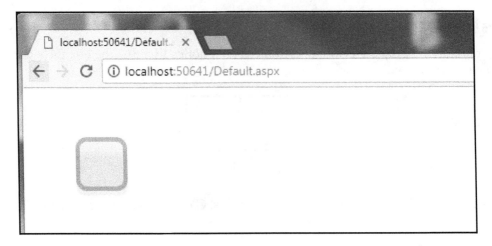

Figure 3.1.11:Uncheck the box and Hello World disappears

Again, for clarity, the final `Default.aspx.cs` code for this chapter is displayed in the following code block:

```
//1. using is a keyword, it's blue
//2. System is a name space that stores already created code
//3. using System brings in existing code
using System;

//4. class is a required container for creating our own code samples
public partial class _Default : System.Web.UI.Page
{
    //5. code below is where we place our own code
    //6. Page_load is code that runs when a page loads from a server
    protected void Page_Load(object sender, EventArgs e)
    {
    }


    protected void CheckBox1_CheckedChanged(object sender, EventArgs
    e)
    {
        if (CheckBox1.Checked) //7. Checks to see
        whether a check box is checked
        {
            Panel1.Visible = true; // 8.code runs when user wants to
            see panel

        }
        else
```

```
        {
            Panel1.Visible = false; //9. Hides panel when user
            unchecks box
        }


    }
}
```

# Summary

In this chapter, you learned about working with the `if/else` blocks.

In the next chapter, you will continue to learn about C# and specifically how to make variable values grow. We'll eventually need that to talk about loops.

# 13
# Making a Variable Grow by Adding 1

In this chapter, you will learn how to make a variable value grow by one. This absolutely makes a difference because when we talk about loops next, this is essentially assumed knowledge.

## Growing a variable by one

Let's begin with a simple HTML page, as shown here in *Figure 3.2.1*. Then, open up a C# page, which looks like *Figure 3.2.2*; some people call this *the code-behind page*. That makes sense, right? It's the C# code behind the HTML. Here, keep in mind that all we will do is to demonstrate the operation of a single concept or a couple of related concepts:

```
Server Explorer   Toolbox     Default.aspx.cs     Default.aspx  ⊕ ×
    1   <%@ Page Language="C#" AutoEventWireup="true" CodeFile="Default.aspx.cs" Inherits="_Default" %>
    2
    3   <!DOCTYPE html>
    4
    5   <html xmlns="http://www.w3.org/1999/xhtml">
    6   <head runat="server">
    7       <title></title>
    8   </head>
    9   <body>
   10       <form id="form1" runat="server">
   11               <asp:Label ID="sampLabel1" runat="server" Text=""> Hello World</asp:Label>
   12       </form>
   13   </body>
   14   </html>
   15
```

Figure 3.2.1: Our starting point for this chapter

```
Toolbox      Default.aspx.cs*  -□  X  Default.aspx
2_Default.aspx                                        _Default
   1   //1. using is a keyword, it's blue
   2   //2. System is a name space that stores already created code
   3   //3. using System brings in existing code
   4   using System;
   5
   6   //4. class is a required container for creating our own code samples
   7   public partial class _Default : System.Web.UI.Page
   8   {
   9       //5. code below is where we place our own code
  10       //6. Page_load is code that runs when a page loads from a server
  11       protected void Page_Load(object sender, EventArgs e)
  12       {
  13
  14       }
  15   }
```

Figure 3.2.2: The starting "behind" page for this chapter

Now insert the following line and comment:

```
int x = 5; //7. Variable is needed so we have something whose values can grow
```

The only reason for having this variable present is that it is needed so that you have something whose values can grow.

The first way of growing a value is simply to type x++. Insert the following line and comment:

```
x++; //8. x++ has the result of making the value of x grow by 1
```

That's it! Simple enough.

Now let's display the updated value of x, and for that we'll enter the following:

```
sampLabel.Text = $"The current value of x is {x}";
```

Again, you follow `sampLabel.Text =` by the $ symbol for string interpolation, and double quotes.

Note that we put x within curly braces so that its value can be merged into the string and shown in the window.

That is relatively easy. Let's take a look at it in action by opening it in Google Chrome, as shown in the following screenshot:

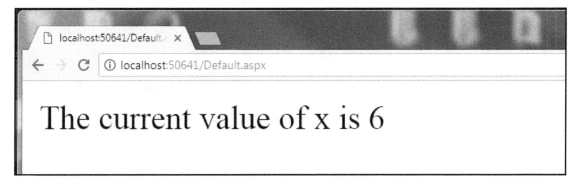

Figure 3.2.3: The resulting value shown in Google Chrome

So, the current value of x is 6. That is true. Close the output window and the **Solution Explorer** panel.

# Another way to grow a variable

In the next stage, you will learn about another thing that you can do to grow a variable. To do this, enter the following line and comment, which explains the purpose of this line:

```
x = x + 1; //9. x=x+1 means: grab x, increase its value by 1 and store back
to x
```

Grow its value by 1 and store the value back to x.

In comment 8, it's the same thing, where it says x++ has a result of making the value of x grow by 1, that value is then stored back to the same x. So, throughout this entire process, there's only the x variable involved, only one variable.

Let's print the updated value. Take the following line from `Default.aspx.cs`, highlight it, press *Ctrl+C* to copy, and then press *Ctrl+V* to paste:

```
sampLabel.Text = $"The current value of x is {x}";
```

> If you want to go back to the beginning of a line you hit **Home**, if you want to go to the end of a line, on your keyboard you hit *End*.

Because you want this output to be accumulated with the previous output or appended to it, insert +=. Also, because you want it to be on its own line, insert a <br> tag as shown in the following code block:

```
sampLabel.Text += $"<br>The current value of x is {x}";
```

Let's take a look at the updated result in Google Chrome:

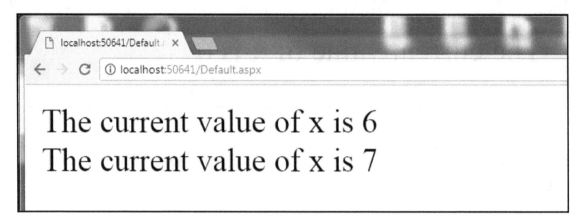

Figure 3.2.4: The current values of x, achieved in two different ways, are displayed

Here, it says the current value of x is 7. That is true. So, you see the value of x growing clearly from 6 to 7. This is our simple code.

Again, for review, the final `Default.aspx.cs` code for this chapter is displayed in the following code block:

```
//1. using is a keyword, it's blue
//2. System is a name space that stores already created code
//3. using System brings in existing code

using System;

//4. class is a required container for creating our own code samples
public partial class _Default : System.Web.UI.Page
{
    //5. code below is where we place our own code
    //6. Page_load is code that runs when a page loads from a
    server
    protected void Page_Load(object sender, EventArgs e)
    {
        int x = 5; //7. Variable is needed so we have something
        whose values can grow
```

```
x++; //8. x++ has the result of making the value of x grow
by 1
sampLabel.Text = $"The current value of x is {x}";

x = x + 1; //9. x=x+1 means: grab x, grow its value by 1 and
store the value back to x
sampLabel.Text += $"<br>The current value of x is {x}";
    }
}
```

# Summary

In this chapter, you learned how to grow a variable by 1. In the next chapter, we'll talk about loops, and ++ will be super important.

# 14

# Repeating Blocks of Code with While Loops

In this chapter, you will learn how to work with while loops. The `While` loops are indispensable in real life. For example, you can use them to read a large number of rows from a file very quickly. But I'll show you a slightly more academic example to keep things comprehensible and understandable.

## Inserting a button

In our case, we'll display a list of squares of some values. Enter the following temporarily at the bottom of our starting HTML file:

```
1*1 = 1
2*2 = 4
3*3 = 9
4*4 = 16
```

Clearly, doing it by hand this way is not good, so delete these lines. Essentially, we need a superior way, a faster way, or a more mechanical and more efficient way. So, go to **View** | **Toolbox**, and select **Button**, as shown in the following screenshot:

Figure 3.3.1: Select Button from Toolbox

Now drag **Button** and drop it into the markup, right above the Label tag, as seen in the following screenshot. Close **Toolbox** and then **Solution Explorer**, as we don't need either of these:

```
Default.aspx.cs*        Default.aspx*  ↔ ✕
     1  <%@ Page Language="C#" AutoEventWireup="true" CodeFile="Default.aspx.cs" Inherits="_Default" %>
     2
     3  <!DOCTYPE html>
     4
     5  <html xmlns="http://www.w3.org/1999/xhtml">
     6  <head runat="server">
     7      <title></title>
     8  </head>
     9  <body>
    10      <form id="form1" runat="server">
    11          <asp:Button ID="Button1" runat="server" Text="Button" />
    12          <asp:Label ID="sampLabel" runat="server" Text=""></asp:Label>
    13      </form>
    14  </body>
    15  </html>
    16
```

Figure 3.3.2: The button dragged into the markup, right above Label

When you switch to the **Design** View, you have a **Button** and a **Label**, as shown in the following screenshot:

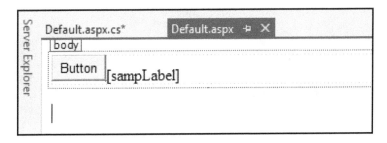

Figure 3.3.3: The button and label shown in the Design view

Now we name the text on the Button so that it's more informative. We'll say here List Squares so that you understand the purpose of what we will do:

```
<asp:Button ID="Button1" runat="server" Text="List Squares" />
```

# Modifying the button

To start the next stage, put a `<br>` tag after the button so that **Button** and **Label** are on separate lines. In other words, now they are vertically stacked and Button has text that's useful, List Squares:

```
<asp:Button ID="Button1" runat="server" Text="List Squares" /> <br/>
```

To make use of the `Button` control, double-click on it (see *Figure 3.3.4*) to bring up `button1_Click`. This is the Event Handler, which you can see directly below the `Button` control in the following screenshot:

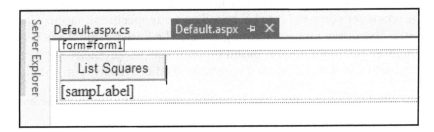

Figure 3.3.4: The button and label are on separate lines

This is the code that runs when somebody clicks on it:

```
protected void Button1_Click(object sender, EventArgs e)
{

}
```

# Creating a while loop

Now let's create the code. Let's type the following:

```
int howManyTimes = 5;
```

Here, `int` is a data type for whole numbers.

Note that I'm naming my variables very meaningfully, and I'm using *camel casing*. Camel casing is called that because the capital letters within the text look like the humps of a camel. It's the capital `M` and `T` within `howManyTimes`. You see?

Now of course, as you can imagine, there are rules for naming variables, but usually, just don't make them too long. Be sure to make them meaningful so that you understand their purpose even if you look at your code two months from now or ten months from now.

So, `int howManyTimes =`, in our particular case, let's say 5. Now, after the statement, add comment 7, if we are counting from the top, to indicate the purpose of this variable:

```
//7. Value tells how many times in all a loop will run
```

The next stage in the process is to create a counter variable, so enter the following:

```
int counter = 1;
```

Keep in mind the fact that when I chose 5 earlier this means absolutely nothing. That number can be whatever you need it to be, based on your specific situation. The fact that the counter is set to `1` also doesn't mean anything either. The initial value that's being assigned can also be whatever you need it to be, based on your specific problem. So, you have to take a look at your situation and think about it carefully. And obviously, you should experiment.

Now add comment 8 after the statement. It serves a generic kind of purpose as follows:

```
//8. This variable keeps the loop going
```

By this I mean that it constructs the loop. Now we'll enter this:

```
while (counter<=howManyTimes)
```

Let's also add comment 9:

```
//9. counter<=howManyTimes is the logical condition that controls the
operation of the loop
```

By logical condition, <= is a less than or equal to sign. If you hover your mouse over it, the tooltip, shown in *Figure 3.3.5*, tells you that when it operates, it produces a Boolean or a `true` or `false` value. Because that is so, you can use it with `counter<=howManyTimes`, which is a Boolean or a `true` or `false` kind of condition. It's either true or it's not.

Furthermore, you will observe that the operator itself is this quantity, operator <=, so that is the operator, the less than equal to. Of course, there are other ones that you learned about in school, like greater than, greater than or equal to >=, and so on.

```
//9. counter<=howmanytimes is the logical condition that controls the operation of the loop
while(counter<=howManyTimes)
}                    ⊙  bool int.operator <=(int left, int right)
```

Figure 3.3.5: Tooltip for <= , or the less than equal to sign

Where it says `int left`, that of course refers to the value of the counter and `int right` refers to the value to the right of `howManyTimes`. Everything that you see highlighted in the tooltip is meaningful and is there for a definite reason.

We have our condition. That is what controls the operation of the loop. Once the condition fails, the loop exits; let's add that as comment 10:

```
//10. once counter variable is greater than howManyTimes, the loop fails
```

This comment means that it exits, that is, we stop looping.

Now you'll say the following between the curly braces. Remember, we're displaying the squares of some basic numbers. To make that happen, type the following:

```
sampLabel.Text += $"<br>{counter}^2";
```

 You cannot use just +, because if you do, you will overwrite the text every single time; only the latest line will be visible. += appends or accumulates, so you see all of the lines of output.

Once again, we put a $ symbol for string interpolation, double quotes to make a string, <br> so that the content is pushed down to the next line, and then, within the curly braces, you type counter and ^2 (squared).

Now, remember here that the quantity represented by {counter} will be replaced with the actual value of the counter variable. The <br> tag serves as a way of pushing output down to the next line, the $ symbol is there to ensure string interpolation, and the +=operator forces stuff to be appended together so that the string gets bigger and bigger and bigger.

When you see something in brown (or orange), this means that it goes out to the screen exactly in that form, except of course stuff like <br>, which is really HTML. So, that produces a visible effect.

# Working with the Math class

Now we will use the Math class. The Math class is great as it has a lot of methods which are useful. Type the following: Math, the name of the class and . (dot). These are methods—things that I can calculate. One of them is Pow (power). In the pop-up tooltip, you'll see double x and double y. What you have to do is to specify two values; counter is the first value, that is, the value which you want to square, and then,^2, which means squared. Your statement should appear as follows:

```
sampLabel.Text += $"<br>{counter}^2={Math.Pow(counter, 2)}";
```

Now let's add comment 11 above this statement so that we understand what we are doing:

```
//11. Math.Pow(counter,2) means square the value of the counter: 1, 1*1=1,
2*2=4, 3*3=9
```

Here, it's a basic squaring operation—basic math. Remember to close with a semicolon.

At the next stage, type `counter++`. Remember, in the previous chapter you learned that `++` has the effect of adding values—that is what it is doing for us. So, now let's add comment 12 following the statement:

```
counter++; //12. counter++ grows the counter by 1 every time the loop runs
```

You have to do what it says in the comment; if you don't, the loop will never stop. In fact, it would never stop because this counter's condition would always be `true`, and the counter would always be less than or equal to `howManyTimes`.

# Running the code

Now let's take a look at the output in Google Chrome:

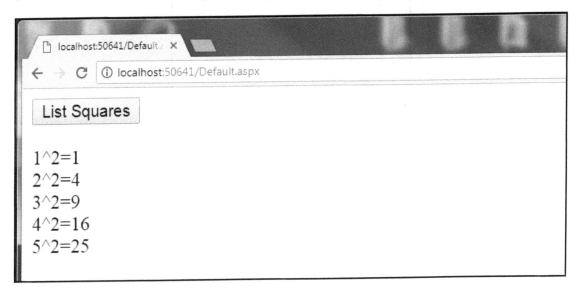

Figure 3.3.6: The list of squares generated as a result of running our code

# Experimenting with the code

If you want to understand anything in more detail, what would you do? You experiment and see what are the effects of changing quantities. Let's change the value in the statement here to say 25 and then run the code again to observe what happens. The result is shown in the following screenshot:

```
int howManyTimes = 25;
```

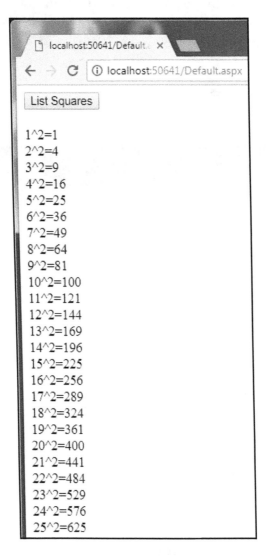

Figure 3.3.7: By changing the value to 25, the list of squares generated increases

This is how you can understand things in more detail. Make more modifications, run the code, observe the result, and then usually the meaning becomes much clearer. Now when you take a look and scroll down, you will see that there are 25 values—that is what it means.

The fact that we're going by 1s is not special. This means that I could change the `counter++` variable so that it goes up by 2 if I wanted to do that. And, if you remove the `<br>`tag in this somewhat complex example and run the code, you will observe that you get everything as the output on a horizontal line, as shown in the following screenshot:

Figure 3.3.8: By removing <br>, the list of squares generated appears on a horizontal line

Close all of the panels, put the `<br>` tag back, and so on. That's how you can learn more about this: remove it, run it, and observe the result so that you understand what the purpose is and why it's present.

Again, for review, the final `Default.aspx.cs` file for this chapter is displayed in the following code block:

```
//1. using is a keyword, it's blue
//2. System is a name space that stores already created code
//3. using System brings in existing code
using System;

//4. class is a required container for creating our own code samples
public partial class _Default : System.Web.UI.Page
{
    //5. code below is where we place our own code
    //6. Page_load is code that runs when a page loads from a server
    protected void Page_Load(object sender, EventArgs e)
    {
    }

    protected void Button1_Click(object sender, EventArgs e)
    {
        int howManyTimes = 25;//7. Value tells how many times in all
        a loop will run
        int counter = 1;//8. This variable keeps the loop going
        //9. counter<=howmanytimes is the logical condition that
        //controls the operation of the loop
```

```
//10. once counter variable is greater than howManytimes
while (counter <= howManyTimes)
{
    //11. Math.Pow(counter,2) means square the value of the
    counter: 1, 1*1=1, 2*2=4, 3*3=9
    sampLabel.Text += $"{counter}^2={Math.Pow(counter, 2)}";
    counter++; //12. counter++ grows the counter by 1 every
    //time the loop runs
}
}
}
```

# Summary

In this chapter, you learned how to work with `while` loops. You inserted and programmed a button, created your first while loop, used the `Math` class to square the results, and ran and modified your code to change the output.

In the next chapter, we'll talk about `for` loops.

# 15

# Repeating Blocks of Code with For Loops

In this chapter, you'll learn how to use the `for` loops; you'll also learn about list boxes.

## Inserting a button

First, let's put a button inside an HTML file. For this, go to **View** | **Toolbox** and select **Button**, as shown in in the following screenshot:

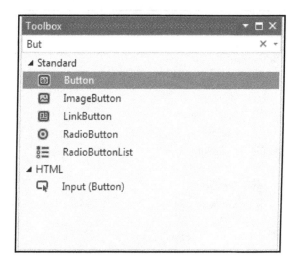

Figure 3.4.1: Selecting Button from Toolbox

Now drag **Button** and drop it into the page, right below `form`, as seen in the following screenshot. As the purpose of a**Button**control would be to click on it, we can fill `ListBox` using a `for` loop. Keep this in mind; this is the objective here.

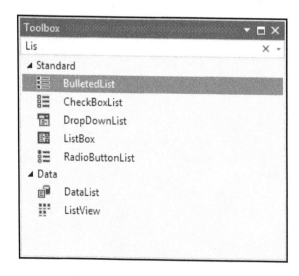

```
Default.aspx.cs  ⊕  ✕  Default.aspx*  ⊕  ✕
 1  <%@ Page Language="C#" AutoEventWireup="true" CodeFile="Default.aspx.cs" Inherits="_Default" %>
 2
 3  <!DOCTYPE html>
 4
 5  <html xmlns="http://www.w3.org/1999/xhtml">
 6  <head runat="server">
 7      <title></title>
 8  </head>
 9  <body>
10      <form id="form1" runat="server">
11          <asp:Button ID="Button1" runat="server" Text="FillBox"/> </br>
12      </form>
13  </body>
14  </html>
15
```

Figure 3.4.2: The Button line has been dragged into the page below form

Change the displayed text such that it says, for example, `FillBox`, so that the purpose is clear. Next, type a `<br>`tag to break down `FillBox` and bring it down to the next line. Then, after **Button**, put **ListBox**. So type `listb` in the **SearchToolbox** box, as shown in the following screenshot:

Figure 3.4.3: Types of lists available in Visual Studio

# Inserting ListBox

There are several types of lists: there's **Bulleted List**, for example, but just put a **ListBox**control to the markup. Your `Default.aspx` file should now look as shown in the following screenshot:

```
Default.aspx.cs     Default.aspx* ⊕ ✕
 1  <%@ Page Language="C#" AutoEventWireup="true" CodeFile="Default.aspx.cs" Inherits="_Default" %>
 2
 3  <!DOCTYPE html>
 4
 5  <html xmlns="http://www.w3.org/1999/xhtml">
 6  <head runat="server">
 7      <title></title>
 8  </head>
 9  <body>
10      <form id="form1" runat="server">
11          <asp:Button ID="Button1" runat="server" Text="FillBox"/> </br>
12          <asp:ListBox ID="ListBox1" runat="server"></asp:ListBox>
13      </form>
14  </body>
15  </html>
16
```

Figure 3.4.4: ListBox has been inserted into the markup

That's all we really need; that's the visual aspect of our interface. Let's take a look at it in the**Design**view. You will see `FillBox` and `Unbound`, as shown in the following screenshot:

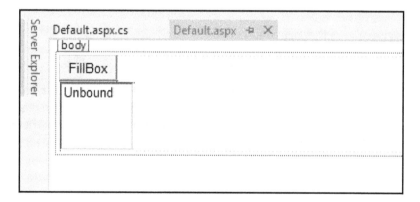

Figure 3.4.5: In the Design view, you see FillBox and Unbound

# Binding in the code

Now, let's bind it in code. Double-click on `FillBox` to bring up the event handler:

```
protected void Button1_Click(object sender, EventArgs e)
{
}
```

# Starting a for loop

This is the code that runs when you want to fill the box with some entries. How do we actually do that? Well, we will begin as follows:

```
for (int i = 1; i <= 20; i++)
```

What we have here essentially is a `for` loop. The `int i = 1` declaration is a variable declaration. In a `while` loop, the variable is declared outside it. Here, it's declared as part of the definition of the loop.

Then we have a logical condition: `i<=10`. We had a logical condition with the `while` loop. So far, if you think about it carefully, this is a very similar concept, logically speaking; that is, it's not altogether different.

Now, the `i++` variable is needed to keep the loop going; it grows the value of `i` as the loop executes.

Insert the following above the `for` loop code:

```
ListBox1.Items.Clear();
```

This is needed for the following reason: if you click on the `FillBox` button to fill the box without that line, the output just gets bigger and bigger--it grows and grows and grows. `ListBox1.Items.Clear();` clears out the items in the box. `ListBox1` is the name of the box. `Items` is the collection of items that you have stored inside it, and `Clear` is a method that can get rid of them--move them away or clear them away.

Now we'll add the 7th comment immediately following this line:

```
//7. Needed to clear box so output does not accumulate
```

For the next stage, let's add some more comments:

```
//8. int i=1 simply means the first value to show in the box will be 1
```

This comment means that the first value to show in the box will be 1. It could be 0, for example, so nothing special about it to be honest:

```
//9. i<=10 is the logical condition that makes the loop until say, i=11,
and then the condition fails
```

The logical condition that makes the loop run is i<=10. The loop ends once the condition has failed. For example, once i assumes the value 11, then the condition will fail; it will stop running:

```
//10. i++ is needed to keep the value of i growing
```

In the context of while loops, we saw exactly the same logic. We saw counter++; here, it's i++. There's nothing special about using i; you can also use counter if you want.

## Filling ListBox using the for loop

Now we'll take our loop and fill the box. How can we accomplish this? Well, take a look.

If you had ListBox1.Items.Clear() earlier, you very likely have a method called Add here:

```
ListBox1.Items.Add(i);
```

Notice the list of methods that you can run that pops up as you type (see *Figure 3.4.6*). You can clear away the items in the list or you can add to them. You can put an item inside the list, then put in `i` and close with a semicolon:

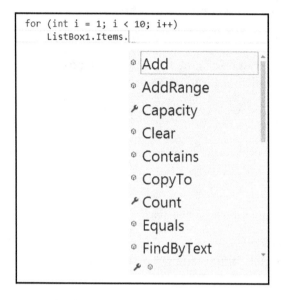

Figure 3.4.6: Popup of the list of methods that you can run

Wait! There's an error message. If you hover your mouse over `i`, the message appears, as shown in the following screenshot:

```
for (int i = 1; i < 10; i++)
    ListBox1.Items.Add(i);
```

[●] (local variable) int i

Argument 1: cannot convert from 'int' to 'string'

Figure 3.4.7: Error message indicating that you cannot convert from int to string

The message says `cannot convert from 'int' to 'string'`--an integer to a string. Well, we can actually do this as follows:

```
ListBox1.Items.Add(i.ToString());
```

First, type `.` (dot), then the method on the screen can be used to operate on `i`. One of them is called `ToString`, as shown in the following screenshot. It converts a numeric value to a string representation.

```
for (int i = 1; i < 10; i++)
    ListBox1.Items.Add(i.);
```
```
⊕ CompareTo
⊕ Equals
⊕ GetHashCode
⊕ GetType
⊕ GetTypeCode
⊕ ToString      string int.ToString() (+ 3 overloads)
                Converts the numeric value of this instance to its equivalent string representation.
```

Figure 3.4.8: The ToString method converts a numeric value to a string representation

Let's add the 11th comment immediately after this line:

```
//11. i.ToString() takes 5 and produces "5"
```

Be sure to insert the double quotes. Remember, it's not how it looks to you but how it looks to the computer. The computer sees the number 5 and "5" (within double quotes) as two different data types.

You'll notice another thing here because there's only one line of logic after the `for` statement. It is a single line of logic. With this line, you don't even needcurly braces:

```
for (int i = 1; i <= 20; i++)
    ListBox1.Items.Add(i.ToString());//11. i.ToString() takes 5 and
    produces "5"
}
```

Let's see this in action. Open Google Chrome and click on `FillBox`. The box, as shown in the following screenshot, has been filled, you see?

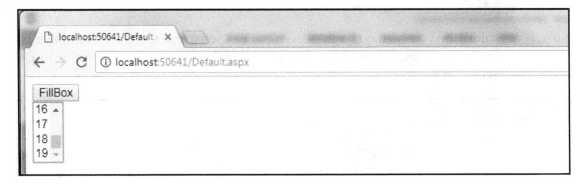

Figure 3.4.9: FillBox has been populated with a ton of values

Obviously, generating values like this by hand can be tedious and time-consuming, and this loop is superior. Or, if you had to read from such a box, clearly, using a loop like the one we just built would be superior.

Also, if you want to know the purpose of anything more clearly, what would you do? Switch the `for` statement over from say 10 to 20; the difference in results usually reveals the purpose of the quantity you have changed, as shown in the following code block:

```
for (int i = 1; i <= 20; i++)
```

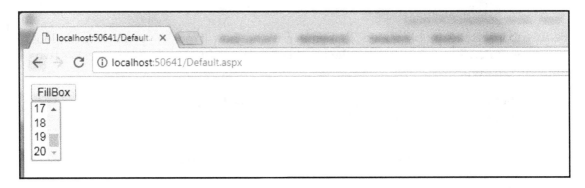

Figure 3.4.10: The Fill Box has now been populated with 20 values

Click on `FillBox`, then the top value will now be `20` and so on.

There is one more thing to note here. Imagine that you want to go by twos. Is that possible? The answer is yes. For example, you can type the following code:

```
for (int i = 1; i <= 20; i=i+2)
```

This will essentially make `i` grow by two every time instead of one. Let's take a look, in Google Chrome, at the values that show on the screen when we do that:

Figure 3.4.11: The values now grow by two

The output goes `1`, then `1` and `2` is `3`, `3` and `2` is `5`, `5` and `2` is `7`—all the way to the end where `17 + 2` is `19`. So now you're going by twos after changing the value in the `for` statement. But it's customary to go by ones, so `i++` is more commonly used.

For review, the final `Default.aspx.cs` code for this chapter is displayed in the following code block:

```
//1. using is a keyword, it's blue
//2. System is a name space that stores already created code
//3. using System brings in existing code
using System;

//4. class is a required container for creating our own code samples
public partial class _Default : System.Web.UI.Page
{
    //5. code below is where we place our own code
    //6. Page_load is code that runs when a page loads from a server
    protected void Page_Load(object sender, EventArgs e)
    {
    }
```

```
protected void Button1_Click1(object sender, EventArgs e)
{
    ListBox1.Items.Clear();//7. Needed to clear box so output
    //does not accumulate
    //8. int i=1 simply means the first value to show in the box
    //will be 1
    //9. i<=10 is the logical condition that makes the loop
    //until say, i=11, and then the condition fails
    //10. i++ is needed to keep the value of i growing

    for (int i = 1; i <= 20; i=i+2)
        ListBox1.Items.Add(i.ToString());//11. i.ToString()
        //takes 5 and produces "5"
}
}
```

# Summary

In this chapter, you learned how to work with `for` loops. You inserted a `Button` and a `ListBox` control, created and modified your first `for` loop, and filled in the list box using the `for` loop.

In the next chapter, we'll talk about `foreach` loops and how they can be used to iterate over collections of items.

# 16
# Iterating Over Collections with foreach Loops

In this chapter, you'll learn about `foreach` loops. These are good for examining collections of items.

## Inserting TextBox

Imagine that you are within `Default.aspx`. Make sure that you are within the form element, as shown in the following code block:

```
<form id="form1" runat="server">
</form>
```

The first thing to be done is this: basically, grab and drag a box--TextBox. For this, go to **View | Toolbox**, type **Tex**, and select **TextBox**, as shown in the following screenshot:

Figure 3.5.1: Select textbox from among the Toolbox options

Now, drag a box and drop it into the page, as shown in the following screenshot:

```
Default.aspx.cs      Default.aspx* ⚏ X
     1  <%@ Page Language="C#" AutoEventWireup="true" CodeFile="Default.aspx.cs" Inherits="_Default" %>
     2
     3  <!DOCTYPE html>
     4
     5  <html xmlns="http://www.w3.org/1999/xhtml">
     6  <head runat="server">
     7      <title></title>
     8  </head>
     9  <body>
    10      <form id="form1" runat="server">
    11          <asp:TextBox ID="TextBox1" runat="server"></asp:TextBox>
    12      </form>
    13  </body>
    14  </html>
    15
```

Figure 3.5.2. TextBox has been dragged and dropped into the page and moved to the appropriate spot

For the purpose of the box, if you miss out on placing it sometimes, it's OK. You see, when it's all highlighted, as in the screenshot, you can still move it around and place it anywhere you like. I'll drop it right below the <form> tag, though.

So now we have a box. From the box, we will read a string and then grab each character in the string individually; this is our objective here.

## Inserting a label

In the next stage, add a label as well. Expand **Toolbox** and then type la, as shown in the following screenshot:

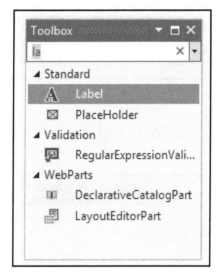

Figure 3.5.3. Select Label from Toolbox

Drag and drop a **Label** control into the markup. Now we have a `Label` tag. To separate the `Label` and `TextBox` controls vertically, insert a `<br>` tag. It should look as shown in the following screenshot:

```
Default.aspx.cs    Default.aspx* ⊡ ×
  1  <%@ Page Language="C#" AutoEventWireup="true" CodeFile="Default.aspx.cs" Inherits="_Default" %>
  2
  3  <!DOCTYPE html>
  4                                                                    Toolbox                    ▾ ☐ ×
  5  <html xmlns="http://www.w3.org/1999/xhtml">                       la                          × ▾
  6  <head runat="server">                                             ⊿ Standard
  7      <title></title>                                                 A    Label
  8  </head>                                                             ⊠    PlaceHolder
  9  <body>                                                            ⊿ Validation
 10      <form id="form1" runat="server">                               🔲   RegularExpressionVali...
 11          <asp:TextBox ID="TextBox1" runat="server"></asp:TextBox>  ⊿ WebParts
 12          <asp:Label ID="Label1" runat="server" Text="Label"></asp:Label>  ▥ DeclarativeCatalogPart
 13      </form>                                                         ▦   LayoutEditorPart
 14  </body>
 15  </html>
 16
```

Figure 3.5.4. Drag and drop Label from Toolbox

Let's look at this in the **Design** View. You have a box and a label under the box, as shown in the following screenshot:

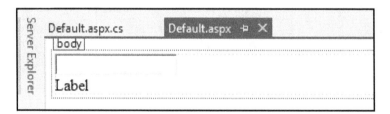

Figure 3.5.5. You should see a box and a label under the box

# Relating TextBox with Label

We'll now relate the box and the label under it by double-clicking on the box. This generates the `TextBox1_TextChanged` event handler. (If you still have one from an earlier chapter, you can just delete it.):

```
protected void TextBox1_TextChanged1(object sender, EventArgs e)
{

}
```

At this stage, we have to read the value from the box first by adding the following to the event handler:

```
string input = TextBox1.Text;
```

What this line does for us is as follows. I'll number it comment 7 because it's up top:

```
//7. Reads value from box and saves to input variable
```

In the next stage, once you have the input text saved to an `input` variable as `string`, you need to grab each character. To do this, use `foreach`. So type the following:

```
foreach (char c in input)
```

The `foreach` loop has a certain standard design, but before we go into this, consider the following scenario: if you take the word `"He"` (note that it is between double quotes). This word really consists of two characters: one character is the letter `H` and the second character is the letter `e`. The word `He`, which is a `string` in C#, really consists of two characters. Each individual component of the string is a character, in other words. And this matters because now I know that I should type `char` between parentheses following `foreach`.

In `foreach (char c in input)`, the `c` variable is a made-up word. If you want, you can use `d` or something else, but I'll just use `c`, which is short for the word "character" essentially. So, there is `foreach char` `c` in the collection. Here the collection is the `input` keyword, so you type `input`. But let's interpret this in simple English, as stated in comment 8:

```
//8. This means grab each letter in the string
```

# Generating a vertical output

Now that we understand why `foreach` is present, in the next stage, let's write additional code, for example, something like `Hello`. What we want to do is essentially produce something like this:

```
H
e
l
l
o
```

We do this so that each character would be on its own line. We are beginning with a horizontal word and then spelling it out vertically instead; that's our objective. Because this is the case, we definitely need to push down to the next line as we do that.

One thing that I want to do, however, is go back to `Default.aspx` first.

Do you see where it says **Label** (as shown previously in in *Figure 3.5.5*)? I want to clear that out. This means that in the **Source** view, we need to remove the `Label` property of the `Text` attribute within the `Label` control and delete it. This makes it disappear, as shown here:

```
asp :Label ID="Label1" runat="server" Text=""></asp:Label>
```

Now, go back to the **Design** view and note that the only thing left is the idea of the label, but it doesn't show on our page. However, the text, that is, the value of the `Text` attribute, does.

Alright, now go back to `Default.aspx.cs`. Here we will say the following:

```
Label1.Text += $"<br>{c}";
```

Remember, the action of the `+=` operator is to stack up input or output, depending on what you need, but the point is that it's accumulating it, not overwriting it. Next, you'll put a `$` symbol for string interpolation and then double quotes to make a `string` return type. Then, because the objective is to write it down to the next line, put a `<br>` tag between double quotes and then place the variable whose value you want to show within curly braces, that is, c. Then, close this with a semicolon.

Remember this `foreach` loop controls only the line right after it. When all you have is one line of logic after a loop, it's assumed that the loop controls only that one line of logic, whatever it happens to be. As I say in comment 9, it prints c to the page in a vertical column this time:

```
//9. Prints c to the page in a vertical column
```

Let's observe this in action. Open Google Chrome, and there's our box at the top. If I type, for example, `Hello` and hit *Enter*, it spells out `Hello` in a vertical column, as I said that it would:

Figure 3.5.6: The input Hello is typed out in a vertical column, thanks to our foreach loop

# Removing parts of the code to determine their impact

If you wish to understand the meaning of each line in more detail, what would you do? You just remove the parts one by one. So first remove the `<br>`& tag. This just reproduces the word, so now we understand that the `<br>` tag is necessary to break down the word over individual lines, run the code, and observe the difference, as shown in *Figure 3.5.7*:

```
Label1.Text += $"{c}";
```

Figure 3.5.7: The output when <br> is removed

Again, remove the + sign (restoring the <br> tag ), and it looks like this now:

```
Label1.Text = $"<br>{c}"
```

Now run it. This simple procedure will eliminate old data for the purpose of things. So type in `Hello` and notice that only the last thing outputs on the screen. There you go:

Figure 3.5.8: The output when the + sign is removed (with <br> restored)

But that's not what we want, so we put the += operator back, and that's how you can investigate these things in more detail:

```
Label1.Text += $"<br>{c}"
```

For review, the final `Default.aspx.cs` code for this chapter is displayed in the following code block:

```
//1. using is a keyword, it's blue
//2. System is a name space that stores already created code
//3. using System brings in existing code
using System;

//4. class is a required container for creating our own code samples
public partial class _Default : System.Web.UI.Page
{
    //5. code below is where we place our own code
    //6. Page_load is code that runs when a page loads from a server
    protected void Page_Load(object sender, EventArgs e)
    {
    }


    protected void TextBox1_TextChanged(object sender, EventArgs e)
    {
```

```
string input = TextBox1.Text;//7. Reads value from box and
saves to input variable
foreach (char c in input)//8. This means grab each letter in
the string
    Label1.Text += $"<br>{c}";//9. Prints c to the page in a
    vertical column


    }
}
```

# Summary

In this chapter, you learned how to work with `foreach` loops. You inserted a `TextBox` and `Label` control in the `Default.aspx` file and then related the two. You also worked with `foreach` loops to produce a vertical output. Finally, you removed parts of your code to determine the impact of doing this.

In the next chapter, we'll talk about examining multiple values with the `switch` blocks.

# 17
# Examining Multiple Variable Values with Switch Blocks

In this chapter, you will learn about the `switch` blocks in a drop-down list. We'll make a `switch` block work with a drop-down list, and you'll see why it is very natural to combine the two.

## Inserting DropBox and Label

Go to **View** | **Toolbox**, type `Dro`, and select **DropDownList**, as shown in the following screenshot:

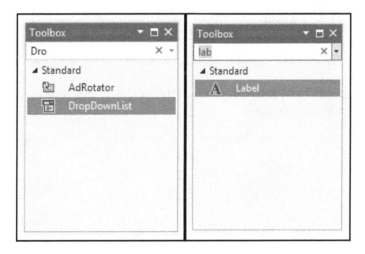

Figure 3.6.1: Select DropDownList from Toolbox

From **Toolbox**, drag **DropDownList** into the form, and under **DropDownList**, also place a **Label** so that your screen looks like the one shown in the following screenshot:

```
Default.aspx.cs*        Default.aspx* + X
     1  <%@ Page Language="C#" AutoEventWireup="true" CodeFile="Default.aspx.cs" Inherits="_Default" %>
     2
     3  <!DOCTYPE html>
     4
     5  <html xmlns="http://www.w3.org/1999/xhtml">
     6  <head runat="server">
     7      <title></title>
     8  </head>
     9  <body>
    10      <form id="form1" runat="server">
    11          <asp:DropDownList ID="DropDownList1" runat="server"></asp:DropDownList>
    12          <asp:Label ID="Label1" runat="server" Text="Label"></asp:Label>
    13      </form>
    14  </body>
    15  </html>
    16
```

Figure 3.6.2: Default.aspx with DropDownList and Label inserted in the page

**DropDownList** allows us to choose from among several options. Next, switch over to the **Design** view:

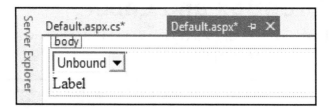

Figure 3.6.3: In the Design view, you can see that the label needs to be pushed down to the next line

Notice that `Label` needs to be pushed down to the next line. So, type in `<br/>`, which can push the label down to its own line:

```
<asp:DropDownList ID="DropDownList1" runat="server"></asp:DropDownList> <br
/>
```

# Populating the drop-down list

In the **Design** View, you can see the `Label` control is now below the box, as shown in *Figure 3.6.4*. Now, if you click on the little arrow (chevron) that points to the right from `Unbound`, a small drop-down list will display. Select **Edit Items...** and in the dialog that appears, you can add items to be displayed in the list:

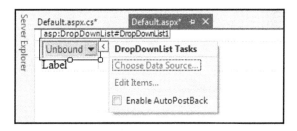

Figure 3.6.4: Select Edit Items...

Click on **Add**. In the `Text` field, type in `Pears`, and notice that the values automatically focus. Click on **Add** again, and enter `Apples`. Let's do one more for `Mangoes`.

Note that the number that appears to the left of these items in the **Members** window is the index; so index 0, index 1, index 2, and so on. Then, just click on **OK**, and make sure that you select **Enable AutoPostBack**. This means that when you interact with the list and make a new choice, you get a fresh copy of the page essentially; that is, you're posting back to the server automatically:

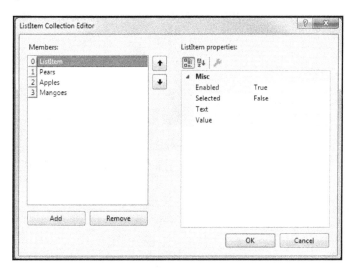

Figure 3.6.5: Adding items to the drop-down list

Before we do anything else, let's open Google Chrome and take a look at the results so far:

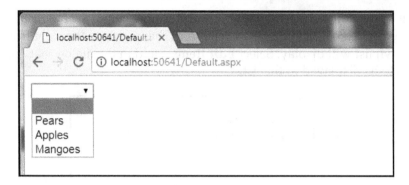

Figure 3.6.6: The drop-down list thus far

The page says `Pears` first, right? Select `Apples`, and notice that when you do that the mouse cursor spins. When you select `Mangoes` that mouse cursor spins, and so on.

# Adding information to display about each drop-down item

Now we will display some information about each choice. Thus, if you select `Pears`, it will display some information, and so on.

Unload the page by clicking the brown (square) stop button, and switch over into `Default.aspx.cs`, which should look like this:

```
protected void DropDownList1_SelectedIndexChanged(object sender, EventArgs
e)
  {

  }
```

If you don't have that, go back into `Default.aspx`, then left double-click on the drop-down list, and it will generate this stub in `Default.aspx.cs`, right beneath the previous event handler stub.

Here is where we are going to process information; so you will enter the following beneath the first closed curly brace:

```
switch (DropDownList1.SelectedValue)
{

}
```

Here, `switch` means to grab something and examine its possible value. In another case, we will type `DropDownList1`, that's our list, . (dot), and one of the things that it stores—`SelectedValue`, so that we can examine a selection.

With that done, we'll enter the following between the curly braces under `switch`:

```
{
    case "Pears" :
}
```

If somebody, for example, chooses the **Pears** option, you need to run some code as follows. We'll give the page a title, so type `Page.Title`. This will be filled at runtime and will change automatically. And now you will enter, for example, `Pears` in double quotes and close with a semicolon:

```
Page.Title = "Pears";
```

Here, `case "Pears":` is sometimes called a *case label*, hence let's add these comments:

```
case "Pears" : //7. case label runs when the user selects Pears on the page
Page.Title = "Pears"; //8. sets title of page as program runs
```

After that, we can display some other information about `Pears`. We have a `Label` control in our page, so start with `Label1.Text` and set that equal to some information about `Pears`, for example, `"Pears cost 25 cents."`, and then terminate this statement with a semicolon:

```
Label1.Text = "Pears cost 25 cents.";
```

If you want to show a cents symbol, there's a really nice feature that you can use. You put a \ (backslash) and then type `u00A2`. At runtime, this portion will be rendered as basically a cents symbol:

```
Label1.Text = "Pears cost 25\u00A2. "
```

In the next stage, due to the design of the `switch` block, put a `break` keyword.

```
break ;
```

So, we have a case label, and we set the title of the page as the program runs with `Page.Title =`.

Now let's add comment 9 for `Label1.Text`. Of course, this simply means to fill a label on the page with some information specific to `Pears`:

```
Label1.Text = "Pears cost 25\u00A2. "; //9. Fill label on page with some
information
```

In the last stage, what that did was simply to leave the `switch` block.

Once you have processed the case, for example, `Pears` is the one that is matched, then you leave the body of the `switch` block. However, let's create one more case for the sake of illustration: even though we have three, I'll only show you two. After that, you can of course, just take this code:

```
switch (DropDownList1.SelectedValue)//Switches based on what the user has
selected on a web page
{
    case "Pears": //7. case label runs when the user selects Pears
    on the page
    Page.Title = "Pears"; //8. sets title of page as program runs
    Label1.Text = "Pears cost 25\u00A2. "; //9. Fill label on
    page with some information
    break; //10. Leave the switch block
```

# Replicating cases

Select the first case block, press *Ctrl+C* to copy, and then *Ctrl+V* down below to paste it. And now we switch, but here's something to learn, as we can see the popup here says that the `switch` statement contains multiple cases with the value `Pears`, as shown in the following screenshot:

```
case "Pears":
    Page.T    ⚙ class System.String
    Label1    Represents text as a sequence of UTF-16 code units.To browse the .NET Framework source code for this type, see the Reference Source.
    break;    The switch statement contains multiple cases with the label value '"Pears"'
```

Figure 3.6.7: This tooltip pop-up indicates that the switch statement contains multiple cases with the value Pears

So, you know that's not allowed; you need to switch this to a new value; that's just what it means to switch. Think about it. So, here we are going to say `Apples`.

In this case, we also need to retitle the page; so give it a dynamic title, such as `Apples`, `Apple information`, or `Information about Apples`-something relevant. Now change the message so that it says `Apples cost 25 cents`, and then you will leave the `switch` block:

```
case "Apples": //11. case label runs when the user selects Apples on the
page
Page.Title = "Apples"; //12. sets title of page as program runs
Label1.Text = "Apples cost 25\u00A2";//13. Fill label on page with some
information
break; //14. Leave the switch block
```

You could also ask, for example, for the case of `Mangoes`, but this is sufficient for our purpose.

# Running your program

Now, let's observe this in action. Open Google Chrome, and notice that first it says `Pears`, that's OK. If I switch to `Apples`, it says `Apples cost 25¢`, as shown in *Figure 3.6.7*. Now we have that nice cents symbol! Go back to `Pears`, where it says `Pears cost 25¢`, and so on. Now close this.

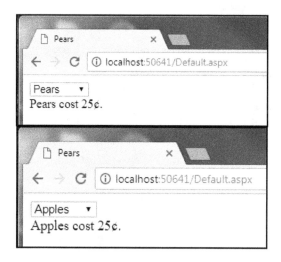

Figure 3.6.7: Select the item from the drop-down, and its particular information is displayed

These are the basics of doing something fairly practical with a `switch` block. Again, because of the nature of a drop-down list and the fact that you can examine multiple values, it kind of marries very naturally with a `switch` block, as I've shown you.

For review, a complete version of `Default.aspx.cs` for this chapter is displayed in the following code block:

```
//1. using is a keyword, it's blue
//2. System is a name space that stores already created code
//3. using System brings in existing code
using System;

//4. class is a required container for creating our own code samples
public partial class _Default : System.Web.UI.Page
{
    //5. code below is where we place our own code
    //6. Page_load is code that runs when a page loads from a server
    protected void Page_Load(object sender, EventArgs e)
    {
    }


    protected void DropDownList1_SelectedIndexChanged(object sender,
    EventArgs e)
    {
        switch (DropDownList1.SelectedValue)
        {
            case "Pears":
                Page.Title = "Pears";//8. Sets title as program runs
                Label1.Text = "Pears cost 25\u00A2.";
                break;//10. Leave the switch block

            case "Apples":
                Page.Title = "Pears";//8. Sets title as program runs
                Label1.Text = "Apples cost 25\u00A2.";
                break;//10. Leave the switch block
        }
    }
}
```

# Summary

In this chapter, you learned about the `switch` blocks in a drop-down list. You began by inserting a `dropbox` and a `label`, then you populated the drop-down list, added information to display about each drop-down item, replicated and edited cases, and ran your program to see how selecting an item from the drop-down list displayed its particular information.

In the next chapter, I'll show you how to use a `TryParse` method to write more stable and professional code.

# 18
# Improving Input Processing with TryParse

In this chapter, you'll learn how to use the `TryParse` method, or a version of that method, to write more stable code.

## Inserting a button and a textbox

Let's begin with a simple HTML page, as shown in *Figure 3.7.1*. Using **Toolbox**, let's place **Button** and **TextBox** in the page. The `Button` control will basically say calculate and will display, for example, some number increased by 10%. Obviously, this depends on what you need. Type `tex` in the **Search Toolbox** field, select **TextBox**, and drag and drop that into the page. Right above it, place a **Button** control so that users have something to click on. Again, type `but` in the **Search Toolbox** field, and drag and drop **Button** into the page. You want to stack them vertically, so at the end of the `Button` statement, type `<br>`:

```
1  <%@ Page Language="C#" AutoEventWireup="true" CodeFile="Default.aspx.cs" Inherits="_Default" %>
2
3  <!DOCTYPE html>
4
5  <html xmlns="http://www.w3.org/1999/xhtml">
6  <head runat="server">
7      <title></title>
8  </head>
9  <body>
10     <form id="form1" runat="server">
11         <asp:Button ID="Button1" runat="server" Text="Button" />
12         <asp:TextBox ID="TextBox1" runat="server"></asp:TextBox><br />
13     </form>
14 </body>
15 </html>
16
```

Figure 3.7.1: Button and TextBox are inserted into the page

You can even leave the names if you want, except the display text on the `Button` control, so that it says something more informative, for example, find 110% of Value.

Now, let's take a look at it in the **Design** view and see what we have:

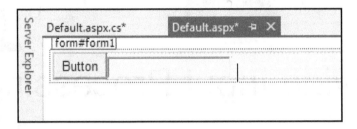

Figure 3.7.2: At this point, there is just a button and a text box

# Inserting the label

We now have a `Button` control, and under it we have a `TextBox` control. We need one more visual element, which is a `Label` control. So, type `<br>` after the `TextBox` control, and then place a `Label` tag under that, so that we have a place to display information. Next, drag and drop **Label** from **ToolBox** into the page. Now we have the `Button`, `TextBox`, and `Label` controls stacked vertically, as shown in the following screenshot:

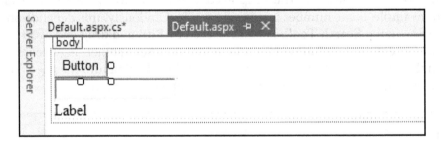

Figure 3.7.3: Now we have a button, a text box, and a label stacked vertically

Your code should now appear as follows:

```
<asp:Button ID="Button1" runat="server" Text="Find 110% Of Value" /><br />
<asp:TextBox ID="TextBox1" runat="server"></asp:TextBox><br />
<asp:Label ID="Label1" runat="server" Text="Label" ></asp:Label>
```

Here, perhaps you want to display nothing, so you can just remove the `Text` attribute altogether, you see?

```
<asp:Label ID="Label1" runat="server" ></asp:Label>
```

Now, in the **Design** view, all you see is `Label1`, the name, and the `ID` attribute of it in code. By runtime, this is no longer visible, so keep that in mind.

Let's just run this first in Google Chrome to observe what we've done so far:

Figure 3.7.4: Basically, we have a button and a box at this point

We have our simple interface in the preceding screenshot. You can click on the `Button` control; below that you have a box—you can input anything here, see? Now, you need to connect the button and the box together along with **Label**; that's not visible here, but remember it's still there. You can close this window.

# Introducing the TryParse method

Now let's switch into `Default.aspx.cs` by double-clicking on the `Button` control, and that brings up the event handler—the code that runs when somebody interacts by clicking on the `Button` control. So, here we'll enter this:

```
protected void Button1_Click(object sender, EventArgs e)
  {
  double xOut;
```

We do not set the value of `double xOut`. So, let's add a comment after this statement on why this variable is necessary:

```
//7. Variable is needed so that TryParse can operate as it's been designed
to do
```

The variable is needed so that `TryParse`, the method that will attempt to convert to a numerical value if it can, will operate as it's been designed to do.

To make use of `TryParse`, type the following under the `double xOut` statement:

```
if (double.TryParse)
```

Remember, `if` runs on Boolean or logical conditions; that is, the `true` or `false` kinds of statements. If you hover your mouse over `TryParse` (refer to *Figure 3.7.5*), you'll notice that it gives back a `bool` value, that is, a Boolean or a `true` or `false` value; that is why it can be used with an `if` statement:

---

ⓘ  bool double.TryParse(string s, out double result) (+ 1 overload)
Converts the string representation of a number to its double-precision floating-point number equivalent. A return value indicates whether the conversion succeeded or failed.

Cannot convert method group 'TryParse' to non-delegate type 'bool'. Did you intend to invoke the method?

---

Figure 3.7.5: TryParse gives back a bool value, and that is why it can be used with if. out is a parameter--if TryParse can set it, it will

As you can also see, you have to fit in a `string` value and then also something called *out double result*. Here, `out` is basically a parameter; it's a value that you can feed into it, and if `TryParse` can set it, it will. And then that value becomes available in your own code so that you can make use of it. Also `double`, of course, is the data type. So, `out` is a new keyword here.

Now let's take a look at this in action. Type `double.TryParse` and then the `string`value. Where will we get the `string` value? This value should come from `TextBox`. So, within the parentheses following `TryParse`, if you want to, you could just directly type `TextBox1.Text`, which means get the text out of the `TextBox` control. And `TryParse`, remember it's called to Try Parse, which doesn't guarantee that it will, but it might, depending on how you input the value. So, `TryParse(TextBox1.Text`, and then we enter, for example, `out xOut))`:

```
if(double.TryParse(TextBox1.Text,out xOut))
```

So, what is this statement saying? Let me describe this in some detail here in comment 8:

```
//8. Line below says: take text from box, and if possible, convert it to a
numerical value
```

There's no guarantee that this will happen for the following reason. If you use this and input the word `ten`, this cannot be converted to the number 10. So, set comment 9 as follows:

```
//9. If "ten", this cannot be converted to the number 10. 10, C# first sees
as "10", so then use TryParse
```

Keep in mind the basic fact that when you aim to enter a value, even if it looks like a number to you, it's not. So, when you enter a value, for example, `"10"` into a `TextBox`, C# first sees 10 between double quotes, or a string. When you hover your mouse over `Text`, it says **string**. You see that?

```
if (double.TryParse(TextBox1.Text, out xOut))//8. Line below says: take text
//9. If "ten", this cannot be c    ⚙ string System.Web.UI.WebControls.TextBox.Text { get; set; }
                                       Gets or sets the text content of the System.Web.UI.WebControls.TextBox control.
```

Figure 3.7.6: When you hover your mouse over Text, it says string

# Using TryParse to convert input into a numerical value

Now, if possible, use `TryParse` to convert that string into a truly numerical form so that you can operate on it mathematically.

In the next stage, imagine that `TryParse` succeeds. It really does two things. When you hover your mouse over it (refer to *Figure 3.7.7*), first of all it indicates whether something has succeeded in terms of being converted to a numerical value, that is a `true` or `false` result. This is the meaning of `bool` at the beginning of this message. `TryParse` tells you first, in essence, "Yes, perhaps I've been able to succeed in converting your input into a numerical value." But, beyond that, if that process succeeds, it also makes available to us the result, the value itself (look at the word `result` in the message):

```
TryParse(TextBox1.Text, out xOut))//8. Line below says: take text from box, and if possible, convert
n",     ⓘ bool double.TryParse(string s, out double result) (+ 1 overload)
        Converts the string representation of a number to its double-precision floating-point number equivalent. A return value indicates whether the conversion succeeded or failed.
```

Figure 3.7.7: TryParse has been successful in converting input into a numerical value and makes available the value itself

Imagine that we have the numerical result available now, and we can make use of it. For example, enter the following between the open and closed curly braces:

```
{
    Label1.Text = $"{xOut} increased by 10% is {xOut * 1.1}";
}
```

Set `Label1.Text` equal to something. For example, type a `$` symbol for `string` interpolation, double quotes to make a `string` data type, and then we'll enter `{xOut}` increased by 10% is. Then, to find the value of x increased by 10%, enter `{xOut * 1.1};`, closing this with a semicolon.

Now the beauty of `TryParse` is that it returns a Boolean `true` or `false` value, this means that there's an `else` block involved. And if your input cannot be converted to a truly numerical form that is mathematically useful, then you can display a message. So, enter the following code:

```
else
{
    Label1.Text = "Input cannot be treated as a numerical value.";
}
```

This immediately improves your program over the way you might have written it previously. It's more stable—it won't crash this time.

Now let's add comments 10 and 11, indicating that the line runs when a successful conversion to numerical form occurs. (These comments here are a bit lengthy, so you can break them over two lines as shown.)

```
Label1.Text = $"{xOut} increased by 10% is {xOut * 1.1}"; //10. Line runs
when input can be converted
//11. successfully to numerical form: 10
```

Now add comment 12 as follows, indicating that the line runs when input cannot be converted to the numerical form.

```
Label1.Text = "Input cannot be treated as a numerical value."; //12. Runs
when input cannot be converted
```

# Running your program

Let's take a look at what happens here. Crank up our code in Google Chrome. There has to be some benefit obviously to writing this.

Our button reads `Find 110% Of Value`, so enter `100`—that's easy. Then click on the button, and it says `100 increased by 10% is 110`, as shown in the following screenshot:

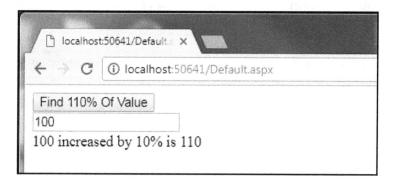

Figure 3.7.8: When 100 is input, the correct result is achieved

However, now input the word `hundred`, and it returns `Input cannot be treated as a numerical value`, as shown in the following screenshot. That is also correct. So, it's more stable in that sense, you see? Now you can close this.

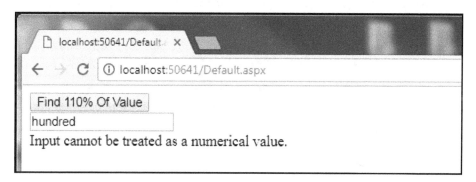

Figure 3.7.9: When the word *hundred* is the input, the correct result is achieved again

Remember `TryParse` is powerful: you have `decimal.TryParse`, `Boolean.TryParse`, and so on. But the thing that matters is understanding it properly. Remember that it does two things: it takes the value (`TextBox1.Text` in this case) and brings it into the method so that we can operate on it, and second, assuming the method has worked successfully, in our example, `out xOut` sets a value that we can use in the code after that. Further, the `bool` return type that you saw in the popup shown in *Figure 3.7.7* tells you whether the conversion has been successful or not.

For review, a complete version of the `Default.aspx.cs` file for this chapter is displayed in the following code block:

```
//1. using is a keyword, it's blue
//2. System is a name space that stores already created code
//3. using System brings in existing code
using System;

//4. class is a required container for creating our own code samples
public partial class _Default : System.Web.UI.Page
{
    //5. code below is where we place our own code
    //6. Page_load is code that runs when a page loads from a server
    protected void Page_Load(object sender, EventArgs e)
    {
    }

    protected void Button1_Click(object sender, EventArgs e)
    {
        double xOut;//7. Variable is needed so that TryParse can
        //operate as it's been designed to do

        if (double.TryParse(TextBox1.Text, out xOut))//8. Line below
        //says: take text from box, and if possible, convert it to a
        //numerical value
        //9. If "ten", this cannot be converted to the number 10. 10,
        //C# first sees as "10", so then use TryParse
        {
            Label1.Text = $"{xOut} increased by 10% is {xOut * 1.1}";
            //10. Line runs when input can be converted
            //11. successfully to numerical form: 10
        }
        else
        {
            Label1.Text = "Input cannot be treated as a numerical value.";
            //12. Runs when input cannot be converted
        }
    }
}
```

# Summary

In this chapter, you learned about how to use a `TryParse` method, to write more stable code. You started by inserting `Button` and `TextBox`, then you inserted `Label`, and finally, you used the `TryParse` method to convert the input into a numerical value.

In the next chapter, we'll talk about the ternary operator.

# 19
# Replacing If/Else Blocks with the Ternary Operator

In this chapter, you will learn how to make use of the **ternary operator** to make decisions. I'll show you how to use it with the `TryParse` method so that you can understand its power better.

## Inserting two text boxes and a button

Let's first create a program that takes two TextBox controllers. Then, we will read the values and operate on them mathematically.

Go to **View**, switch over to **Toolbox**, and then add two text boxes. Type `tex` and drag **TextBox** into the form, and then, insert a `<br>`tag and put another **TextBox** control under it. After that, grab a **Button** control from the **Toolbox** control and drag it under the second **TextBox** control in the form. Your screen should appear as shown in the following screenshot:

```
Default.aspx.cs*        Default.aspx* ╄ ✕
    1  <%@ Page Language="C#" AutoEventWireup="true" CodeFile="Default.aspx.cs" Inherits="_Default" %>
    2
    3  <!DOCTYPE html>
    4
    5  <html xmlns="http://www.w3.org/1999/xhtml">
    6  <head runat="server">
    7      <title></title>
    8  </head>
    9  <body>
   10      <form id="form1" runat="server">
   11          <asp:Button ID="Button1" runat="server" Text="Button" OnClick="Button1_Click" /><br />
   12          <asp:TextBox ID="TextBox1" runat="server"></asp:TextBox><br />
   13          <asp:TextBox ID="TextBox2" runat="server"></asp:TextBox>
   14      </form>
   15  </body>
   16  </html>
   17
```

Figure 3.8.1: Your form after dragging in two text boxes and a button

# Creating the interface

Next, we will click on the button to do a calculation. Now, change the display of the text on the button from `Button` to, for example, `Find Sum`. So that line in the code will look like the following block of code:

```
<asp:Button ID="Button1" runat="server" Text="Find Sum" /><br />
```

Switch over to the **Design** view, and it appears as shown in the following screenshot:

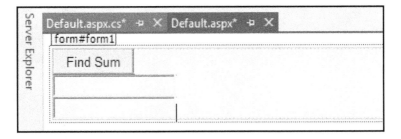

Figure 3.8.2: The result of your code in the Design view

Now we need to be able to display the results somewhere. Let's go to the **Source** view, insert a `<br>` tag, and then place a `Label` control after the `Button` control. For that, type `lab`, drag and drop a `Label` control into the page, and clear out the default property for `Text` on the label and replace it with the words `Find Sum`:

```
<asp:Label ID="Label1" runat="server" Text="Find Sum"></asp:Label>
```

Now, go over to the **Design** view and, as you can see in the following screenshot, look at our simple user interface:

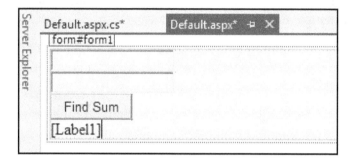

Figure 3.8.3: Our simple user interface

# Combining the ternary operator with TryParse

Now, we'll create the code. Double-click on the **Find Sum** button, and that brings up the event handling code—the code to be created and run; this is to take an action when somebody clicks on the button. The code looks like the following; we have to read the two values and then take an action:

```
protected void Button1_Click(object sender, EventArgs e)
{
    double xOut, yOut;
}
```

The purpose of these variables is to try to set the values using `TryParse`. Add comment 7 as follows, at the end of the line to that effect:

```
//7. Purpose of these variable is to try to set them using try parse
```

Remember, `TryParse`, if it is able to convert, assigns a value; but if it's not able to convert, it saves a zero to the variable. Keep in mind that it does that. OK?

There's a value of some kind saved, but zero obviously is not the one that you want in most cases. So, now we'll say the following:

```
double x = double.TryParse(TextBox1.Text, out xOut) ? xOut :0;
```

Note that we combine `TryParse` with `double`, as in `double.TryParse`. Now that you have to read from the first box, we say `TextBox1.Text`. This is OK because in `Default.aspx`, when you drag elements into a page, they're given an automatic `ID`. So, `ID="TextBox1"`and `ID="TextBox2"`. After `TextBox1.Text`, first type , (a comma), then `out`, and then for the result, end with `xOut`. This yields the value that you can potentially produce from the attempts to convert using `TryParse`.

Now, if this successfully produces a numerical value, you want to save that over to `x`, as an example; so, you can put ? (question mark) and then you can type, for example, `xOut`. On the other hand, when it not successful, you can just save the value `0`.

If you wanted to, you could type `xOut` instead of the value `0`, believe it or not, but the only thing is that this will become difficult to understand, correct?

Remember, when the code runs, if the following process succeeds, then the value of the initial `xOut` is saved over to `x` and that value could be `5` or `10` or `15`. On the other hand, if this process fails, then the second `xOut` is given a value `0`; so that would save `0` over to `x`. I prefer to keep things clear-cut, so I'll just use `0`, not the second `xOut`:

```
double x = double.TryParse(TextBox1.Text, out xOut) ? xOut :0;
```

Now, let's add a couple of comments above this line:

```
//8. Line below combines the ternary operator with TryParse
//9. If conversion works, xOut has the intended value and it's then saved
to x
//10. If conversion fails, xOut has the value 0, but I've chosen to just
save 0 to x
```

In the next stage, we'll repeat the same process. We want to add two values. So, now you will say the following:

```
double y = double.TryParse(TextBox2.Text, out yOut) ? yOut : 0;
```

This time, you'll say `TextBox2` to grab a value from the second box as a text or string value, and set it inside the method. Type out and yOut. If this line is successful, then the yOut value will be saved over to the y variable.

Now, let's look at one more thing that I haven't mentioned. Start by hovering your mouse over `TryParse`, and you'll see the pop-up tip, as shown in the following screenshot:

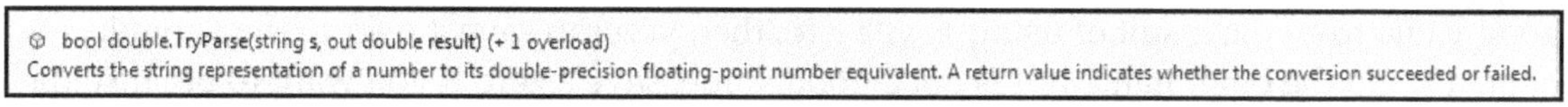

⊙ bool double.TryParse(string s, out double result) (+ 1 overload)
Converts the string representation of a number to its double-precision floating-point number equivalent. A return value indicates whether the conversion succeeded or failed.

Figure 3.8.4: Pop-up tooltip shown when you hover your mouse over TryParse

# The Boolean power of TryParse

Remember that it's a Boolean kind of quantity that `TryParse` gives back to you. Also, recall that `TryParse`, the ternary operator operates on a very simple logic. Take a look at the following figure:

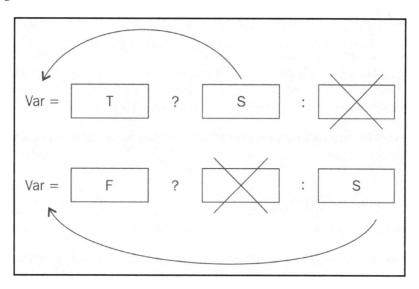

Figure 3.8.5: Illustration of the TryParse Logic

Here, the first blocks represent our condition, which can have either a `true` (**T**) or a `false` (**F**) value. Next, you have a question mark. Following that, the second block represents the value that is saved (**S**) to the variable only if the condition is true. Then you have a colon, and then the final value that is saved to the variable only if the condition is false. This is how it operates.

Regardless of how sophisticated it seems, that's what it's doing. So, if `yOut` is produced as a good value from the result of using `TryParse`, then you can save it over to the variable named `y`. On the other hand, if it is not a good value, save a zero if you want to because the conversion might fail. If the conversion fails, then `yOut` is just given the value `0`. You can just type `yOut` also, but then it gets very confusing, so I make it clear by typing `0` and that's it. OK, it's a matter of preference.

In the next stage here, we'll add the following comments (changing `xOut` to `yOut`):

```
//11. Line below combines the ternary operator with TryParse
//12. If conversion works, yOut has the intended value and it's then saved
to y
//13. If conversion fails, yOut has the value 0, but I've chosen to just
save 0 to y explicitly
double y = double.TryParse(TextBox2.Text, out yOut) ? yOut : 0;
```

First, the same logic basically applies to this line (`yOut`) as to the one earlier (`xOut`), so keep that in mind. In this case, you'll put `yOut` as the intended value and then it's saved to `y`. If the conversion fails, `yOut` has the value `0`, but I've chosen just to save `0` to `x`, or in this case `y`, explicitly. So, it's easy to understand.

Now that we have these two, perhaps, potentially correct numerical values, we can make use of them. You can enter `Label1.Text` and just display the sum. So, type the following:

```
Label1.Text = $"Your sum is {x + y}";
```

Note that we use string interpolation again with the `$` symbol. You can do a calculation right within the curly braces.

Comment 14 above this statement would be as follows:

```
//14. x+y are added, and the result is saved into the string for printing
```

# Running your program

Now let's observe this happen. Let's open Google Chrome and add the values of 5 and 10 and find the sum. It says that Your sum is 15, as shown in following screenshot:

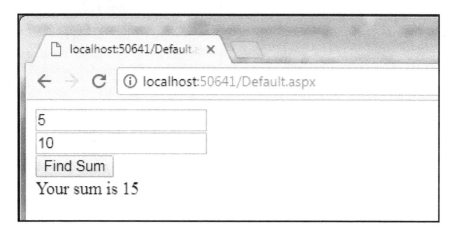

Figure 3.8.6: Here a good value is produced as a result of using TryParse and saved over to a variable

However, if you input some mumbo jumbo instead of 5 and the number like 10 again, it will say that your sum is 10. So, it doesn't try to add something that clearly is not numerical with something that is numerical.

For review, a complete version of the Default.aspx.cs file for this chapter is displayed in the following code block:

```
//1. using is a keyword, it's blue
//2. System is a name space that stores already created code
//3. using System brings in existing code
using System;

//4. class is a required container for creating our own code samples
public partial class _Default : System.Web.UI.Page
{
    //5. code below is where we place our own code
    //6. Page_load is code that runs when a page loads from a server
    protected void Page_Load(object sender, EventArgs e)
    {
    }


    protected void Button1_Click(object sender, EventArgs e)
    {
```

```
        double xOut, yOut;//7. Purpose of these variable is to try to
        //set them using try parse
        double x = double.TryParse(TextBox1.Text, out xOut) ? xOut : 0;

        //8. Line above combines the ternary operator with TryParse
        //9. If conversion works, xOut has the intended value and it's
        //then saved to x
        //10. If conversion fails, xOut has the value 0, but I've
        //chosen to just save 0 to x explicitly
        //11. Line below combines the ternary operator with TryParse
        //12. If conversion works, yOut has the intended value and it's
        //then saved to y
        //13. If conversion fails, yOut has the value 0, but I've
        //chosen to just save 0 to y explicitly
        double y = double.TryParse(TextBox2.Text, out yOut) ? yOut : 0;
        Label1.Text = $"Your sum is {x + y}";
        //14. x+y are added, and the result is saved into the string
        // for printing
    }
}
```

# Summary

In this chapter, you learned how to make use of the ternary operator to make decisions. You saw how to use it with the `TryParse` method.

In the next chapter, we'll talk about using various logical operators.

# 20
# Operators That Evaluate and Assign in Place

In this chapter, you'll learn about several different kinds of operators that are commonly used. Let's take a look at these in action.

## Inserting Button and Label

Crank up a project. Go to **View** | **Toolbox** and drag a Label control into the markup. Also, above the Label markup, let's place a Button control. The initial Default.aspx page is shown in the following screenshot:

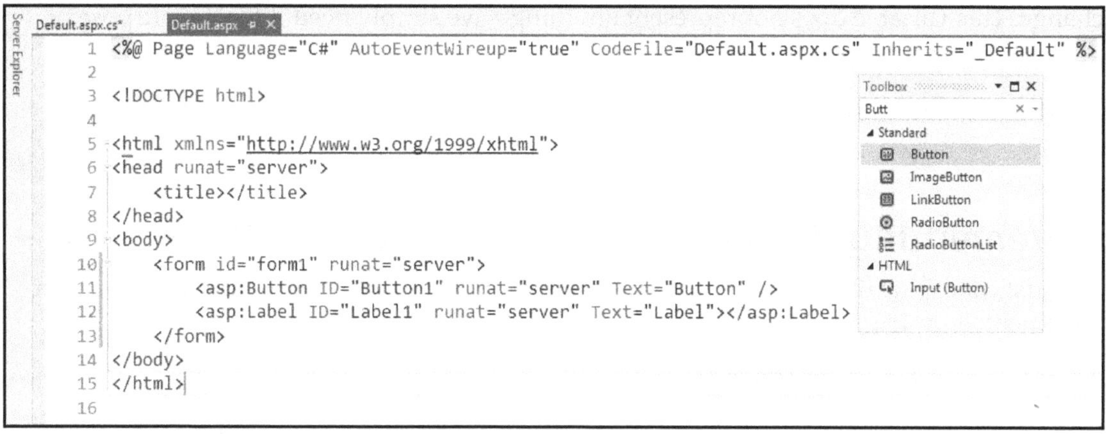

```
Default.aspx.cs*        Default.aspx  ⊕ ✕
     1  <%@ Page Language="C#" AutoEventWireup="true" CodeFile="Default.aspx.cs" Inherits="_Default" %>
     2
     3  <!DOCTYPE html>
     4
     5  <html xmlns="http://www.w3.org/1999/xhtml">
     6  <head runat="server">
     7      <title></title>
     8  </head>
     9  <body>
    10      <form id="form1" runat="server">
    11          <asp:Button ID="Button1" runat="server" Text="Button" />
    12          <asp:Label ID="Label1" runat="server" Text="Label"></asp:Label>
    13      </form>
    14  </body>
    15  </html>
    16
```

Figure 4.1.1: Our initial Default.aspx page for this chapter

We will click on the `Button` control, and then we'll show some output in the `Label` control. Remember that these things in code are called `Button1` and `Label1` so that the `ID` attribute remembers how you refer to it in your C# code.

Go back to the **Design** view and then double-click on the `Button` control, as shown in the following screenshot:

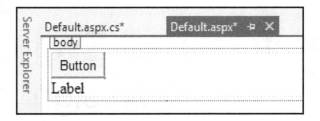

Figure 4.1.2: Our current code shown in the Design view

Notice in the preceding screenshot that I left the text as `Button`. We can fix that. When you double-click on **Button**, that brings up the code Event Handler down below. I will change comment 6 so that it says the following:

```
//6. Button1_Click is code that runs when a page loads from a server
```

# Introducing operators

Now we'll illustrate some **operators**; for this, we need a variable whose value we can change. This variable does not represent anything—we simply need it for the purpose of illustrating the concepts:

```
double x = 25; //7. Declares and sets a variable so we can illustrate some
basic concepts
```

# Incrementing the value of a variable by 1 with ++

The first concept is this: imagine that you want to print a value of a variable after it's been incremented by 1:

```
Label1.Text = $"x={++x}";
```

Here, ++ is the pre-increment operator; it acts on x to increase its value by 1. The updated value is then stuck into the string, and it's printed using string interpolation, as you can see, by the $ sign in the statement. We will describe the action of this operator in comment 8 as follows:

```
//8. ++x runs first, which means x will show 26, NOT 25
```

Let's observe this in action in Google Chrome. If I click on **Button**, it says x=26, as shown in the following screenshot. This confirms that it's working as expected:

Figure 4.1.3: The result confirms that ++x runs first

# Incrementing the value of a variable by 2 with +=

Imagine that you want to do something like increasing the value of a variable by 2. How can we do that? We can, for example, say the following:

```
Label1.Text += $"<br>x+2={x += 2}";
```

Remember to use +=, as we will append what we want to output at this line to what already has been the output. The $ symbol here is for string interpolation, double quotes to make a string, and <br> to push down to the next line so that everything is on its own horizontal line. Now we will show the value of x increased by 2. How do we do that? For example, we can say x+2 would have some value. To do that, within the curly braces, type x, then +=2, and then close with a semicolon.

Let's describe what we have done above that line as comment 9:

```
//9. Code below x+=2 means the same thing as x=x+2: grab x, add 2 to it,
and store back to x
```

There's only one variable involved here named x. That's it—there aren't multiple variables; even if they're written multiple times, it doesn't mean anything.

Let's now observe the results. Also, remember that when x+2= is brown (or orange), it's printed to the screen exactly; when it's black within curly braces as {x += 2}, this means that you'll do a mathematical operation and then take the final value and stick it into the string value. The <br> tag pushes the control down to the next line within a web page.

Now let's observe this in Google Chrome. You'll see the Button control, and it says x=26 and x+2=28. That's correct. 26 + 2 is 28:

Figure 4.1.4: The correct results for the preceding line are displayed

Now, let's fix up the Default.aspx file a little bit. For this, switch over to the **Source** view, and as shown in the following code block, put a <br> tag after Button:

```
<asp:Button ID="Button1" runat="server" Text="Button"
OnClick="Button1_Click" /><br />
```

Notice also that when we clicked on the Button control to generate the Event Handler—the code, it added OnClick ="Button1_Click", which means connect what you see here to what is shown in the Event Handler in Default.aspx.cs. That's why we need this name, Button1_Click, in the Event Handler in Default.aspx.cs and in Default.aspx. This is how you establish the connection between the two.

# Working with the -- operator

In the next stage here, I'll show you a couple of operators. Imagine that you want to take a value of x and decrease it by 1, before printing it or something along those lines. So, you can do it as follows:

```
//10. --x has the action of decreasing x by 1 and then printing the updated
value
```

Because `--` is in front of x, it runs first. Then the updated value of x is printed. Let's check that out:

```
Label1.Text += $"<br>x-1={--x}";
```

Again, here we will say `+=` to append, the `$` symbol for string interpolation, `<br>` to push the control down to the next line, and now `--x`, which is the same as saying subtract 1 from x. It's like writing x-1. Now let's observe the results in Google Chrome. Click on **Button** and it says x=26, x+2=28, x-1=27, as shown in the following screenshot:

Figure 4.1.5: Taking the value of x and decreasing it by 1

# Working with the == operator

Now let's take a look at one more operator. For example, you can also do logical comparisons. There are so many of them, and of course, I can't present all of them to you in this book; however, the logic pretty much follows these lines, and I will demonstrate one now.

For comment 11, enter the following:

```
//11. == checks whether two quantities are equal or not
```

Let's check this out by typing the following:

```
Label1.Text += $"<br>Does x equal 3? " + (x == 3);
```

Once again, here we will say `Label1.Text`, `+=` to append, string interpolation with the `$` symbol, and `<br>` to push down to the next line. Now we just want to check, for example, whether x equals the number 3. So, we say `Does x equal 3?`, and to that question, we can say, for example, + and then x==3. Close this with a semicolon.

Here, if you hover your mouse over ==, you'll see the pop-up tip shown in *Figure 4.1.6*. The == symbol is an operator, and it compares two values. The words **double left** simply is whatever the value of x happens to be, and the words **double right** refers to 3. When == operates, it's an operator; it operates on two things: something on its left and something on its right. The result of running this operation is a Boolean data type (`bool`); either x is 3 or it's not. That's it. So, it's a true or false kind of comparison that you're making:

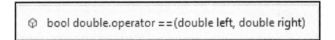

Figure 4.1.6: The pop-up tip shown when you hover your mouse over ==

Again, to emphasize this, remember that = means assignment and == means comparing two values; they have different meanings, as they do in some languages.

Now, let's take a look in Google Chrome. Click on **Button**, and it says Does x equal 3?, as shown in the following screenshot. The result is False because here x is 26:

Figure 4.1.7: The results of running the program

For review, a complete version of `Default.aspx.cs` file for this chapter is displayed in the following code block:

```
//1. using is a keyword, it's blue
//2. System is a name space that stores already created code
//3. using System brings in existing code
using System;

//4. class is a required container for creating our own code samples
public partial class _Default : System.Web.UI.Page
{
    //5. code below is where we place our own code
    //6. Button1_Click is code that runs when a page loads from a
    //server
    protected void Page_Load(object sender, EventArgs e)
    {
    }

    protected void Button1_Click(object sender, EventArgs e)
    {
        double x = 25; //7. Declares and sets a variable so we can
        //illustrate some basic concepts
        Label1.Text = $"x={++x}";//8. ++x runs first, which means x
        //will show 26, NOT 25
        //9. Code below x+=2 means the same thing as x=x+2: grab x, add
        //2 to it, and store back to x
        Label1.Text += $"<br>x+2={x += 2}";
        //10. --x has the action of decreasing x by 1 and then printing
        //the updated value
        Label1.Text += $"<br>x-1={--x}";

        //11. == checks whether two quantities are equal or not
        Label1.Text += $"<br>Does x equal 3? " + (x == 3);
    }
}
```

# Summary

In this chapter, you learned about several different kinds of common operators. You learned how to increment by 1, using ++ and by 2, using +=, and you also worked with the -- and == operators.

In the next chapter, we'll talk about another kind of logical operator.

# 21

# Checking Two Conditions with the Logical AND Operator

In this chapter, I will show you how to use the logical AND operator.

## Setting up the project

Bring up a project, and this time let's build a simple interface with two text boxes, a **button** and a **label**. Go to **View | Toolbox**. Type `tex` in the **Search Toolbox** field, and drag two `TextBox` controls into the page. You will read a couple of values from the boxes, and then you'll just check whether they're empty or not.

Now, you will need to place a Button control that someone can click on. So again, in the **Search& Toolbox** field, type but and drag the Button control into the page. After that, place a Label control so that you have a place to display content, and add it into the page. Now you have a very simple interface. Your initial screen for this project should now look like the one shown in the following screenshot:

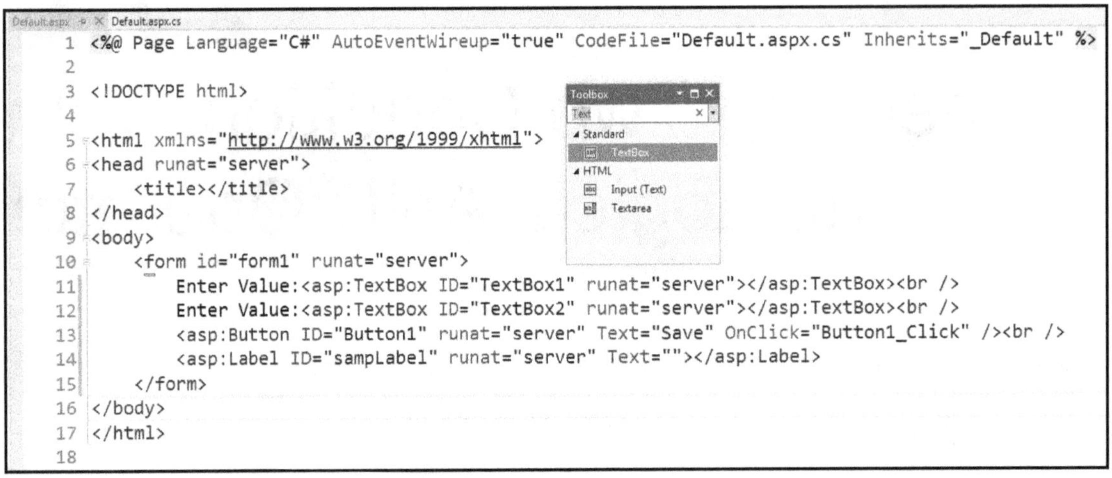

```
Default.aspx    X  Default.aspx.cs
     1  <%@ Page Language="C#" AutoEventWireup="true" CodeFile="Default.aspx.cs" Inherits="_Default" %>
     2
     3  <!DOCTYPE html>
     4
     5  <html xmlns="http://www.w3.org/1999/xhtml">
     6  <head runat="server">
     7      <title></title>
     8  </head>
     9  <body>
    10      <form id="form1" runat="server">
    11          Enter Value:<asp:TextBox ID="TextBox1" runat="server"></asp:TextBox><br />
    12          Enter Value:<asp:TextBox ID="TextBox2" runat="server"></asp:TextBox><br />
    13          <asp:Button ID="Button1" runat="server" Text="Save" OnClick="Button1_Click" /><br />
    14          <asp:Label ID="sampLabel" runat="server" Text=""></asp:Label>
    15      </form>
    16  </body>
    17  </html>
    18
```

Figure 4.2.1: The initial project screen

# Building your simulation

Now, before each of the TextBox control, let's put a little bit of text. Let's say Enter Value: before each TextBox control. Next, change the visible text on the Button control so that it says, for example, Save, as shown here:

```
<asp:Button ID="Button1" runat="server" Text="Save" /><br />
```

You are pretending that you're going to save to a database. Eventually, you'll add in real code, but here it's just a simulation, that's all.

Now take a look at it in the **Design** view, and it must look like the following screenshot. You'll have two text boxes, a **Save** button, and a `Label` control:

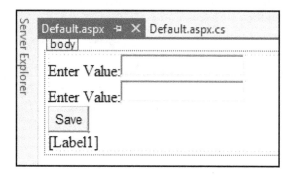

Figure 4.2.2: Our interface thus far in the Design view

# Determining if there is something in the text boxes

Now double-click on the **Save** button. Inside, you see the event handler, and you'll create a code that ensures that both the boxes have entries. In other words, you'll ensure that neither box is empty. So, enter the following:

```
if(TextBox1.Text!="" && TextBox2.Text !="")
```

Here, the `!=` symbol is read as *does not equal*, and `TextBox1.Text !=""` in simple English is asking, "is something present in the box?" This is simply confirming that the text in the box is something different from nothing; in other words, confirming that there is something there. Then, you will use the `&&` (AND) symbol. This is what that means—the logical AND operator. Next, for the second text box also you'll say, `TextBox2.Text !=""`.

Now, set comment 7 as follows:

```
//7. Line below ensures entries are present in both boxes
```

This is what the line is checking.

# Displaying the results

Now, imagine that there are entries in both the boxes. In that case, you need to display some text. So, for example, type the following code:

```
Label1.Text = "Your entries have been saved";
```

Here, you're pretending that you're saving to a database. In real life, that's not so easy; you've got to write a lot more code. On the other hand, if one of the boxes is empty or both the boxes are empty, you have to display a relevant message. So, first you will say `else`, and then within a set of curly braces, you will say the following:

```
else
{
    Label1.Text = "Both entries must be specified.";
}
```

Remember to close this with a semicolon. That's it. This is our simple program!

Now, let's add a couple of comments in simple English, starting with number 8:

```
Label1.Text = "Your entries have been saved"; //8. Line runs when both
boxes are filled
```

On the other hand, comment 9 should read as follows:

```
Label1.Text = "Both entries must be specified.";
//9. Runs when one box, or the other box, or both boxes are empty
```

Now, the `&&` symbol, which is a logical AND operator, short-circuits. This means the following. If `TextBox1.Text!=""` is false, that is a logical condition, the right-hand side of `&&` is not checked, and you skip to the `else` block directly.

If `TextBox1.Text!=""` is true and `TextBox2.Text !=""` is true, then the code executes the following:

```
Label1.Text = "Your entries have been saved";
```

So, the only time this runs is if the left-hand side is true and the right-hand side is true.

Now, imagine that `TextBox1.Text!=""` is false. So again, that will skip down to `else` directly, and the right-hand side of `&&` would not even be checked. That is called **short-circuiting**.

Now, one more thing here. If `TextBox1.Text!=""` is true, but the right-hand side is false, then again you'll skip down to `else`.

Let's go through this process now. Open Google Chrome. We will see the boxes, as shown in the following screenshot:

Figure 4.2.3: The interface before entering any values

Now you can experiment with possible values. First, don't enter anything in the first box or the second box—leave them both empty and click on **Save**. It says, Both entries must be specified., as shown in the following screenshot. This confirms that the else block is executed—you can see that in the message:

Figure 4.2.4: The result of clicking on Save with no values entered in either box

Now, put something into the top box, for example `Hello`, but leave the second box empty, and look at the values. Again, it says `Both entries must be specified`, as shown in the following screenshot. This confirms that the `else` block has run again:

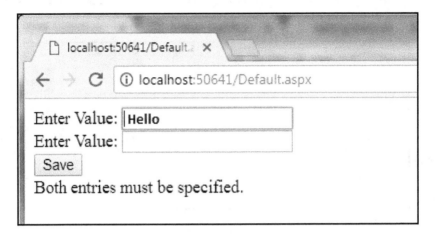

Figure 4.2.5: The result of clicking on Save with Hello entered into the top box

Now, let's put something into the bottom box, for example `15`, empty out the first box, and then click on **Save**. Again, this confirms that the `else` block has run. The results are shown in the following screenshot. So, we have tried three cases, and in all of them the `else` block is executed.

Figure 4.2.6: The result of clicking on Save with the top box empty and 15 entered into the bottom box

Now, put in entries in both the boxes and then click on **Save**. As shown in *Figure 4.2.7*, it says Your entries have been saved. So, the only time that the code runs is when you have entries in both the boxes on the page. If you don't have them in both the boxes, every single time when the code is run, the else portion of the block is executed.

Figure 4.2.7: The result of clicking on Save with something entered into both the boxes

These are the basics of using the logical && operator and specifically understanding how it executes.

For review, a complete version of Default.aspx.cs for this chapter is displayed in the following code block:

```
//1. using is a keyword, it's blue
//2. System is a name space that stores already created code
//3. using System brings in existing code
using System;

//4. class is a required container for creating our own code samples
public partial class _Default : System.Web.UI.Page
{
    //5. code below is where we place our own code
    //6. Button1_Click is code that runs when a page loads from a
    //server
    protected void Page_Load(object sender, EventArgs e)
    {
    }

    protected void Button1_Click1(object sender, EventArgs e)
    {
        if (TextBox1.Text != "" && TextBox2.Text != "")
            //7. Line below ensures entries are present in both boxes
            Label1.Text = "Your entries have been saved. ";//8. Line
```

```
//runs when both boxes are filled

        else
        {
            Label1.Text = "Both entries must be specified. ";
            //9. Runs when one box, or the other box
            // or both boxes are empty
        }
    }
}
```

# Summary

In this chapter, you learned how to use the logical && operator. You set up a project, pretended to save to a database, wrote code to determine if there was something in the two text boxes, and learned what short-circuiting means.

In the next chapter, you'll learn about the logical || (OR) operator.

# **22**

# Checking Two Conditions with the Logical OR Operator

In this chapter, you will learn how to use the logical || (OR) operator and the CheckBox control.

## **Working with check boxes**

We will place a couple of CheckBox controllers into the form. Open up **Toolbox** and drag a CheckBox control into the page so that it looks like this:

```
<body>
 <form id="form1" runat="server">
     <asp:CheckBox ID="CheckBox1" runat="server" />
 </form>
```

If you switch over to the **Design** view, you'll see the section of the screen as shown in the following screenshot:

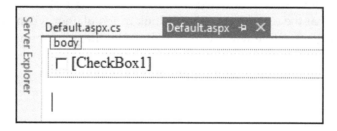

Figure 4.3.1 The screen produced by the preceding code, in the Design view

Now, let's launch this so that you can see how it's rendered in Google Chrome. Keep in mind that the rendering of these things—their visual appearance—can vary sometimes from browser to browser.

Now, we have a CheckBox control, as shown in *Figure 4.3.2*. You basically check it or uncheck it. Clearly, what is true about this is that it has two possible states: two possible values—checked and unchecked.

Figure 4.3.2: CheckBox in the checked state

Now, go back to the **Source** view, and we will build up the interface. Put a `<br>` tag at the end and add one more CheckBox control. So again, drag another box into the page and then put another `<br>` tag at the end of the line.

Next, also add a Text attribute to each CheckBox control. For example, type the following:

```
<body>
 <form id="form1" runat="server">
 <asp:CheckBox ID="CheckBox1" runat="server" text="Smoker"/> <br />
 <asp:CheckBox ID="CheckBox2" runat="server" Text="Over 45" /><br />
 </form>
```

Go back to the **Design** view, and now we have two CheckBox controllers, as shown in *Figure 4.3.3*. Notice that the CheckBox controls look much plainer when you design them; they look a little more attractive when you actually view them in a browser:

Figure 4.3.3: The two checked check boxes in Google Chrome

There is one more thing for you to note here: add a button under the boxes so that we can analyze the results. Change the Text property of the Button control so that it says Submit, for example, and then put another <br> tag. Finally, insert a Label control for the purpose of showing the results. For this, type lab in the **Toolbox** search field, and drag a Label control into the markup. Your code should now appear as follows:

```
<body>
   <form id="form1" runat="server">
      <asp:CheckBox ID="CheckBox1" runat="server" text="Smoker"/>
      <br />
      <asp:CheckBox ID="CheckBox2" runat="server" Text="Over 45" />
      <br />

      <asp:Button ID="Button1" runat="server" Text="Submit" />
      <br />
      <asp:Label ID="Label1" runat="server" Text="Label">
      </asp:Label>
   </form>
```

Now switch over to the **Design** view to look at our markup, our basic HTML, as shown in the following screenshot. This is its appearance:

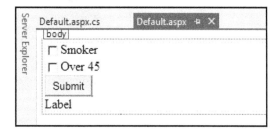

Figure 4.3.4: Our current markup in the Design view

Let's view it again in Google Chrome, as can be seen in *Figure 4.3.5*. When it gets a little more complex, it's good to view things in stages as you build them. You get a couple of the `CheckBox` controllers, and you can click on the **Submit** button. This looks pretty good!

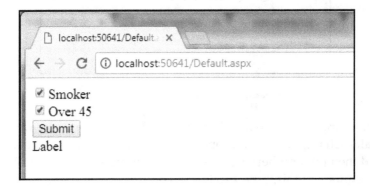

Figure 4.3.5: Our interface in Google Chrome

# Introducing the logical || (OR) operator

Clearly, you need to be able to examine the values whether something is checked or not and so on. So, to do that exactly now in C#, you'll double-click on the **Submit** button, and that brings up the event handler. Let's add comment 5 as follows:

```
//5. Code below runs when submit button is clicked
 protected void Button1_Click(object sender, EventArgs e)
```

The code is as follows:

```
if(CheckBox1.Checked || CheckBox2.Checked)
```

In the preceding `if` statement, the `Checked` property is a true or false type of quantity. Hover your mouse over it, and it says `bool` for Boolean. This is why you can use it with an `if`. In simple English, this is asking whether there is a check mark in the box or no.

In C#, to say OR, you type two vertical lines like this: ||.

Let's express the preceding statement in simple English in comment 6:

```
//6. In English, we'd say: is box 1, or box2, or potentially both boxes,
checked
if (CheckBox1.Checked || CheckBox2.Checked)
```

Now, we have to take an action. Imagine that both the boxes are checked, or maybe the first or the second one, it doesn't really matter. Let's display a relevant line of text:

```
{
    Label1.Text = "You do not qualify for a discount";
    //7. Runs when one box, or the other, or both are checked
}
```

Be sure to close the `Label1.Text` line with a semicolon. Let's also add comment 7 at the end of that line to indicate when this runs.

On the other hand, imagine that neither box is checked. In other words, both the boxes are empty. Start with `else`, and then between the curly braces enter the following line, closing with a semicolon. Then, add comment 8 at the end of this line:

```
else
{
    Label1.Text = "You do qualify for a discount"; //8. Runs when
    neither box is checked
}
```

Here, for review, is what your code should look like at this point:

```
//1. using is a keyword, it's blue
//2. System is a name space that stores already created code
//3. using System brings in existing code
using System;

//4. class is a required container for creating our own code samples
public partial class _Default : System.Web.UI.Page
{
    protected void Page_Load(object sender, EventArgs e)
    {
    }

    //5. Code below runs when submit button is clicked
    protected void Button1_Click(object sender, EventArgs e)
    {
        //6. In English, we'd say: is box 1, or box2, or potentially
        //both boxes, checked
        if (CheckBox1.Checked || CheckBox2.Checked)
        {
```

```
        Label1.Text = "You do not qualify for a discount";
        //7. Runs when one box, or the other, or both are checked
    }

    else
    {
        Label1.Text = "You do qualify for a discount";
        //8. Runs when neither box is checked
    }
}
}
```

# Experimenting with the logical || (OR) operator

I know this still seems a little abstract. However, the best thing to do is actually to type the code or run it and experiment with potential box values.

Open Google Chrome and let it load. First of all, if I don't check either box, they're both blank, and I click on **Submit**, it says You do qualify for a discount, as shown in the following screenshot:

Figure 4.3.6: Neither box is checked, and the message is "You do qualify for a discount"

Now imagine that I check `Smoker` and click on **Submit**. It says You do not qualify for a discount. Maybe this is for applying for health insurance or something.

Figure 4.3.7: The Smoker box is checked, and the message is "You do not qualify for a discount"

Now imagine that I only check `Over 45` and click on **Submit**. Again, it says You do not qualify for a discount, as shown in the following screenshot:

Figure 4.3.8: When the Over 45 box is checked, the message is "You do not qualify for a discount"

Finally, imagine that I select both the boxes and click on **Submit**. Once again, it says You do not qualify for a discount, as shown in the following screenshot:

Figure 4.3.9: When both the boxes are checked, the message is "You do not qualify for a discount"

So, these are the basic operations of the logical || (OR) operator. In other words, if the left-hand side of the `if` statement is true (refer to the following code block), but the right-hand side is false, then the whole operator evaluates to true, which means `Label1.Text = "You do not qualify for a discount"` runs:

```
if (CheckBox1.Checked || CheckBox2.Checked)
```

On the other hand, if the left-hand side of the `if` statement is false, but the right-hand side is true, then `Label1.Text = "You do not qualify for a discount"` will still execute. Only one of these conditions has to be true for the line immediately within the `if` block to run.

Now, if the left-hand side of the `if` statement is true, but the right-hand side is false, the || (OR) operator **short-circuits**. This means that because the left-hand side of it is true, then `Label1.Text = "You do not qualify for a discount"` runs and the right-hand side is not even checked; it just runs the `if` block. Again, this is called **short-circuiting**.

One more thing to consider here is this: if both sides of the `if` statement are false, then the `else` block is the one that executes. This is why I started with two `CheckBox` controls because if you write the code and check the values of the boxes, you can experiment, and then that allows you to develop a deeper understanding of the operation of the logical || (OR) operator.

# Summary

In this chapter, you learned how to use the logical || (OR) operator and experimented with it to some extent. You also learned how to work with the `CheckBox` control.

In the next chapter, you'll learn about the basics of arrays.

# 23
# Declaring, Setting, and Reading Arrays

In this chapter, you will learn about the basics of arrays. An *array* is like a block of memory. So, we'll begin by creating a couple of TextBox controls and then reading the values from the boxes into an array.

## Setting up the basic interface

Go to **View** | **Toolbox**. Grab a **TextBox** control, and drag it into the page. Then repeat this action with another **TextBox** control. Next, beneath that, place a **Button** control, and then under that, place a **Label** control so that you have a place to display some output.

This is the basic user interface. Let's change a couple of things here, though. First of all, put the <br /> tags to insert line breaks so that the markups are on separate lines. The Label control doesn't need one because there's nothing underneath it, so it can stay there as-is. Now change the text on the Button tag so that it says, for example, Summarize. Your Default.aspx page should appear as the following screenshot:

```
Default.aspx.cs*        Default.aspx  □ X
 1  <%@ Page Language="C#" AutoEventWireup="true" CodeFile="Default.aspx.cs" Inherits="_Default" %>
 2
 3  <!DOCTYPE html>
 4
 5  <html xmlns="http://www.w3.org/1999/xhtml">
 6  <head runat="server">
 7      <title></title>
 8  </head>
 9  <body>
10      <form id="form1" runat="server">
11          <asp:TextBox ID="TextBox1" runat="server"></asp:TextBox><br />
12          <asp:TextBox ID="TextBox2" runat="server"></asp:TextBox><br />
13          <asp:Button ID="Button1" runat="server" Text="Summarize" OnClick="Button1_Click" /><br />
14          <asp:Label ID="Label1" runat="server" Text=""></asp:Label>
15      </form>
16  </body>
17  </html>
18
```

Figure 5.1.1: Your basic Default.aspx interface

Next, we will read some values, store them to an array, and then, for example, show the total of the values and the average of the values.

Go to the **Design** view, and what you see should look like the following screenshot:

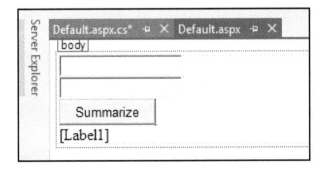

Figure 5.1.2: The basic interface in the Design view

You now have two `TextBox` controls and `Button` and `Label` controls. Let's preview this quickly in Google Chrome to make sure that it can be seen clearly:

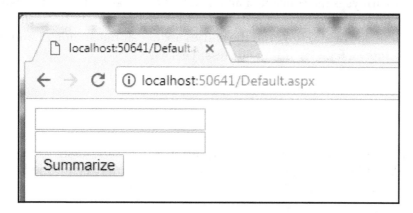

Figure 5.1.3: The basic interface preview in Google Chrome

# Creating the array

Now you can close the preview and unload it. Next, double-click on the button labeled `Summarize` in the **Design** view. So, now we are inside the Event Handler for the click event; when somebody clicks on the button, we respond to it with the code that follows. First, remember that we have two `TextBox` controls, so we will create an array, read the values, and operate on them. For this, type `decimal`, which is a data type. Next, put brackets to indicate that you're creating an array. Then, type `values`, which is the name of the array. On the right-hand side, type `new`, essentially to make the array live in memory. Then type `decimal` and 2 within a second set of brackets. Finally, close this with a semicolon:

```
decimal[] values = new decimal[2];
```

So, what is the purpose of this line? To explain this, let's insert comment 5 at the end of the line, as follows:

```
//5. This line creates an array of length 2, or it can store 2 entries
```

An array is basically a block of memory, and you can store values inside that block of memory.

# Setting up an index

A big thing with arrays is the concept of an *index*. So how does that matter? Take a look. Remember, the array we just created is designed to store two entries, because there's a 2 where it says `new decimal`. However, the entries are not stored at index 1 and index 2; the word index is simply a fancy word for address. That's it.

Let's actually add this as comment 6 on the next line:

```
//6. index in this context is just the same as saying address: 0,1 and NOT
1,2
```

In our particular case, because the length of the array is 2, the addresses or the indexes go from 0 to 1 as 0,1 and *not* 1,2. So, even though we might naturally be inclined to count 1, 2, 3, and so forth, in C# you begin at 0, not at 1:

```
values[0] = decimal.Parse(TextBox1.Text);
```

Note that here, the index is 0. So, this will store the first value at index number 0. And now we'll make it read from the box. So, we say `decimal.Parse` and then `TextBox1.Text`, and end with a semicolon.

In real life, you probably want to use the `TryParse` method and make this code more sophisticated, because this could crash as we have it. If somebody entered 10, that would be OK; but if somebody entered the word ten, it would potentially crash. So `TryParse` will be a better and more realistic way.

We will say the following now at the end of this line:

```
//7. Converts and saves value from box to array at index 0
```

Now we can repeat this for the second box; so, enter the following, adding a similar comment to the previous one:

```
values[1] = decimal.Parse(TextBox2.Text); //8. Converts and saves value
from box to array at index 1
```

Now when you talk about this in spoken language, you have to be extremely careful. So, `values[0]` is the first entry at index 0 and `values[1]` is the second entry at index 1, so keep that in mind. That's how you would describe it in spoken language.

How can you make use of it? Well, keep this basic fact in mind: it doesn't matter how fancy it looks; ultimately, `values[0]` simply represents whatever number has been typed into the first box and `values[1]` represents whatever number has been typed into the second box. That is all that it can possibly mean. Ultimately, it's just a number.

So, if we want to `total` the two `decimal` values, on the right-hand side we need to do basic addition as follows:

```
decimal total = values[0] + values[1];
```

# Using arrays to do addition

The action here is very simple: add two values in the array and then store them to the `total` variable. That's it. Insert comment 9 at the end of this line:

```
decimal total = values[0] + values[1];//9. Add the two values in the array
and store to total variable
```

After this, of course, you want to display it to the user. To do so, type the following:

```
Label1.Text = $"Total is {total:C}";
```

Again, use the `$` symbol for string interpolation and double quotes for a string. We are working with a monetary example, so we'll format this as currency and close with a semicolon. Enter comment 10 at the end of this line as follows:

```
//10. Displays total value formatted as currency
```

Now, let's run this and observe what happens. Open Google Chrome, enter a couple of values in both the boxes, and click on `Summarize`, as shown in the following screenshot. The total is $110.00. Correct? Exit the screen and unload:

Figure 5.1.4: The total of the values entered into the boxes is $110.00

# Using arrays to display an average

There is one more thing here. Imagine that you want to display the average; how can you do that using a natural feature of arrays? The fact that our array is two units long (it can store two entries) is something that we should be able to use. So, we will say the following here:

```
Label1.Text += $"Average is {total / values.Length:C}";
```

Note that we use += to append the line that we are about to create to the previous line. Next comes the $ symbol for string interpolation and double quotes for a string. Then we say, for example, "Average is ", and then within the curly braces, we stick in our calculation, which is {total / values.Length:C}";. What this says is to take the total and divide by values.length. Now that is also a monetary amount, OK? So, the format is currency, or C, and we close with a semicolon.

Let me describe this in a little more detail by entering comment 11 below that line:

```
//11. Line below total/values.Length because total is the result of adding
the entries
```

This is the same as doing very simple math, for example, taking 23, adding 34 to it, and then dividing it by 2 to find the average of those two numbers: (23 + 34)/2. That's it.

Further, comment 12 should read as follows:

```
//12. values.Length tells you how many entries there are
```

So, this is just a simple arithmetic average; the simplest kind of average that you can possibly do.

Now let's observe this in action. Open Google Chrome. I also format this as currency, because it is still money, right? Because, when you add $10 and $15, the average is another monetary amount. Here, when we enter 56 and 455 and click on **Summarize**, it says **Total is $511.00** and **Average is $255.50**.

The only thing missing is the <br> tag so that average goes to its own line in a web page. Let's add that now as follows:

```
Label1.Text += $"<br>Average is {total / values.Length:C}";
```

Now, enter some values and click on **Summarize**. That's it. So, now it's working as expected, as shown in the following screenshot:

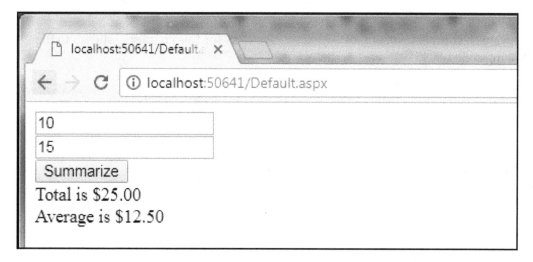

Figure 5.1.6: Average now appears on its own line

# Viewing the page source

Behind the scenes, right-click and select **View page source**. Remember that most of the source is automatically generated; you don't have to worry about it. The stuff that you put in is rendered to this very simple HTML. So, if you know anything about HTML, the following snippet should strike you as immediately familiar; there's nothing peculiar about it. It's just plain HTML that the browser ultimately receives in this context:

```
<%@ Page Language="C#" AutoEventWireup="true" CodeFile="Default.aspx.cs"
Inherits="_Default" %>

<!DOCTYPE html>

<html xmlns="http://www.w3.org/1999/xhtml">
<head runat="server">
    <title></title>
</head>
<body>
    <form id="form1" runat="server">
        <asp:TextBox ID="TextBox1" runat="server"></asp:TextBox><br />
        <asp:TextBox ID="TextBox2" runat="server"></asp:TextBox><br />
        <asp:Button ID="Button1" runat="server" Text="Summarize"
        OnClick="Button1_Click" /><br />
```

```
            <asp:Label ID="Label1" runat="server" Text=""></asp:Label>
        </form>
    </body>
    </html>
```

For review, a complete version of `Default.aspx.cs` for this chapter is shown in the following code block:

```
//1. using is a keyword, it's blue
//2. System is a name space that stores already created code
//3. using System brings in existing code
using System;

//4. class is a required container for creating our own code samples
public partial class _Default : System.Web.UI.Page
{
    protected void Page_Load(object sender, EventArgs e)
    {
    }

    protected void Button1_Click(object sender, EventArgs e)
    {
        decimal[] values = new decimal[2];
        //5. This line creates an array of length 2, or it can store 2
        //entries
        //6. index in this context is just the same as saying address:
        //0,1 and NOT 1,2
        values[0] = decimal.Parse(TextBox1.Text);
        //7. Converts and saves value from box to array at index 0
        values[1] = decimal.Parse(TextBox2.Text); //8. Converts and
        //saves value from box to array at index 1
        decimal total = values[0] + values[1];// 9.Add the two values
        //in the array and store to total variable
        Label1.Text = $"Total is {total:C}";//10. Displays total value
        //formatted as currency
        Label1.Text += $"<br>Average is {total / values.Length:C}";
        //11. Line below total/values.Length because total is the
        //result of adding the entries
        //12. values.Length tells you how many entries there are
    }
}
```

# Summary

In this chapter, you learned about the basics of arrays. An *array* is like a block of memory. To build an array, you created a couple of `TextBox` controls and then read the values from the boxes into the array. You learned about setting up an index and using the array to do addition and to find an average.

In the next chapter, we'll talk about using loops with arrays.

# 24
# Iterating Over Arrays with foreach Loops

In this chapter, you will learn how to make loops and arrays work.

## Setting up the beginning interface

Let's begin with a simple markup, like the one shown in the following screenshot, and into it we will place a button and a label:

```
Default.aspx.cs*        Default.aspx* ⊕ ×
    1  <%@ Page Language="C#" AutoEventWireup="true" CodeFile="Default.aspx.cs" Inherits="_Default" %>
    2
    3  <!DOCTYPE html>
    4
    5  <html xmlns="http://www.w3.org/1999/xhtml">
    6  <head runat="server">
    7      <title></title>
    8  </head>
    9  <body>
   10      <form id="form1" runat="server">
   11
   12      </form>
   13  </body>
   14  </html>
   15
```

Figure 5.2.1: Our simple beginning markup

Go to **View** | **Toolbox**, and drop in a Button control and a Label control beneath it. Now, put a `<br>` tag after the Button line, remove the text that says Button between the double quotes, and replace it with Show, or something along those lines. Next, remove the text attribute of the Label control so that it goes away. Your Default.aspx page should now look similar to the following screenshot:

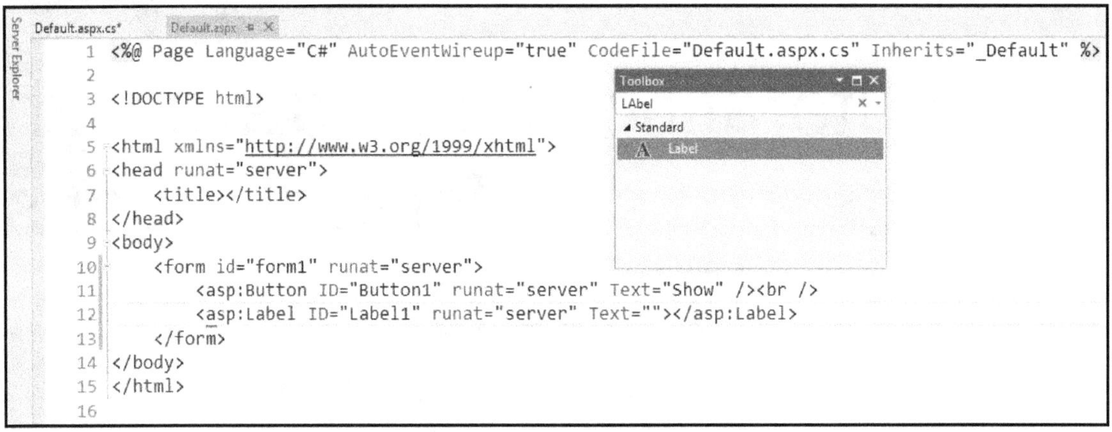

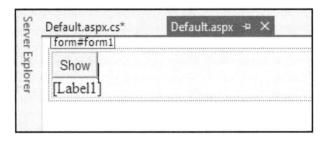

Figure 5.2.2: The modified mark with a button and a label

Now, in the **Design** view, we have a very simple interface consisting of a Button control and a Label control, as shown in the following screenshot:

Figure 5.2.3: Our simple interface in the Design view

# Creating an array of strings

Double-click on the **Show** button to bring up the event handler. Here, we'll create our code; so enter the following code:

```
string[] s = { "h", "e", "y" };
```

Here, `string[]` simply means an array of strings. We name it s, and follow this with a list—an initializer. Put the entries between curly braces; in this case, you entered `{"h", "e", "y"}`. You placed all of these entries in double quotes and closed it with a semicolon. Each of the entries, `"h"`, `"e"`, `"y"`, is a string. Don't be thrown by the fact that these are individual characters. The fact that *does* matter is that they're between double quotes. This means that each of them is a `string`, not a character.

C# does indeed have a `character` data type, and for that you would put, for example, `'g'` (between single quotes). In other words, the way that it's stored in the system is different; so, double quotes or single quotes absolutely makes a big difference! Keep that in mind.

Now let's add comment 5 after this line as follows:

```
//5. Makes array of strings
```

# Introducing the foreach loop

We can examine these values now. We can do different things with them, but imagine that all you want to do is just print them. So, we will say the following:

```
foreach (string c in s)
```

Writing `string` here reflects the fact that each of the entries between the curly braces in the preceding line is a `string`. After `string`, you type c, which is basically a variable that is scoped to the loop; it exists within the context of the loop only. When a loop operates, that's when c exists as a variable. Now let's add comment 6 above this line as follows:

```
//6. As loop runs, c stands for h, then e, and then the letter y
```

The purpose of c is that it represents each of those characters as the loop operates.

So, `foreach string c in` (`in` is a keyword here), and then a collection of items; the collection is represented by s.

# Displaying the results

Perhaps all that you want to do is to display them; so enter the following beneath the foreach statement:

```
Label1.Text += $"<br>{c}";
```

Note that we use += to append the current line to the previous lines as the loop operates. Type the $ symbol for string interpolation, double quotes, <br> to make sure that the output is stacked in a column vertically, and then the value to be shown, c, which goes within the curly braces. Remember, the black portions in the code are replaced at runtime with an actual value such as "h", "e", or "y". Close this with a semicolon.

Now let's add a couple of more comments; so comment 7 at the end of the foreach statement is as follows:

```
//7. Needed so each letter can grabbed
```

Also, comment 8 at the end of the Label1.Text line should say something like the following:

```
//8. Prints each letter in a column
```

# Running the program

Now let's observe this in action. Open Google Chrome. Click on the **Show** button, and it says h-e-y vertically (see the following screenshot), and that's it. Simple enough!

Figure 5.2.4: Our foreach loop in action

For review, a complete version of the `Default.aspx.cs` file for this chapter is displayed in the following code block:

```
//1. using is a keyword, it's blue
//2. System is a name space that stores already created code
//3. using System brings in existing code
using System;

//4. class is a required container for creating our own code samples
public partial class _Default : System.Web.UI.Page
{
    protected void Page_Load(object sender, EventArgs e)
    {
    }

    protected void Button1_Click(object sender, EventArgs e)
    {
        string[] s = { "h", "e", "y" };
        //5. Makes array of strings
        foreach (string c in s)//6. As loop runs, c stands for h, then
        //e, and then the letter y
            Label1.Text += $"<br>{c}"; //7. Needed so each letter can
            //grabbed
            //8. Prints each letter in a column
    }
}
```

# Summary

In this chapter, you learned how to make loops and arrays work. You created an array of strings, learned how to use a `foreach` loop, and displayed the results when you ran the program.

In the next chapter, we will talk about creating simple methods.

# 25
# Creating and Using a Simple Method

In this chapter, you will learn about creating and running your own methods.

## Setting up the user interface

Let's begin with `Default.aspx`. Open **Toolbox** (remember, *Ctrl+Alt+X*) and then insert a `Label` control simply as a place to hold some output. Let's also place a `TextBox` control above the `Label` control. Grab a `TextBox` control, and drag and drop it into the page. Now, the last thing to do to set this up is to put a `<br>` tag at the end of the `TextBox` line. Our simple user interface is shown in the following screenshot:

```
Default.aspx.cs*     Default.aspx  ▬ ✕
    1  <%@ Page Language="C#" AutoEventWireup="true" CodeFile="Default.aspx.cs" Inherits="_Default" %>
    2
    3  <!DOCTYPE html>
    4
    5  <html xmlns="http://www.w3.org/1999/xhtml">
    6  <head runat="server">
    7      <title></title>
    8  </head>
    9  <body>
   10      <form id="form1" runat="server">
   11          <asp:Label ID="Label1" runat="server" Text="Label"></asp:Label> <br />
   12          <asp:TextBox ID="TextBox1" runat="server"></asp:TextBox> <br />
   13      </form>
   14  </body>
   15  </html>
   16
```

Toolbox ▾ ☐ ✕
Text                    × ▾
▲ Standard
  ▭ TextBox
▲ HTML
  ▭ Input (Text)
  ▭ Textarea

Figure 5.3.1: Our simple user interface

# Creating a method

Now switch to the **Design** view, and double-click on **TextBox**. This generates the event handler, and here you'll create your code. But first, right above it, we will create a **method**, as shown as follows. A method is simply a chunk of code. Usually, it has a very definite purpose that is expressed very clearly through the name of the method:

```
private static double GetIncreasedValue(double x)
```

Let's begin with some of the requirements. First, we start with `private`, and the fact that this is `private` indicates that this method can be called only within the code that you see; it cannot be accessed by code, for example, in other programs. After `private`, we put `static`. The word `static` in this context means that you can call the method. When you call it, you can simply type the name of the method.

Next, we say `double`. This is the return type, which tells you that when the method operates, it basically produces a `double` data type as a result of its operations. This is then followed by the name. So, here we say `GetIncreasedValue`, which is the name of our method. As this is the name, we know that this method will produce some kind of increase in the value.

If you want, you can make it more exact, you can say `Get110PercentOfAValue`, for example. That, in essence, is what ours will do. So, here we'll just say `GetIncreasedValue`, followed by parentheses. The next bit is a data type such as `double` and then x; `double` in this context is the data type of the parameter named x. You can imagine that the parameter is basically a placeholder through which values are passed into the body of the method so that it can operate on them.

Let's add several comments above this line. I'll be very exact this time:

```
//5. private means this method is reachable only within this class
//6. static means we can call this method directly by just its name
//7. double is the data type of the value returned by a method
//8. GetIncreasedValue is the name of the method
//9. double x is the data type and name of a parameter
//10. Parameters serve as place holders through which values are passed
into methods
```

This is basically the header of our method. Next, you will define the body.

# Defining the body of the method

Now we have to define the body of the method—the logic that defines the body of the method. So, between the curly braces, we'll say the following:

```
return x * 1.1;
```

This is what we mean by increased value. Now, notice that I used the `return` keyword. This means that the value of x is multiplied by 1.1 and it is returned to the calling code. So, let's add comment 11 after this line, as shown here:

```
return x * 1.1; //11. Sends the value of x*1.1 back to the calling code
```

By the **calling code**, I mean the place where the method is invoked or called. Go to where it says `TextBox1_TextChanged` in the event handler. Now let's add comment 12 under this, as follows:

```
//12. Line below reads value from box and converts to numerical form and
saves to variable
```

# Working with the Convert class

Beneath comment 12, you'll add the following line:

```
double value = Convert.ToDouble(TextBox1.Text);
```

Notice the class called `Convert`. If you hover your mouse over `Convert`, it says **Converts a base data type to another base data type.** So, basically this is a nice class: a collection of functionality that we can use to convert between different data types.

Now, in our particular case, we say `Convert.ToDouble`, and specifically we'll take the input from the box; so we finish with `TextBox1.Text`.

Remember that this line will read from the `TextBox` control, and the value will be converted to a `double` data type and then saved over to the variable named `value`. So, all of that will happen within that single line.

# Increasing the value of a variable with the GetIncreasedValue method

Once we have this numerical value, we want to increase it, say, by 10 percent or multiply it by `1.1`. To accomplish this step, we say the following:

```
double result = GetIncreasedValue(value);
```

First, I begin this statement with `double`. Why? I do this because I know that I'll use the method that we created earlier (repeated as follows for clarity). I'm using that method because it also has a return type of `double` (highlighted). In other words, this confirms that the `double` data type in our method matches the `double` data type in the statement we're about to create.

```
private static double GetIncreasedValue(double x)
{
    return x * 1.1; //11. Sends the value of x*1.1 back to the
    calling code
}
```

So we say `double result` = and then write the name of the method, `GetIncreasedValue`. Then, since the pop-up tip says `double x`, I will put `value` in parentheses and close with a semicolon:

```
double result = GetIncreasedValue(value);
```

The big idea here is this: when you hover your mouse over `ToDouble` in the `double value = Convert.ToDouble(TextBox1.Text);` statement, you will observe that it's got a `double` data type that it produces and that matches the `double` data type at the beginning of that statement. You see? When you hover your mouse over `GetIncreasedValue`, the way we defined it, it produces a `double` data type as well. So, it matches the `double` data type in the preceding statement. If it does not, many times you may get an error.

Here, `GetIncreasedValue` is the name of our method, and `value` in this context is called an **argument**. So, let's set comments 13 and 14 above this line as follows:

```
//13. value is called the argument because it's the value passed into the
method so the method
//14. can operate on it and produce a result
```

# Outputting the results

As a last step, once we have this result back from our method, we can produce some kind of output. So, we'll say the following:

```
Label1.Text = $"{value} increased by 10% is {result}";
```

Remember, at runtime, `value` in the preceding statement will be replaced with the actual value of a variable and then increased by 10 percent. Then, within the second set of curly braces is `result`. Close this with a semicolon.

This line simply, of course, prints the value to the user increased by 10 percent; so let's add the comment 15 at the end of this line:

```
//15. Shows value to user increase by 10%
```

Keep this basic fact in mind: when I click in the `TextBox` control my first step is to read the value, and the second step is basically to call the method. This means that processing will be switched to the point addressed by the following part of the code:

```
private static double GetIncreasedValue(double x)
{
    return x * 1.1; //11. Sends the value of x*1.1 back to the
    calling code
}
```

After the preceding lines operate, you go back down to the `double result = GetIncreasedValue(value);` line of your program, where the result is saved to the `double result` variable. That variable, in turn, is used later in the `Label1.Text` line, where it also says `{result}`. This is the sequence of operations here.

# Running your program

Now, open Google Chrome. You'll see our box, as shown in Figure 5.3.2. Enter a value, such as 56, and it says 56 increased by 10% is 61.6:

Figure 5.3.2: The value of what is entered in the box is increased by 10 percent using the GetIncreasedValue method

Of course, if you enter ten, you'll get an error, like the one shown in *Figure 5.3.3*. That input generates a format exception. So obviously, it's something that we have to learn to handle, but for now, just be aware of it.

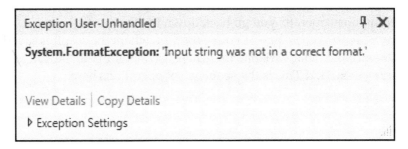

Figure 5.3.3: Format exception error produced from an erroneous input

For review, a complete version of the Default.aspx.cs file for this chapter is displayed in the following code block:

```
//1. using is a keyword, it's blue
//2. System is a name space that stores already created code
//3. using System brings in existing code
using System;

//4. class is a required container for creating our own code samples
```

```
public partial class _Default : System.Web.UI.Page
{

    //5. private means this method is reachable only within this
    //class
    //5. private means this method is reachable only within this
    //class
    //6. static means we can call this method directly by just its
    //name
    //7. double is the data type of the value returned by a method
    //8. GetIncreasedValue is the name of the method
    //9. double x is the data type and name of a parameter
    //10. Parameters serve as place holders through which values are
    //passed into methods
    private static double GetIncreasedValue(double x)
    {
        return x * 1.1; //11. Sends the value of x*1.1 back to the
        //calling code
    }
    protected void TextBox1_TextChanged(object sender, EventArgs e)
    {
        //12. Line below reads value from box and converts to
        //numerical form and saves to variable
        double value = Convert.ToDouble(TextBox1.Text);
        //13. value is called the argument because it's the value
        //passed into the method so the method
        //14. can operate on it and produce a result
        double result = GetIncreasedValue(value);
        Label1.Text = $"{value} increased by 10% is {result}";//15.
        Shows value to user increase by 10%
    }
}
```

# Summary

In this chapter, you learned about creating and running your own methods. You created a method, defined the body of the method, worked with the `Convert` class, and increased the value of a variable with the `GetIncreasedValue` method.

In the next chapter, you will learn how to work with arrays and how to pass them into methods, and also, how to operate on arrays and then return some kind of useful quantity based on the array.

# 26

# Passing Arrays into Methods

In this chapter, you will learn how to work with arrays and how to pass them into methods. You will also learn how to operate in arrays and then return some kind of useful quantity based on the arrays.

## Setting up the user interface

Let's begin with this very simple interface. Here's our markup, and all I have in there already is a Button and Label control:

```
Default.aspx.cs        Default.aspx*  + X
     1  <%@ Page Language="C#" AutoEventWireup="true" CodeFile="Default.aspx.cs" Inherits="_Default" %>
     2
     3  <!DOCTYPE html>
     4
     5  <html xmlns="http://www.w3.org/1999/xhtml">
     6  <head runat="server">
     7      <title></title>
     8  </head>
     9  <body>
    10      <form id="form1" runat="server">
    11          <asp:Button ID="Button1" runat="server" Text="Button" /> <br />
    12          <asp:Label ID="Label1" runat="server" Text=""></asp:Label>
    13      </form>
    14  </body>
    15  </html>
    16
```

Figure 5.4.1: Our simple starting user interface

In the **Design** view, our interface appears as shown in the following screenshot:

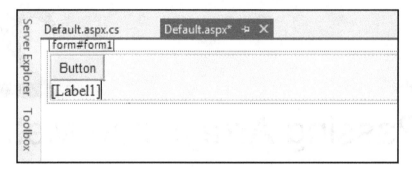

Figure 5.4.2: Our interface in the Design view

Now, just double-click on the Button control to generate the event handler so that you can write some code. When you do that, it generates the event handler as shown in the following code block:

```
protected void Button1_Click(object sender, EventArgs e)
{
}
```

# Creating the method to find the total of values inside an array

We'll create a method right above the line beginning with protected void. The purpose of this method will be to find the total of some values inside an array. To create the method, we'll do the following:

We saw private, static, and double ;before. Let's name this method as Sum. Now, because we'll accept an array, we cannot create on it. Type double as an example, followed by open and closed brackets, and then values. Our parameter is named values, and a data type essentially is an array of doubles:

```
private static double Sum(double[] values)
```

Next, we'll find the Sum of the values, but first let's add the following comment above this line:

```
//5. values is the array that is the parameter
```

# Summing up the values

Comment 5 indicates that `values` is the array we're essentially going to pass. To find the `sum`, enter the following line of code within the curly braces below the line beginning with `private static double`:

```
double sum = 0;
```

Be sure to close the line with a semicolon. Here, it's very important that you begin with 0 rather than some other value. Why so? Imagine that you want to add 1+2+3. Well, what you're actually doing here is putting 0+ before this. Although this is not how we write it on paper, this is how computers understand it. So, when we begin from 0, we have 0+1+2+3. . . . If you don't, you'll get an error; consider you have 4 in the place of 0, but you're adding 1+2+3, you'll have an error, which is not what you intended. So, you need to begin with 0. That is why we entered `double sum = 0` as the initial value of `Sum`. Let's add this as comment 6 at the end of the preceding line:

```
//6. Begin sum with 0 so its value does not change the sum
```

# Using a foreach loop to grab entries inside the array

Now, because we have an array with the name `values`, naturally we will use a loop of some kind. For this, enter the following below this line:

```
foreach (double d in values)
```

Remember that `double` here is a data type, and we know that it should be that because our array stores `doubles`—that's the reason. As the loop operates, `d` basically refers to each value individually. To document the purpose of this line, let's add comment 7 after it as follows:

```
//7. Grabs each entry inside the array
```

# Adding up the values as the loop operates

For the next stage, enter the following:

```
sum += d;
```

Let's add the following comment right after this line to document why this line matters; why it is necessary:

```
//8. sum+=d has the action of adding up the values as the loop operates
```

You have to insert += in this line. If you don't, then you'll be overwriting, and things will not be saved properly. So, += helps to create a sum.

# Returning the value

At the end, of course, we return the value; so type the following and that's it:

```
return sum;
```

Follow this line with comment 9:

```
//9. Returns sum at the end of the method
```

Now, keep in mind that if our array, for example, has 10 values, then the preceding `foreach` statement will run 10 times. Because the loop says there are 10 entries and `sum +=` `d` is linked with the `foreach`, they run together, essentially. Keep that in mind.

# Filling the array

How do you make use of all this? Go to the event handler, and we'll make an array. Now, of course, in real life, this would come from, for example, a database or a web page entry box. Here, though, we'll do it this way to save time. Enter the following between the curly braces:

```
double[] vals = { 4, 5, 9, -10, 2 };
```

Here, we call our array `vals`. On the right-hand side, we initialize it with a list as shown and close with a semicolon. Add comment 10 at the end of this line as follows:

```
//10. Creates an array of doubles so we have something to add up
```

# Outputting the results

To make use of our `Sum` method, let's enter the following in the next line:

```
Label1.Text = $"Sum of values is {Sum(vals)}";
```

Again, we use the `$` symbol for string interpolation and double quotes to make a string. Next, you can say `Sum of values is`. Then you can just embed the method call directly into the string; for this, insert curly braces and type `Sum(vals)` between them. Close with a semicolon.

Let's describe the action of this line as comment 11 above this line, as follows:

```
//11. Line below calls the Sum method and the result is then printed on the
web page
```

The result is a `double`. Remember, in the `private static` **double** `Sum(double[]` `values)` line, the word `double` highlighted here is the result, which tells you the data type of the result, `return sum;`, is returned by the method of the sum, which is a `double` data type. This is ultimately what is stuck into the `"Sum of values is {Sum(vals)}"` string so that you can print it.

After this, you write the name of the method you pass into the array, and that's it.

# Running your program

Let's observe this in action. Open Google Chrome. When the page is loaded, as shown in *Figure 5.4.3*, click on the **Show Sum** button, and it says Sum of values is 10. Correct? Remember, in this simple sense, you should be able to check the code and make sure that it works as expected. So, if you add 4 + 5 + 9 + -10 + 2, the result is 10. Check this up on your calculator to confirm that it works as expected.

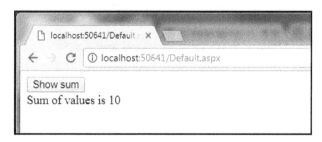

Figure 5.4.3: Our program adds the sum of values correctly

For review, a complete version of the `Default.aspx.cs` file for this chapter is displayed in the following code block:

```
//1. using is a keyword, it's blue
//2. System is a name space that stores already created code
//3. using System brings in existing code
using System;

//4. class is a required container for creating our own code samples
public partial class _Default : System.Web.UI.Page
{
    //5. values is the array that is the parameter
    private static double Sum(double[] values)
    {
        double sum = 0;//6. Begin sum with 0 so its value does not
        //change the sum
        foreach (double d in values)//7. Grabs each entry inside the
        //array
            sum += d;//8. sum+=d has the action of adding up the
            //values as the loop operates

        return sum;//9. Returns sum at the end of the method
    }

    protected void Button1_Click(object sender, EventArgs e)
    {
        double[] vals = { 4, 5, 9, -10, 2 };//10. Creates an array of
        //doubles so we have something to add up
        Label1.Text = $"Sum of values is {Sum(vals)}";//11. Line
        //below calls the Sum method and the result is then printed
        on the web page
    }
}
```

# Summary

In this chapter, you learned how to work with arrays and how to pass them into methods. You also learned how to operate on arrays and then return some kind of useful quantity based on the arrays.

In the next chapter, you will learn about reference type and value type variables.

# 27

# Reference Type and Value Type Variables

In this chapter, you will learn about reference type and value type variables.

## Setting up the user interface

Let's first open up a simple project. This time, put nothing in it but a **Label** within the form, as shown in the following screenshot:

```
Default.aspx.cs    Default.aspx*  + X
    1  <%@ Page Language="C#" AutoEventWireup="true" CodeFile="Default.aspx.cs" Inherits="_Default" %>
    2
    3  <!DOCTYPE html>
    4
    5  <html xmlns="http://www.w3.org/1999/xhtml">
    6  <head runat="server">
    7      <title></title>
    8  </head>
    9  <body>
   10      <form id="form1" runat="server">
   11          <asp:Label ID="Label1" runat="server" Text=""></asp:Label>
   12      </form>
   13  </body>
   14  </html>
   15
```

Figure 5.5.1: Our simple project—only a label appears within the form

In the **Design** view, all that we currently have is shown in the following screenshot:

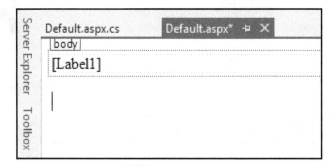

Figure 5.5.2: The current interface in the Design view

Now, double-click slightly to the right of **Label**. This brings up the Page_Load event handler. If it ever disappears for you, just double-click somewhere to the right of the **Label**, and it comes up again.

# Reference type versus value type variables

Since we will be talking about reference type and value type variables in this chapter, you have to understand the difference between the two in their behavior.

## Reference type variables

To begin, we'll create methods; so, start by entering the following:

```
private static void ChangeArray(int[] arr)
```

Here, we say `private` and then `static` and `void` this time. The `void` keyword simply means that our method will perform an action, but it will not send a numerical value, such as 10, back to where it's called. It will do *something*, but not send a numerical value, such as 10, back.

Next, we add `ChangeArray` as the name of the method. We pass in an array of integers (`int`) and then `arr`. That's all our method will do to illustrate the concept.

Let's add comment 5 before going further. Obviously, you've seen a lot of this before, but perhaps you haven't seen `void`. So, type the following above this line:

```
//5. void means do not send a value like 10 back to the calling code
```

In this case, remember that `arr` is the parameter and the data type is an integer (`int`) of arrays.

Now, below this line, type the following:

```
arr[0] = 10;
```

What is the purpose of this line? This line essentially will confirm the following, which we'll put as comment 6:

```
//6. This line changes the value stored at index 0. This change is visible
in the calling code.
```

In other words, when you're passing things by reference, for example, this means that you're giving one thing multiple names; however, all of those names basically allow you to change that one thing. As a result, this means that if you change something through one name, that change becomes visible through other names. For example, imagine you might be named Tom Adam John, and you might respond to Tom or Adam or John. Thus, you have multiple names, but they all point to you. The same principle holds here with arrays. When you deal with arrays, if a change is made through one name, that change is visible through other names.

## Value type variables

Now, let's also make another method as follows:

```
private static void ChangeValue(double x)
{
    x = 30;
}
```

You've seen most of this, except perhaps the `x = 30;` line; so add comment 7 at the end of this line as follows:

```
//7. Setting the value 30 to x will not change the argument where the
method is called
```

For clarity, the following code block shows what your code should look like up to this point:

```
//1. using is a keyword, it's blue
//2. System is a name space that stores already created code
//3. using System brings in existing code
using System;
```

```
//4. class is a required container for creating our own code samples

public partial class _Default : System.Web.UI.Page
{
    private static void ChangeArray(int[] arr)
    {
        //5. void means do not send a value like 10 back to the
        //calling code
        arr[0] = 10;//6. This line changes the value stored at index
        //0. This change is visible in the calling code.

    }
    private static void ChangeValue(double x)
    {
        x = 30;//7. Setting the value 30 to x will not change the
        //argument where the method is called
    }
    protected void Page_Load(object sender, EventArgs e)
    {
    }

}
```

Now, let's take a look at this in action. I know these things seem a little abstract at first, but you need some more code to illustrate these concepts. So, we will add the following within the curly braces of the event handler:

```
int[] arr1 = { 1, 2 };
```

Here, `int[] arr1` is set equal to a very simple array. Next, below this, call the following:

```
ChangeArray(arr1);
```

Add comment 8 after the `int[] arr1` line as follows:

```
//8. Creates a simple array
```

After the `ChangeArray(arr1);` statement, add the following comment:

```
//9. Calls a method and passes in the array
```

Now, the question is, will the change that is made in `arr[0] = 10;` be visible in the code we write next? This is what we will check. To verify this, add the following:

```
Label1.Text = $"The value at index 0 is {arr1[0]}";
```

Let's put the question in other words as comment 10, as follows:

```
//10. Does arr1[0] shows 1 or does it show 10
```

What we ask here is, does it show the original 1 (highlighted here in `int[] arr1 = { 1,)` or will it show 10 (highlighted here in `arr[0] = 10;`)?

Again, for clarity, here is how the lines we've just added should appear in your program:

```
protected void Page_Load(object sender, EventArgs e)
{
    int [] arr1 = { 1, 2 }; //8. Creates a simple array
    ChangeArray(arr1); //9. Calls a method and passes in the array
    Label1.Text = $"The value at index 0 is {arr1[0]}"; //10. Does
    arr1[0] shows 1 or does it show 10
}
```

Let's take a look at the action here in Google Chrome. You'll see `The value at index 0 is 10`, as shown in the following screenshot:

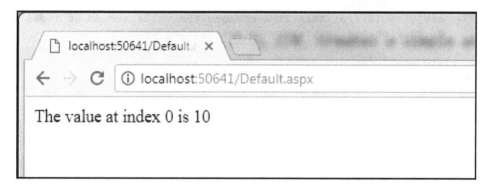

Figure 5.5.3: The program run confirms that the value is 10

What this confirms is that when you deal with arrays (they are **reference types**), when a change is made in `arr[0] = 10` in the array, the change should also be visible through `arr1[0]` even inside the event handler. So, if you change it inside the `ChangeArray(arr1)` method, the change is visible also in `{arr1[0]}`.

Imagine that Step 1 in the following code block represents `ChangeArray(arr1);`, Step 2 represents `arr[0] = 10;` (this is the change in value stored at index 0), and Step 3 represents `{arr1[0]}` all the way back inside `Page_Load`, which confirms that the value has been changed. This is one behavior.

```
//1. using is a keyword, it's blue
//2. System is a name space that stores already created code
//3. using System brings in existing code
using System;

//4. class is a required container for creating our own code samples

public partial class _Default : System.Web.UI.Page
{
    private static void ChangeArray(int[] arr)
    {
        //5. void means do not send a value like 10 back to the
        calling code

        // This is Step 2:
        arr[0] = 10;//6. This line changes the value stored at index
        0. This change is visible in the calling code.
    }
    private static void ChangeValue(double x)
    {
        x = 30;//7. Setting the value 30 to x will not change the
        argument where the method is called
    }
    protected void Page_Load(object sender, EventArgs e)
    {
        int[] arr1 = { 1, 2 };//8. Creates a simple array
        //This is Step 1:
        ChangeArray(arr1);//9. Calls a method and passes in the array
        //This is Step 3:
        Label1.Text = $"The value at index 0 is {arr1[0]}";//10. Does
        arr1[0] shows 1 or does it show 10
    }

}
```

Now, let's look at another kind of behavior, which is that of a simple data type. We will try something much easier this time. Start by entering the following, including comment 11:

```
double z = 25; //11. Creates a variable
```

Next, below that, type the following, including comment 12:

```
ChangeValue(z); //12. z is the argument that is passed into the method
named ChangeValue passed as a copy
```

The question is, as before: will passing z into `ChangeValue` in the code repeated as follows have any impact on the value of z?

> Think of it as shown in the following code snippet, the `double x` parameter being passed is a reference to the z variable in the `ChangeValue(z);` function call mentioned here:

```
private static void ChangeValue(double x)
{
    x = 30;
}
```

How can we answer this? Let's print this value after `ChangeValue` operates:

```
Label1.Text += $"<br>The value of z is now {z}";
```

Here, you have += to append, and then you say `"The value of z is now {z}"`, putting z within curly braces, and close with a semicolon. Now, because we've done this before, obviously, I'm predicting that the value of z will not be changed. But let's observe it in any case.

Open Google Chrome, and you'll see the message shown in the following screenshot:

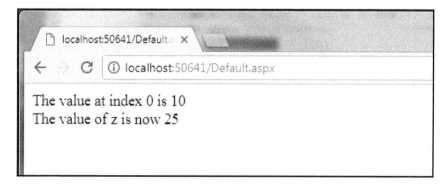

Figure 5.5.4: Our program results as they appear in Google Chrome

We also saw that the value of z was not changed. In other words, imagine Step 1 represents ChangeValue(z); in the final code block at the end of this section. When you code ChangeValue (refer to the following code snippet), what goes into the body of ChangeValue through the x is basically a copy of z. So, you can imagine that what this receives is a copy of the data of z, which means that z itself, the original value, never changes.

```
private static void ChangeValue(double x)
{
    x = 30;
}
```

This is very different, so contrast this with doing the other thing, that is when you code ChangeArray(arr1); (refer to the line with the following function call ChangeArray(arr1); in the final block of code at the end of this section). This now represents Step 1, and the array value now goes into the ChangeArray method (refer to the following code snippet):

```
private static void ChangeArray(int[] arr)
{
arr[0] = 10;
}
```

Essentially, what is passed is a reference, which means that the second stage here, Step 2; in essence, if this changes the array, it is visible in the highlighted arr1[0] of the following statement, and this would represent Step 3:

```
Label1.Text = $"The value at index 0 is {arr1[0]}";
```

So, with arrays, a change made in one place becomes visible in multiple places. With simple data types such as doubles, what is passed into the body of a method is a copy of the data, which means that the original is not changed. This represents some very different behaviors in that sense.

The following code block represents all the code we have worked on so far in this chapter:

```
//1. using is a keyword, it's blue
//2. System is a name space that stores already created code
//3. using System brings in existing code
using System;
//4. class is a required container for creating our own code samples
public partial class _Default : System.Web.UI.Page
{
    //5. void means do not send a value like 10 back to the calling
    code
    private static void ChangeArray(int[] arr)
```

```
    {
        arr[0] = 10;//6. This line changes the value stored at index
        //0. This change is visible in the calling code.

    }
    private static void ChangeValue(double x)
    {
        x = 30;//7. Setting the value 30 to x will not change the
        //argument where the method is called
    }
    protected void Page_Load(object sender, EventArgs e)
    {
        int[] arr1 = { 1, 2 };//8. Creates a simple array
        //ChangeArray(arr1);//9. Calls a method and passes in the array

        Label1.Text = $"The value at index 0 is {arr1[0]}";//10. Does
        //arr1[0] shows 1 or does it show 10

        double z = 25; //11. Creates a variable
        ChangeValue(z); //12. z is the argument that is passed into the
        //method named ChangeValue passed as a copy

        Label1.Text += $"<br>The value of z is now {z}";//12. z is the
        //argument that is passed into the method named ChangeValue
        // passed as a copy
    }

}
```

# Summary

In this chapter, you learned about reference type and value type variables.

In the next chapter, you will learn how to create more powerful methods using the params keyword.

# 28
# Creating More Flexible Methods with the params Keyword

In this chapter, you'll learn how to use the `params` keyword to create more powerful and flexible methods.

## Designing the starting markup

Let's begin with a simple markup page. Open **Toolbox** (*Ctrl+Alt+X*) and drag a **Button** control into the form so that you have something to click on. Change the displayed text so that the `Button` control says `Show Product`, for example. Then, place a `Label` control below the `Button` control line so that you have a place where the output should go. Your markup page should now look like the one shown in the following code block:

```
Default.aspx.cs    Default.aspx  ⊕ ✕
    1  <%@ Page Language="C#" AutoEventWireup="true" CodeFile="Default.aspx.cs" Inherits="_Default" %>
    2
    3  <!DOCTYPE html>
    4
    5  <html xmlns="http://www.w3.org/1999/xhtml">
    6  <head runat="server">
    7      <title></title>
    8  </head>
    9  <body>
   10      <form id="form1" runat="server">
   11          <asp:Button ID="Button1" runat="server" Text="Show Product" />
   12          <asp:Label ID="Label1" runat="server" Text="Label"></asp:Label>
   13      </form>
   14  </body>
   15  </html>
   16
```

Figure 5.6.1: Our simple markup for this chapter

When you're learning, it's not good to have all the lines crammed together. So, separate the two lines by inserting a `<br>` tag at the end of the `Button` markup line. I've tried doing this by placing `Label` right after `Button`, but that gets really confusing when you're learning, so even a little `<br>` tag is helpful.

# Creating the product method

Now, go to the **Design** view and double-click the `Show Product` button so that it brings up the `Button1_Click` Event Handler—the code that runs when somebody clicks on the button. Above it, we'll create a method with the name `Product`, using the `params` keyword. We'll start by inserting comment 5 as follows:

```
//5. params keyword allows us to pass a variable number of values into a
method
```

Specifically, there's no reason why you shouldn't be able to do this—as described in comment 6 here:

```
//6. Product(1,2) or Product(1,2,4) or Product(-3,4,3,6)
```

These are just some numbers, right? It doesn't matter; you should be able to pass a variable number of values to the method. The word *product* in English simply means what you get when you multiply numbers together, OK? If you want, you can even insert negative numbers. So, you should be able to multiply some numbers together. Also, the number of values you're multiplying should be flexible. It shouldn't be fixed so that you can multiply only two values; you should be able to multiply 50 values if you want. So, this is a great method.

Let's take a look at what I mean. Enter the following:

```
private static double Product(params double[] arr)
```

You've seen `private` and `static` before. After those comes `double`, which is the data type returned by the method that we are about to create. We name the method `Product`, and use the new keyword `params`. Then, we make an array, `double`, and name the array, `arr`.

So, `params double[] arr` is what gives us flexibility, specifically the `params` keyword, when we call the method.

Now, let's define the body of the method. Between curly braces, type the following:

```
double product = 1;
```

Again, remember that if you want to multiply numbers together, you've got to begin with something; you cannot begin with 10. For example, if multiply 2 × 4, you would want the value of 8 to come out; however, if you begin with 10, it will be 2 × 4 × 10, you won't end up with what you want. The way to do that in C# is to begin with 1. So, *1 × 2 = 2; 2 × 4 = 8.* This is an example.

Now imagine that you want to multiply *5 × 4 × 3*. In C#, you begin with *1* to keep the product correct. You have *5 × 4 = 20; 20 × 3 = 60; 60 × 1 = 60.* You cannot begin with some value like 5 or 2 or whatever, because that would not work—it would throw off the product. You cannot even begin with 0, because if you do, 0 times anything is still 0, so that won't be useful. So, you begin with 1.

Let's add comment 7 after this line as follows:

```
double product = 1; //7. 1*2*4=8, 1*5*4*3=60, begin with 1 as the initial
value of product
```

Then, because we have an array of doubles, use a `foreach` loop. So, enter the following below this line, including comment 8:

```
foreach (double d in arr) //8. Grab each value inside the array
```

Of course, this simply means grab each value inside the array.

Next, you accumulate, or you build up, the product. To do this, you type the following, including comment 9:

```
product *= d; //9. This line makes the product grow until the loop ends
```

The preceding line has the effect of building the product. So, essentially, the way we are multiplying this is as follows:

```
4,5,6
1 * 4 = 4
4 * 5 = 20
20 * 6 = 120
```

Imagine that the array has values such as 4, 5, and 6. So, first you'd do *1 × 4*, which produces a result of 4. Next, you would take that value, 4, and do *4 × 5*, which produces a result of 20. Finally, you'd do *20 × 6*, which produces a result of 120. See? You begin it in that sequence of steps; that is how it operates. It does this in that fashion from left to right. Once again, this also demonstrates that you've got to begin with 1.

At the end, you return the product; so, type the following, including comment 10:

```
return product; //10. Sends the product back to the calling code
```

Now, add a blank line to separate the `double product` and the `foreach` lines in your existing code.

Remember, the following lines are treated as a unit; essentially, this means that if the loop has 10 values, this unit will run 10 times, and so on:

```
foreach (double d in arr)//8. Grab each value inside the array
product *= d;//9. This line makes the product grow until the loop ends
```

Now, go to the Event Handler and enter the following under the open curly brace:

```
double x = 5, y = 10, z = 15;
```

Here we're just declaring and setting some variables, and that's OK to do because they're all of the same data type. Thus, you can just declare and set them on a single line; you don't have to keep typing `double y`, `double z`, and so on.

Add comment 11 at the end of this line as follows:

```
//11. Declares and sets values of the same data type
```

# Using the product method to multiply variables

In the next stage, we'll make use of the `Product` method. So, enter the following line:

```
Label1.Text = $"{x}*{y}={Product(x, y)}";
```

Here, you begin by typing `Label1.Text =`, followed by a `$` symbol for string interpolation, double quotes to make a string, and then you say, for example, `{x}*{y}`. Remember, if it's black, it's replaced with the value of x at runtime; if it's brown (or orange on macOS), it goes to the screen exactly as it is written. Then, within curly braces, you enter the name of the method and then pass in the values `(x, y)`, and close with a semicolon. Now, enter comment 12 at the end of the line as follows:

```
//12. Calls Product with x and y as the arguments
```

In this case, we're operating on two values. Let's observe this in action in Google Chrome. Click on `Show Product`, and you'll get `5*10=50`:

Figure 5.6.2: A simple example of the Product method at work

Now, we want to be able to multiply, for example, 10 values, or however many you want. To make it simple, we'll work with three values for now. So, we will say the following:

```
Label1.Text += $"<br>{x}*{y}*{z}={Product(x, y, z)}";
```

Again, we begin by typing `Label1.Text` (don't forget to put a `<br>` tag so that it goes down to the next line on a web page), but this time use `+=` to append, the `$` symbol for string interpolation, and double quotes to make a string. Then we say {x}*{y}*{z}=, and then, within curly braces, we place a call to Product as {Product(x, y, z)}. Follow this line with comment 13:

```
//13. Calls Product with x, y and z as arguments
```

Now the `Products(x, y, z)` function accepts three values passed in. Nonetheless, the result is that it works. Again, remember, if it's brown (or orange on macOS), this simply means that it will appear on the page exactly as written in the code. Let's observe this in Google Chrome, as shown in the following screenshot:

Figure 5.6.3: The result of using the Product method with three variables

This is how you create a more flexible and powerful method. Label1.Text can be used, for example, with a method called split that operates on strings, and so on, in real life. It's very useful.

For review, a complete version of the Default.aspx.cs file for this chapter is displayed in the following code block:

```
//1. using is a keyword, it's blue
//2. System is a name space that stores already created code
//3. using System brings in existing code
using System;
//4. class is a required container for creating our own code samples
public partial class _Default : System.Web.UI.Page
{
    //5. params keyword allows us to pass a variable number of values
    //into a method
    //6. Product(1,2) or Product(1,2,4) or Product(-3,4,3,6)
    private static double Product(params double[] arr)
    {
        double product = 1; //1*2*4=8, 1*5*4*3=60, begin with 1 as the
        //initial value of product
        foreach (double d in arr) //8. Grab each value inside the array
            product *= d; //9. This line makes the product grow until
            // the loop ends
        return product; //10. Sends the product back to the calling
        //code

    }
    protected void Button1_Click(object sender, EventArgs e)
    {
        double x = 5, y = 10, z = 15;//11. Declares and sets values of
        //the same data type
        Label1.Text = $"<br>{x}*{y}={Product(x,y)}";//12. Calls product
        //with x and y as the arguments
        Label1.Text += $"<br>{x}*{y}={Product(x, y, z)}";//13. Calls
        //Product with x, y and z as arguments
    }
}
```

# Summary

In this chapter, you learned how to use the `params` keyword to create more powerful and flexible methods. You created a `Product` method and used it to multiply variable values.

In the next chapter, you will learn how to create more powerful methods using the `out` keyword.

# 29

# Creating More Flexible Functions with the out Keyword

In this chapter, you'll learn how to create more powerful methods using the `out` keyword. And by powerful, I mean methods that are essentially more useful because they not only can return a value but can also set other values that can become available in your code.

## Setting up the beginning interface

Let's again begin with a simple interface. Drag a **Button** control into the form, and change the text on the `Button` markup to say `Summarize`. Also, add a `Label` control below this line, and remove the `text` attribute. Your `Default.aspx` file should appear as shown in the following code block:

```
Default.aspx.cs*        Default.aspx ☐ ✕
     1  <%@ Page Language="C#" AutoEventWireup="true" CodeFile="Default.aspx.cs" Inherits="_Default" %>
     2
     3  <!DOCTYPE html>
     4
     5  <html xmlns="http://www.w3.org/1999/xhtml">
     6  <head runat="server">
     7      <title></title>
     8  </head>
     9  <body>
    10      <form id="form1" runat="server">
    11          <asp:Button ID="Button1" runat="server" Text="Summarize"/><br />
    12          <asp:Label ID="Label1" runat="server" ></asp:Label>
    13      </form>
    14  </body>
    15  </html>
    16
```

Figure 5.7.1: Our simple starting interface

If you switch to the **Design** view, you have a `Button` control that says `Summarize` and a `Label` right under the `Button` control, as seen in the following screenshot:

Figure 5.7.2: The starting interface in the Design view

# Introducing language-integrated queries

Now, double-click on the `Summarize` button, which brings up the Event Handler. To make working with arrays a little more efficient than before, in fact, a lot more efficient, I've added a new element; so, make sure that you add the following lines at the very top:

```
using System;
using System.Linq;
```

This language-integrated query has a collection of extremely powerful methods, for example, to make working with things such as arrays and collections of various kinds much more efficient.

# Using the out parameter

Right above the start of the Event Handler, we'll create a method called `Summarize`. For this, type the following:

```
private static double Summarize(double[] values, out double average)
```

Here, `double` will take an array called `values`. This line is followed by a pair of open and close curly braces, between which you will eventually enter code.

First, let's add comments 6 and 7 as follows:

```
//6. out keyword indicates that average value will be set inside Summarize
//7. average is also available in other methods
```

As we mentioned in comment 7, because `average` is an `out` kind of parameter, it's also available in other methods. Keep that in mind.

Our method also returns a value using the `return` keyword. That's what I meant by creating more powerful methods. One value is returned as usual using the `return` keyword; but other values, such as `average`, are also still available after they are set inside `Summarize`. So, this method does two very useful things.

Also take note of what we express here in comment 8:

```
//8. keep in mind this method also still returns a value of type double to
the calling code
```

In this comment, we are referring to the following `double` data type (highlighted). You see that?

```
private static double Summarize(double[] values, out double average)
```

# Working with the average extension method

Now let's create the code. Enter the following:

```
average = values.Average();
```

Here, `Average` is a method, and as you should be able to see in `using System.Linq;`, `Linq` is no longer faded. This means that `Average` has been called, and that confirms that `Average` is stored within `Linq`. Hover your mouse over `Average();`. Even though the tooltip says a lot of different things, as illustrated in *Figure 5.7.3*, what matters is `double` at the start of the first line, and `average`, which is also of type `double`, correct? So, the two data types are matched as always. This is obviously a big theme in C#: match your data types, or you might get errors of some kind.

```
(extension) double System.Collections.Generic.IEnumerable<double>.Average() (+ 10 overloads)
Computes the average of a sequence of double values.

Exceptions:
  ArgumentNullException
  InvalidOperationException
```

Figure 5.7.3: Tooltip for Average(); in the preceding line of code

Now let's add comment 9 at the end of this line as follows:

```
//9. Uses Average extension method to find average of values inside array
```

For our purposes, the `Average` extension method is a very useful thing, and that's what matters. The `Average` extension method is used to set the value of the `average out` parameter. Let's add comment 10 right below this:

```
//10. This average found is used to set the value of average out parameter
```

Let's also now type the following line:

```
return values.Sum();
```

This line, of course, simply sends the `Sum` value back to the calling code. Let's enter this as comment 11 at the end of this line:

```
//11. This line sends the sum back to the calling code
```

Hover your mouse over `Sum`, and it tells you that after it operates, it produces a `double` data type. That is why you see that in the line repeated following this screenshot, we have a `double` data type—the two data types are matched:

Figure 5.7.4: Tooltip for Sum() in the preceding line of code

```
private static double Summarize(double[] values, out double average)
```

# Working with the var keyword

For the next stage, enter the following line of code:

```
var vals = new double[] { 4, 5, 6, 8, 8, 9, 10, -40 };
```

The `var` keyword is an implicit data typing, and that's fine. After `vals =`, you will create an array on the right-hand side. We name it `new double` and then make a list of values within curly braces and the initializer. So, for example, we type `{ 4, 5, 6, 8, 8, 9, 10, -40 }`. You can put in any values (it doesn't matter what they are), and close with a semicolon.

Now let's add comment 12 at the end of this line as follows:

```
//12. Creates an array to operate on
```

In real life, this might be read, for example, from a database of all kinds of things—a table, or a page, and so on. Note that in the preceding code line, I used the `new` keyword, and then `double`, which is the data type. Then I inserted square brackets and made the list of the actual values stored inside the array—this is the initializer.

On the left-hand side, we use the `var` keyword, and this is useful when you don't want to figure out what the data type is. You can type `var` and C# will decide what `var` represents based on what it finds on the right-hand side. So remember, C# is strongly typed.

If you hover your mouse over `var` it says `double[]`. So, `var` recognizes the fact that this is an array of `double` values.

# Outputting the results of the Summarize method

In the next stage, we'll make use of our `Summarize` method. So, type the following:

```
Label1.Text = $"Sum of values={Summarize(vals)}";
```

Here, within the curly braces, we place a call to `Summarize` and type `(vals)`, which is of course the array you're passing in, and then type `out`.

Now we need one more thing. Right now, if you leave this line ending with just `(vals)`, you will get an error. When you hover your mouse over `Summarize`, the tooltip popup says, *There's no argument given that corresponds to the required formal parameter 'average' of '_Default.Summarize(double[],out double)'*. In other words, you're missing this bit (out `double average`): the `average` value, the `out` parameter that is needed. To make this work, you've got to make a new variable. So, enter the following line above the `Label1.Text` line. That's it. You don't even have to set its value:

```
double average;
```

Let's first add comment 13 after this line as follows:

```
//13. This will be used to call Summarize. Its value does not have to bet
set here.
```

Now go back, and after `vals`, type out average, as shown here:

```
Label1.Text = $"Sum of values={Summarize(vals, out average)}";
```

Also, you want to display the average, so how can you do that? Well, remember the benefit of the method is that after it runs, it not only returns the sum of the values but it also makes the value of average available. For this, type the following:

```
Label1.Text = $"Average of values is ={average}";
```

We couldn't do this before; this is obviously a more powerful way of writing code.

Enter comment 14 above the first Label1.Text line as follows:

```
//14. Line below calls Summarize with value array and sets the average
value
```

The second Label1.Text line actually displays average; so, let's add comment 15 at the end of that line:

```
//15. Line displays average
```

# Running and modifying your program

Now crank up Google Chrome, and let's observe the result, as shown in *Figure 5.7.5*. Keep in mind that until now, you've had no way of doing this; that is, producing this type of behavior. You would have had to, for example, create two methods.

Figure 5.7.5: New behavior achievable with the out keyword

Now add a `<br>` tag before `Average` to push down a line, change = to += to append, and then relaunch this in the browser. Click on `Summarize` again, and it shows the results, as shown in the following screenshot. The results displayed are correct:

Figure 5.7.6: The preceding result is modified by adding <br> and changing = to +=

Remember, as you begin to create your code, you want to use small values that you can check easily, right? You should be able to enter these values into a calculator, find the average, and make sure that it's OK. So, for example, sum the values and make sure that whatever your code is producing also corresponds to the simple, calculator-based results.

For review, a complete version of the `Default.aspx.cs` file for this chapter is displayed in the following code block:

```
//1. using is a keyword, it's blue
//2. System is a name space that stores already created code
//3. using System brings in existing code
using System;
using System;
using System.Linq;
//4. class is a required container for creating our own code samples
public partial class _Default : System.Web.UI.Page
{
    //6. out keyword indicates that average value will be set inside
    //Summarize
    //7. average is also available in other methods
    //8. keep in mind this method also still returns a value of type
    //double to the calling code
    private static double Summarize(double[] values, out double
    average)
    {
        average = values.Average();//9. Uses Average extension method
        //to find average of values inside array
        //10. This average found is used to set the value of average
        //out parameter
```

```
        return values.Sum();
        //11. This line sends the sum back to the calling code
    }

    protected void Button1_Click(object sender, EventArgs e)
    {
        var vals = new double[] { 4, 5, 6, 8, 8, 9, 10, -40 };//12.
        Creates an array to operate on
        double average; //13. This will be used to call Summarize. It's
        value does not have to br set here.
        //14. Line below calls Summarize with value array and sets the
        average value
        Label1.Text = $"Sum of values={Summarize(vals, out average)}";
        //15. Line displays average
        Label1.Text += $"<br>Average of values is={average}";
    }
}
```

# Summary

In this chapter, you learned how to create more powerful methods by using the out keyword. You were introduced to language-integrated queries. You began working with the out parameter, learned about the Average Extension method, and used the var keyword in a program.

In the next chapter, you will learn how to use the out and ref keywords.

# 30
# Combining the ref and out Keywords to Write Flexible Functions

In this chapter, you'll learn how to use the `out` and `ref` keywords.

## Setting up the starting interface

Let's begin with `Default.aspx` and drag a **Button** control into the page. Change the `Text` parameter on the button to say `Show Summary`. Then, under the `Button` tag, place a `Label` control. Your screen should now look like the following screenshot:

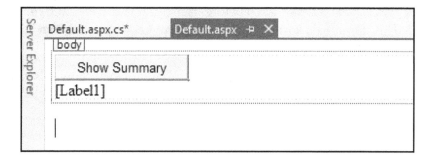

Figure 5.8.1: The initial interface for this chapter

We've done this before, right? There's nothing new. The basic markup is shown in the following screenshot:

```
Default.aspx.cs*          Default.aspx  ⊕ ✕
  1  <%@ Page Language="C#" AutoEventWireup="true" CodeFile="Default.aspx.cs" Inherits="_Default" %>
  2
  3  <!DOCTYPE html>
  4
  5  <html xmlns="http://www.w3.org/1999/xhtml">
  6  <head runat="server">
  7      <title></title>
  8  </head>
  9  <body>
 10      <form id="form1" runat="server">
 11          <asp:Button ID="Button1" runat="server" Text="Show Summary" OnClick="Button1_Click"/><br />
 12          <asp:Label ID="Label1" runat="server" ></asp:Label>
 13      </form>
 14  </body>
 15  </html>
 16
```

Figure 5.8.2: The basic markup for this chapter

# Creating the GetValueAndInterest method

Let's go over to the **Design** view and then double-click on the **Button** control. This, of course, brings up the event handler. First, we'll create a method above it called `GetValueAndInterest`. For this, enter the following:

```
private static void GetValueAndInterest(out decimal interest, ref decimal
value)
```

You've seen `private`, `static`, and `void` before. Here, `GetValueAndInterest` is the name of our method. This is followed by `out decimal`, then `interest`, and then `ref decimal value`. Follow this with open and close curly braces.

Before we go further, let's add a couple of comments to understand how this is helpful. So, start by entering comment 5 as follows:

```
//5. interest is the result of a calculation done inside the method, so
it's an out parameter
```

We don't have to set `interest` where the method is called; you can set the value inside `GetValueAndInterest`. You don't have to initialize it when you call the method; you do it within the method.

Now enter comment 6 as follows directly beneath it:

```
//6. value is needed to calculate the interest, but it's set in
Button1_Click
```

# The ref and out keywords

In the preceding line of code, `value` is different because it is `ref`; so it's modified with the `ref` keyword. This means that its value has to be set basically before the method is called, and when it's passed into the method, it's changed, and then it becomes available again where it's called. So keep that in mind.

The `out` keyword is a little different. This does not have to be set where the method is called; it's set inside the method, and then that new value becomes available throughout our code—a different behavior to some extent.

# Calculating principle and interest

Now, enter the following code and comment 7 between the curly braces:

```
interest = 0.05M * value; //7. Finds interest and saves it to the interest
out value
```

Next, enter this line and comment 8 beneath it:

```
value = value + interest; //8. Line updates how much money there with the
new interested added to it
```

This line now simply updates the principle or the value. So, we updated the `interest` variable and then we updated `value`. Now these values become available down in `Button1_Click`; so, let's check that out.

Now, within the curly braces of the Event Handler, enter the following:

```
decimal principle = 4500;
```

The `decimal principle` variable is the amount invested, and let's say it's $4,500. In real life, of course, this might come from a database; we might read it, for example, from a web page or some kind of text box, but this is sufficient for our purposes to save some time.

Now let's add comment 9 directly above this line:

```
//9. This is the money on which we want to find the interest
```

At the next stage, you'll call the methods, but even before you do that, add the following line under `decimal principle`:

```
decimal interest;
```

This is our `out` parameter, our `out` value; so add comment 11 at the end of this line. (We'll come back and add comment 10 later.)

```
//11. This is our out value. It does not have to be set here.
```

Notice that the value is set inside the `GetValueAndInterest` method because that's where the interest is calculated; it doesn't have to be set here.

In the next stage, we'll enter the following:

```
GetValueAndInterest(out interest, ref principle);
```

In the preceding line, we started with `GetValueAndInterest` and then passed in the quantities of interest. So, we typed `out interest` and then `ref principle`. Notice that `principle` is going in with the `ref` keyword, and it has to be modified in the sense that its value is set.

After that, `ref` and pretty much behave in the same way; with this level of explanation, it's sufficient.

Now let's go back and add comment 10 at the end of the `decimal principle` line:

```
//10. This goes in with ref keyword, so it's value has to be set here
```

# Outputting the results

You pass interest and principle basically, one by `out` and one by `ref` into `GetValueAndInterest`. Their values are set, and now they become available to you in `Button1_Click`; so you can display them. Next, enter the following line:

```
Label1.Text = $"Final Amount is {principle}";
```

Remember, the final amount is the `principle` variable, so we entered `principle` here.

Now why does this work? Why can I type `principle`? The reason is that when I typed `ref principle`, that went into the method (`value = value + interest;`). It got updated, and then the change that is made in the method becomes visible down below in `{principle}`. See that? So, `principle` actually represents the new updated value, not the old one. That's why we call this `Final Amount`.

Let's add comment 12 at the end of this line as follows:

```
//12. Prints updated value
```

Obviously, these things are somewhat subtle, and you have to practice them a little more to understand them thoroughly. But first, you've got to begin by becoming aware of their existence. Next, enter the following line:

```
Label1.Text += $"<br>Interest is {interest}";
```

Here, we start with `Label1.Text` and then say `+=` to append. We follow this with a `$` symbol for string interpolation and double quotes to make a string. Next, we insert a `<br>` tag to push down to the next line, and then say `Interest is` and put in the interest. To format this output as currency, we need to insert `:C` for both the principle and interest lines, as shown as follows; also, add comment 13:

```
Label1.Text = $"Final Amount is {principle:C}"; //12. Prints updated value
Label1.Text += $"<br>Interest is {interest:C}"; //13. Prints interest to
screen
```

# Running your program

Let's observe all of this in action. So, head to Google Chrome. When you click on `Show Summary`, it says `Final Amount is $4,725.00` and `Interest is $225.00`, as shown in the following screenshot:

Figure 5.8.3: The output of combining the ref and out keywords

So these are some of the basics of using the ref and out keywords. Remember, in some sense they are the same, but in an important sense, they are not the same. With out, the value doesn't have to be set, as in decimal interest;. With ref, essentially the value does have to be set, as in decimal principle = 4500. In either case, what is essentially true is that whether you use out or ref, in the Label1.Text lines, the principle is now the updated value and interest is also the result of using our method above. You see? So, whatever changes are made, for our purposes, they are essentially made within the body of the method. Those changes are likewise communicated down to the Label1.Text lines. So, keep that in mind. The ref keyword is very useful when making C# programs that work with Microsoft Office programs.

For review, a complete version of the Default.aspx.cs file for this chapter is displayed in following code block:

```
//1. using is a keyword, it's blue
//2. System is a name space that stores already created code
//3. using System brings in existing code
using System;
using System;
using System.Linq;
//4. class is a required container for creating our own code samples
public partial class _Default : System.Web.UI.Page
{

    //5. interest is the result of a calculator of a calculation done
    //inside the method, so it's an out parameter
    //6. value is needed to calculate the interest , but it's set in
    //Button1_Click
    private static void GetValueAndInterest(out decimal interest, ref
decimal value)
    {
        interest = 0.05M * value; //7. Finds interest and saves it to
        //the interest out value
        value = value + interest; //8. Line updates how much money
        //there with the new interested added to it
    }

    protected void Button1_Click(object sender, EventArgs e)
    {
        //9. This is the money on which we want to find the interest
        decimal principle = 4500;
        decimal interest;//10. This is our out value. It does not have
        //to be set here.
        GetValueAndInterest(out interest, ref principle);
        Label1.Text = $"Final Amount is {principle}";//12. Prints
        //updated value
```

```
        Label1.Text += $"<br>Interest is {interest:C}"; //13. Prints
        //interest to screen
    }
}
```

# Summary

In this chapter, you learned how to use the `out` and `ref` keywords. You created a method called `GetValueAndInterest`, learned about the differences between the `ref` and `out` keywords, and learned how to calculate principle and interest.

In the next chapter, we'll talk about the `out` keyword in c# 7.0.

# 31

# The out Keyword in C# 7

In this chapter, we're going to learn how to use the `out` keyword in C# 7.0.

## Creating the program template

To begin, make a new project in Visual Studio. We'll keep it super simple. Go to **File > New > Project.**; *Ctrl + Shift + N* is the key combination, of course. This will bring up the **New Project** window:

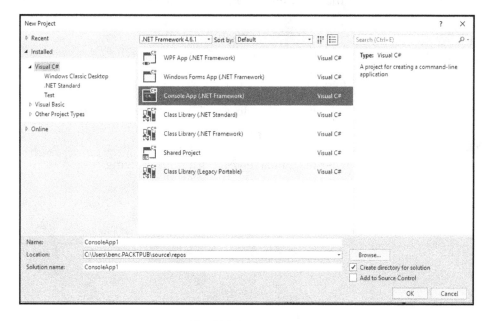

Figure 3.1: Setting up a new project

From this list, make sure you have **Visual C#** selected as a template, then select **Console App**. We'll just use a simple console app here for speed. You can leave the other settings as they are and click on **OK**. This generates a basic template:

```
using System;
using System.Collections.Generic;
using System.Linq;
using System.Text;
using System.Threading.Tasks;

namespace ConsoleApp1
{
    class Program
    {
        static void Main(string[] args)
        {
        }
    }
}
```

The thing I like about this version of Visual Studio is that it is very fast. In the previous version, this process would sometimes take what seemed like a minute. The first thing that we're going to do is simplify this to just what we need. So, first of all, we can cut most of the lines from the `using` block at the top. Remove all but the first line to leave this:

```
using System;
```

Then, let's amend this line to read the following:

```
using static System.Console;
```

We're going to use `WriteLine` later in our code, and it's stored within the `Console` class. Next, remove the `namespace` line; it's too complicated for our simple example. Also, remove the associated opening and closing curly braces. Finally, get rid of `string[] args` as we don't need this either. This should leave you with the following:

```
using static System.Console;
class Program
{
    static void Main()
    {
    }
}
```

The default template that Microsoft provides is simple, but it's also made to cover a lot of options that we don't need here. So, it's good practice to simplify the code to its most basic structure. Once that's done, highlight it and press *Shift + Tab* on your keyboard; this formats it nicely for you.

 Remember, the `class Program` line here is needed as the basic scaffolding for our code. Also, `static void Main()` is the entry point to the program. That's how the operating system hooks it and loads it into memory.

# Writing the Summarize function

The first thing that we're going to do is create a function or method that will allow us to summarize an array. Create a new line under the `class Program` opening curly brace and type the following:

```
static void Summarize(double[] values, out double sum, out double average)
{

}
```

So, our function will accept an array of doubles, which we'll call `values`. We then have a couple of variables for `sum` and `average`. Note that both of these use the `out` keyword.

Next, within the curly braces of our `Summarize` function, type the following:

```
sum = average = 0;
```

This will simply set our two values to 0. Next, we are going to form the sum. For this, type the following:

```
foreach(var d in values)
```

So here we are telling the program to go in and grab each value in the `values` array using `foreach`, then we are going to perform an action on that value. In this case, we're going to add it to the `sum` variable so that the `sum` variable functions like an accumulator. That's why it's important to have it set in a way it is equal to 0 initially, not some other value. If you have it set to a different value, you will not have the correct sum. Okay, so underneath the preceding line, type the following:

```
sum += d;
```

Remember that += is needed so that the values are accumulated and the value of the sum variable increases with each addition. Of course, that's if all the values are positive; if some of them are negative, then the value would decrease. So the Sum += d line grows the value of the sum variable as the foreach loop operates.

Once you have the value of the sum variable, which is all the entries added together, you can find the average. Let's go ahead and do that here. On the next line, type the following:

```
average = sum / values.Length;
```

The basic definition of an average is to add up the values and then divide them by the number of values that you have. This is exactly the same logic; it's just expressed in C#. You can get the number of values in the array by simply accessing its Length property, which in our case is values.Length.

This is how our function will be complete.

# Implementing the function

To make use of our new Summarize function, we're going to add some code between the Main() curly braces. Type the following:

```
double[] arr = { 1, 5, 3, -6, 3, 6 };
```

Here, we're just creating a simple array and initializing it with a set of values. It doesn't really matter what they are, and I've included a negative value here for fun. Terminate this with a semicolon. Now that we have our test array, we can go ahead and run our Summarize function on it. On the next line, type the following:

```
Summarize(arr, out double sum, out double average);
```

We're passing in our new arr array that we've already set to the correct double type, and we're also declaring our two out variables.

 Notice that in previous versions of C#, these variables would have to be declared outside of this function call, above it. In this case, because we're using the latest version of C#, you don't have to do this anymore. So it's simpler.

Remember that the big thing about these `out` keywords is that when their values, in our case `sum` and `average`, are set inside our `Summarize` method, those values are also reachable inside other methods, such as `Main`.

On the next line underneath our `Summarize` call, write the following:

```
WriteLine($"Sum={sum} \n Average={average}");
```

We can just type `WriteLine` here because we have already included `static` `System.Console` in the `using` block. Here we have `$` that indicates string interpolation. This is really important, so make sure you have `$` and that the `{sum}` and `{average}` parts are black and not maroon in color. Maroon means print to the screen exactly as it appears. Black means replace with specific numerical values.

# Running the program

That's about it! Let's go ahead and run our program. Go to **Debug > Start Without Debugging** or do *Ctrl + F5*. Give it a second to build and then you should get your results:

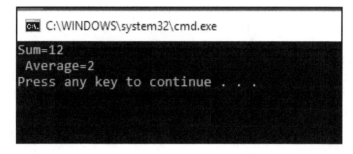

Figure 3.2: The debug Window

It says the sum is 12 and the average is 2. These are simple values, so you can just check them on a calculator. Go ahead and check them. Add them up and make sure that the sum is 12. Then, you can average them out. We have six values in our array, so 12 divided by 6 is 2. This is the average.

Here's the full program code for this chapter for your reference:

```
using static System.Console; //needed for getting WriteLine into our code

class Program
{
    static void Summarize(double[] values, out double sum, out double
```

```
average)
{
    //out keyword means that when the values of sum and average are
    //set inside Summarize
    // those values are reachable inside other methods like Main
    sum = average = 0; //zero out the values of sum and average
    foreach (var d in values) //grab each value in the values array
        sum += d; //this line grows the value of the sum variable
        //as the foreach loop operates

    average = sum / values.Length; //add up values, and then divide
    //by the number of values
}
static void Main()
{
    double[] arr = { 1, 5, 3, -6, 3, 6 }; //array to summarize
    Summarize(arr, out double sum, out double average); // call
    //Summarize method
    WriteLine($"Sum={sum} \n Average={average}");
}
}
```

# Summary

When you design this kind of a program, first you try to keep your sample array small and make sure that you double-check your math on a calculator. That's a good indicator that the code is sound. This is it for this simple example of using the out keyword in C# 7. In the next chapter, we'll dive deeper into arrays in C# with a look at multidimensional arrays and how to use them.

# 32
# Multidimensional Arrays

In this chapter, we'll talk about two-dimensional arrays.

## Understanding two-dimensional arrays

A two-dimensional array is a familiar term; it's something like an Excel table, like the one shown in *Figure 5.9.1*. In Excel, for example, the address of the top-left cell is A1. The address of the cell immediately to its right is B1. Then the address of the cell immediately below A1 would be A2, and that of the cell to its right would be B2:

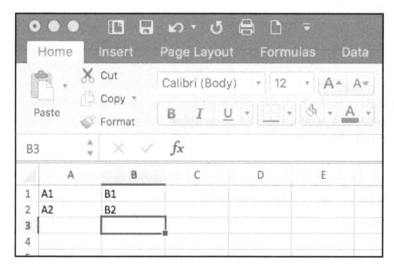

Figure 5.9.1: An Excel table is a two-dimensional array

In C#, as with other programming languages, things are a little different. The top-left cell has the address 0,0 and the address of the cell immediately to its right is 0,1. The first number in 0,0 represents the row number; actually, the row index. So, row 1 means 0 index. The second number in 0,0 represents the column. In other words, the first column has an index of 0. If you move over to the right, the 0 in 0,1 still represents the first row, which has an index of 0, not 1. And then the 1 in 0,1 represents the second column, which in Excel is called **B**. Then, where it says A2 in Excel, that is, row 2, column 1, that will be 1,0, and then the cell immediately to its right will be 1,1, as shown in the following screenshot:

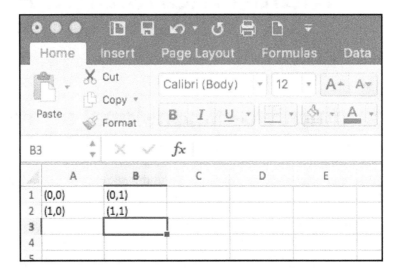

Figure 5.9.2: The addresses of cells in a C# two-dimensional array

So keep in mind that, as with regular arrays, there's an offset of 1. In other words, you don't begin with an index of 1, you always begin with an index of 0 in C#. These are the addresses of the cells. Now, let's express this in C#.

# Setting up the initial interface

In the **Source** view, all I need to keep things as efficient as possible is a Button control and a Label control, as shown in the following screenshot:

```
 1 <%@ Page Language="C#" AutoEventWireup="true" CodeFile="Default.aspx.cs" Inherits="_Default" %>
 2
 3 <!DOCTYPE html>
 4
 5 <html xmlns="http://www.w3.org/1999/xhtml">
 6 <head runat="server">
 7     <title></title>
 8 </head>
 9 <body>
10     <form id="form1" runat="server">
11         <asp:Button ID="Button1" runat="server" Text="Show Calculations" OnClick="Button1_Click" /><br />
12         <asp:Label ID="sampLabel" runat="server"></asp:Label>
13     </form>
14 </body>
15 </html>
16
17
```

Figure 5.9.3: The initial Default.apsx page for this chapter

In the **Design** view, it looks as shown in the following screenshot. It has a `Button` control with a `Label` control under it:

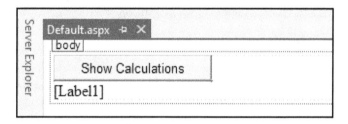

Figure 5.9.4: Our starting program in the Design view

Now, double-click on `Show Calculations`, and that brings up the Event Handler. When you do this, remember that `OnClick="Button1_Click"` in the `Button` tag in `Default.apsx` is the connection between the markup and the C#.

# Coding a two-dimensional array

Now, type the following code between the curly braces in the Event Handler:

```
double [,] arr = new double[2, 2];
```

Here, we say `double`, which is a data type, and then use brackets and separate them with a comma. Then, we type `arr =` and, for example, `new double`. To specify its size, we enter, for example, `[2, 2]` and close with a semicolon.

So, this is just like a table in Excel that has two rows and two columns. In that sense, it's nothing new. So, we'll follow this line with comment 5:

```
//5. Declares and sets 2 by 2 array, 2*2=4, so array has 4 cells
```

Here, there are four cells to be filled. Let's fill the cells next. We will say the following to do this:

```
arr[0, 0] = 45; arr[0, 1];
```

Here, `arr` is the name of the array, and then we specify the index. For the first cell, remember, (0, 0) means the first row and the first column in C#: index 0 for the row index and 0 for the column. Let's set a value, for example, 45. This doesn't really matter that much, obviously.

Now, because this gets a little more complex—even the way you write the code makes a difference—it's helpful if you place the adjacent cell on the same row within your code. So, we type `arr` and then, in brackets, row 0, and column 1, closing with a semicolon. Let's enter this as comment 6 at the end of this line as follows:

```
//6. Filling the first row, which has an index of 0, column indexes go from
0 to 1
```

Notice that if you leave `arr[0, 1]` unassigned, you get an error, as shown in the following screenshot. Specifically, it says, **Only assignment, call, increment, decrement, and new object expressions can be used as a statement**. So, now you have a clearer definition of what a statement is, correctly formatted in C#:

```
 struct System.Int32
Represents a 32-bit signed integer.To browse the .NET Framework source code for this type, see the Reference Source.

Only assignment, call, increment, decrement, and new object expressions can be used as a statement
```

Figure 5.9.5: Error message generated if you leave arr[0, 1] unassigned

Let's assign a value to `arr[0, 1]`, for example, 34:

```
arr[0, 0] = 45; arr[0, 1]=34;
```

To move to the next row, we'll say the following:

```
arr[1, 0] = 23;arr[1, 1] = 78;
```

Here, we start by saying `arr` and then in brackets, the row index 1; remember, this really means the second row. Then we type a comma and put, for example, column index 0, which really means the first column. We set some value there, such as 23 (it doesn't really matter), and end with a semicolon. Now to fill the last cell, we type `arr`, and then a row with index 1, which really means the second row, and a column with index 1, which really means the second column. Then, we fill that with some value, for example, 78.

Now, let's add comment 7 at the end of this line as follows:

```
//7. Filling second row, which has index 1, column indexes go from 0 to 1
```

Remember that in the code, when you look down at the addresses, the row indexes change; when you look across, the column indexes change. It is really just like a table in Excel. This is how you can relate it to, something immediately familiar, hopefully.

So what can you do with these? Well, a common thing might be, for example, to add up the values; so, type the following:

```
double sum = 0;
```

You begin with a sum value of 0 and add something else. Add comment 8 at the end of the preceding line:

```
//8. Begin with a value of 0 so the sum is not changed
```

Then, use a `foreach` loop. This is really nice, even though it seems so complicated; if you want to add up the values, you can use a single `foreach` loop. So, enter the following, including comments 9 and 10:

```
foreach (double d in arr) //9. This means grab each entry one at a time
sum += d; //10. Add the entries together
```

Basically, these two lines mean grab each entry and add them all together.

# Printing out your results

At the end, you can print the results. For this, we can enter something like the following:

```
sampLabel.Text = $"Sum is {sum}";
```

Here, we just print the `sum` variable. So, within the curly braces, we place the `sum` variable. Follow this line with comment 11:

```
//11. Prints sum to web page
```

The preceding code line, of course, simply prints the `sum` value to a web page. Remember, this means, the sum of all the entries; a single loop handles all of them as well. It's a really nice feature. You might have learned previously about *nesting loops*. Well, believe it or not, you can do it this way, too.

# Running the program

Let's now open Google Chrome and click on `Show Calculations`; it says `The Sum is 180`, as shown in the following screenshot:

Figure 5.9.6: The sum result of our multidimensional array program

Well, when you work with small values, of course, you should be able to confirm that they are correct. So, if you take 45 and you add 23 and 34 and 78 from the lines that begin with `arr` in your program, you will see that the sum is 180.

# What else can you do?

We can find the format of one of the things there. For this, we can enter the following:

```
sampLabel.Text += $"<br>The value at index (0,1) formatted as currency is
{arr[0, 1]:C}";
```

Here, we start with `sampLabel.Text` and then use `+=` to append. Then, we put in a `<br>` tag to move down to the next line, a `$` symbol for string interpolation, double quotes to make a `string` data type, and say, for example, `The value at index (0,1) formatted as currency is`. As we are looking at `index (0,1)`, we type `{arr[0, 1]:C}`.

Now, let's add comment 12 above this line as follows:

```
//12. Line below prints entry at index 0,1 formatted as currency
```

Let's take a look at this in Google Chrome, and click on `Show Calculations`. As you can see in the following screenshot, `$34.00` is formatted as currency:

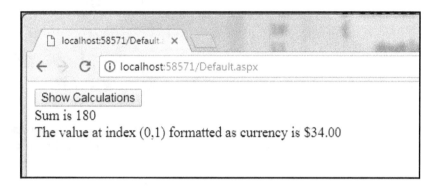

Figure 5.9.7: $34.00 is formatted as currency

Basically, what you could do previously with simple numerical values and variables, you can also do now. Of course, if you want, you can combine individual entries using various kinds of math—you can add, subtract, multiply, and divide them as usual.

For review, a complete version of the `Default.aspx.cs` file for this chapter is displayed in the following code block:

```
//1. using is a keyword, it's blue
//2. System is a name space that stores already created code
//3. using System brings in existing code
using System;
//4. class is a required container for creating our own code samples
public partial class _Default : System.Web.UI.Page
{

    protected void Button1_Click(object sender, EventArgs e)
    {
        double[,] arr = new double[2, 2];//5. Declares and sets 2 by 2
```

```
        //array, 2*2=4, so array has 4 cells
        arr[0, 0] = 45; arr[0, 1] = 34; //6. Filling the first row,
        //which has an index of 0, column indexes go from 0 to 1
        arr[1, 0] = 23; arr[1, 1] = 78;//7. Filling second row, which
        //has index 1, column indexes go from 0 to 1
        double sum = 0;//8. Begin with a value of 0 so the sum is not
        //changed

        foreach (double d in arr) //9. This means grab each entry one
        //at a time
            sum += d; //10. Add the entries together

        sampLabel.Text = $"Sum is {sum}";//11. Prints sum to web page
        sampLabel.Text += $"<br>The value at index (0,1) formatted as
        currency is {arr[0, 1]:C}";
    }
}
```

# Summary

In this chapter, we talked about two-dimensional arrays and how they are similar and different in an Excel spreadsheet and in C#. You learned how to code and modify them, and you printed out your results.

In the next chapter, you will learn about the dynamic and var keywords.

# 33
# Writing Easier Code with the Var and Dynamic Keywords

In this chapter, you'll learn about the `dynamic` and `var` keywords.

## Setting up the project

Let's bring up a project. We'll start by getting rid of the `<div>` tags in `Default.aspx`. Then we'll insert two text boxes; for this, go to **Toolbox** and type `tex` in the **Search ToolBox** field. Drag and drop the first `TextBox` control into the form. End the line with a `<br>` tag to break that to the next line. Now, copy the `TextBox` control line and paste a copy of it right beneath it. So, there are two text boxes now, right? Remember that the `ID` attributes are automatically changed from `TextBox1` to `TextBox2` when you copy and paste.

Go back to **Toolbox**, type but in the **Search ToolBox** field, and then drag and drop a
Button control below the second text box. Change the text on the Button control to say
Increase, and end the line with a `<br>` tag . Finally, once more in the **Search Toolbox** field,
type Lab and drag and drop a Label control below the Button control line, as shown in the
following screenshot:

```
Default.aspx ⊕ × Default.aspx.cs
  1  <%@ Page Language="C#" AutoEventWireup="true" CodeFile="Default.aspx.cs" Inherits="_Default" %>
  2
  3  <!DOCTYPE html>
  4
  5  <html xmlns="http://www.w3.org/1999/xhtml">
  6  <head runat="server">
  7      <title></title>
  8  </head>
  9  <body>
 10      <form id="form1" runat="server">
 11          <asp:TextBox ID="TextBox1" runat="server"></asp:TextBox><br />
 12          <asp:TextBox ID="TextBox2" runat="server"></asp:TextBox><br />
 13          <asp:Button ID="Button1" runat="server" Text="Increase" /><br />
 14          <asp:Label ID="Label1" runat="server" Text=""></asp:Label>
 15
 16      </form>
 17  </body>
 18  </html>
 19
```

Figure 5.10.1: The Default.aspx file for this project

Now take a look at the results. When you go to the **Design** view, it should look as shown in
the following screenshot:

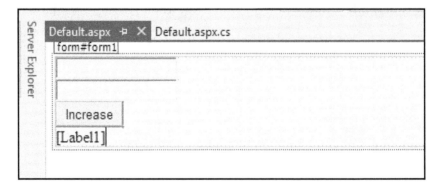

Figure 5.10.2: The basic interface in the Design view

# Working with the dynamic keyword

Now, let's double-click on the `Button` control. In `Default.aspx.cs`, get rid of the `Page_Load` Event Handler and then enter the following:

```
private static dynamic Increase(dynamic x)
```

Here, `private` means it is accessible only here, `static` allows us to call the function directly through the name, and `Increase` is the name of the function.

After this, enter the following between curly braces:

```
return x * 1.1;
```

Here, we will be restricting our attention to numerical values; however, `dynamic` is powerful: it can accommodate pretty much any data type.

In our case, this is what we will do. Enter the following between the curly braces beneath the `protected void Button1_Click` line:

```
dynamic z = Convert.ToDouble(TextBox1.Text);
```

Now, if you hover your mouse over `dynamic` here, the popup says that `dynamic` represents an object whose operations will be resolved at runtime; in essence, not now—not until the program runs.

Next, enter the following directly beneath the preceding line:

```
sampLabel.Text = $"{z} increased by 10% is {Increase(z)}";
```

This will work perfectly well. Then, enter the following:

```
z = Convert.ToInt32(TextBox2.Text);
```

Look at this very carefully. Instead of typing `double` again, I chose `Int32`, which is an `integer` type. Remember, if you hover your mouse over `dynamic`, the pop-up message again says that `dynamic` represents an object whose operations will be resolved at runtime. It's the same with the function.

In this line, z represents an `integer` data type, whereas the z in the preceding `dynamic z` line represents a `double` data type. A system with the `dynamic` keyword is smart enough to be able to switch from one type to another easily. So, it's a more flexible code, essentially.

Remember, we have one single method—we don't need a function with a `double` or `integer` data type, and so on. So, we will call the following below this line:

```
sampLabel.Text += $"<br>{z} increased by 10% is {Increase(z)}<br>";
```

Note that this line includes a += operator; otherwise, it's exactly the same code—the rest of it is the same. The only difference is that, in the first case, z will be treated as a `double` data type, and in the second case, it is an `integer` data type. And z can store both of them: it can accommodate them easily. You can then switch the data type from one to the other within your code pretty easily and elegantly.

Now, open your browser and give this a go so that you can visualize the results thus far. Let's enter 10 in both boxes and click on `Increase`:

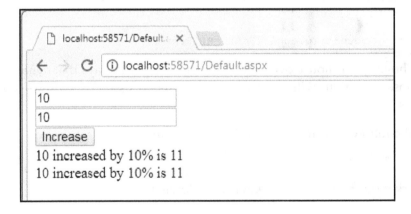

Figure 5.10.3: The results of running the program so far

Yes, it's true that it looks the same to the eye; however, keep in mind that the first box converts the input to a `double` data type while the second box converts it to an `integer` data type, so they're not the same internally. For example, when we enter 10.89 in both the boxes, the number we enter in the first box gets accepted. However, when we enter that same number in the second box, it generates an error, as shown in the following screenshot:

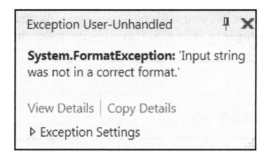

Figure 5.10.4: Error generated when program tries to convert input to an integer

There are ways to handle this. You can use `TryParse`, `TryCatch`, and so on, to make it superior. You'll learn about these eventually, but keep in mind that the big idea so far is that a single variable can represent different data types equally well. The dynamic keyword allows extending C# so it can work with other languages like IronPython, which has its own set of powerful features. The details, however, are beyond the scope of this book.

# Working with the var keyword

Now, let's enter the following line:

```
var title = "Welcome";
```

If you hover your mouse over `var`, it says **class System.String**, whereas with `dynamic`, you'll recall that it's not known until runtime. Thus, `var` and `dynamic` do not serve the same function.

Next, enter the following:

```
Page.Title = title;
```

Here, `title` is the title that we have created, so that's `Page.Title`. Now, what we will try to do is to assign a new data type to the word `title`. For this, enter the following:

```
title = 25;
```

If you hover your mouse over 25, you will see a message indicating that **you cannot implicitly convert type integer to string**, as shown in the following screenshot:

> ◾ struct System.Int32
> Represents a 32-bit signed integer. To browse the .NET Framework source code for this type, see the Reference Source.
>
> Cannot implicitly convert type 'int' to 'string'

Figure 5.10.5: Error message indicating that you cannot convert type integer to string

This means that with the var keyword, the type of data is already known right now—you cannot change it. So, the preceding line will not run. Let's comment this line out as follows:

```
// title = 25; this is not possible because title is already recognized as
a string
```

Now, in the z = Convert.ToInt32 line entered earlier, the type of the z variable can be changed, right? So, go back and add the comment shown at the end of this line:

```
z = Convert.ToInt32(TextBox2.Text); //the type of variable z can be
changed, z is given an integer now
```

Now go back to the dynamic z = Convert.ToDouble line and add the following comment:

```
dynamic z = Convert.ToDouble(TextBox1.Text);//z is given a double
```

In fact, z can be given a string data type, or a great number of different things. I've just been doing this with numerical ones that are fairly easy to understand at first.

So the word var is very powerful, as it basically means that you have less to remember as a programmer because the system is smart enough to recognize what a data type is. For example, in the following line, when you hover your mouse over the right-hand side and the left-hand side, it says **class System.string**. You see that?

```
var title = "Welcome";
```

This can also be used for many different expressions. You can, for example, type the following:

```
foreach (var c in Page.Title)
```

This is for each character in the title of the page, basically. Let's do some action. Enter the following below this line:

```
sampLabel.Text += $"{c.ToString().ToUpper()}";
```

Here, note that we used `+=` to append to the previous results. Thus, the number of things that can be done is great. In this case, I took each character and then converted it to a `string` data type, because strings and characters are not the same, and then I also converted it to uppercase.

If you want, you can try it this way:

```
sampLabel.Text += $"{c.ToUpper()}";
```

In the `foreach (var c in Page.Title)` line, when you hover your mouse over `c`, you see that the popup says **struct System.Char**. So, in this case, the system is smart enough to recognize that `c` is a character. When you try to call `ToUpper` on the character, it doesn't quite work, as shown in the following screenshot:

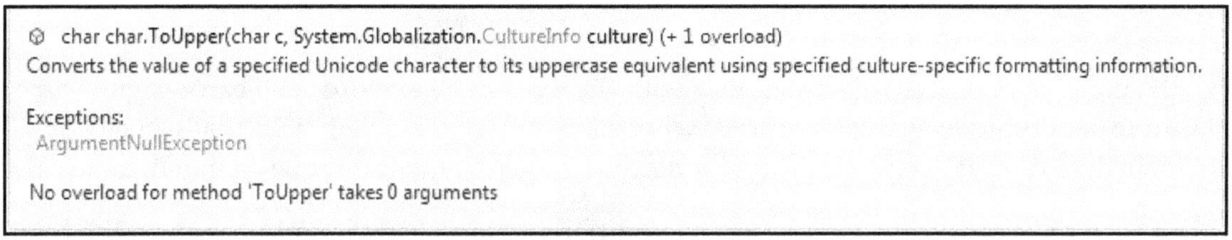

Figure 5.10.6: Error message indicating that there is no overload method for 'ToUpper'

# Running the program

To make the preceding line work, you need to add `ToString()`. First, you have the character; next you convert it to a string, and then you convert it to uppercase. Finally, you can display the character:

```
sampLabel.Text += $"{c.ToString().ToUpper()}";
```

This is one way of doing it. Now let's take a look at the results. In Google Chrome, enter 1 in the first box, 50 in the second box, and click on the `Increase` button. As you can see, 1 `increased by 10% is 1.1` and 50 `increased by 10% is 55`. Finally, you see that `WELCOME` now appears in all uppercase, as shown in the following screenshot:

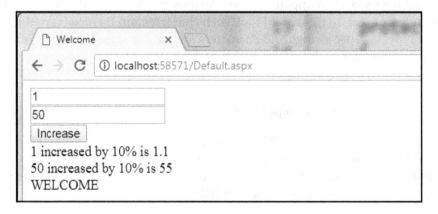

Figure 5.10.7: The results of running the program

So, the big idea here is to remember that with the `dynamic` keyword, you can assign multiple data types to a single variable, whereas with `var`, you cannot do that—once you assign a data type, it's recognized, and after that the data type cannot be changed.

The `dynamic` keyword can be used in many different ways. For example, to return the type of data from a function or a parameter type. It's the same thing with `var`. You can declare something to be `var`; you can also use it in a `foreach` loop and in similar contexts.

For review, a complete version of the `Default.aspx.cs` file for this chapter is displayed in the following code block:

```
//1. using is a keyword, it's blue
//2. System is a name space that stores already created code
//3. using System brings in existing code
using System;
//4. class is a required container for creating our own code samples
public partial class _Default : System.Web.UI.Page
{
    private static dynamic Increase(dynamic x)
    {
        return x * 1.1;
    }

    protected void Button1_Click(object sender, EventArgs e)
```

```
{
    dynamic z = Convert.ToDouble(TextBox1.Text);//z is given a
    //double
    sampLabel.Text = $"{z} increased by 10% is {Increase(z)}";
    //the type of variable z can be changed, z is given an integer
    //now
    z = Convert.ToInt32(TextBox2.Text);
    sampLabel.Text += $"<br>{z} increased by 10% is {Increase(z)}
    <br>";
    var title = "Welcome";
    Page.Title = title;
    // title = 25; this is not possible because title is already
    //recognized as a string
    foreach (var c in Page.Title)
    {
        sampLabel.Text += $"{c.ToString().ToUpper()}";
    }
}
}
```

# Summary

In this chapter, you learned about the `dynamic` and `var` keywords.

In the next chapter, we will talk about creating classes, and we will imagine classes as templates for making objects.

# 34

# Creating a Class with a Constructor and a Function

In this chapter, we will talk about creating classes. We will imagine classes as templates for making objects.

## Our initial markup

Let's begin with a very simple markup, shown here in the **Source** view:

```
1  <%@ Page Language="C#" AutoEventWireup="true" CodeFile="Default.aspx.cs" Inherits="_Default" %>
2
3  <!DOCTYPE html>
4
5  <html xmlns="http://www.w3.org/1999/xhtml">
6  <head runat="server">
7      <title></title>
8  </head>
9  <body>
10     <form id="form1" runat="server">
11         <asp:Button ID="Button1" runat="server" Text="Show Balance" /><br />
12         <asp:Label ID="Label1" runat="server" Text=""></asp:Label>
13     </form>
14 </body>
15 </html>
16
```

Figure 6.1.1: The initial simple markup for this chapter

If we switch over to the **Design** view, all we have is a button that says Show Balance, and under it a Label control where the balance can actually be displayed, as shown in the following screenshot:

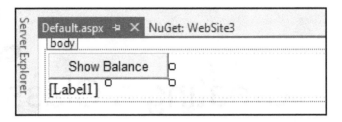

Figure 6.1.2: The initial interface in the Design view

# Creating a class

Now, double-click on Show Balance. Here, we will create a class that represents bank accounts. Start by deleting comment 4, which is not suitable for our purposes, and then enter the following under using system:

```
class BankAccount
```

Here, class is a keyword, so it's blue of course, and BankAccount is an identifier—it's a name you make up. In other words, this means if I want to, I can put Bob or VideoGameCharacter there—whatever I need to represent. So, in our case, BankAccount is what I put there.

In the context of what we are creating, let's describe the purpose of this line in the new comment 4:

```
class BankAccount//4. Class functions as a template for creating bank
accounts
```

# Creating the class structure

In the next stage, you will create the actual structure within the curly braces and then start defining the things that describe a bank account. So, for example, type the following:

```
private decimal balance;
```

What is the purpose of this line? To describe it, let's add comments at the end of this line as follows:

```
//5. private means this variable is reachable only within the bank account
class
```

Also, `decimal` is just a data type, so let's follow this with comment 6:

```
//6. decimal is the data type
```

Then, `balance` is the name of our variable. We'll say this here in comment 7:

```
//7. balance is the name of our instance variable or some people call it a
field
```

In the context of classes, `balance` is not just called a variable, but it's also called an *instance variable*. Or, as some people call it, a *field*. Its purpose is to store information. So comment 8 should say the following:

```
//8. balance stores information about each bank account
```

You have a value in your balance, another person has a different value, and yet another person has a different value; it's a changing quantity, so we call it an instance variable.

# Working with an instance

Now, what is an instance? An *instance* is just, for example, one specific bank account. How do we actually make bank accounts? Enter the following:

```
public BankAccount(decimal bal)
```

Here, we start with `public` and then `BankAccount`, and then we specify a parameter, just as with regular methods.

Since `BankAccount` here is `public`, this means that this code can be accessed outside the `BankAccount` class and that it specifically has the `name` constructor. Let's add comment 9 at the end of this line as follows:

```
//9. This is the constructor, which runs when a bank account is made
```

In other words, that's the code that executes.

# Setting the account balance

Next, within the curly braces beneath the line beginning with `public`, let's set the balance; for this, let's type the following:

```
{
    balance = bal;
}
```

We set the value of an instance variable within the body of the constructor. Let's add comment 10 at the end of the preceding line of code as follows:

```
//10. This line sets the value of instance variable whenever a new bank
account is created
```

This is the purpose of the line. It's like when you go to a bank, basically, and you open a new account; you give them some initial amount of money. Let's assume that's the case here. This is exactly the same thing; the same logic, expressed obviously in code.

# Displaying the balance using a method

Now, besides that, imagine that you go to an ATM, for example. You need to be able to view your balance. Well, we need a similar action or mechanism here. So, we create a method. Let's enter the following:

```
public string GetBalance()
```

Here, we create a method. A *method*, in the context of a class is, as you can imagine, an action that something can perform. Well, if you have a bank account, then the action it can perform is to display your balance to you, or some other action, such as increasing your balance or decreasing your balance, depending on what you're doing.

For our purposes, however, the basic thing is to display the balance, so we write the preceding line. Within the curly braces beneath this, because we have `string` here and it represents or returns a string when it runs, you have to add code to do this. So, enter the following:

```
return $"Balance: {balance:C}";
```

Here, we enter `return`, and then the `$` symbol for string interpolation and double quotes to make a string. Next, we say `Balance:` and then within a set of curly braces, we stick in the `balance` instance variable and put in `:C` to format it as currency. We close this with a semicolon. The precision of language matters very much.

Notice that if you highlight the `balance` instance variable in the code, it gets highlighted in several places; in fact, all of the occurrences of it get highlighted. Try it. And then `C`, of course, formats the results or output.

Enter comment 11 at the end of this line as follows:

```
//11. This method is public and gets the balance formatted as a string
```

The method gets the balance formatted not just as a number, but as the whole `$"Balance: {balance:C}"` string. See that? Remember, in this context, the `$` symbol, as before, is used for string interpolation; it has nothing to do with money. `C` is what is responsible for showing the balance formatted as currency—two different functions.

Now, let's add comment 12 at the end of this line as follows:

```
//12. Shows balance formatted as currency
```

To break down what we have created thus far: we basically have a template, which contains the entire class, that is, everything under the `BankAccount` class. See? It's got a `private` instance variable, `private decimal balance;`, and this stores information about each bank account. It's also got a constructor, `public BankAccount(decimal bal)`, which runs when a bank account is actually created, and, finally, we have a method called `GetBalance`, which essentially is an action that a bank account can perform. So, we have a template for creating bank balance accounts—that's what we are creating.

# Making a bank account object

Now, to make a `BankAccount` object, enter the following within the curly braces beneath `Button1_Click`:

```
BankAccount ba = new BankAccount(4500);
```

This will create a bank account in memory so that it actually exists. Keep in mind where you place this. It will be created every time you click on `Button1_Click`, The whole process will go on every time. And now where it says `decimal bal`, we have to specify the balance, so we say `4500` and then close with a semicolon. Now, let's enter comment 13 at the end of this line as follows:

```
//13. Creates a new bank account
```

# Crunching the numbers

In the preceding code line, on the left-hand side, we have our data type called `BankAccount`, then the name of a variable `ba`, and then =, which is the assignment operator. On the right-hand side, this is where we actually make the object live in memory so that it exists with the `new` keyword; so we have `new BankAccount`. Notice that `new` here is blue—it's a keyword. Next, we pass in an argument, such as `4500`, and that is used to set the value of the instance variable for each bank account.

Beneath that, enter the following:

```
Label1.Text = ba.GetBalance();
```

Here, `ba` is the name of our object—our bank account, and . (dot) brings up a list of methods that can be executed on the `BankAccount` object, as shown in *Figure 6.1.3*:

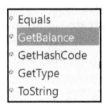

Figure 6.1.3: The list of methods that can be executed on the BankAccount object

These are the actions that it can perform. One of these actions, of course, is `GetBalance`. If you hover your mouse over `GetBalance`, it gives back a string, as shown in *Figure 6.1.4*. And remember that `Label1.Text` is also a string, so the data types are matched as usual.

Figure 6.1.4: GetBalance gives back a string

In the preceding mouse hover, `BankAccount.GetBalance()` means that within the `BankAccount` class in our code, there is a method called `GetBalance`, and the . (dot) between `BankAccount` and `GetBalance()` is member access: the member to be accessed. The member is a thing, like a method; so, in our case, the member is called `GetBalance`. The parts of `string.BankAccount.GetBalance()` consist of return type, data type, name of class, . (dot), and then `GetBalance`, respectively. Now, let's set comment 14 as follows:

```
//14. Runs GetBalance method on the bank account object
```

I have given a huge number of comments here to try to be as thorough as possible.

# Running the program

Let's open Google Chrome, and then click on `Show Balance`. It says `Balance: $4,500.00`, as shown in the following screenshot:

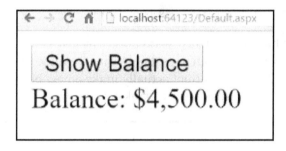

Figure 6.1.5: The correct bank account balance is shown, formatted as currency

So, everything's working as expected. Regardless of how sophisticated this looks, you can right-click and select **View page source**. Remember that all of this is auto-generated (as shown in *Figure 6.1.6*)—you don't have to worry about it. But really, the big thing here is what is highlighted in the screenshot— `Balance: $4,500.00`:

```
14
15      <input type="submit" name="Button1" value="Show Balance" id="Button1" /><br />
16      <span id="Label1">Balance: $4,500.00</span>
17
```

Figure 6.1.6: Auto-generated source code

This is returned by our method; it comes from calling our methods, specifically `$"Balance: {balance:C}"`. You see that? This is what goes into the web page, basically—the balance.

# Private versus public

Again, remember, when it comes to fields and storing information, you make the fields `private` in general so that they cannot be altered willy-nilly by code that could be unfriendly. Methods like this are usually `public` so that they can be accessed; otherwise, you would not be able to, for example, get the balance.

Imagine that you change `public string GetBalance()` to `private`; now, the popup shown in shown in *Figure 6.1.7* says that the method is inaccessible due to its protection level. It's not useful anymore, as now you cannot get the balance. For our simple purposes, you make it `public`:

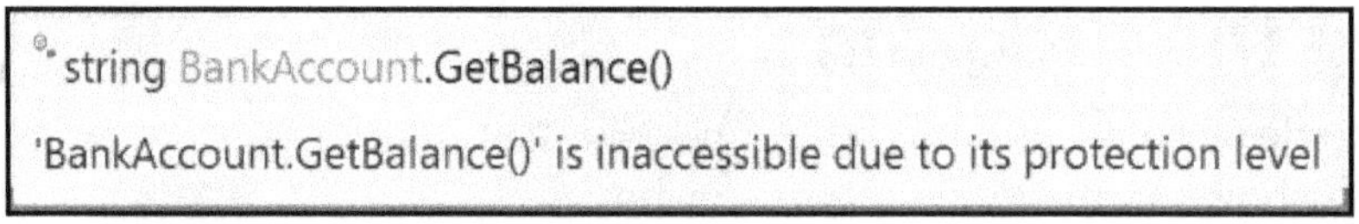

string BankAccount.GetBalance()

'BankAccount.GetBalance()' is inaccessible due to its protection level

Figure 6.1.7: Error message displayed when you change GetBalance() from public to private, making the method inaccessible

Now, imagine that you have the `public BankAccount(decimal bal)` constructor, and that you change it to `private`. Now it says that it is inaccessible due to its protection level, as shown in *Figure 6.1.8*. Now you cannot actually make a new bank account; you must make it `public` so that you can make a new bank account.

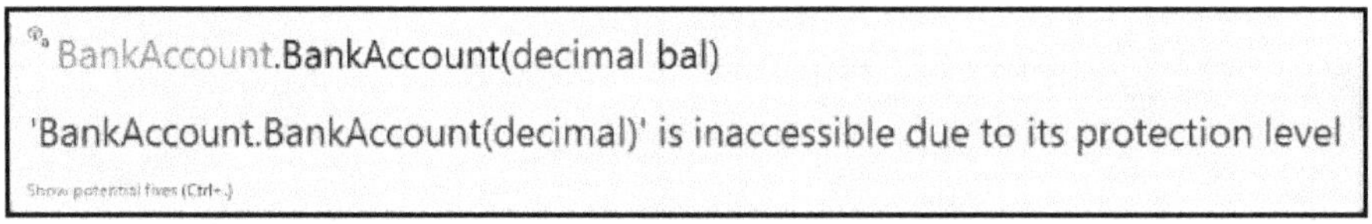

BankAccount.BankAccount(decimal bal)

'BankAccount.BankAccount(decimal)' is inaccessible due to its protection level

Show potential fixes (Ctrl+.)

Figure 6.1.8: Error message displayed when you change BankAccount from public to private, making the method inaccessible

Also, if you change the field in `private decimal balance;` to `public`, that would be a problem, right? Because now, you can type `ba` and notice that the `balance` field shows up in IntelliSense that list of features you can use, and now you can set it to a new value that you want. In other words, code from other applications could come along and change the balance. That would obviously be a severe problem for people, so that's not the way to do it. Keep fields, as a general rule, `private` and secure, and then access them securely in a controlled fashion with a method like this one.

For review, a complete version of the `Default.aspx.cs` file for this chapter is displayed in the following code block:

```
//1. using is a keyword, it's blue
//2. System is a name space that stores already created code
//3. using System brings in existing code
using System;

class BankAccount//4. Class function as a template for creating bank
accounts
{
    private decimal balance;//5. private means this variable is
    //reachable only within the bank account class
    //6.decimal is the data type
    //7. balance is the name of our instance variable or some people
    //call it field
    //8. balance stores informatino about each bank account.

    public bank Account(decimal bal)//9. This is the consturctor, which
    //runs when a bank account is made
    {
        balance = bal;//10. This line sets the value of instance
        //variable whenever a new bank account is created
    }
    public string GetBalance()
    {
        return $"Balance:{balance:C}";//12. Shows balance formatted as
        //currency
    }
}
public partial class _Default : System.Web.UI.Page
{

    protected void Button1_Click(object sender, EventArgs e)
    {
        BankAccount ba = new BankAccount();//14. Runs Getbalance method
        //on the bank account object
        Label1.Text = ba.GetBalance();
        //the bank account object.

    }
}
```

# Summary

In this chapter, we talked about creating classes, and we imagined classes as templates for making objects. You created a class, developed its structure, learned about instance variables, set bank account balances and displayed them using a method, made a bank account object, and finally, you ran the program to "crunch the numbers."

In the next chapter, we'll talk about creating and using the `static` classes.

# 35
# Creating a Class with a Static Method

In this chapter, you will learn about creating and using `static` classes.

## Setting up a simple initial interface

Bring up a project, and into the `<form>` element, place a couple of visual things. First of all, let's put a `TextBox` control. We will create a class that basically collects some methods that perform definite operations, such as reversing the sequence of characters in a string.

The `TextBox` control that you dragged into the form is for user input on the page. In the next stage, you'll add a `Button` control so that the user can click on, for example, `Reverse`. So, drag and drop a `Button` control directly below the `TextBox` control inside the form. After the `Button` control, let's also add a `Label` control, so that we can show the string reversed. So, drag and drop a `Label` control directly below the `Button` control in the form.

Close the **ToolBox** window, and our simple interface is shown in the following screenshot:

```
Default.aspx.cs    Default.aspx  ⊕ ✕  NuGet: WebSite3
    1  <%@ Page Language="C#" AutoEventWireup="true" CodeFile="Default.aspx.cs" Inherits="_Default" %>
    2
    3  <!DOCTYPE html>
    4
    5  <html xmlns="http://www.w3.org/1999/xhtml">
    6  <head runat="server">
    7      <title></title>
    8  </head>
    9  <body>
   10      <form id="form1" runat="server">
   11          <asp:TextBox ID="TextBox1" runat="server"></asp:TextBox><br />
   12          <asp:Button ID="Button1" runat="server" Text="Button" /><br />
   13          <asp:Label ID="Label1" runat="server" Text="Label"></asp:Label>
   14      </form>
   15  </body>
   16  </html>
   17
```

Figure 6.2.1. Our simple interface for this project

Now switch over to the **Design** view, and it appears as shown in the following screenshot:

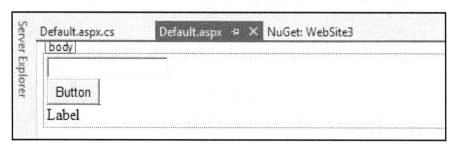

Figure 6.2.2. Our simple interface in the Design view

What we can do now is remove the word Button from the Text property, for example, and make it say Reverse as follows:

```
<asp:Button ID="Button1" runat="server" Text="Reverse" /><br />
```

That's all we will do. Also, get rid of the Text attribute under Label, as shown here:

```
<asp:Label ID="Label1" runat="server"></asp:Label>
```

So, you have the text box, the Button control that says Reverse, and the Label markup as shown earlier.

# Introducing static classes

Again, switch over to the **Design** view, and double-click on the `Reverse` button. At the top of `Default.aspx.cs` (under `using System;`), we will put a new kind of class. So, enter the following:

```
static class StringUtil
```

The `StringUtil` keyword is the short form for utilities. Let's add comment 4 at the end of this line as follows:

```
//4. Class represents a collection of operations or methods only
```

Because class represents a collection of operations or methods only, it's a `static` class. In other words, you would not make a `StringUtil` object. Remember, in the previous chapter, we created an object using the `new` keyword. *String utilities* is basically a collection of operations or methods; you would not make an object of the `string utility` type because, what would that be? That's difficult to imagine. If you have, for example, a `person` class, you can imagine writing `new person;` you can describe any person very easily—hair color, speech, some language, height, and so on.

So, `static class StringUtil` functions only as a container for collecting methods that operate on strings. That's all it's doing. There are no fields. In other words, there are no fields as you might have for a person, such as ID, name, and social security number. So, no fields or information, just operations, OK? Class represents a collection of operations or methods only.

# Creating the Reverse method

We'll create one method; so type the following within the curly braces below `static class StringUtil`:

```
public static string Reverse(string s)
```

The name of our method is `Reverse`. It produces a string and it operates on a string. It's `static`, which means that we'll be able to call it by writing the name of the class and then the name of the method—we'll see that momentarily. Here, `public` of course means that it's accessible in code outside of the class.

Let's add a few comments above this line, starting with comment 5, to see what we've created here. Type the following:

```
//5. Public means reachable anywhere
//6. static means we can call the method by writing: StringUtil.Reverse
//7. string is what we're going to produce and the method name is //Reverse
//8. string s is the data type and name of parameter
```

Remember, in comment 6, `StringUtil` is the name of the class and `Reverse` is the name of the method to be called.

# Coding the Reverse method

After `public static string Reverse(string s)`, within the curly braces, we'll write the code that reverses a string as follows:

```
var chars = s.ToCharArray();
```

We can do this in various ways, but one way is to use `var`, which you'll remember is a handy way of replacing, for example, `decimal`, `double`, `integer`, and `array`. Just use `var` instead. Here, I say `chars`, which is short for characters, and I'll take the string that we pass in, which is called `s`. Among the many different things that you can do to it, you can convert it to an array. So, we say `ToCharArray` and close with a semicolon.

Here, when you hover your mouse over `s.ToCharArray()`, it says: **Copies the characters of this instance to a Unicode character array**, as shown in *Figure 6.2.3*. So, basically it takes our string and converts it to an array of characters.

```
char[] string.ToCharArray() (+ 1 overload)
Copies the characters in this instance to a Unicode character array.
```

Figure 6.2.3: Tooltip popup shown when you hover your mouse over s.ToCharArray()

Let's add comment 9 at the end of this line so that we understand its purpose:

```
//9. Converts string to array of characters and saves to chars
```

The preceding code line converts a string to an array of characters and saves it to `chars`. So, now when you hover your mouse over `var`, the popup says `char[]`. This indicates that you have created an array to hold individual characters of the string that we have passed in.

# Reversing the array

In the next stage, we will reverse the array, so enter the following:

```
Array.Reverse(chars);
```

Here, we typed `Array` followed by `.` (dot), then `Reverse`, followed by the name of the array that we want to reverse; in our case, it's called `chars`.

 Make sure that `using System;` is up at the very top after the initial comments. If it's not there, restore it. If you restore it, you will see that `Array` is back. This confirms that it's stored within `System`, also.

So, what does the preceding line of code do here? Let's add comment 10 at the end of this line as follows:

```
//10. This has the action of reversing the array: 1,2,3 after reversing
it's 3,2,1
```

Here, you're switching the order of things. The last bit, then, once you have the letters reversed, is to send them back as a `new string` method. To accomplish that, enter the following beneath this line:

```
return new string (chars);
```

# Undoing the reversed string

The preceding code line takes the action that we'll document in comment 11 as follows:

```
//11. This creates a new string from the reversed array and sends it back
to the calling code
```

Again, I try to be as detailed with comments as possible.

To make use of all of this, down below within the curly braces of the event handler, we'll type the following very easily and quickly:

```
Label1.Text = StringUtil.Reverse(TextBox1.Text);
```

Here, we typed `Label1.Text =`, and since we have to read the value from the box, hit it with the `Reverse` method, and then display it back to the user; to accomplish all of this in one fell swoop, we say `StringUtil`, or in other words, string utilities, and then `Reverse(TextBox1.Text)`. That's it.

So, let's add a few comments above this line, starting with comment 12:

```
//12. Text1.Text reads value from box
//13. That value is passed into Reverse method
//14. After Reverse runs, it produces a string back to the user
```

# Running the program

Now, let's run this. Open Google Chrome. Enter a word, such as `hello`, and click on `Reverse`; it says olleh (see *Figure 6.2.4A*). If you enter `1,2,3` and click on Reverse, it says `3,2,1` (see *Figure 6.2.4B*), and so on:

Figures 6.2.4A and 6.2.4B: Reversing the sequence of characters in a string

So, it's working as expected. Now, remember, even if you input `1,2,3`, these look like numbers to you, but they're not. Behind the scenes, these are treated as a string; they're stored internally as a string.

These are the basics of a `static` class. Remember, a `static` class is basically used to collect methods that have very definite definitions, that do definite things, but do not think of making a new string utility object; it just wouldn't be sensible to do so. We're just collecting functionality operations together. This is also used commonly, for example, with the `Math` class, and other classes like that.

For review, a complete version of the `Default.aspx.cs` code file for this chapter is displayed in the following code block:

```
//1. using is a keyword, it's blue
//2. System is a name space that stores already created code
//3. using System brings in existing code
using System;
static class StringUtil //4. Class represents a collection of operations or
//methods only
{
    //5. Public means reachable anywhere
    //6. static means we can call the method by writing: StringUtil.Reverse
    //7. string is what we're going to produce and the method name is
Reverse
    //8. string s is the data type and name of parameter
    public static string Reverse(string s)
    {
        var chars = s.ToCharArray();//9. Converts string to array of
characters
        //and saves to chars
        Array.Reverse(chars);//10. This has the action of reversing the
array:
        //1,2,3 after reversing it's 3,2,1
        return new string(chars);//11. This creates a new string from the
        //reversed array and sends it back to the calling code
    }
}

public partial class _Default : System.Web.UI.Page
{

    protected void Button1_Click(object sender, System.EventArgs e)
    {
        //12. Text1.Text reads value from box
        //13. That value is passed into Reverse method
        //14. After Reverse runs, it produces a string back to the user
        Label1.Text = StringUtil.Reverse(TextBox1.Text);
    }

}
```

# Summary

In this chapter, we talked about creating and using `static` classes. To reverse the characters in a string, you created a Reverse method, coded the method, reversed an array, and "reversed" the string.

In the next chapter, we'll talk about properties.

# 36

# Creating a Class with an Object Property

In this lesson, we're going to talk about properties.

## Setting up a simple markup page

We'll begin with a very simple markup page, like the one shown in the following screenshot:

```
Default.aspx.cs        Default.aspx ⚙ ✕ NuGet: WebSite3
    1  <%@ Page Language="C#" AutoEventWireup="true" CodeFile="Default.aspx.cs" Inherits="_Default" %>
    2
    3  <!DOCTYPE html>
    4
    5  <html xmlns="http://www.w3.org/1999/xhtml">
    6  <head runat="server">
    7      <title></title>
    8  </head>
    9  <body>
   10      <form id="form1" runat="server">
   11          <asp:TextBox ID="TextBox1" runat="server" OnTextChanged="TextBox1_TextChanged"></asp:TextBox><br />
   12          <asp:Label ID="Label1" runat="server"></asp:Label>
   13      </form>
   14  </body>
   15  </html>
   16
```

Figure 6.3.1: Our simple starting markup page for this lesson

What we have here is a `TextBox` control, then we have a `Label` control after the `TextBox` control--a very simple interface. We will collect a value, which will be the radius of a circle, then display some relevant information about the circle. Really easy stuff.

OK, go over to the **Design** view. What we currently have is shown in the following screenshot:

Figure 6.3.2: Our starting interface in Design view

Again, we have a TextBox control and a Label control. Now left double-click on the box to bring up the event handling code. Do this next. Now it looks like the following screenshot:

```
1  //1. using is a keyword, it's blue
2  //2. System is a name space that stores already created code
3  //3. using System brings in existing code
4  using System;
5
6  public partial class _Default : System.Web.UI.Page
7  {
8
9
10     protected void TextBox1_TextChanged(object sender, EventArgs e)
11     {
12
13     }
14 }
```

Figure 6.3.3: Our starting Default.aspx.cs page

# Creating a class

The first thing to do is to create a class. Enter the following under the `using System;` directive:

```
class Circle
{


}
```

Remember, the purpose here is to model circles. That's the objective. Now, let's add comment 4 at the end of this line, as follows:

```
//4. This class functions as a template for making circle objects
```

There you go! In the next stage, we're going to add an instance variable or a field, so we'll say the following below the open curly under the `Circle` class:

```
private double radius;
```

This is a field or an instance variable. Follow this line with comment 5, as shown here:

```
//5. This is the instance variable that defines each circle object
```

The `radius` is simply the distance from the center of the circle to a point on the circle, that is, from the center to a point on a circumference. OK.

In the next stage, we are going to say the following:

```
public double Radius
```

 Observe that we use the big `R` in `Radius` here.

This means something else here, so add comment 6 at the end of this line, as follows:

```
//6. Radius is the property that represents the radius of a circle
```

# Introducing properties

A *property* is basically a mechanism for reading the value of a field, of a backing field, or setting its value in an intelligent way. What do I mean by this? Enter the following after the open curly braces under `public double Radius`:

```
{
    get
    {
        return radius
    }
```

Observe that we use the small "r" in `radius` here.

Here, you say and just read the value. So, here `return radius` is used to retrieve the value of the `radius` variable. Enter comment 7 after this line as follows:

```
//7. This line retrieves the value of a circle radius
```

Now, why is a property different? It's because properties can be intelligent. And by intelligent, I mean that you can create code that controls access to the backing field. In the context of what we are creating here, `radius` (`little "r"`) is the backing field for the property. There's a portion called `set`:

```
}
    set
{
```

So, big `R` means property. In our case, that little "r" is the backing field--the little `radius` variable. In the next stage, between curly braces under `set`, we are going to say the following:

```
if (value >= 0)
```

In other words, if the value is greater than or equal to 0, then set `radius`. The value exists because of the way properties have been defined in C#. It's a keyword, thus it's blue (Windows). It just exists. It's available already--it's not something we introduced.

Enter comment 8 at the end this line as follows:

```
//8. Checks whether the value we're attempting to set is more than or equal
to 0
```

This is reasonable for a radius. A radius goes from the center to a point on the circle; it can be zero, which is really a point itself, or it can be something more than 0, which means you have a circle.

So, if the value there is greater than or equal to 0, then we can say the following between curly braces under this line:

```
radius = value;
```

Follow this line with comment 9, as follows:

```
//9. This runs if the value being set is ok
```

In other words, we have defined the value in terms of being greater than or equal to 0. On the other hand, if somebody attempts, for example, to input -10, that is not an acceptable value for `radius`. Radii are 0, but this really means that you have a point in that case. Some people call it a "degenerate circle," or they're more than 0, such as 5, 10, or 15, but not -10. That's it! You can now enter the following below the closed curly braces for the preceding line:

```
else
{
    radius = 0;
}
```

Next, add comment 10 at the end of this line:

```
//10. The radius field gets the value 0 when a user attempts, for example,
to assign a value like -5
```

Note that -5 is not a reasonable quantity or something that can be measured with a ruler: -5 does not work. OK?

# Using the Circle class

Now, in the next stage, we will make use of this class. So, go down to the following line:

```
protected void TextBox1_TextChanged(object sender, EventArgs e)
```

# Making a Circle object

Enter the following within curly braces below this line:

```
Circle circ = new Circle();
```

So we're creating a new `Circle` object. Now, remember, because this is going into `TextBox1_TextChanged`, and every time you press *Enter*, this will run again. Keep this in mind. That's OK for us--it doesn't really matter very much. We're just illustrating some basic concepts here.

Now add comment 11 at the end of this line, as follows:

```
//11. Makes a new circle object
```

Then, what we'll do is as follows. We'll set something. So, to set the radius, type the name of the object, that is, . (dot), and then notice that a little wrench shows together with the word `Radius`. When you select this from the list, it says **get** and **set** in a tooltip (refer to the following screenshot):

Figure 6.3.4: The tooltip

This indicates that you're working with a property, and instead, it:

```
circ.Radius = double.Parse(TextBox1.Text);
```

In real life, you would use `TryParse`. One of the problems with using `TextBox` control, for example, is that somebody could input `hello`, which obviously cannot be converted into numerical form. So, in real life, you would have added `TryParse` to make the code more sophisticated and more powerful, obviously as a way of writing a more professional application. OK, but in this case, this is sufficient for our purposes.

Notice on the left-hand side that we have the name of an object, then . (dot), which again is member access, and then `Radius`, which is the name of our property. Also, notice that if you highlight `circ.Radius` and if you look all the way up, `Radius` is also highlighted in the line `public double Radius`, which indicates that we're talking about the same thing.

For the next stage, enter the following:

```
Label1.Text = $"Circumference is {2 * Math.PI * circ.Radius}";
```

In the preceding line, the circumference of the circle is obtained with the {2 * Math.PI * circ.Radius} expression. The Math class has a constant within it called PI; that is, a value that never changes, which is called PI. PI is equal to about 3.14. Lastly, you multiply that by the radius. So, to read the value of the property for our Circle object, type the name of the object, . (dot), and then the name of the property again.

Now, let's add a meaningful comment here to be sure that you understand where things are at present. Enter comment 12 directly above the circ.Radius... line:

```
//12. Line below uses circ.Radius, which means that the set portion of the
property is called
```

Remember when we had said used the set word above. See that? That was the block that is called when you *set* the value.

At this stage, the get portion is called. Now enter comment 13 above the Label1.Text... line:

```
//13. Because circ.Radius is used, and not SET, the Get portion of the
Radius property is called
```

Since Radius is used and not set, it's not being set. It has already been set; you are just making use of an existing value, so the portion of the Radius property is called.

That's why you need get and set--you need both. You need the get block, so to speak, the "getter," and then the "setter," as some people will call it. You need both, and each one serves a definite, different purpose.

OK, let's observe this in action now. Open Google Chrome. Once the page is loaded, input a variable, let's say 5, and hit *Enter*. As seen in the following screenshot, it displays Circumference:

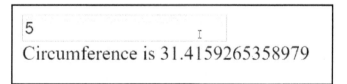

Figure 6.3.5: The circumference of a circle with a radius of 5

If you try to input –5, it says that `Circumference` is 0, which is also correct. You cannot have a negative value for a radius--it's not physically possible. However, if you input a word such as `hello`, you'll see an app crash error, as shown in the following screenshot:

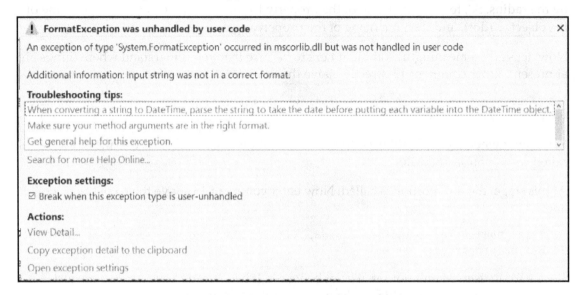

Figure 6.3.6: App crashes error as the result of bad input

This is as it must be. You can correct it, of course, by implementing `TryParse` instead as an example.

> It's extremely important to type in all the code line by line. It really makes a big difference in your learning how to program in C#.

For review, a complete version of the `Default.aspx.cs` file for this lesson is displayed in the following code block:

```
//1. using is a keyword, it's blue
//2. System is a name space that stores already created code
//3. using System brings in existing code
using System;
class Circle//4. This class functions as a template for making circle
objects
{
    private double radius;
    //5. This is the instance variable that defines each circle object
    public double Radius;
```

```
//6. Radius is the property that represents the radius of a circle
{
    get
    {
        return radius;//7. This line retrieves the value of a circle
radius
    }
    set
    {
        if (value >= 0)//8. Checks whether the value we're attempting
to set
        //is more than or equal to 0
        {
            radius = value;//9. This runs if the value being set is ok
        }
        else
        {
            radius = 0;//10. The radius field gets the value 0 when a
user
            //attempts, for example, to assign a value like -5
        }
    }
}
}

public partial class _Default : System.Web.UI.Page
{

    protected void TextBox1_TextChanged(object sender, EventArgs e)
    {
        Circle circ = new Circle();
        //11. Makes a new circle object
        //12. Line below uses circ.Radius, which means that the set
        //portion of the property is called
        circ.Radius = double.Parse(TextBox1.Text);
        //13. Because circ.Radius is used, and not SET, the Get portion
of the
        //Radius property is called
        Label1.Text = $"Circumference is {2 * Math.PI * circ.Radius}";
    }
}
```

# Summary

In this lesson, you learned about properties. You also created a class called `Circle`.

In the next lesson, you're going to learn about `static` fields and then `static` properties that could be used to access those fields. You will also learn about what happens when we shut down *IS Express*.

# 37
# Creating a Class with Static Fields, and Properties

In this lesson, you're going to learn about `static` fields and then `static` properties, which could be used to access those fields. You will also learn about what happens when you shut down *IIS Express*. So let's take a look.

## Setting up the interface for this project

Remember, *IS Express* is the one that comes by default with the Visual Studio web server. So bring up a project. What we are going to do here is put a box under . It will start with your truck name--I'll make trucks, alright? So, put a `TextBox` control in here, like this. That's it:

```
Truck Name: <asp: TextBox ID="TextBox1" runat="server">< /asp:TextBox><br
/>
```

Now, below this, place a `Button` control, as follows:

```
<asp:Button ID="Button1" runat="server" Text="Button" /<br />
```

Remember to add the `<br>` tag at the end of the preceding lines in order to stack the content vertically.

When somebody clicks on the Button control, we'll count the number of trucks that have been made. That's all it's going to do. So, change the Text property on the Button tag to something more meaningful, such as Count. Your starting code for this project should then look like the following screenshot:

```
1 <%@ Page Language="C#" AutoEventWireup="true" CodeFile="Default.aspx.cs"
Inherits="_Default" %>
2
3 <!DOCTYPE html>
4
5 <html xmlns="http://www.w3.org/1999/xhtml">
6 <head runat="server">
7     <title>Our First Page</title>
8 </head>
9 <body>
10    <form id="form1" runat="server">
11    Truck Name: <asp: TextBox ID="TextBox1" runat="server">< /asp:TextBox><br
/>
12     <asp:Button ID="Button1" runat="server" Text="Count" /<br />
13
14          <asp:Label ID="sampLabel" runat="server" </asp:Label>
15
16
17    </form>
18 </body>
19 </html>
20
```

Figure 6.4.1: The Starting interface for this project

So, in **Design** view, as shown in the following screenshot, you have a box, Truck Name, and Count. That's it, a simple user interface!

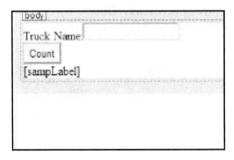

Figure 6.4.2: Our simple user interface

# Creating the Truck class

In the next stage, what you are going to do is this: go to **Solution Explorer**, right-click the name of the website, select **Add**, and then click on **Class**. Name this class `Truck` and then click on **OK**. When the Visual Studio message comes up, click on **Yes**. Your screen should look as shown in the following screenshot:

```
 6 /// <summary>
 7 /// Summary description for Truck
 8 /// </summary>
 9 public class Truck
10 {
11
12      public Truck(string name)
13      {
14
15      }
16
17 }
```

Figure 6.4.3: Public class Truck

We're going to learn about the `static` concept. Do you see where it says `public class Truck`? You're going to type the following lines beneath the open curly brace:

```
private string make;
private static int count;
public Truck(string name)
{
    make = name;
    count++;
}
public static int TruckCount
{
    get
    {
        return count;
    }
}
```

Here's what is happening with each of the preceding lines:

1. After `private string`, follow with the make of the truck, such as whether it's a Honda, Ford, or Dodge.

2. Next, enter `private static int count`. Now when you make the trucks, two things will happen: you'll set the name of the truck and then increase the count of the trucks. So, you'll say `public Truck(string name)` and then within curly braces beneath that, enter the following:

   ```
   make = name;
   count++;
   ```

3. Now `count++` means that every time a new truck is made, the `count` variable is increased by 1.

4. Now you want access to the `count` variable `private static int count`, which is `static`, so that it acts at the class level. So you want secure access to it. Notice that right now it's `private`. This means it's accessible only where this line is positioned and not anywhere else. So to make it securely accessible, below the closed curly brace, let's make a `public static int TruckCount` property, as follows:

   ```
   public static int TruckCount
   ```

5. Now, between the opened and closed curly braces, enter get.

6. Then, between the nested opened and closed curly braces below this line, enter the following:

   ```
   return count
   ```

   - You'll notice that because this `count` field is `static`, the property that goes along with it is also `static` and it acts at the class level, which means that you can write the *name of class.name of the static property*, which is backed by the `static int count` statement.

7. Alright, that's it for the class. So right-click on any of the `using System` namespace above and select **Organize Usings** > **Remove Unnecessary Usings**. You don't need them.

OK, so this is the heart of our application, nothing else. That's it.

Now return to `Default.aspx`, go to the **Design** view (see *Figure 6.4.2*) and then left double-click on `Count`. This will bring up the event handler for the `Count` button.

Now to make it do something, we'll say the following between opened and closed curly braces:

```
Truck tr = new Truck(TextBox1.Text);
```

This line initializes the constructor using the value in the `TextBox` control.

Below this, enter the following:

```
sampLabel.Text = $"There are {Truck.TruckCount} truck(s).";
```

Start with `sampLabel.Text` to make use of the `static` property. Follow this with a `$` symbol, double quotes, and `There are`, for example, trailed by the name of the class, that is, `{Truck. (dot) TruckCount}`. Notice in the pop-up tip that `TruckCount` shows up as a `static` property. See? Then, it shows up `truck(s)`.

Sometimes people put s within parenthesis as an indicator that the first one will be singular, but after that they will be plural. You have one truck or multiple trucks. See that?

## Counting trucks

Alright, now to make use of this, take a look. Open your browser. Your screen should be similar to the image shown in the following screenshot:

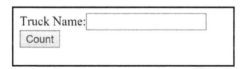

Figure 6.4.4: The interface of the Truck public class

Alright, so first if I enter the brand name of a truck, let's say, `Honda`, it's going to display the name of the truck brand. Now let's hit `Count`. You see that it says `There are 1 truck(s)`. Now just keep hitting `Count`. You should see the count increase: 1, 2, 3, and so on. That's coming from the `static` properties keeping track of the total number of trucks. So, it's smart enough to realize that 15 `Truck` objects, for example, have been made and that the `static` property keeps track of all those objects.

# Closing IS Express (Windows users)

For Windows users, if you unload this from memory by clicking on the brown square button, notice that in the taskbar, the IIS Express icon is still there, as shown in *Figure 6.4.5*. So, if you launch this again, enter Honda and hit Count. It is keeping track of them between page loads. So beware of that.

Figure 6.4.5: IIS Express remained active, even when the program was unloaded from memory

To clear this so that it goes back to 1, what do you do? You unload the program, click on the **IIS Express** icon in the taskbar, and where it says Stop Site, you select that. Alternatively, you can exit it completely, as shown in the following screenshot:

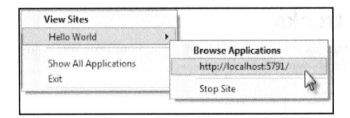

Figure 6.4.6: Exiting or stopping IIS Express in Windows

Alright, once you exit this, the Internet Information Services stuff is shut down, and when you launch, enter Honda and hit Count. It will go back to 1. Alright, so keep this in mind-- that's how you can clear it so that you start back at 1, if that's your objective.

# Documenting your program

Alright, so these are the basics. Let's review what we have made here and add comments:

1. We have a `Truck` class, but then we have a `private` string make, so we should add the following comment to the end of this line:

   ```
   //make of truck
   ```

2. Next, you have a class level field. This means that you call it directly through the class name, so add the comment below `private static int count`, which in this case keeps track of the total number of instances of a class, that is, the total number of trucks that have been made:

   ```
   //class level field
   ```

3. Now add the following comment to the end of the `make = name` line:

   ```
   //set instance field
   ```

4. Next, add the following comment to the end of the `count++` line:

   ```
   //increment instance count
   ```

   line increments the instance count in the number of trucks that have been made.

5. Note that `public static int TruckCount` is a `static` property, so its purpose is as follows. Add the comment that follows above `public static int TruckCount`:

   ```
   //control access to static field with static property
   ```

6. Now, back in the `Default.aspx.cs` page, at the end of the `Truck tr = new Truck(TextBox1.Text)` line, add the following comments:

```
//make a new truck
//use static property below with Truck.TruckCount
//name of class.name of static property
```

- Remember, `Truck` is the name of the class, which has member access, and then `TruckCount`. So, the basic logic is `.` (dot) and then the name of the `static` property. You can also do this with fields, but fields are usually protected, so fields are private, and properties are used to control access to the fields.

This summarizes the basics of these concepts.

# Lesson review

For review, a complete version of `Truck.cs` for this lesson is displayed in the following code block:

```
/// <summary>
/// Summary description for Truck
/// </summary>
public class Truck
{
    private string make;//make of truck
    private static int count;//class level field
    public Truck(string name)
    {
        make = name;//set instance field
        count++;//increment instance count
    }
    //control access to static field with static property
    public static int TruckCount
    {
        get
        {
            return count;
        }
    }
}
```

The complete version of `Default.aspx.cs` for this lesson is displayed in the following code block:

```
//using is a directive
//System is a name space
//name space is a collection of features that our needs to run
using System;
//public means accessible anywhere
//partial means this class is split over multiple files
//class is a keyword and think of it as the outermost level of grouping
//:System.Web.UI.Page means our page inherits the features of a Page
public partial class _Default : System.Web.UI.Page
{
    protected void Button1_Click(object sender, EventArgs e)
    {
        Truck tr = new Truck(TextBox1.Text);//make a new truck
                    //use static property below with Truck.TruckCount
                    //name of class.name of static property
        sampLabel.Text = $"There are {Truck.TruckCount} truck(s).";
    }
}
```

# Summary

In this lesson, you learned about `static` fields and then `static` properties that could be used to access those fields. You also learned about what happens when you shut down IIS Express. You created a `public Truck` class, used it to count trucks by make, and finished by going back and documenting your program.

In the next lesson, you're going to learn about the basics of inheritance. You will be focusing solely on the concept of a relationship between a parent class and a child class. You will also focus on the concept of centralizing code so that it doesn't have to be written multiple times.

# 38

# Centralizing Common Code with Inheritance

In this lesson, you're going to learn about the basics of inheritance. We will focus solely on the concept of inheritance as a relationship between a parent class and a child class. You will also learn about the concept of centralizing code so that it does not have to be written multiple times.

## Setting up the interface for this lesson

Alright, so now think of a project. The basic HTML for this project is shown in the following screenshot:

```
1  <%@ Page Language="C#" AutoEventWireup="true" CodeFile="Default.aspx.cs" Inherits="_Default" %>
2
3  <!DOCTYPE html>
4
5  <html xmlns="http://www.w3.org/1999/xhtml">
6  <head runat="server">
7      <title>Our First Page</title>
8  </head>
9  <body>
10     <form id="form1" runat="server">
11
12     <div> style="text-align: center;">
13         <asp:Label ID="sampLabel" runat="server" </asp:Label>
14     <div>
15
16     </form>
17 </body>
18 </html>
19
```

Figure 6.5.1: The basic HTML for the project in this lesson

The first thing that we are going to do is add files. Go to **Solution Explorer**, right-click on the name of the website, select **Add**, and then click on **Class**. Name the Vehicles class and then click on **OK**. When the Visual Studio message comes up, click on **Yes**.

# Creating the Vehicles class file

Now we have a basic class called Vehicles, as shown in the following screenshot:

```
/// <summary>
/// Summary description for Vehicles
/// </summary>
public class Vehicles
{

    public Vehicles()
    {
        //
        // TODO: Add constructor logic here
        //
    }
}
```

Figure 6.5.2: Public class Vehicles

Every vehicle virtually has two things: A make, which is whether it's a Honda or a Ford, and the model, for example, Accord, Focus, and so on. So, you have a Honda Accord, Ford Focus, and so on.

# Introducing instance variables

Now enter the following beneath the open bracket under public class Vehicles:

```
private string make;
private string model;
```

These are two **instance variables** placed inside the Vehicles class.

Let's make the constructor here. So now you're going to type this after the preceding lines:

```
public Vehicles(string mk, string mod)
```

This is a **parametrized constructor**. You have to set the instance variables inside it. So type the following between curly braces beneath this line:

```
make = mk; model = mod;
```

So, to review, add the following comment as shown. These are two instance variables:

```
private string make; //instance variables
```

Inside the constructor, you set the instance variables. So, enter the following comment directly above the `public Vehicles` constructor line:

```
//set instance variables inside constructor
```

# Writing a function to get the make of a vehicle

The next thing that we are going to do is write a function. So, below the closed parentheses under instance variables, enter the following:

```
public string GetMake()
```

This line will get the make of a vehicle. Between curly braces below this line, enter the following:

```
return make;
```

That's it. Since `public string GetMake()` is a function, it's `public` and accessible anywhere. Enter the following comment above it:

```
//make function to get vehicle make
```

So that's our basic code. This is a `Vehicles` class. Alright, that's it for the class.

Now let's clean this up, so right-click on any of the `using System` lines above and select **Organize Usings > Remove Unnecessary Usings**.

# Creating the Truck class file

Now we're going to make a class called `Truck`. So, enter the following at the bottom of the `Vehicles.cs` file:

```
public class Truck : Vehicles
```

Because a truck is a kind of vehicle, it possesses the common features of a vehicle, such as tires, steering wheel, brakes, and so on. We say `public class Truck` inherits from `Vehicles`. Here, in this context, the colon symbol (`:`) means inherits. Alright? So `Truck` inherits from `Vehicles`.

Therefore, `Truck` is a kind of vehicle. Notice that if you hover your mouse over the word `Truck` in the line, it indicates that you now have to make a constructor, as shown in the following screenshot:

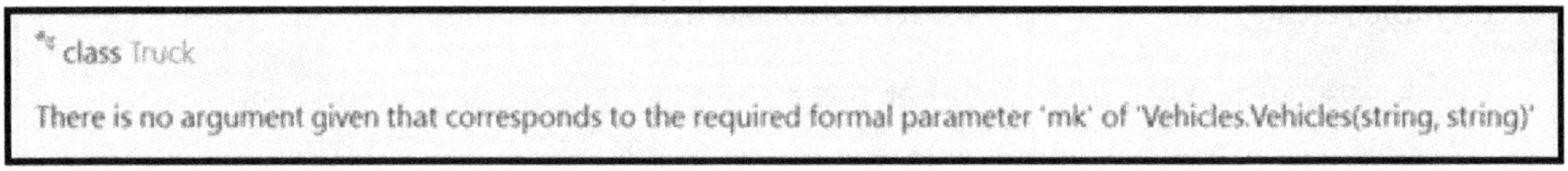

Figure 6.5.3: Pop-up tip indicating that you now have to make a constructor

Now, between curly braces within the body that follows this line, enter the following:

```
public Truck(string mk, string mod) : base(mk, mod) { }
```

The big idea here is *centralization*. Because we have a class `Truck`--a truck is a kind of vehicle--we can make use of the fields we just saw under `public class Vehicles`, as they are also accessible in the `Truck` class. So, after `public Truck(string mk, string mod)`, put a colon (`:`) as shown earlier, and then type `base(mk, mod)`. This will have the effect of calling the base class constructor. In other words, `Truck` is a kind of vehicle, so when I make `Truck`, I don't have to write the `make = mk; model = mod` line. Rather, I can make use of it as it's defined inside `Vehicles`.

So, I'm reusing the following right block of code:

```
public Vehicles(string mk, string mod)
{
    make = mk; model = mod;
}
```

It's written one time, and I don't have to create it again. Right? That's a benefit of inheritance.

In the next stage in the code, we also want to make use of `GetMake`. One way of doing it is to enter the following below the `public Truck` line:

```
public string GetTruckMake()
```

Again, you don't have to recreate the code. You can just enter the following below this line:

```
base.GetMake();
```

So, to repeat, we are calling the base class, that is, the `make` function or the `GetMake` function in this case.

If you want, when you hover your mouse over this line, you can have a list. Do you see where it says **Name can be simplified?** You can click on the lightbulb, and the message shown in *Figure 6.5.4* pops up. You don't even need the base; you can just call it directly without it. **Click on the Simplify member access 'base.GetMake'**, message, and it changes it to return `GetMake()`:

```
return GetMake();
```

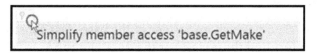

Figure 6.5.4: Pop-up tip indicating that the name can be simplified

Remember, we are now reusing this `GetMake` function so that we don't have to code it separately inside the `Truck` class.

# Creating the sedan class file

Now, to emphasize these points, let's add one more class called `Sedan`. To do this, copy (*Ctrl+C*) the `public class Truck : Vehicles` block and paste it (*Ctrl+V*) to declare a new class. Alright, now if you click on **Truck** in the newly pasted line, notice that this is instructive too because it says that the namespace, that is, the global namespace, indicates that this file already contains a definition for Truck, as seen in Figure 6.5.5. Then, we would have multiple classes with the same name. So let's change the name of this public class to Sedan.

Figure 6.5.5: Pop-up warning that the file already contains a definition for Truck

We'll call ours `Sedan`. Again, `public class Sedan : Vehicles` means that since a sedan is a vehicle, it inherits from the `Vehicles` class.

Now, between curly braces within the body that follows this line, enter the following:

```
public Sedan(string mk, string mod) : base(mk, mod) { }
public string GetSedanMake()
```

Notice that other than changing `Truck` to `Sedan`, the rest of it is exactly the same, except `GetSedanMake`. That's it!

So, to review, remember the big idea. We have a class called `Vehicles`, two instance variables, namely a make and a model, a constructor, and a function. OK, `public string GetMake()` specifically is what we call an **accessor function** because it accesses, that is, it reads the value of the make.

We have a class called `Truck`, which makes use of the base class constructor, and it also makes use of the `make` function (base class) or the `GetMake` function. Then, we have another class called `Sedan`, which also makes use of the base class constructor, and we have `GetSedanMake`, which makes use of `GetMake` in the base class `Vehicles`.

# The structure of our program

OK, so please understand why we have designed this structure here. `Vehicles` is a class. We've got a lot of stuff here: two instance variables, a constructor, and a function. These features can be reused in the child classes. They don't need to be recoded.

Now go to **Solution Explorer**, right-click on **Vehicles.cs**, and select View Class Diagram. This is kind of instructive here. In the following screenshot, you can visualize the relationships among the classes in this project:

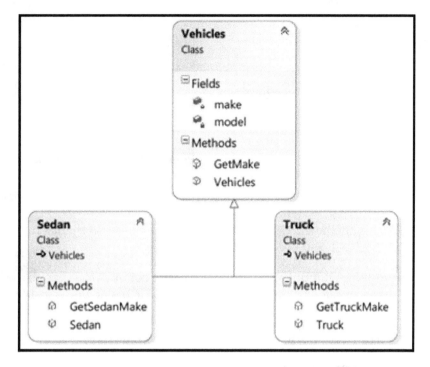

Figure 6.5.6: The relationships among the three classes in this project

You can see **Vehicles** is at the top and then **Sedan** and **Truck** inherits from it. The classes are linked by inheritance lines. Whatever class is being defined, the box can be expanded to reveal the information displayed in the figure. For example, in the **Vehicles** class, you can see the **make** and **model**, right? There you go. And the items under the classes shown can also be called through the base class using the base keyword because the code is centralized inside Vehicles.

# Designing the interface for user input

Alright, so with this in place, to make use of this structure, we're going to go to `Default.aspx` and do the following. First, I'm going to place `TextBox` below `form id= line`. Type the following:

```
Enter Sedan Make and Model: <asp: TextBox ID="SedanBox" runat="server"><
/asp:TextBox><br />
```

We start this line by showing as many useful things as possible. Then, following `Enter Sedan Make and Model:`, place the `TextBox` control, making sure to put in a `<br>` tag at the end of the line.

Now repeat this for `Truck`, as follows:

```
Enter Truck Make and Model: <asp: TextBox ID="TruckBox" runat="server"><
/asp:TextBox><br />
```

Alright, now you're going to put a `Button` control next to the following code:

```
<asp:Button ID="Button1" runat="server" Text="GetMake"
OnClick="Button1_Click" /><br />
```

Now, the only function of the `Button` control is to get the make. So change the `Text` property from `Button` to `GetMake`.

Below this in the form, we'll input stuff into the box with commas to separate the input types: the `Sedan` make model inside one box and the `Truck` make model inside the other box.

Let's go to the **Design** view. The basic interface is shown in the following screenshot:

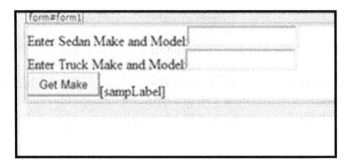

Figure 6.5.7: Our basic interface in Design view

You can get rid of the centering by deleting the two `<div>` tags in `Default.aspx`. We don't need them--they don't matter to us. Alright. So, the basic code for the user interface is now shown in the following screenshot:

```
1  <%@ Page Language="C#" AutoEventWireup="true" CodeFile="Default.aspx.cs" Inherits="_Default" %>
2
3  <!DOCTYPE html>
4
5  <html xmlns="http://www.w3.org/1999/xhtml">
6  <head runat="server">
7      <title>Our First Page</title>
8  </head>
9  <body>
10     <form id="form1" runat="server">
11     Enter Sedan Make and Model: <asp: TextBox ID="SedanBox" runat="server">< /asp:TextBox><br />
12     Enter Truck Make and Model: <asp: TextBox ID="TruckBox" runat="server">< /asp:TextBox><br />
13     <asp:Button ID="Button1" runat="server" Text="GetMake" OnClick="Button1_Click" /><br />
14
15     <asp:Label ID="sampLabel" runat="server" </asp:Label>
16
17
18     </form>
19  </body>
20  </html>
21
```

Figure 6.5.8: The basic code for the user interface

Back in the **Design** view, left double-click on the `GetMake` button. (You don't need the `protected void Page_Loaded` code, so get rid of it.) Take a look at the following screenshot. This is where we will make use of everything.

```
{
    protected void Button1_Click(object sender, EventArgs e)
    {

    }
}
```

Figure 6.5.9: Here is where you will enter and make use of everything you've set up until now

If you wanted to, and as shown in the HTML in *Figure 6.5.8*, you could rename `TextBox1` to `SedanBox` because it's more meaningful, and then likewise, rename `TextBox2` in the line below it to `TruckBox`.

# Creating an array of strings

The first thing to do is this: we're going to make an array of strings. First, we will start with the `Sedan` string as follows:

```
string[] sedanMakeModel = SedanBox.Text.Split(new char[] { ',' });
```

The `','` symbol will have the effect of splitting the input in the box into separate words because you're going to put the make and the model inside one box with a comma separating them. This will split into a string array.

Now, let's repeat this for `Truck`, right below the following line:

```
string[] truckMakeModel = TruckBox.Text.Split(new char[] { ',' });
```

# Displaying the results

To make use of this means the following: to display it to the user, for example, you can say that you have to make the objects and display them. Now you can enter the following:

```
Truck tr = new Truck(truckMakeModel[0], truckMakeModel[1]);
```

Start with `Truck tr = new Truck`. Then, you want to initialize the make and the model, so you're going to say `truckMakeModel`, index 0, `truckMakeModel`, index 1, and then close with a semicolon. That's it!

It's going to initialize the truck, then you repeat this for `Sedan`. So basically, it's the same code. Be sure to change the words so that they are appropriate for `Sedan`, as follows:

```
Sedan sed = new Sedan(sedanMakeModel[0], sedanMakeModel[1]);
```

So again, we get the make and the model for each vehicle. Also, remember to change from `tr` for `Truck` to `sed` for `Sedan`--something like that.

Now to display them, you can type the following:

```
sampLabel.Text = $"Your sedan is a {sed.GetSedanMake()}";
```

> One of the members you can now see in the pop-up list is called **GetMake**. If you want, you can do it that way, as it comes from the `Vehicles` class, or you can use `GetSedanMake` as well. Both of them, in fact, are available.

Now you can repeat this as follows:

```
sampLabel.Text += $" Remember the += accumulates and the br pushes down to
the next line Your truck is a {tr.GetTruckMake()}";
```

Remember, += accumulates and the <br> pushes down to the next line.

# Running the program

So these are the basics. Now, run the program in your browser. Enter Honda, Accord, in the **Enter Sedan Make and Model** box and then enter Ford, Explorer in the **Enter Truck Make and Model box**. Then click on Get Make. The results should look like **Your sedan is a Honda Accord and your truck is a Ford Explorer**, as shown in the following screenshot:

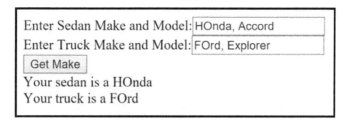

Figure 6.5.10: The results of running our program

That's it! It's working as expected. So these are the basics of this concept.

# Lesson review

For review, a complete version of Vehicles.cs for this lesson is displayed in the following code block:

```
/// <summary>
/// Summary description for Vehicles
/// </summary>
public class Vehicles
{
        private string make;//instance variables
        private string model;
        //set instance variables inside constructor
```

```
        public Vehicles(string mk, string mod)
        {
            make = mk; model = mod;
        }
        //make function to get vehicle make
        public string GetMake()
        {
            return make;
        }
} //truck inherits from Vehicles because it's a kind of vehicle
public class Truck : Vehicles
{
        public Truck(string mk, string mod) : base(mk, mod) { }
        public string GetTruckMake()
        {
            return GetMake();
        }
} //Sedan inherits from Vehicles because it's a kind of vehicle
public class Sedan : Vehicles
{
    public Sedan(string mk, string mod) : base(mk, mod) { }
    public string GetSedanMake()
    {
        return GetMake();
    }
}
```

The complete version of Default.aspx.cs for this lesson is displayed in the following code block:

```
//using is a directive
//System is a name space
//name space is a collection of features that our needs to run
using System;
//public means accessible anywhere
//partial means this class is split over multiple files
//class is a keyword and think of it as the outermost level of grouping
//:System.Web.UI.Page means our page inherits the features of a Page
public partial class _Default : System.Web.UI.Page
{
    protected void Button1_Click(object sender, EventArgs e)
    {
        //get make and model of sedan
        string[] sedanMakeModel = SedanBox.Text.Split(new char[] { ','
        });
        //get make and model of truck
        string[] truckMakeModel = TruckBox.Text.Split(new char[] { ','
        });
```

```
        //make truck with values inside make and model array for trucks
        Truck tr = new Truck(truckMakeModel[0], truckMakeModel[1]);
        //make sedan with values inside make and model array for sedan
        Sedan sed = new Sedan(sedanMakeModel[0], sedanMakeModel[1]);
        //call GetSedanMake and GetTruckMake
        sampLabel.Text = $"Your sedan is a {sed.GetSedanMake()}";
        sampLabel.Text += $"<br>Your truck is a {tr.GetTruckMake()}";
    }
}
```

# Summary

In this lesson, you learned about the basics of inheritance. We focused solely on the concept of inheritance as a relationship between a parent class and a child class. You also learned about the concept of centralizing code so that it does not have to be written multiple times. This lesson showed you as many useful, practical, and valuable things as possible. For example, you created a Vehicles class, learned about instance variables, which were used to input the make and model, and parameterized constructors. You wrote a function to get the make of a vehicle, learned what is an accessor function, created a Truck and Sedan class file, designed the interface for user input, and created an array of strings.

In the next lesson, you're going to learn about **virtual** functions.

# 39

# Centralizing Default Code with Virtual Functions

In this chapter, you're going to learn about virtual functions.

## Setting up a basic HTML for this project

Let's bring up a project. The basic HTML for this project is shown in the following screenshot:

```
1  <%@ Page Language="C#" AutoEventWireup="true" CodeFile="Default.aspx.cs" Inherits="_Default" %>
2
3  <!DOCTYPE html>
4
5  <html xmlns="http://www.w3.org/1999/xhtml">
6  <head runat="server">
7      <title>Our First Page</title>
8  </head>
9  <body>
10     <form id="form1" runat="server">
11
12     <div style="text-align: center;">
13         <asp:Label ID="sampLabel" runat="server"></asp:Label>
14     </div>
15
16     </form>
17 </body>
18 </html>
```

Figure 6.6.1:

# Creating the Vehicle function

So, we're going to talk about vehicles and sedans in particular. What I want you to do is this: Go to **Solution Explorer**, right-click on the name of the website, select **Add**, and then click on **Class**. Name the class Vehicle, then click on **OK**. When the Visual Studio message comes up, click on **Yes**. Bring it into the project. The initial Vehicle class code is shown in the following screenshot:

```
1
2
3
4
5
6   /// <summary>
7   /// Summary description for Vehicle
8   /// </summary>
9   public class Vehicle
10  {
11    public Vehicle()
12    {
13        //
14        // TODO: Add constructor logic here
15        //
16    }
17  }
```

Figure 6.6.2: The initial Vehicle class code

Now, for every vehicle, there's a make, right? Enter the following beneath the open curly bracket under public class Vehicle:

```
private string make;
```

You place this inside the Vehicle class because every vehicle has a make--a Honda, a Ford, and so on. We are going to initialize it in the constructor. First, get rid of the comment lines shown in the figure as you will not need them. Then, type string mk to set the value of the variable inside the parenthesis of the existing line, as follows:

```
public Vehicle(string mk)
```

Between the curly braces beneath the preceding line, enter the following:

```
make = mk;
```

Now, `private string make` is an instance variable, then you have the constructor declared as follows: `public Vehicle(string mk)`. The `make = mk` line is like the instance variable setting within the constructor.

# Writing a virtual function

Now we are going to write the following below the closed curly brace under `make = mk;`:

```
public virtual string ShowInformation()
```

Here, `public` means accessible from anywhere; `string` means the function returns a `string` value, and the name of the string is `ShowInformation`. But what about `virtual`? That's a new keyword. This keyword indicates that this function provides some default functionality and you can make use of this default functionality. But also, in child classes, this function can be refined. So in between curly braces, under `public virtual string ShowInformation`, we will simply enter the following:

```
return $"Make:{make}";
```

This will just get you the make of the vehicle.

Now let's clean this up. Right-click on any of the **using System** lines and select Organize Usings > Remove Unnecessary Usings.

# Using the Virtual function

To make use of this virtual function, you have to make a new class. Enter the following code:

```
public class Sedan : Vehicle
```

Sedans have a make, model, and so on, right? But they perhaps have some more specific information, for example, the number of doors. Some sedans are hatchbacks so they could have five doors. Just to keep things simple, we'll say the following:

```
private int numberOfDoors;
```

Now after the `numberOfDoors` variable is declared, enter the following code:

```
public Sedan(string mk, int doors) : base(mk)
```

Start with `public Sedan`. Then, you need to initialize the make of the sedan, for example, whether it's a Honda, Ford, Subaru, or something like that. To do this, type `(string mk, int doors)`. Now, to see that you can do this, split the initialization as follows:

- Add * : `base(mk)` to pass the make so it could be initialized at the end of the `Sedan` parameterized constructor line
- Then, the number of doors can be initialized within this parameterized constructor (between curly braces):

    - `numberOfDoors = doors;`

For review, this section of the code should appear as follows:

```
private string make;
public Vehicle(string mk)
{
    make = mk;
}
public virtual string ShowInformation()
{
    return $"Make:{make}";
}
public class Sedan : Vehicle
{
    private int numberOfDoors;
    public Sedan(string mk, int doors) : base(mk)
    {
        numberOfDoors = doors;
    }
}
```

This is splitting the initialization of `Sedan` because the `Sedan` constructor, as you can see, will first call the base class constructor, then the `make` value. So set the value, then the number of doors will be set within this body of the code. This means it's being split.

# Overriding a method

Now we are going to override the ShowInformation function. We will say the following inside the scope of the Sedan class:

```
public override string ShowInformation()
```

Notice that ShowInformation() shows up by default in the popup as you type, so select it. When you do so, return base.ShowInformation(); is automatically placed between curly braces below the preceding line. You want to make use of this. You want to use $"Make:{make}"; from the return line in the preceding code. So, you want to call the base class version of ShowInformation because you want to show the make of the vehicle. Then, you're going to make the following refinements:

```
return base .ShowInformation() + " " + $"<br>Number Of
Doors:{numberOfDoors}";
```

In the preceding line, after you write Number Of Doors, you can make another variable called {numberOfDoors}. Enclosed in double quotes, close it with a semicolon.

Notice that the return $"Make:{make}"; virtual function is defined. It has some basic information provided that would be useful to virtually all the vehicles. Next, the overridden version that starts with return base.ShowInformation() calls the base class one because it makes sense. You want to show the make of the vehicle, but then it also adds a touch of refinement if you show the number of doors.

So really, the override in public override string ShowInformation() refers back to the public virtual string ShowInformation() virtual function, which then provides some basic functionality that might be applicable in many cases. Then, an overridden version adds a touch of refinement. There you go!

# Exploring the Vehicle class diagram and the base class object

Again, to call a base class function, type `base`. Then, type the name of the function, just as we've done previously. To make use of all of this class hierarchy, it would be useful if you right-click on **Vehicle.cs** in **Solution Explorer** and select **View Class Diagram**. You will see the class diagram, as shown in the following screenshot:

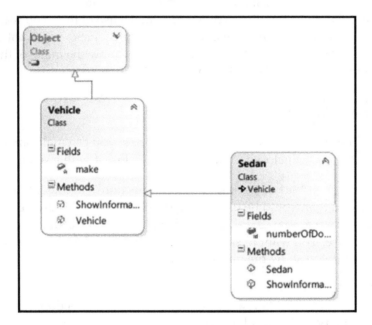

Figure 6.6.3: The Vehicle Class Diagram

You can see that there's a relationship between **Vehicle** and **Sedan**. Also, there's something else about this diagram of which you should be aware. Take a look. We made the `Vehicle` class as the parent class of `Sedan`. Now take an even closer look. If you right-click on **Vehicle** and choose **Show Base Class**, `Object` is the base class. In fact, `Object` is the base class at the root of the entire .NET hierarchy.

What does `Object` provide? If you expand it, you will see all the features that it provides. These are accessible to you as well. For example, when you type `ToString` in a variable, it's coming from here. That is, it's coming from a definite place: `ToString`. Alright, I'm not going to go into it further now, but know that it's present--it's the parent class; it's the root of the entire hierarchy.

So, we have `Object` in this case and `Vehicle` derives from it; then, `Sedan` derives from `Vehicle`.

# Building the user interface

In the next stage, we are going to make use of an interface as well, so go to **Solution Explorer** and open `Default.aspx`. Now, let's make a user interface. Open **Toolbox** and type `tex` for `TextBox` in the search field. Add two text boxes below the `<form>` tag, one for the make and one for the number of doors, as follows:

```
Make:<asp:TextBox ID="TextBox1" runat="server"></asp:TextBox><br />

Door Number: <asp:TextBox ID="TextBox2" runat="server"></asp:TextBox><br />
```

Be sure to separate these with a `<br>` tag.

Next, put a `Button` control below these lines, as follows:

```
<asp:Button ID="Button1" runat="server" Text="Make Vehicle" /><br />
```

Since we're going to make `Vehicles`, change `Text` on `Button` to something more meaningful, such as `Make Vehicle`. There you go! The basic code for the user interface is now shown in the following screenshot:

```
1  <%@ Page Language="C#" AutoEventWireup="true" CodeFile="Default.aspx.cs" Inherits="_Default" %>
2
3  <!DOCTYPE html>
4
5  <html xmlns="http://www.w3.org/1999/xhtml">
6  <head runat="server">
7      <title>Our First Page</title>
8  </head>
9  <body>
10     <form id="form1" runat="server">
11     Make:<asp:TextBox ID="TextBox1" runat="server"></asp:TextBox><br />
12     Door Number: <asp:TextBox ID="TextBox2" runat="server"></asp:TextBox><br />
13     <asp:Button ID="Button1" runat="server" Text="Make Vehicle" OnClick="Button1_Click" /><br />
14     <asp:Label ID="sampLabel" runat="server"></asp:Label>
15
16
17     </form>
18 </body>
19 </html>
```

Figure 6.6.4: Basic code for the user interface

Next, switch to the **Design** view. You have two `TextBox` controllers. Make the `Make Vehicle` button as shown in the following screenshot:

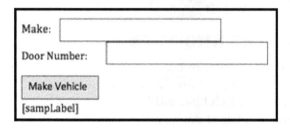

Figure 6.6.5: Our interface in Design view

# Making the Vehicles

Now left double-click on the **Make Vehicle** button and make a vehicle. But first, start by entering `Sedan` between curly braces under `protected void Button1_Click...`. If you go to **Vehicle.cs** and change `public class Sedan : Vehicle` so that it is not `public`, back in `Default.aspx.cs`, if you hover your mouse over `Sedan`, you will see the pop-up message, shown in *Figure 6.6.6*, that in `Sedan` is a type that is not valid in this context; that's why we have this declared `public` in `Vehicle.cs`:

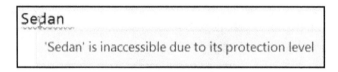

Figure 6.6.6: Message in Default.aspx.cs

Now that the `Sedan` class is accessible inside other classes, you can say the following:

```
Sedan sed = new Sedan(TextBox1.Text, int.Parse(TextBox2.Text));
```

 On the left-hand side, you declare it and on the right-hand side that you actually made it. You bring it into memory.

We get the string we make--let's say, Honda--from the first `TextBox` control and the number of doors from the second `TextBox`. We have to parse it, so we say `int.Parse(TextBox2.Text));`.

This will simply make our `Vehicle` class. Remember, whenever you have nested code, the compiler processes the code from the inside to the outside. So `TextBox2` gets the text. `Parse` converts it into a number and passes it to the constructor. It's the same with `TextBox1`. That's a string already, so we pass it into the constructor from the `Sedan` class.

## Displaying the output

Alright, with that in place, we can display it as follows:

```
sampLabel.Text = sed.ShowInformation();
```

That's it! This is allowed because `Text` is of the type `string` and `ShowInformation` also returns a string. That's why the value is matched correctly in terms of data types.

## Running the program

Now, let's launch it in your browser. Enter a make, such as `Honda`, and it's a four-door vehicle. The result is `Honda Number Of Doors:4`, as shown in the following screenshot:

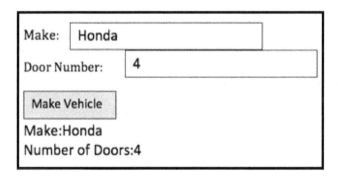

Figure 6.6.7: The result of running our program

So these are the basics of using a virtual function in a somewhat realistic context. Let's have a review at this point because this is a somewhat realistic example. When you look at your files in **Solution Explorer**, you should have the solution file, the website, and the `App Code` folder. Within it, you should have `ClassDiagram`, `Vehicle.cs`, which is your C# code, a `Bin` folder, and `Default.aspx`. The other files are provided by default, and you really don't have to touch them.

# Lesson review

For review, a complete version of the `Vehicle.cs` file for this lesson is displayed in the following screenshot:

```
/// <summary>
/// Summary description for Vehicle
/// </summary>
public class Vehicle
{
    //instance variable
    private string make;
    //vehicle constructor
    public Vehicle(string mk)
    {
        make = mk;
    }
    //virtual function that provides some basic featrues
    public virtual string ShowInformation()
    {
        return $"Make:{make}";
    }
}
public class Sedan : Vehicle
{
    private int numberOfDoors;
    public Sedan(string mk, int doors) : base(mk)
    {
        numberOfDoors = doors;
    }
    //this version overrides the virtual one above
    //it calls the base class function, and adds a touch of
    //refinement
    public override string ShowInformation()
    {
        return base.ShowInformation() + " " + $"<br>Number Of Doors:
        {numberOfDoors}";
    }
}
```

The complete version of the `Default.aspx.cs` file for this lesson is displayed in the following screenshot:

```
//using is a directive
//System is a name space
//name space is a collection of features that our needs to run
using System;
//public means accessible anywhere
//partial means this class is split over multiple files
//class is a keyword and think of it as the outermost level of grouping
//:System.Web.UI.Page means our page inherits the features of a Page
public partial class _Default : System.Web.UI.Page
{
    protected void Button1_Click(object sender, EventArgs e)
    {
        Sedan sed = new Sedan(TextBox1.Text, int.Parse(TextBox2.Text));
        sampLabel.Text = sed.ShowInformation();
    }
}
```

# Summary

In this lesson, you learned about virtual functions. You created a `Vehicle` class, used a `virtual` keyword, overrode a method, learned about the base class object, built the user interface, and wrote the code to make the vehicles and display the output when you ran the program.

In the next lesson, you're going to learn about abstract classes, which are classes that represent abstract concepts.

# 40
# Model Concepts with Abstract Classes

In this chapter, you're going to learn about `abstract` classes. These are classes that represent abstract concepts.

## Introducing the basic HTML for this lesson's project

Let's take a look at the implementation. The following is an illustration of our basic HTML file:

```
 1  <%@ Page Language="C#" AutoEventWireup="true" CodeFile="Default.aspx.cs" Inherits="_Default" %>
 2
 3  <!DOCTYPE html>
 4
 5  <html xmlns="http://www.w3.org/1999/xhtml">
 6  <head runat="server">
 7      <title>Our First Page</title>
 8  </head>
 9  <body>
10      <form id="form1" runat="server">
11
12          <asp:Label ID="sampLabel" runat="server"></asp:Label>
13
14      </form>
15  </body>
16  </html>
```

Figure 6.7.1: The basic starting HTML for this project

# Adding the ThreeDShapes class

First, let's add a class. Go to **Solution Explorer**, right-click on the name of the website, select **Add**, and click on **Class**. Name the class `ThreeDShapes` and click on **OK**. When the Visual Studio message comes up, click on **Yes**. There you go! We have `public class ThreeDShapes`. The relevant portion of the initial `ThreeDShapes` class code is shown in the following screenshot:

```
1 public class ThreeDShapes
2 {
3      public ThreeDShapes()
4      {
5
6
7
8      }
9 }
```

Figure 6.7.2: The initial ThreeDShapes class code

# Introducing abstract classes

Now we're going to make `ThreeDShapes` an `abstract` class because we're going to be dealing with the concept of a three-dimensional shape, such as a cube, cylinder, or sphere. However, each of these shapes is very different. So, specifically, the way that you calculate the volume of these shapes differs drastically. We have the concept of a three-dimensional object, but the specifics, that is, the calculational specifics, vary widely.

It's a concept, and we are going to make it `abstract`. So currently where it says `public class`, change it as follows:

```
public abstract class ThreeDShapes
```

We don't need the constructor here. Starting with the `public ThreeDShapes()` line and on down, you can delete it.

There's more to this, but I'll show you the basics. Enter the following in curly braces below `public abstract class ThreeDShapes`:

```
public abstract double GetVolume();
```

The abstract keyword, as you can see, means that no limitations are provided; therefore, this makes sense. After all, when you move over, for example, from a sphere to a cube to a cylinder and so on, the volumes that are found vary drastically. It doesn't make sense to provide any default implementation.

If you can think of some default code that's sensible, go with a virtual function. If you can't, go with an abstract one, like the one we are discussing in this section..

Let's clean this up. Right-click on all the using System lines above and select **Organize Usings > Remove Unnecessary Usings**. Let's add this one at the top:

```
using static System.Math;
```

Notice that at first, the preceding code is grayed out because it's not being used yet, but it will be used momentarily and then it will be darker.

# Determining volumes

Now to make use of our simple abstract class in the context of two other classes, we're going to start by using the code we'll discuss in the next section below public abstract double GetVolume.

# Calculating the volume of a sphere

```
public class Sphere : ThreeDShapes
```

Sphere inherits from ThreeDShapes. One of the defining characteristics of a sphere is radius, that is, the distance between the center and a point on the surface. Now type the following between curly braces under the preceding line of code:

```
private double radius;
```

Then you can initialize the following code, so you can type the following directly beneath it:

```
public Sphere(double r)
```

Now, within curly braces below the following line, you can set the value of radius. Enter the following:

```
radius = r;
```

This sets the instance variable for this particular sphere. Notice that the word `Sphere` in the preceding `public class Sphere : ThreeDShapes` line has a squiggly line underneath it. If you hover your mouse over **Sphere**, it will show the following message:

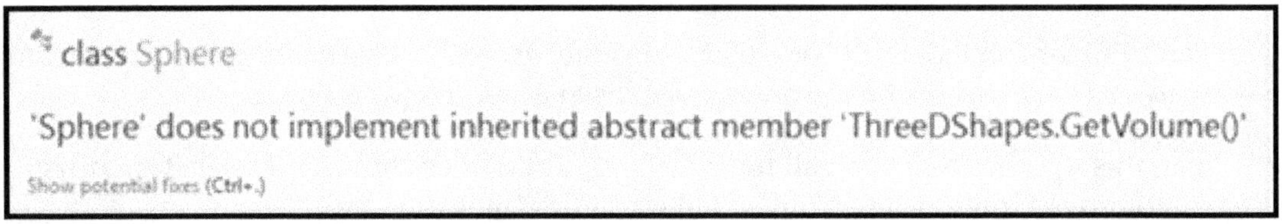

Figure 6.7.3: Error message for class Sphere

If you click on the **Show potential fixes** link in the lower-left corner of the message, it will even show you what to do, as you can see in the following screenshot:

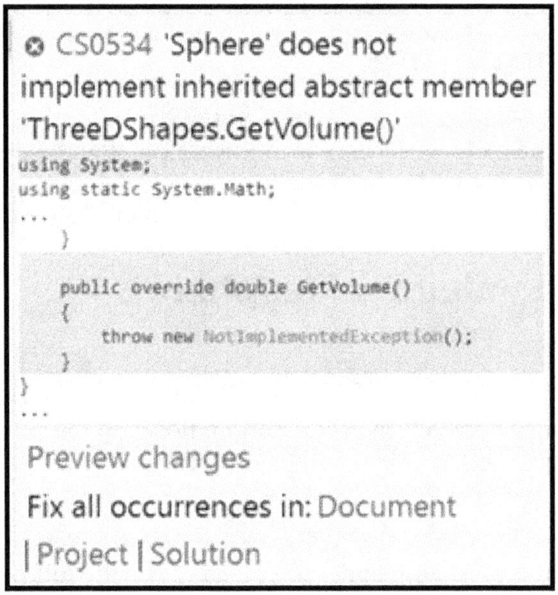

Figure 6.7.4: Potential fixes to problem displayed in Figure 6.7.3

Click on the box that says **public override double**, shown in *Figure 6.7.4*, and it provides an override. Delete the line that says **throw new NotImplementedException();**. We don't want this. We actually want to provide an implementation that's useful, one that will return a result. So enter the following between curly braces below `public override double GetVolume()`.

# Taking advantage of the radius using the static System.Math

For a sphere, the volume is calculated as follows:

```
return (4.00) / (3.00) * PI * Pow(radius, 3);
```

The `Pow` keyword is short for the power function. In this case, you're going to take `radius` of the sphere and cube it, so `radius`, 3 is the same as radius$^3$. This means that the radius length is raised to the third power or multiplied by itself three times.

If I do not insert `using static System.Math;` at the top of the `ThreeDShapes.cs` file, then I will not be able to use `PI` in this line of code. Instead, I would have to type `Math.PI`. But because I added the `using static System.Math;` line, I don't need `Math` in front of `PI`; I can just write `PI`.

Of course, you can extend this. Besides `spheres`, for example, you can easily visualize real-world uses of spheres, such as a basketball or globe.

# Calculating the volume of a cube

A cube is like a box where all the edges are of equal length. First, enter the following beneath the `Sphere` class:

```
public class Cube : ThreeDShapes
```

Clearly, a cube is a kind of three-dimensional object. Next, in open curly braces beneath the preceding line, enter the following:

```
private double edge;
```

Directly below this line, you can configure the cube as follows:

```
public Cube(double edgeLength)
```

In the preceding line, `edgeLength` is the name of the parameter.

Now, between curly braces below the preceding line, enter the following to set the value:

```
edge = edgeLength;
```

Now we have to implement `GetVolume` for cubes. To do this, type the following in closed curly braces after the preceding line:

```
public override double GetVolume()
```

This provides a default implementation, not a `NotImplementedException` error. You can delete the preceding line. We'll talk about it later. For our purposes, you can now say the following within curly braces below the preceding line:

```
return Pow(edge, 3);
```

Note that as you type `Pow()`, the pop-up tip says `(double x, double y)`. In our case, this means `(edge, 3)`.

Alright, to find the volume of a cube, multiply the edge by itself three times. In other words, it's like edge-cubed. That's it!

For review, a complete version of our basic class hierarchy (including comments) for this lesson, `ThreeDShapes.cs`, is displayed in the following code block:

```
//because we have System.Math, we can type
//Pow(...) instead of Math.Pow(...)
using static System.Math;
//class represents a concept
public abstract class ThreeDShapes
{
    //all 3d shapes have volume, so makes sense to have
    //a function that represents this abstract concept
    public abstract double GetVolume();
} //Sphere inherits from ThreeDShapes
public class Sphere : ThreeDShapes
{
    private double radius;
    public Sphere(double r)
    {
        radius = r;
    }
    //this function provides a highly specific implementation of GetVolume
    public override double GetVolume()
    {
        return (4.00) / (3.00) * PI * Pow(radius, 3);
    }
} //Cube inherits from ThreeDShapes
public class Cube : ThreeDShapes
{
    private double edge;
    public Cube(double edgeLength)
```

```
    {
        edge = edgeLength;
    }
    //this provides a highly specific implementation of GetVolume
    public override double GetVolume()
    {
        return Pow(edge, 3);
    }
}
```

If you want, you can do this with the `abstract` class at the top, but the `abstract` class is more application-specific. Furthermore, it helps to bind your code into a more hierarchically and logically connected structure.

Notice that the `using System` directive is still grayed out, so right-click on it and remove this one too. Still, `using static System.Math` is necessary. Then, we have an `abstract` class because it represents an `abstract` concept, then `Sphere` inherits from `ThreeDShapes` because it is a kind of a 3D shape.

Next, the defining characteristic for spheres is the `radius` variable, so set the `radius` variable inside the constructor. Then, override `GetVolume` to provide a concrete implementation. This means specific mathematical detail, such as `return (4.00) / (3.00) * PI * Pow(radius, 3);`. Repeat this in the next call for cubes, using the same logic.

# Entering data

Now, to make use of this, go to `Default.aspx`. First, delete the `<div>` tag lines. Then, we need to read some input, so type the following below the form line:

```
Enter Sphere Radius:<asp:TextBox ID="TextBox1"
runat="server"></asp:TextBox><br />
```

Put a `TextBox` control there to read the value to the user. Remember to include the `<br>` tag at the end of the line. There you go!

Next, type the following line directly beneath the preceding line:

```
Enter Cube Edge Length:<asp:TextBox ID="TextBox2"
runat="server"></asp:TextBox><br />
```

Next, put in a `Button` control that will calculate this when you click on it. Go to **Toolbox**, type `but` in the search field, and drag it in under the preceding two lines:

```
<asp:Button ID="Button1" runat="server" Text="Find Volumes" /><br />
```

Change the `Text` property on the `Button` control markup to something more meaningful, such as `Find Volumes`, and end with a `<br>` tag. That's it!

So, you have two `TextBox` controls where you will put in a little bit of text, `Button`, and a `Label` control. In the **Design** View, you will see our simple user interface, as shown in the following screenshot:

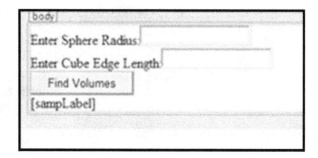

Figure 6.7.6: Our interface in Design view

Now, left double-click on the **Find Volumes** button and go to `Default.aspx.cs` for this lesson. Delete the lines that start with the comment above `protected void Page_Load` so that you can start with `protected void Button1_Click....`

# Making a new sphere

Now we're going to do this. Enter the following between curly braces under `protected void Button1_Click...`, let's make a `Sphere` class object:

```
Sphere sp = new Sphere(double.Parse(TextBox1.Text));
```

Start by typing `Sphere` and call it `sp = new Sphere`. Now we have to initialize the `radius` variable of this `Sphere` class. According to the labels on the boxes in `Default.aspx`, `Enter Sphere Radius` would be `TextBox1`, so we need to say `double.Parse` and then `TextBox1.Text`. Close with a semicolon.

Remember `TextBox1.Text` means to get the text. Parse implies converting it into a numerical value, and `new Sphere` indicates you to actually make a new `Sphere` object.

# Making a new cube

You can repeat this for the cube using the same logic. So, just select this line, copy (*Ctrl+C*) the code, and paste (*Ctrl+V*) it. You'll need to replace `Sphere` with `Cube` and `new Sphere` with `new Cube`:

```
Cube cb = new Cube(double.Parse(TextBox2.Text));
```

Alright! Now to display the results, enter the following below the preceding line:

```
sampLabel.Text = "Volume of sphere is " + sp.GetVolume();
```

You can attach the value by typing +. Notice that the `GetVolume` method shows up as a member function in the pop-up list as you type, so select it. Close with a semicolon.

# Displaying the results

Continue by entering the following below the preceding line:

```
sampLabel.Text += "<br>Volume of cube is " + cb.GetVolume();
```

Because this is a new line of code in this `Label` control, remember to include += and then make sure that you put a `<br>` tag there. So, += appends to the existing text and the `<br>` tag pushes it down the next line. That's it!

# Running the program

Now, let's run the program. Open your browser from `Default.aspx`. If you enter 4 in the sphere radius, 5 as the cube length, and click on the **Find Volumes** button, you will see the results shown in the following screen. So, it's working as expected.

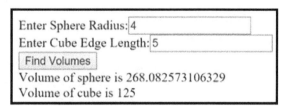

Enter Sphere Radius: 4
Enter Cube Edge Length: 5
Find Volumes
Volume of sphere is 268.082573106329
Volume of cube is 125

Figure 6.7.7: The results of running our program

These are the basics of `abstract` classes, which represent `abstract` concepts. It's something that everybody agrees exists, but here I chose sphere, cube, and so on to work with more concrete classes because there is a specific way of finding the volume of a sphere and a cube. Likewise, the same logic could be used for a cylinder, cone, and so on.

## Lesson review

The complete version of the `Default.aspx.cs` file for this lesson is displayed in the following code block:

```
//using is a directive
//System is a name space
//name space is a collection of features that our needs to run
using System;
//public means accessible anywhere
//partial means this class is split over multiple files
//class is a keyword and think of it as the outermost level of grouping
//:System.Web.UI.Page means our page inherits the features of a Page
public partial class _Default : System.Web.UI.Page
{
    protected void Button1_Click(object sender, EventArgs e)
    {
        //make a new sphere object
        Sphere sp = new Sphere(double.Parse(TextBox1.Text));
        //make a new cube object
        Cube cb = new Cube(double.Parse(TextBox2.Text));
        //display volume of sphere
        sampLabel.Text = "Volume of sphere is " + sp.GetVolume();
        //display volume of cube
        sampLabel.Text += "<br>Volume of cube is " + cb.GetVolume();
    }
}
```

## Summary

In this lesson, you learned about `abstract` classes, which are classes that represent abstract concepts. You created a class called `ThreeDShapes`. You wrote code to calculate the volumes of a sphere and a cube. You studied how to override an error. And finally, you worked with `using static system.math`.

In the next lesson, you're going to learn about how you can return your own data type from a method.

# 41
# Using Custom Types as Return Types

In this lesson, you're going to learn about how you can return a data type from a function. We'll use a data type that we have already made. We'll also take a look at some other things along the way.

## Setting up the project

Start a project, and within the HTML, place the following code in the form. We're going to make a library for music! We're going to make a song library. It will be called `Title 1`. Next to it, we're going to put a `TextBox` control for collecting the names of the songs from the user, for example, or something like that. There you go:

```
Title 1:<asp:TextBox ID="TextBox1" runat="server"></asp:TextBox><br />
```

`Title 2` will be a really simple library consisting of only two songs, as follows:

```
Title 2:<asp:TextBox ID="TextBox2" runat="server"></asp:TextBox><br />
```

Be sure to terminate both the lines with a `<br>` tag.

Of course, one thing that you can do once you have a library is to sort it. For this, put in a `Button` control below these lines:

```
<asp:Button ID="Button1" runat="server" Text="Sort" OnClick="Button1_Click"
/><br />
```

Change the `Text` property in the preceding line from `Button` to `Sort`. End this line with a `<br>` tag. That's it!

You don't need the `<div>` tag lines; delete them. The following screenshot shows what your `Default.aspx` HTML should look like for this project:

```
 1 <%@ Page Language="C#" AutoEventWireup="true" CodeFile="Default.aspx.cs" Inherits="_Default" %>
 2
 3 <!DOCTYPE html>
 4
 5 <html xmlns="http://www.w3.org/1999/xhtml">
 6 <head runat="server">
 7     <title>Our First Page</title>
 8 </head>
 9 <body>
10     <form id="form1" runat="server">
11     Title 1:<asp:TextBox ID="TextBox1" runat="server"></asp:TextBox><br />
12     Title 2:<asp:TextBox ID="TextBox2" runat="server"></asp:TextBox><br />
13         <asp:Button ID="Button1" runat="server" Text="Sort" OnClick="Button1_Click" /><br />
14
15         <asp:Label ID="sampLabel" runat="server"></asp:Label>
16
17
18     </form>
19 </body>
20 </html>
21
```

Figure 6.8.1: The basic HTML for this project

Our simple user interface in the **Design** view is shown in the following screenshot:

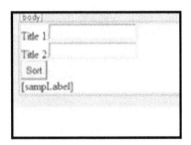

Figure 6.8.2: The basic HTML for this project

# Creating the SongLibrary class

Now, we're going to make the `SongLibrary` class in C#. As an example, go to **Solution Explorer**, right-click on the name of the website, select **Add**, and then click on **Class**. Name the `SongLibrary` class and then click on **OK**. When the Visual Studio message comes up, click on **Yes**.

The relevant portion of the initial SongLibrary class code looks like the following:

```
 9 public class SongLibrary
10 {
11      public SongLibrary()
12      {
13
14
15
16      }
17 }
```

Figure 6.8.3: The initial SongLibrary class code

We'll go through the process of entering a block of code one line at a time. Start by entering the following from the top:

```
using System;
public class SongLibrary
{
    private string[] songs;
    public SongLibrary(string[] tunes)
    {
        songs = tunes;
    }
}
```

Because the preceding code is somewhat sophisticated, we're going to do the following:

1. Start by deleting all of the default code that the program puts in.
2. Now the only thing that you need on top is using System; it's the only namespace that you need.
3. Next, we're going to make the class of type public, so after the using System namespace declaration type public class SongLibrary, followed by a set of curly braces.
4. Then, make an instance variable, which is an array of strings. You can type private string[] songs;.
5. To initialize this, we'll type public SongLibrary(string[] tunes), again followed by a set of curly braces.
6. Then, take the songs and set them equal to the tunes using songs = tunes;.

So, we have an instance variable that's an array of strings, the titles of the songs, and a constructor of the library that sets the library. This completes the steps for creating the library.

# Sorting SongLibrary

In the next stage, within the `SongLibrary` class we'll create a new function that will sort the library; enter the following:

```
public SongLibrary SortLibrary()
```

In this case, notice that the return type of this function is `SongLibrary`, so it operates and then returns `SongLibrary`--it has been sorted in some way. So, let's simulate the sorting process. Now enter the following within the preceding function:

```
Array.Sort(songs);
```

Notice that as you type in `songs`, the songs array is accessible from the pop-up list.

Now type the following beneath `Array.Sort(songs);` line:

```
return this;
```

The word `this` in the preceding line refers to the current object.

The current object, the current instance of the `SongLibrary` class, has the songs array accessible from the lines in the preceding code: `private string[] songs`, `songs = tunes`, and `Array.Sort(songs)`. When I say `this`, it means the current `SongLibrary` object, which appears in the `public class SongLibrary`, `public SongLibrary(string[] tunes)`, and `public SongLibrary SortLibrary()` lines. Lastly, we return the value of the `songs` array with a `return this;` statement. If you hover your mouse over this, the popup says **class SongLibrary**, so it matches the return type above `SongLibrary`. Do you see that?

# Check it yourself

Your code for `SongLibrary.cs` up to this point should be as follows:

```
using System;
public class SongLibrary
{
    private string[] songs;
    public SongLibrary(string[] tunes)
```

```
    {
        songs = tunes;
    }
    public SongLibrary SortLibrary()
    {
        Array.Sort(songs);
        return this ;
    }
}
```

# Displaying the song library

Now let's add one more function here. So besides sorting the library, of course, you can also display it. So we'll make a function that displays stuff now and call it `DisplaySongs`. Add the following after the `SortLibrary` function:

```
public string DisplaySongs()
```

Next, within curly braces, enter the following:

```
string list = null;
```

Right below the preceding line, make a foreach loop as follows:

```
foreach (var str in songs)
```

Again, notice that `songs` is accessible from the pop-up list as you type. So, for each variable string in the `songs` array, or basically for each song, what we're going to do is build a display. To do this, type the following within curly braces:

```
list += $"<br>{str}";
```

This will display a string that represents all the things inside the `songs` array. At the end, you can return this, so you can say the following after the closed curly brace:

```
return list;
```

That's it! For review, the final version of `SongLibrary.cs`, including comments, is shown in the following code block:

```
using System; //namespace import
public class SongLibrary //name of our type
{
    private string[] songs; //instance varialbe is an array
    public SongLibrary(string[] tunes)
    {
```

```
        songs = tunes;//set instance variable through parameter
    }
    public SongLibrary SortLibrary()
    {
        Array.Sort(songs);//sort songs array
        return this;//return sorted song library
    }
    public string DisplaySongs()
    {
        string list = null;//make string null at first
        foreach (var str in songs)
        {
            list += $"<br>{str}";//build up results
        }
        return list;//return list
    }
}
```

The preceding code block is our `SongLibrary`, really a basic one--a constructor, a couple of functions, and so on. Of course, you can create other ones that would allow you to, for example, search for a certain sequence of characters within a song title. Also, if you have some experience in C#, there are things called lists, which are more flexible than arrays. We will examine lists in the next lesson.

Now, we move on to the next stage. We'll go to the `Default.aspx` file and go to the **Design** view where you'll see the interface we created earlier, as shown in *Figure 6.8.2*. Now left double-click on the **Sort** button. Of course, this takes you to the `Default.aspx.cs` screen. You can get rid of the event handler that appears on this screen.

Enter the following block of code, after the open curly brace under the `protected void Button1_Click` line:

```
string [] songs = new string[] { TextBox1.Text, TextBox2.Text };
SongLibrary songLib = new SongLibrary(songs);
songLib.SortLibrary();
sampLabel.Text = songLib.DisplaySongs();
}
}
```

I'd enter the preceding block of code, one line at a time.

1. Make an array of strings, which consists of the song titles.
2. Then, make a new `SongLibrary` object in the next line, and to initialize it, pass in the array, that is, `songs`.

3. Now, let's sort the library in the next line. (Notice as you type that `SortLibrary` is a member in the pop-up list that appears, so select it.)
4. Now to display the results, type the `sampLabel.Text` line followed by `songLib.DisplaySongs();`.

So, in other words, we've offloaded the displaying of the songs, that is, the building of the string that represents this, into the `SongLibrary` class, which is where it really belongs. We've written some custom code here to accomplish this. There you go!

# Running the program

So, let's view this now in a browser and take a look at the results:

Figure 6.8.5: The results of running our program

For **Title 1**, I entered wake me up by Avicii and then cry cry baby. When I hit the **Sort** button, you see that it shows cry cry baby first below the `Title` fields and wake me up second, so it's acting as expected. It's sorting the music.

# Lesson review

The complete version of the `Default.aspx.cs` file for this lesson is displayed in the following code block:

```
//using is a directive
//System is a name space
//name space is a collection of features that our needs to run
using System;
//public means accessible anywhere
//partial means this class is split over multiple files
//class is a keyword and think of it as the outermost level of grouping
//:System.Web.UI.Page means our page inherits the features of a Page
public partial class _Default : System.Web.UI.Page
```

```
    {
        protected void Button1_Click(object sender, EventArgs e)
        {
            //songs array made from text boxes
            string[] songs = new string[] { TextBox1.Text, TextBox2.Text };
            //pass songs array into constructor of SongLibrary
            SongLibrary songLib = new SongLibrary(songs);
            //sort the library
            songLib.SortLibrary();
            //display the sorted songs
            sampLabel.Text = songLib.DisplaySongs();
        }
    }
```

# Summary

In this lesson, you learned about how to return a data type from a function using a data type that you made. You created the `SongLibrary` class and wrote functions to sort the song library and display the results.

In the next lesson, you're going to learn about lists.

# 42
# Using Lists to Operate on Data Efficiently

In this lesson, you are going to learn about lists. Lists are more flexible than arrays because, with lists, you can size a list dynamically, and perform a great variety of operations easily and efficiently.

## Summarizing the values in a list

Let's start by making three boxes on the page. For this, enter the following in the form:

```
Value 1: <asp: TextBox ID="TextBox1" runat="server">< /asp:TextBox><br />
```

This is where you're going to put the first value. Close this with a `<br>` tag, of course. Then, copy this and paste it beneath the preceding code line. Note that when you're pasting numbers, it automatically changes from `TextBox1` to `TextBox2`. A nice little feature, right? Change this line to start with `Value 2`. Now paste it down below the preceding code line one more time and change this line to start with `Value 3`.

Next, drag a `Button` control below these lines so that somebody can click to summarize the values of the list. We'll define `Summarize` here as, for example, finding the maximum, minimum, average, sum, and so on of the values in the list. We'll do this just to illustrate some of the functions that can be applied to lists very easily.

Now change the `Text` property in the `Button` markup; change this to, say, `Summarize`. Again, add a `<br>` tag. Your `Default.aspx` screen should now look like the following screenshot:

```
1 <%@ Page Language="C#" AutoEventWireup="true" CodeFile="Default.aspx.cs"
Inherits="_Default" %>
2
3 <!DOCTYPE html>
4
5 <html xmlns="http://www.w3.org/1999/xhtml">
6 <head runat="server">
7     <title>Our First Page</title>
8 </head>
9 <body>
10     <form id="form1" runat="server">
11     Value 1: <asp: TextBox ID="TextBox1" runat="server">< /asp:TextBox><br />
12     Value 2: <asp: TextBox ID="TextBox2" runat="server">< /asp:TextBox><br />
13     Value 3: <asp: TextBox ID="TextBox3" runat="server">< /asp:TextBox><br />
14     <asp:Button ID="Button1" runat="server" Text="Summarize" /<br />
15     <asp:Label ID="sampLabel" runat="server" </asp:Label>
16
17
18     </form>
19 </body>
20 </html>
21
```

Figure 6.9.1: Your starting Default.aspx page for this lesson

Click on the **Design** view and you will see the basic user interface, as shown in the following screenshot:

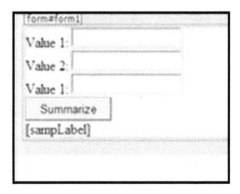

Figure 6.9.2: The basic interface for this lesson

As you can see, there are three boxes for collecting the values and a `Summarize` button. Now, left double-click on the `Summarize` button; this takes you to the `Default.aspx` screen with the event handler code in place.

# Introducing a generic namespace

To make use of lists, you have to introduce a new namespace. The one that concerns us is shown in the following code. Type the following below `using System`:

```
using System.Collections.Generic;
```

# Starting a list of doubles

Now, within curly braces, under `protected void Button1_Click`, type the following:

```
List <double> d = new List<double>();
```

Note that as soon as you type `List<>`, as seen in *Figure 6.9.3*, a tooltip pops up that says `T`. It refers to the type of elements in the list:

List< T >
Represents a strongly typed list of objects that can be accessed by index. Provides methods to search, sort, and manipulate lists.
**T:** *The type of elements in the list.*

Figure 6.9.3: Tooltip pop-up for List<T>

In our case, we are making a list of `doubles`. It's a new notation, but that's fine; it's a list of `doubles`. That's what it means. Let's name the list d, followed by an = sign. Now, on the right-hand side, write `new List<double>()` and close with a semicolon. Notice that the size is not specified. So, one nice thing about lists is that they can grow automatically to accommodate new values. It's a nice feature.

# Filling the list

The next step is to fill the list; add the following beneath the previous line of code:

```
d.Add(Convert.ToDouble(TextBox1.Text));
```

Start with `d.` and then `Add()`. In our case, we need to add `double`. To make this happen, type `Convert.ToDouble` and then write `TextBox1.Text`. Of course, this will convert a number from the inside to the outside. So, we get the text, convert it into `double`, and add it to the list from the inside to the outside. It's the same logic there every single time.

Now press *Ctrl+C* to copy this line and then *Ctrl+V* to paste it down below the previous line of code. Now repeat this for the other boxes and change to `TextBox2` and `Textbox3`, respectively.

# Displaying the max, min, average, and sum

The preceding code will just make the list for us using the `Add` function. And we can display some useful results: max, min, average, and sum. Take a look at how easy all of this can be. The first thing to type, for example, is the following:

```
sampLabel.Text = $"Sum={d.Sum()}";
```

Notice that `Sum` doesn't show up in the pop-up list. So, to populate the list, you need a `generic` namespace. To make use of `Sum`, we're going to introduce a new namespace called `Linq`. Enter the following directly below `using System.Collections.Generic`:

```
using System.Linq;
```

`System.Linq` is a language-integrated query. We'll learn more about these later. For now, this is just the basics. Now when you type, notice that `Sum` shows up in the list. So, you can select it and that's it. Then, we'll find the sum of the list really easy, no more loops of any kind.

We can repeat this, for example, for other quantities that might be of concern for the list, such as, the average of the list. Again, to do this, type the following:

```
sampLabel.Text += $"<br>Average={d.Average()}";
```

When you type `Average` now, notice that it shows up in the list; it's automatically done for you, for the `Average` function.

Let's do a couple more. Let's just see some of the things that are possible. Let's also do, of course, the min and max values. Type the following:

```
sampLabel.Text += $"<br>Min={d.Min()}";
sampLabel.Text += $"<br>Max={d.Max()}";
```

This was so easy, right? Now, remember, the cursor has to move down after the first line accumulates the value; that is why you need to stick in <br> tags before Average, Min, and Max.

Now, let's give this a run just to see the results so far and to make sure that everything is working as expected. Let's launch it. So there are the three boxes, as seen in *Figure 6.9.4*. When you enter some easy values, such as 1, 2, and 3, and hit Summarize, it says Sum=6. You can count them like this: *1+2+3=6*. Next, it says Average=2, which is the value in the middle box, the Minimum=1, and Maximum=3. As you can see, you've been able to do all of this very elegantly and quickly:

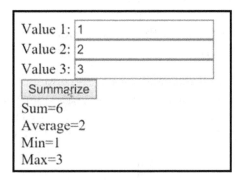

Figure 6.9.4: Our program now calculates the sum, average, min, and max values of items in the list

Clearly, the process we discussed is superior to sitting down and writing your own routines. There are many other things that can be done with lists; for example, see the following.

# Squaring the results

Imagine that you want to perform an action of some kind on each value on your list. Maybe, you want to display the square of the value and subtract it from the average. You do this commonly in statistics, for example. For this, enter the following:

```
d.ForEach(x => sampLabel.Text += $"<br>{x}^2={x * x}");
```

Start by typing d. (d-dot) and then ForEach. Then, there's a particular syntax that says action, as seen on the tooltip popup in the following screenshot:

```
void List<double>.ForEach(Action<double> action)
Performs the specified action on each element of the List<T>.
action: The Action<in T> delegate to perform on each element of the List<T>.
```

Figure 6.9.5: The syntax for action. An action is something that you do

We're going to put x within parentheses. Now this is a bit of a new notation: x followed by an = sign. This, in turn, is immediately followed by an arrow: =>. So basically, you're going to perform some action on each x. In our case, what we can do is say sampLabel.Text += again, followed by the $ symbol and, within double quotes, build up a string. This is really tight code, and works very nicely.

Next, within double quotes, we'll start with a <br> tag and then put x within a set of curly braces. Next, you'll insert ^2, for squared, indicating the square of a number, followed by an = sign. Then, stick in x * x within a second set of curly braces to display the square of x. Close the quotes, close the parentheses, and close the line with a semicolon.

Remember, if it's brown (or orange on a Mac), this means that it shows exactly that way on the screen. If it's within black curly braces (Windows), then it's rendered as the actual value at runtime.

The ForEach(x) statement means grab each x element from the list and then perform sampLabel.Text += $"<br>{x}^2={x * x}");, which means display it. Display the x value and then the square of x, and so on.

Let's take a look at this in your browser, as shown in the following screenshot:

```
Value 1: 1
Value 2: 2
Value 3: 3
 Summarize 
Sum=6
Average=2
Min=1
Max=3
1^2=1
2^2=4
3^2=9
```

Figure 6.9.6: The program now successfully calculates the square of the sum, average, min, and max values of items in the list

When you put in some values, say 1, 2, and 3, the output is as follows: the square of one is 1, the square of two is = 4, and the square of 3 is = 9. So, it's working as expected.

# Nesting lists

If you want, you can nest things. So this is another thing that you can do with lists. Add the following line beneath the previous line of code:

```
d.ForEach(x => sampLabel.Text += $"<br>{x}-{d.Average()}={x -
d.Average()}");
```

Start with d.ForEach. Then imagine that you want to display the value of x minus the average, or something like that. Again, put x within parentheses, followed by the => notation. Then, type sampLabel.Text and += so that it continues to append the $ symbol, open quotes, and then <br>. Post this, type something like x – (minus) the average. So, to find the averages, say {x}-{d.Average()}.

Remember, {x – d.Average()} will show the x value separately, and it will show the Average value separately. Because the negative value is in brown, it will show on the screen as value – (minus) average.

We can actually do the computation that we've put within single curly braces: x – d.Average. Close this with a semicolon. There you go!

You can also nest what we'll discuss next. This code, as you can see, is very tight; it's extremely expressive, and it does a lot without too many lines. Let's run this one more time, as seen in the following screenshot:

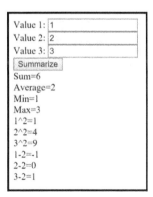

Figure 6.9 7: The program now successfully calculates the square of the sum, average, min, and max values of items in the list

Enter 1, 2, 3 and then hit Summarize. The results now consist of the sum, average, min, max, 1-squared, 2-squared, 3-squared, and then 1 - 2 = -1, 2 - 2 = 0, and 3 - 2 = 1. These are deviations of these values from the average value. These are some of the basics of what you can do with lists.

For review, a complete version of the Default.aspx.cs file for this lesson is displayed in the following code block:

```
//using is a directive
//System is a name space
//name space is a collection of features that our needs to run
using System;
using System.Collections.Generic;//needed for lists
using System.Linq;//needed for functions like Sum
            //public means accessible anywhere
            //partial means this class is split over multiple files
            //class is a keyword and think of it as the outermost level
            //of grouping
            //:System.Web.UI.Page means our page inherits the features of
            //a Page
public partial class _Default : System.Web.UI.Page
{
    protected void Button1_Click(object sender, EventArgs e)
    {
        List<double> d = new List<double>();//make list
        d.Add(Convert.ToDouble(TextBox1.Text));//add values to list
        d.Add(Convert.ToDouble(TextBox2.Text));
        d.Add(Convert.ToDouble(TextBox3.Text));
        sampLabel.Text = $"Sum={d.Sum()}";//show sum of list
        sampLabel.Text += $"<br>Average={d.Average()}";//show average
        //of list
        sampLabel.Text += $"<br>Min={d.Min()}";//show minimum value of
        //list
        sampLabel.Text += $"<br>Max={d.Max()}";//show maximum value of
        //list
        d.ForEach(x => sampLabel.Text += $"<br>{x}^2={x * x}");//show
        //each x squared line below shows each x decreased by the
        //average of the list
        d.ForEach(x => sampLabel.Text += $"<br>{x}-{d.Average()}={x -
        d.Average()}");
    }
}
```

# Summary

In this lesson, you learned about lists. You learned why lists are more flexible than arrays. You summarized values in a list, learned about generic namespaces, started a list of doubles, and filled the list. You also displayed the max, min, average, and sum operators, then squared the results, and finally, you explored nested lists.

In the next chapter, you are going to learn about polymorphism. You will focus on two types of polymorphism, or objects, being treated as different forms depending on the context. The practical benefit of this is that you will write less code.

# 43
# Writing Less Code with Polymorphism

In this lesson, you are going to learn about *polymorphism*, which means "having many forms." We will focus on two kinds of polymorphism, or objects being treated as different forms, depending on the context. The practical benefit of this is that you will write less code.

## Setting up the markup for this project

Here, we'll create a project. Start with the simple HTML markup shown in the following screenshot:

```
1  <%@ Page Language="C#" AutoEventWireup="true" CodeFile="Default.aspx.cs" Inherits="_Default" %>
2
3  <!DOCTYPE html>
4
5  <html xmlns="http://www.w3.org/1999/xhtml">
6  <head runat="server">
7          <title>Our First Page</title>
8  </head>
9  <body>
10     <form id="form1" runat="server">
11
12         <asp:Label ID="sampLabel" runat="server"></asp:Label>
13
14     </form>
15 </body>
16 </html>
17
```

Figure 6.10.1: The simple HTML markup for our project

# Creating the product class

Now, go to the **Solution** Explorer, right-click on the name of the website, select **Add**, and then click on **Class**. Name the class `Product` and click on **OK**. When the Visual Studio message comes up, click on **Yes**.

So the relevant portion of the initial `Product` class code looks as shown in the following screenshot, which is sufficient for our purposes:

```
 9 public class Product
10 {
11
12     public Product()
13     {
14
15     }
16
17 }
```

Figure 6.10.2: The initial Product class code

What's true about every product is that you have a price, a name, and so on. For our purposes, enter the following below the open curly brace under `public class Product`:

```
private decimal price;
```

There you go! Of course, the only thing we'll do within the body of the constructor is type the following:

```
price = pri;
```

This line is used to set the value of the instance variable. Now let's make a `virtual` function. Enter the following after the closing curly brace of the preceding line:

```
public virtual string GetDesc()
```

Within a set of curly braces under the preceding line, enter the following:

```
return $"<br>Price:{ price:C}";
```

Remember, the brown type (Windows) or orange (Mac) on the screen is displayed exactly as it appears between double quotes. Anything that is black within curly brackets is replaced at runtime with a specific value.

# Making a book class

We're going to make two classes that derive from the Product class. Enter the following after the latest curly brace:

```
public class Book : Product
```

Here, Book is derived from Product because a book is a kind of product after all. It's got all the essential characteristics of a product. For the Book class, we'll define an instance variable that reads as follows. Enter this within curly braces under the preceding line:

```
private string title;
```

The title is an important characteristic of a book, though it's not necessarily the case that every product has a title. Still, every book has a title, and that's why we're making it more specific to the Book class.

Let's initialize this to the base class. So right under the preceding line, enter the following:

```
public Book(string t, decimal p) : base(p)
```

With this, the title variable is initialized within a set of curly braces under the preceding line:

```
title = t;
```

We're splitting the initialization of the Book object here basically by doing the common portion of it, which is the price, inside the Product class. However, for the title variable, we do the more refined part of the items inside the Book class.

Further, to override the preceding function, you will now say the following under the closing curly brace under title = t:

```
public override string GetDesc()
```

The GetDesc() function shows up in the drop-down list as you type. Note that the following line is inserted automatically within curly braces under this line:

```
return base.GetDesc()
```

Now leave this bit--it's fine. Every book has a price, and you can display that there. Leave that bit and add the following to it so that it reads as follows:

```
return base.GetDesc() + $"<br>Title:{title}";
```

Remember, at runtime, `base.GetDesc()` will be called. This means that we're going to get the price of the book. Also, if you go back to the line containing the just mentioned price, notice that we formatted it as a currency by inserting `:C` after `price`. Then the `title` variable will also be shown.

We have now created the `Book` class. For review, your code should appear as follows:

```
public class Book : Product
{
    private string title;
    public Book(string t, decimal p) : base(p)
    {
        title = t;
    }
    public override string GetDesc()
    {
        return base.GetDesc() + $"<br>Title:{title}";
    }
}
```

## Making a Shoe class

We're going to repeat what we did, say, for a `Shoe` class, alright? So select the `Book` class lines, *Ctrl* + *C* to copy, and *Ctrl* + *V* to paste the block of code, as follows. We'll call this class `Shoe`:

```
public class Shoe : Product
{
    private string make;
    public Shoe(string mk, decimal p) : base(p)
    {
        title = t;
    }
    public override string GetDesc()
    {
        return base.GetDesc() + $"<br>Make:{make}";
    }
}
```

A shoe is a kind of product, right? Make the following adjustments in each line to change the preceding `Book` class into the `Shoe` class:

1. First, change the class name from `public class Book : Product` to `public class Shoe : Product`.
2. Shoes don't really have `titles`, but they do have a make: Nike, Adidas, or others. So change the line `private string title` to `private string make`.
3. Next, change the line that starts with `public Book` to `public Shoe`. Also, change the string `t` to `string mk`.
4. Then change the line `title = t` to `make = mk`. Set that inside the body.

In order to use inheritance, the `base` class constructor will be called to set the price because that field, the `price` field, is shared.

1. Next, we'll use the same code to override `GetDesc`.
2. In the `return` line that follows, just change `Title` (uppercase T) to `Make` and `title` (lowercase t) to `make` as well.

We've created a relatively easy hierarchy. To review, we have a `Product` class, which defines an instance variable that we just set. Also, it defines a `virtual` function. Remember, the `virtual` functions are those that provide some sensible default functionality, which we can be used in the `Shoe` class. That's why, in the overridden versions, first we write `return base.GetDesc` because every product has a price. That's why we put it inside the `Product` class. We can reuse this code; there's no need to keep writing it separately. The code now should look like what's presented above `Shoe`; it's the same logic but a different object.

# Capturing product information

With the `Shoe` and `Book` classes in place, we have a parent class, `Product`, and two derived classes, `Book` and `Shoe`. Now, go to **Solution Explorer** and open `Default.aspx`. We're going to add stuff. Enter the following to the form:

```
Book Title:<asp:TextBox ID="TextBox1" runat="server"></asp:TextBox><br />

Book Title:<asp:TextBox ID="TextBox2" runat="server"></asp:TextBox><br />
<hr />

Shoe Make:<asp:TextBox ID="TextBox3" runat="server"></asp:TextBox><br />
 Shoe Price:<asp:TextBox ID="TextBox4" runat="server"></asp:TextBox><br />
<hr />
```

We have `Book Title`, `Book Price`, `Shoe Make`, and `Shoe Price`, each followed by a `TextBox` control. Put in the `<br>` tags to stack the little controls vertically on the page. You can delete the `<div>` tag lines. Though we haven't focused much on HTML recently, if you do want to separate these items with horizontal rules, you can do that by inserting `<hr>` tags as in the preceding code block.

Now go to the **Design** view and what we have at present will be as shown in the following screenshot:

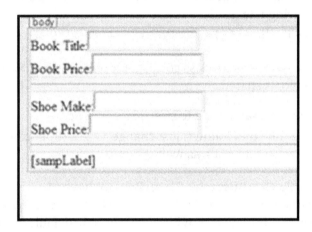

Figure 6.10.3: Our program to this point in Design view

Now we need to get a `Button` control in there also to display the results and values in the boxes. So go to the **Toolbox** window, type `but` in the search field, and then drag and drop **Button** below `<hr>`, after the last `TextBox` control, as follows:

```
<asp:Button ID="Button1" runat="server" Text="Show Formatted" /><br />
```

The `Button` control here will display more nicely formatted input, so change the `Text` property on the `Button` control to say `Show Formatted` and end the line with a `<br>` tag. With the markup changes in place, we see the output as shown in *Figure 6.10.4*. Now if you go to the **Design** view, it will look like the following screenshot:

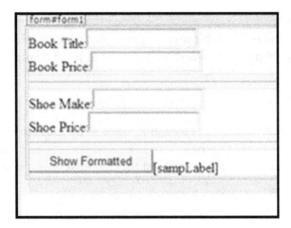

Figure 6.10.4: The interface with the Show Formatted button added

# Making a list of products

Next, double-click on `Show Formatted`. Imagine that you have to make a list of shoes and a list of books. You don't want to make separate lists. Use polymorphism, and the better way to use it is what we'll discuss next. In `Default.aspx.cs`, under `using System`, say the following:

```
using System.Collections.Generic;
```

Then, between curly braces beneath the line that starts with `protected void Button1_Click`, enter the following:

```
List <Product> lp = new List<Product>();
```

You're going to make a list of products (`lp`), which equals a new list of products. Because `Product` is the parent class of `Shoe` and `Book`, you can type the following below this line:

```
lp.Add(new Book(TextBox1.Text, decimal.Parse(TextBox2.Text)));
```

Now take a look. You can type `new book`. You can stick `new Book` into a list of products because `Book` is derived from `Products`. This is *polymorphism* because the `Book` class derives from the `Product` class. You can stick the `Book` data members and member functions into a list of `Products`; that's polymorphism. The `Book` class is not only a book, but it's also a product, so it's got multiple forms. polymorphism means having many forms.

To get the title of the book, refer to `TextBox1.Text`; to get the price of the book, type `decimal.Parse` and then `TextBox2.Text`.

Let's repeat this. Select `lp.Add(new Book(TextBox1.Text...` line and paste it directly beneath the preceding line of code. Now change `TextBox1` in this line to `TextBox3` to get the make of `Shoe`. Next, change the word `Book` to `Shoe`. Now change `TextBox2` in this line to `TextBox4`:

```
lp.Add(new Shoe(TextBox3.Text, decimal.Parse(TextBox4.Text)));
```

Confirm that the information is correct by going back to the **Source** view in `Default.aspx`. There you can see that `Book Title` has `TextBox1` and `Book Price` has `TextBox2`. That's right. Then, `TextBox3` and `TextBox4` are used for the make and price of `Shoe`.

Notice that a shoe can be stuck into a list of products because a shoe is a kind of product. Again, that's polymorphism. The `Shoe` class object is being treated as a shoe, but it derives from the `Product` class, so it can be stuck into a list of Products. Therefore, it has two forms in that sense--it's polymorphism in action.

# Displaying the results

One thing that we can do, of course, is display the results. I'll show you a way of displaying the results, which will be another example of polymorphism. Go back to `Default.aspx.cs` and enter the following below the last line you typed:

```
lp.ForEach(x => sampLabel.Text += x.GetDesc());
```

We saw `ForEach` used in a previous lesson. Now remember, in the preceding statement, `x` means the `Book` and `Shoe` objects. It's not a number like 2 or 4 but an object, a complex object. Note that `x` is to present objects and the `=>` symbol to indicate that an action should be taken.

In our case, what we are going to do is display results. This specifically means that we're going to call `GetDesc` from each class. Hover your mouse over `GetDesc`. You see where it says `string Product.GetDesc()` in the popup? But then the question at runtime is this: will this version of the get description, `public virtual string GetDesc()`, get called from the `Product` class or is the system smart enough to realize that the correct version to be called is `public override string GetDesc()`, first from the `Book` class and then from the `Shoe` class? This is another instance of polymorphism, right? At runtime, when the program runs, `x` in `x.GetDesc()` will represent `Book` or `Shoe` more completely, and the call will be resolved to the child class. So the correct derived version of `GetDesc` will be called. Let's go build an app. Take a look.

# Running the program

Alright, polymorphism, as you have learned, is an interesting but subtle concept. Open the program in your browser. Start with the top box; put in a book title, say, `Amazing Tales`. In the next box, imagine that the book price is something like `$45.89`. The make of the shoe is `Nike`. Finally, the price is something like `$87.99`. When you click on the `Shoe Formatted` button, you'll see the screen shown in the following screenshot:

Figure 6.10.5: The results of running our program

This confirms that the correct derived version of `GetDesc`, in the `public override string GetDesc()` line, has been called. So, again, to stress this point, the benefit is that you made a single list. A single list of products can accommodate many different kinds of products so that you write less code. Putting a book, a shoe, or any other product in a list of products is an example of polymorphism; also, the fact that at runtime the correct version of `GetDesc` is called is another form of polymorphism. This is because the x object in `x.GetDesc()` represents both the `Book` and `Shoe` classes and is correctly resolved to the child class. So, you have two forms of polymorphism.

# Chapter review

For review, a complete version of the `Default.aspx` code file for this lesson is displayed in the following code block:

```
<%@ Page Language="C#" AutoEventWireup="true" CodeFile="Default.aspx.cs"
Inherits="_Default" %>

<!DOCTYPE html>

<html xmlns="http://www.w3.org/1999/xhtml">
<head runat="server">
    <title>Our First Page</title>
</head>
<body>
    <form id="form1" runat="server">
    Book Title:<asp:TextBox ID="TextBox1" runat="server"></asp:TextBox>
    <br />
    Book Price:<asp:TextBox ID="TextBox2" runat="server"></asp:TextBox>
    <br />
    <hr />
    Shoe Make:<asp:TextBox ID="TextBox3" runat="server"></asp:TextBox>
    <br />
    Shoe Price:<asp:TextBox ID="TextBox4" runat="server"></asp:TextBox>
    <br />
    <hr />
    <asp:Button ID="Button1" runat="server" Text="Show Formatted"
    OnClick="Button1_Click" /><br />
    <asp:Label ID="sampLabel" runat="server"></asp:Label>
    </form>
</body>
</html>
```

The complete version of the `Product.cs` file for this lesson, including comments, is displayed in the following block of code:

```
//make parent class
public class Product
{
    //place price here because it's common to all products
    private decimal price;
    //set value of instance variable
    public Product(decimal pri)
    {
        price = pri;
    }
    //make this method virtual
```

```
    //because it makes sense to put the display of the price
    //in a centralized location, since the Price is common to all products
    public virtual string GetDesc()
    {
        return $"<br>Price:{price:C}";
    }
}
public class Book : Product
{
    private string title;
    public Book(string t, decimal p) : base(p)
    {
        title = t;
    }
    //override GetDesc from product
    //by providing a more specific implementation that also shows the
    //book title
    public override string GetDesc()
    {
        return base.GetDesc() + $"<br>Title:{title}";
    }
}
public class Shoe :Product
{
    private string make;
    public Shoe(string mk, decimal p) : base(p)
    {
        make = mk;
    }
    //override GetDesc from product
    //by providing a more specific implementation that also shows the
    //shoe make
    public override string GetDesc()
    {
        return base.GetDesc() + $"<br>Make:{make}";
    }
}
```

The complete version of the `Default.aspx.cs` file for this lesson, including comments, is displayed in the following block of code:

```
//using is a directive
//System is a name space
//name space is a collection of features that our needs to run
using System;
using System.Collections.Generic;//add this for generic lists
        //public means accessible anywhere
        //partial means this class is split over multiple files
```

```
        //class is a keyword and think of it as the outermost level of
        //grouping :System.Web.UI.Page means our page inherits the
        //features of a Page
public partial class _Default : System.Web.UI.Page
{
    protected void Button1_Click(object sender, EventArgs e)
    {
        //make a list of products
        List<Product> lp = new List<Product>();
        //make a book and a shore, and store them inside the list of
        //products
        lp.Add(new Book(TextBox1.Text, decimal.Parse(TextBox2.Text)));
        lp.Add(new Shoe(TextBox3.Text, decimal.Parse(TextBox4.Text)));
        //call the correct, derived version of GetDesc on each product
        //in the list
        lp.ForEach(x => sampLabel.Text += x.GetDesc());
    }
}
```

# Summary

In this lesson, you learned about polymorphism, referring to something that has many forms. We focused on two kinds of polymorphism, or objects being treated as different forms, depending on context, with a practical benefit of having to write less code. You created a parent `Product` class and two child classes: `Book` and `Shoe`. You used polymorphism to make and display a list of products.

In the next lesson, you are going to learn about interfaces.

# 44

# Using Interfaces to Express Common Behaviors

In this chapter, you will learn about interfaces. Interfaces are contracts. These contracts are widely applicable, meaning that many different, unrelated kinds of class can implement an interface. So let's build a hierarchy.

## Building a hierarchy

Let's create a project. The following is the default HTML we'll use:

```
1  <%@ Page Language="C#" AutoEventWireup="true" CodeFile="Default.aspx.cs" Inherits="_Default" %>
2
3  <!DOCTYPE html>
4
5  <html xmlns="http://www.w3.org/1999/xhtml">
6  <head runat="server">
7      <title>Our First Page</title>
8  </head>
9  <body>
10     <form id="form1" runat="server">
11
12         <asp:Label ID="sampLabel" runat="server"></asp:Label>
13
14     </form>
15 </body>
16 </html>
17
```

Figure 6.11.1: The default HTML for a project

Go to **Solution Explorer**, right-click on the name of the website, select **Add**, and then click on **Class**. Name the class `PrintableObjects` and click on **OK**. When the Visual Studio message comes up, click on **Yes**.

We really want to get the C# file more than anything else. With this in place, you can basically select all of the default code in the class and delete it. Refer to the following code:

```
public interface IPrintable
```

Here, `public` is accessible from anywhere, `interface` is a keyword, and `IPrintable` is its name. Many interfaces have "able" at the end, and the reason is that we think of the relationship between classes and interfaces as "can be used as." For example, a document is a printable thing. It can be used as a printable thing, but so can a person. A person can also be printable. A person can be used as a printable object, depending on how you choose to define things.

So, you have `public interface IPrintable`. Next, we'll declare the following between curly braces after the preceding line:

```
string Print();
```

That's it! So this is a simple method signature. Now if you go to **Solution Explorer**, you'll see `PrintableObjects.cs` listed under `App_Code`.

# Implementing the interface

To make use of `IPrintable`, we are going to type the following under the closing curly brace of the preceding line:

```
public class Person : IPrintable
```

This is the printable interface. This means that this person can be treated as a printable object. Let's see how we can ensure this happens. Notice that, once you do this, because this is an interface and a contract, its members have to be implemented in the classes that use that interface.

OK, so if you right-click on `IPrintable` in the preceding line, a pop-up menu will appear. Select **Quick Actions...**, then click on **Implement interface** in the submenu that appears. It will provide a bit of a code for you, as shown in the following screenshot:

```
 3 public interface IPrintable
 4 {
 5     string Print();
 6 }
 7 public class Person : IPrintable
 8 {
 9     public string Print()
10     {
11         throw new NotImplementedException;
12     }
13 }
```

Figure 6.11.2: After you click on Implement interface, it provides this bit of code for you

We don't want the `throw new NotImplementedException;` line, so let's delete it.

In our case, to print a `Person` object, you'll need to do what comes next. But first, let's define a `Person` class. Very simple. Enter the following under the closed curly brace below `public class Person : IPrintable`:

```
private string name;
```

Now, let's set the name; enter the following beneath it:

```
public Person(string name)
```

Within curly braces below this line, enter the following to set the values:

```
name = nam;
```

That's it! So you have a class called `Person`, which implements the printable interface. This means that a person can be used as a printable object.

In `public string Print()`, we have the `Print` method, so within curly braces below this line, enter the following:

```
return $"<br>Name:{ name}";
```

You can delete `using System;` if you haven't done so already.

Now, with this in place, let's add one more line. The big idea with interfaces is they are widely applicable. In other words, many completely unrelated classes can be printable. Let's take a look. Enter the following at the bottom of the code:

```
public class Document : IPrintable
```

Notice again that `Person` and `Document` do not have much in common. They are two completely different constructs, but both can be treated as printable objects.

Now we have to implement `Print` for `Document`. First, let's define it as follows between curly braces under the preceding line:

```
private string text;
```

Directly below this line, type the following:

```
public Document(string t)
```

Now set the value between curly braces below this line. In our case, we will set it as follows:

```
text = t;
```

That's it. Now to implement `printable`, right-click on `IPrintable` in the `public class Document` line, select **Quick Actions...**, and then click on **Implement interface** in the submenu that appears.

Change the line that says `throw new NotImplementedException;` to this:

```
return "<br>" + text;
```

Remember, if it's between double quotes, it's text; however, when the browser receives it, of course, it's seen as HTML.

# Check yourself

With all of this in place, now take a look. The complete version of `PrintableObjects.cs`, including comments, is displayed in the following code block. Check to be sure that you're on track with entering the code for this class:

```
//using is a directive
//System is a name space
//name space is a collection of features that our needs to run
using System;
using System.Collections.Generic;
//public means accessible anywhere
//partial means this class is split over multiple files
```

```
//class is a keyword and think of it as the outermost level of grouping
//:System.Web.UI.Page means our page inherits the features of a Page
public partial class _Default : System.Web.UI.Page
{
    protected void Button1_Click(object sender, EventArgs e)
    {
        //lines below make two printable objects
        IPrintable per = new Person(TextBox1.Text);
        IPrintable book = new Document(TextBox2.Text);
        //lines below make a generic list that can hold printable
        //objects
        List<IPrintable> pr = new List<IPrintable>();
        pr.Add(per);
        pr.Add(book);
        //line below operates on list to invoke Print on each printable
        //object
        pr.ForEach(x => sampLabel.Text += x.Print());
    }
}
```

# Setting up the HTML

Go to **Solution Explorer** and select `Default.aspx`. Type `tex` in the **Search Toolbox** field and drag and drop `TextBox` into the form. At the very beginning of this line, type `Name:`; this will be the name of the person in the box. The line should now appear as follows:

```
Name:<asp:TextBox ID="TextBox1" runat="server"></asp:TextBox><br />
```

Add another text box directly beneath this line. Type `Text:` at the start of this line. This line represents the text of the document, so keep it simple. Now it looks like this:

```
Text:<asp:TextBox ID="TextBox2" runat="server"></asp:TextBox><br />
```

 You can delete the `<div>` tag lines if they exist. They're not necessary for our purposes.

In the next stage, we're going to insert a `Button` control that will show these things. So put a `Button` control below the preceding line, as follows:

```
<asp:Button ID="Button1" runat="server" Text="Print" /><br />
```

Note that here we've made `Print` as the word on `Button`.

## Check yourself

The complete version of `Default.aspx` for this chapter is displayed in the following code block. Check to be sure that you have entered all of the HTML correctly:

```
<%@ Page Language="C#" AutoEventWireup="true" CodeFile="Default.aspx.cs"
Inherits="_Default" %>

<!DOCTYPE html>

<html xmlns="http://www.w3.org/1999/xhtml">
<head runat="server">
    <title>Our First Page</title>
</head>
<body>
    <form id="form1" runat="server">
    Name:<asp:TextBox ID="TextBox1" runat="server"></asp:TextBox><br />
    Text:<asp:TextBox ID="TextBox2" runat="server"></asp:TextBox><br />
        <asp:Button ID="Button1" runat="server" Text="Print"
        OnClick="Button1_Click" style="height: 26px" /><br />
        <asp:Label ID="sampLabel" runat="server"></asp:Label>
    </form>
</body>
</html>
```

Now go to the **Design** view. As shown in the following screenshot, we have a very simple interface, including two `TextBox` controllers and a `Print` Button:

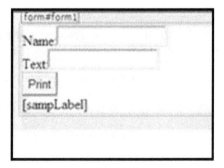

Figure 6.11.5: Our simple interface in the Design view

# Building the interface

Left double-click on the `Print` button. Now we're going to work with the interface inside the Event Handler. The relevant starting portion of the Event Handler is shown in the following screenshot:

```
10 public partial class _Default : System.Web.UI.Page
11 {
12     protected void Button1_Click(object sender, EventArgs e)
13     {
14
15     }
16 }
```

Figure 6.11.6: The starting portion of the Event Handler

Now enter the following after the open curly brace under the line that begins with `protected void Button1_Click`:

```
IPrintable per = new Person(TextBox1.Text);
```

Notice that as you type `IPrintable`, it shows up on the left-hand side as a type; on the right-hand side, the object is essentially made because the `new` keyword actually makes the object, which is `Person`.

You can repeat this as follows:

```
IPrintable book = new Document(TextBox2.Text);
```

This shows that you can now make printable objects. Even though these are widely different--, persons, books, and so on--, they are all printable. Now, below `using System`, enter the following:

```
using System.Collections.Generic;
```

Guess what. You can make a list of printable objects so that you can conduct a search and do a lot of other stuff. Enter the following under the `IPrintable` book:

```
List <IPrintable> pr = new List<IPrintable>();
```

Then, to add values to the `List` object, enter the following lines:

```
pr.Add(per);
pr.Add(book);
```

Notice that, as you type `pr`, you will see all the items that are available on the lists in a pop-up menu, which will now become available here as well, operating on these printable objects. You see that? Here, we've added two objects: `Person` and `Book`.

Earlier, we also learned about `ForEach` applied to lists. On the next line, we can do stuff like the following:

```
pr.ForEach(x => sampLabel.Text += x.Print());
```

Remember that x in this context represents a printable object.

Notice that, when you hover your mouse over `Print`, it says `string IPrintable.Print()`. Remember, ultimately the system is smart enough to resolve this call correctly in such a way that, in `PrintableObjects.cs, public string Print()` is called from `Person` and `public string Print()` is called from the `Document` class.

So, you can declare objects of type `iPrintable`, you can make lists of printable objects, you can operate on these lists of printable objects using constructs such as `ForEach`, and so on.

# Running the program

Alright, let's crank this up in your browser. Now, enter `John Smith, It was a beautiful day.` as the text and click on the `Print` button. The results are shown in the following screenshot:

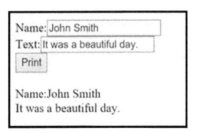

Figure 6.11.7: The results of running our program

There you go. It's working as expected, which is good.

# Lesson review

So, to review, you have an interface, which is essentially a contract, and the purpose is to bind things together to some extent. The relationship between classes and interfaces is that it "can be used as follows," so a `Person` reference variable *can be used as* a printable object, and also, likewise a `Document` reference variable can be used as a printable object.

Once you have an interface when you implement it, the members have to be implemented or you're going to get an error. `IPrintable` objects will be underlined in red. With this in place, you can then make objects of the type `IPrintable`, and you can make lists that store printable objects and other things.

The complete version of `Default.aspx.cs` for this lesson, including comments, is displayed in the following code block:

```
//using is a directive
//System is a name space
//name space is a collection of features that our needs to run
using System;
using System.Collections.Generic;
//public means accessible anywhere
//partial means this class is split over multiple files
//class is a keyword and think of it as the outermost level of grouping
//:System.Web.UI.Page means our page inherits the features of a Page
public partial class _Default : System.Web.UI.Page
{
    protected void Button1_Click(object sender, EventArgs e)
    {
        //lines below make two printable objects
        IPrintable per = new Person(TextBox1.Text);
        IPrintable book = new Document(TextBox2.Text);
        //lines below make a generic list that can hold printable
        //objects
        List<IPrintable> pr = new List<IPrintable>();
        pr.Add(per);
        pr.Add(book);
        //line below operates on list to invoke Print on each printable
        //object
        pr.ForEach(x => sampLabel.Text += x.Print());
    }
}
```

# Summary

In this lesson, you learned about interfaces. Interfaces are contracts. These contracts are widely applicable, meaning many different kinds of classes can implement an interface. You built a hierarchy, implemented an interface, set up the HTML, and built up an interface.

In the next lesson, you are going to learn about indexers, which essentially allow you to treat an object as if it were an array.

# 45

# Iterating over Instances with Indexers

In this lesson, you are going to learn about *indexers*, which essentially allow us to treat an object as if it were an array.

## Setting up a records project

Let's create a project. Go to **Solution Explorer**, right-click on the name of the website, select **Add**, and click on **Class**. Name the class `Records` and click on **OK**. When the Visual Studio message comes up, click on **Yes**. You will be storing records of some kind--it doesn't really matter what type of records you'll be storing. Click on **OK**, then on **Yes**.

Now one of the instance variables for this class will be an array. So enter the following below the open curly brace under `public class Records`:

```
public double [] records = new double[] { 1, 8, 9, 1, -8, -3, -458 };
```

It really doesn't matter what values you put into the array.

Again, for our purposes, you can probably delete the constructor for the class. You know this because we already have the value of the instance variables set inside the class itself; you don't have to make it.

# Making the indexer

Now you're going to make the *indexer*. Enter the following directly beneath the preceding line:

```
private double this [int i]
```

Remember, `public` is accessible anywhere and `double` is the value that it returns. Then, type the keyword `this` and `int i` within brackets, which is how you access the entries.

Now within curly braces below this line, enter the following:

```
get
{
    return records[i];
}
```

Here `records` is the name of an internal array and the index is `[i]`.

Next, below this, you can also have `set`. For this, enter the following:

```
    set
    {
        records[i] = value;
    }
}
```

The value is blue (Windows) or teal (Mac). It's a keyword that exists by default. Inside, you can assign new values to the array. This is the basic class.

You don't need any of the `using System` namespace lines at the very top, so click on the light bulb and select **Remove Unnecessary Usings**.

Now we would like to get the length of the internal array, `records`. We can do this through a property, for example. We can say the following below the closing curly brace under the preceding `set` code:

```
    public int Length
    {
        get
        {
            return records.Length;
        }
    }
```

Here, we have a class called `records`, an instance variable for the class of this array of `doubles`. Now we have an indexer that allows us to access values and set values. We also have a property that can get the length of the internal array. Notice that these properties and indexers have pretty much the same structure with `get` and `set`.

# Reading the values back to the user

Go to `Default.aspx`. The only thing that we will do here is read the values back to the user. To do this, go to **Toolbox** and put a `Button` control into the form. Change the `Text` property on the `Button` control to something more meaningful, such as `Get Records`. (You can delete the `<div>` tag lines.) This line should appear as follows:

```
<asp:Button ID="Button1" runat="server" Text="Get Records" /><br />
```

That's all you really need, so it's really easy. Now go to the **Design** view and double-click on the **Get Records** button. The snippet of `Default.aspx.cs` that you will work with is as follows:

```
public partial class _Default : System.Web.UI.Page
{
    protected void Button1_Click(object sender, EventArgs e)
    {

    }
}
```

# Making a new Records object

Alright! So we're going to make a new `Records` object between a set of curly braces, as follows:

```
Records recs = new Records();
```

To make use of this object, to step through it, and access the internal array, you can type the following directly below the preceding line, Notice that you can use `recs.Length` because the records object has a Length property:

```
for (int i = 0; i < recs.Length; i++)
```

Now, you can display the records. So between a set of curly braces below the preceding line, type the following:

```
sampLabel.Text += "<br>" + recs[i];
```

Remember that the `recs` object we just saw is an object of60; `Records`, but because it has an indexer operating behind the scenes, you can write the name of the object and treat it almost like an array, as you can see in `recs[i]`.

# Running the program

Let's give it a go here in `Default.aspx`. Open your browser and click on `Get Records`. Your screen should look like the one shown in the following screenshot:

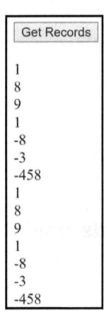

Figure 6.12.1: The output accumulates every time you click the Get Results button

Notice that the output is getting accumulated each time you click on the **Get Records** button. To ensure that this does not happen, print the string in the `Label.Text` function every time. So, go to `Default.aspx.cs`, and below the open curly brace under the line that begins with `protected void Button1_Click...`, enter the following:

```
sampLabel.Text = "";
```

Now when you run this, the output of clicking the **Get Records** button will not accumulate as before.

You've just seen a very simple and straightforward example of how to use an indexer in this lesson, but indexers can get quite elaborate and can be used in many contexts. So remember that the big idea here is that you can make an object into an indexed construct so that you can then step through the object because that object stores an array as an instance variable.

# Chapter review

For review, a complete version of the `Default.aspx` file for this lesson is displayed in the following code block:

```
<%@ Page Language="C#" AutoEventWireup="true" CodeFile="Default.aspx.cs"
Inherits="_Default" %>

<!DOCTYPE html>

<html xmlns="http://www.w3.org/1999/xhtml">
<head runat="server">
    <title>Our First Page</title>
</head>
<body>
    <form id="form1" runat="server">
        <asp:Button ID="Button1" runat="server" Text="Get Records"
        OnClick="Button1_Click" /><br />
        <asp:Label ID="sampLabel" runat="server"></asp:Label>
    </form>
</body>
</html>
```

The complete version of the `Records.cs` file for this lesson, including comments, is displayed in the following screenshot:

```
/// <summary>
/// Summary description for Records
/// </summary>
public class Records
{
    //this is the array that is internal
    private double[] records = new double[] { 1, 8, 9, 1, -8, -3, -458 };
    public double this[int i]
    {
        get
        {
            return records[i];//this gets value stored at index i
        }
        set
        {
            records[i] = value;//this sets the value stored at index i
        }
    }
    public int Length
    {
        get
        {
            return records.Length;//used to get length of internal
            array
        }
    }
}
```

The complete version of the `Default.aspx.cs` file for this lesson, including comments, is displayed in the following code block:

```
//using is a directive
//System is a name space
//name space is a collection of features that our needs to run
using System;
//public means accessible anywhere
//partial means this class is split over multiple files
//class is a keyword and think of it as the outermost level of grouping
//:System.Web.UI.Page means our page inherits the features of a Page
public partial class _Default : System.Web.UI.Page
{
    protected void Button1_Click(object sender, EventArgs e)
    {
        sampLabel.Text = "";//clear label
        Records recs = new Records();//make new records object
```

```
            //use for loop to iterate over records object
    for (int i = 0; i < recs.Length; i++)
    {
        //because recs has an internal array,
        //array access notation can be used by writing recs[i]
        sampLabel.Text += "<br>" + recs[i];
    }
}
}
```

# Summary

In this lesson, you learned about indexers, which essentially allow us to treat an object as if it were an array. You set up a `Records` project, made an indexer, read values back to the user, and made a new `Records` object.

In the next lesson, you are going to learn about making applications more stable by handling bad conditions, but these conditions are usually of the foreseeable type, so you know that they can happen in advance. We call these exceptions.

# 46

# Building Stabler Apps with Exception Handling

In this chapter, we will use exception handling to build more stable applications with throw and catch exceptions. Then you will run a block of code.

## Setting up the HTML for this chapter

The basic HTML for this lesson is shown in the following screenshot:

```
1 <%@ Page Language="C#" AutoEventWireup="true" CodeFile="Default.aspx.cs" Inherits="_Default" %>
2
3 <!DOCTYPE html>
4
5 <html xmlns="http://www.w3.org/1999/xhtml">
6 <head runat="server">
7     <title>Our First Page</title>
8 </head>
9 <body>
10     <form id="form1" runat="server">
11
12     </form>
13 </body>
14 </html>
```

Figure 6.13.1: The basic HTML starting point for this lesson

The first thing that we are going to do is add a couple of boxes. We'll have two boxes for entering input, then we'll try to divide the values. That's the objective here. So go to **Toolbox**, type tex in the Search field, and then drag and drop a Textbox control into the form. Then, drag a second TextBox control directly below it. (Delete the <div> tag lines, as we won't be using them.)

Insert a `Button` control directly below the second `TextBox` control. Remember, the big idea here is to make applications that are stabler and more professional. That's the reason for having exceptions; otherwise, your stuff will be crashing all over the place and people will get frustrated and leave.

In the **Design** view, you can see that the interface is very plain. Change the `Text` property on the `Button` control to something more meaningful, such as `Divide`. Also, insert `Value 1:` in front of the first `TextBox` control and `Value 2:` in front of the second `TextBox` control, as follows:

```
Value 1:<asp:TextBox ID="TextBox1" runat="server"></asp:TextBox><br />
Value 2:<asp:TextBox ID="TextBox2" runat="server"></asp:TextBox><br />
```

This is the basic HTML for this project. Your `Default.aspx` page should now look like the following screenshot:

```
1  <%@ Page Language="C#" AutoEventWireup="true" CodeFile="Default.aspx.cs" Inherits="_Default" %>
2
3  <!DOCTYPE html>
4
5  <html xmlns="http://www.w3.org/1999/xhtml">
6  <head runat="server">
7      <title>Our First Page</title>
8  </head>
9  <body>
10     <form id="form1" runat="server">
11         Value 1:<asp:TextBox ID="TextBox1" runat="server"></asp:TextBox><br />
12         Value 2:<asp:TextBox ID="TextBox2" runat="server"></asp:TextBox><br />
13         <asp:Button ID="Button1" runat="server" Text="Divide" /><br />
14         <asp:Label ID="sampLabel" runat="server"></asp:Label>
15
16
17     </form>
18 </body>
19 </html>
```

Figure 6.13.2: Your Default.aspx page with boxes and a button added

Go to the **Design** view again, and your interface should look like the following screenshot:

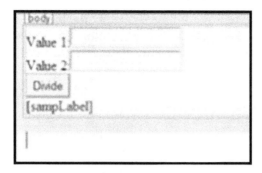

Figure 6.13.3: Your program interface in Design view

Alright, double-click on the **Divide** button. Delete the Event Handler for `Page_Load`. Then, the first thing we're going to do is enter the following between a set of curly braces below the line that begins with `protected void Button1_Click...`:

```
double x, y;// variables for reading input
```

Note the comment indicating that we basically need these variables for reading input.

# Using a try block

Furthermore, because there's no guarantee that the input from the user can be successfully converted, depending on what somebody enters, you have to type `try` directly below the `double x,y;` declaration statement, as follows:

```
double x, y;// variables for reading input
try
```

You can put any stuff that is to be tried, but not guaranteed, to be successful within a `try` block.

Now enter the following between curly braces directly below `try`:

```
x = Convert.ToDouble(TextBox1.Text);
y = Convert.ToDouble(TextBox2.Text);
```

# Throwing an exception

For the next stage, enter the following directly below the lines of code mentioned in the preceding section. But this stage could generate errors. This is because if y is zero, then it is not allowed in mathematics. So, next what we'll do is also type the following:

```
if (y == 0)
{
    throw new DivideByZeroException();
}
```

What is this? `DivideByZeroException` is a class. If you hover your mouse over this class, the pop-up tooltip says this: **Initializes a new instance of the DivideByZeroException class**. To throw an exception means to pass it to the code that will catch it, handle it, and make some use of it.

Next, type `else` below the closed curly brace that follows and enter the following:

```
else
{
    sampLabel.Text = $"{x}/{y}={x / y}";
}
}
```

If y is not equal to 0, you can use `sampLabel.Text` to display it, for example.

# Using a catch block

Here, after the `try` block, we'll enter the following after the last closing curly brace:

```
catch (DivideByZeroException ex)
```

You made a new `DivideByZeroException` object, then you're throwing an exception, and last, it's going to be caught down here in the `catch` block. So, to `catch` means to handle some of the values that are passed.

Enter the following between a set of curly braces below this line:

```
{
    sampLabel.Text = ex.Message;
```

So, it's a message property that this object carries, the `DivideByZeroException` object, and you can display that message.

The `DivisionByZeroException` argument is used when you have problems with division by zero. But what if the input cannot be converted? You can handle that too. You can type the following, for example, after the closing curly brace for the `DivideByZero` catch block mentioned in the preceding line of code:

```
catch (FormatException ex)
```

Then you can say the following between a set of curly braces below the preceding line:

```
sampLabel.Text = ex.Message;
sampLabel.Text += "<br>" + ex.StackTrace;
```

There you go! If somebody types, for example, the word "five" instead of entering the number 5, it's going to produce a format exception.

# Using a finally block

The last block is called the `finally` block, and this block runs no matter what happens in the preceding part of the code; that is, the `finally` block always runs. Enter the following beneath the closed curly brace below the preceding lines:

```
finally
{
    sampLabel.Text += "<br>Your operation is complete.";
}
}
```

Alright, so to be sure that your code is correct, review *Figure 6.13.4*, which shows all of the code that you were supposed to enter into the `Default.aspx.cs` file up to this point (the figure also includes comments):

```
11      protected void Button1_Click(object sender, EventArgs e)
12      {
13          double x, y;// variables for reading input
14          try
15          {
16              //both lines below could generate format exceptions
17              x = Convert.ToDouble(TextBox1.Text);
18              y = Convert.ToDouble(TextBox2.Text);
19              if (y == 0)
20              {
21                  //throw a new object of DivideByZeroException type
22                  throw new DivideByZeroException();
23              }
24              else
25              {
26                  sampLabel.Text = $"{x}/{y}={x / y}";
27              }
28          }
29          //this catch runs when a user inputs 0
30          catch (DivideByZeroException ex)
31          {
32              sampLabel.Text = ex.Message;
33          }
34          //this block runs when a user inputs a word like "five" instead of "5"
35          catch (FormatException ex)
36          {
37              sampLabel.Text = ex.Message;
38                      }
39          finally
40          {
41              //this line always runs, no matter what happens above
42              sampLabel.Text += "<br>Your operation is complete.";
43          }
44      }
45 }
```

Figure 6.13.4: Current Default.aspx.cs code for this lesson

# Running the program

Now let's execute and examine the results, as shown in *Figure 6.13.5*. If you enter some values, such as 2 and 45, and hit the `Divide` button, it will say `2/45 = 0.4444 ...`, a numerical value, and `Your operation is complete`. That's good!

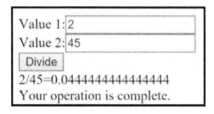

Figure 6.13.5: The results of running our program

Now try this. Enter some letters in the first box, for example, the word "five," and click on the `Divide` button. The result appears in *Figure 6.13.6*. Now it says `The Input string is not in a correct format. Your operation is complete`. So, this doesn't work:

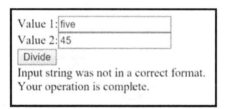

Figure 6.13.6: The results of running the program with incorrectly-formatted data

Now try this. Put 0 in the first box and 6 in the second one. Now it says `Attempted to divide by zero,` as shown in the following screenshot, and your application has now crashed:

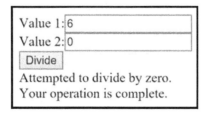

Figure 6.13.7: The application has now crashed

So here are the benefits of what we've done. The `try` blocks are code lines that try to run, which could potentially generate errors or exceptions. You put exceptional situations within `try`, then you can put a series of `catch` blocks to handle the different exceptions. This usually means displaying a message, but it's not the only thing that you can do. For example, go back to your `Default.aspx.cs` page.

# Working with the StackTrace property

Look at the `sampLabel.Text = ex.Message;` code line. If you want more than just a message, let's say that you want some diagnostic output, type the following directly below the `sampLabel.Text = ex.Message;` line:

```
sampLabel.Text += "<br>" + ex.StackTrace;
```

`StackTrace` is a property, so let's take a look at this in a browser now, as shown in the following screenshot:

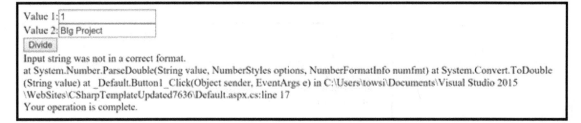

Figure 6.13.8: StackTrace tells you exactly where in the code a problem has occurred

This property is very helpful. If you put in some incorrectly formatted data, you can see from the figure that it tells you exactly where in the code a problem has occurred, specifically at line 17 in this case. There you go! That's `StackTrace`.

So these are the fundamentals. Again, remember that the big idea here is to make applications that are stabler and more predictable by having `try`, `catch`, and `finally`, which always runs. Furthermore, if you are aware of certain exceptions, you can throw them by typing `throw new` and then the name of the exception.

# Investigating exceptions to determine their inheritance

If you want to learn more about exceptions, right-click on the name of an exception class, select **Go To Definition**, and you will see something similar to what is shown in *Figure 6.13.9*. For example, FormatException inherits from SystemException. If you drill down to SystemException and **Go To Definition** on that, you'll discover that SystemException inherits from Exception and so on:

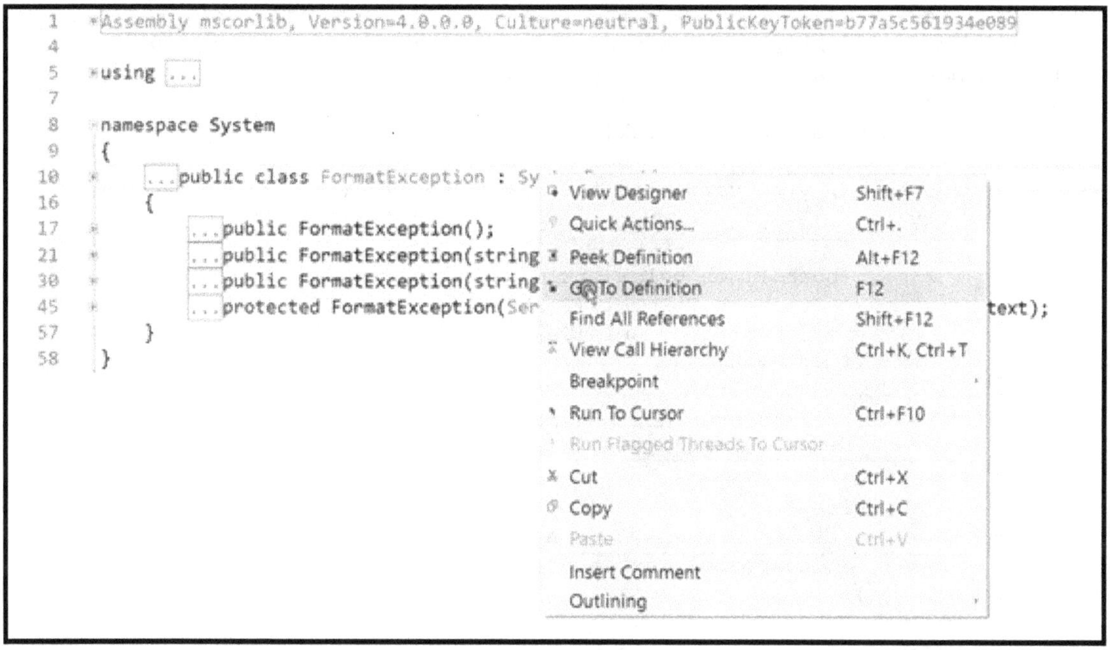

Figure 6.13.9: Drilling down on exception classes to determine their inheritance

So there's the basic hierarchy of classes as far as exceptions go. Of course, if you wanted to, you could write your own exception class that inherits from one of the existing ones.

# Chapter review

For review, the complete version of `Default.aspx.cs` for this lesson, including comments, is displayed in the following code block:

```
//using is a directive
//System is a name space
//name space is a collection of features that our needs to run
using System;
//public means accessible anywhere
//partial means this class is split over multiple files
//class is a keyword and think of it as the outermost level of grouping
//:System.Web.UI.Page means our page inherits the features of a Page
public partial class _Default : System.Web.UI.Page
{
    protected void Button1_Click(object sender, EventArgs e)
    {
        double x, y;// variables for reading input
        try
        {
            //both lines below could generate format exceptions
            x = Convert.ToDouble(TextBox1.Text);
            y = Convert.ToDouble(TextBox2.Text);
            if (y == 0)
            {
                //throw a new object of DivideByZeroException type
                throw new DivideByZeroException();
            }
            else
            {
                sampLabel.Text = $"{x}/{y}={x / y}";
            }
        }
        //this catch runs when a user inputs 0
        catch (DivideByZeroException ex)
        {
            sampLabel.Text = ex.Message;
        }
        //this block runs when a user inputs a word like "five" instead
        //of "5"
        catch (FormatException ex)
        {
            sampLabel.Text = ex.Message;
            sampLabel.Text += "<br>" + ex.StackTrace;
        }
        finally
        {
            //this line always runs, no matter what happens above
```

```
        sampLabel.Text += "<br>Your operation is complete.";
    }
  }
}
```

# Summary

In this lesson, you learned about how to make applications stabler by handling bad conditions, but these conditions are usually of the foreseeable type, so you know that they can happen in advance. So, we call these bad conditions *exceptions*.

You wrote the code to divide values, studied the `try`, `catch`, and `finally` blocks, learned about throwing an exception, worked with the `StackTrace` property, and investigated exceptions to determine their inheritance in this lesson.

In the next chapter, you are going to learn about several concepts. You will learn about automatic properties, named parameters, and optional parameters. You will make a little application that will allow you to conduct a search, for example, searching Amazon or some other site.

# 47
# Using Named and Optional Parameters

In this lesson, you are going to learn about several concepts. We will study automatic properties, named parameters, and optional parameters. We will make a little application that will allow us to perform a search as if we were searching Amazon or some other site.

## Setting up the Book class

Let's create a project. Make a file, go to **Solution Explorer**, right-click on the name of the website, select **Add**, and click on **Class**. Name the class Book and click on **OK**. When the Visual Studio message comes up, click on **Yes**.

The section of the Book class where we'll begin our work looks as shown in the following screenshot:

```
 9 public class Book
10 {
11          public Book()
12      {
13
14      }
```

Figure 6.14.1: Relevant starting section of the Book class

As our first step to making our Book object, enter the following under the open curly brace below public class Book:

```
public string Title { get; set; }
```

Remember, `public` means accessible anywhere. The `get` and `set` within curly braces is what we call an *automatic property*, which means that to set its values, you can set the value of the property directly inside the constructor; you don't need a backing field explicitly defined.

Alright, let's set a couple of other quantities, a couple of other instance variables. Enter the following beneath the preceding line:

```
string bookType;
```

The `bookType` string variable will indicate, for example, whether it's a traditional or electronic book.

Then, set the publication date. To do this, enter the following below the `string bookType;` line:

```
int pubDate;
```

So `pubDate` indicates the publication date. These are the things that are going to define our `Book` class.

## Making the constructor

Now let's make a constructor. Inside the constructor, the first step is to make the parameter list, so enter the following within parentheses after `public Book()`:

```
public Book(string title, int publicationDate, string type = "Traditional
Book")
```

Notice that `publicationDate` is an integer because that's the way it's measured. `Traditional Book` is what we call a default value or an *optional parameter*. So, by default, the value of this will be `Traditional Book`.

To set the value of the `Title` property, within curly braces beneath the preceding line, type the name of the property and set it equal to the parameter, as follows:

```
Title = title;
```

This is basically saving us lines of code by not having to create an explicit `Title` backing field.

Next, to set the value of `pubDate`, enter the following as the next line:

```
pubDate = publicationDate;
```

Then, for `bookType`, enter the following in the next line:

```
bookType = type;
```

That's it! We've made our `Book` object. Because we do have a couple of fields and an automatic property, we want to override `ToString`. For this, enter the following below the closed curly brace present after the preceding line:

```
public override string ToString()
```

Remember, `ToString` comes to us from the object class--that's where it's defined--and the object class `ToString` is `virtual`, so we're going to refine the implementation by typing `all`. Here, if you use the default version, it's not very useful--it doesn't produce nice results. We need clearer results, and that's why we're overriding it. Enter the following with a set of curly braces under the preceding line:

```
return $"Title:{ Title}<br>Type:{bookType}<br>Publication Date:{pubDate}";
```

This will produce a nice result on each book in terms of displaying something useful to the user, specifically the title, the type of book, and the publication date of the book.

You don't need any of the `using System` namespace lines and `//<summary>` comments at the top of the file. As you can see, they are grayed out, so you can delete them.

This is our `Book` class, as shown in *Figure 6.14.2*. Again, remember in `public string Title { get; set; }`, we have `Title`, which is an automatic property. It's automatic because its value is set directly within a constructor: `Title = title`. We have never done this before:

```
using System;
public class Book
{
    public string Title { get; set; }//create automatic property
    string bookType;
    int pubDate;
    public Book(string title, int publicationDate, string type
    "Traditional Book")
```

```
    {
        Title = title;//set value of automatic property
        pubDate = publicationDate;
        bookType = type;
    }
        //override tostring to display book info
    public override string ToString()
    {
        return $"Title:{Title}<br>Type:{bookType}<br>Publication Date:
        {pubDate}";
    }
}
```

So `string type = "Traditional Book"` is what we call an *optional parameter*. As you can see, it says the type, name, and then some default value assigned to it.

# Building the search code

Go to `Default.aspx`. (Delete the `<div>` tag lines, as we won't be using them.) Now put a `Search` box and a `Button` control that says `Search`. We'll be simulating a little database. So, under the `<form id...` tag line, enter the following:

```
Search For:<asp:TextBox ID="TextBox1" runat="server"></asp:TextBox><br />
```

Type `Search For:`, go to **Toolbox**, and drag a `TextBox` control to this line. Let's also add a `Search` button. Go to **Toolbox** and drag a `Button` control below this line:

```
<asp:Button ID="Button1" runat="server" Text="Search" /><br />
```

Change the `Text` property on the `Button` markup to `Search`. That's it!

# Our program interface

Here's the basic HTML interface for this lesson:

```
1  <%@ Page Language="C#" AutoEventWireup="true" CodeFile="Default.aspx.cs" Inherits="_Default" %>
2
3  <!DOCTYPE html>
4
5  <html xmlns="http://www.w3.org/1999/xhtml">
6  <head runat="server">
7      <title>Our First Page</title>
8  </head>
9  <body>
10     <form id="form1" runat="server">
11         Search For:<asp:TextBox ID="TextBox1" runat="server"></asp:TextBox><br />
12         <asp:Button ID="Button1" runat="server" Text="Search" /><br />
13
14         <asp:Label ID="sampLabel" runat="server"></asp:Label>
15
16
17     </form>
18 </body>
19 </html>
20
```

6.14.3: The basic HTML file for this lesson

Go to the **Design** view, and the interface will look like the following screenshot:

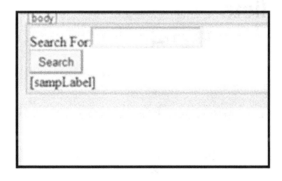

6.14.4: Our simple interface in Design view

Left double-click on the `Search` button, which will bring up the event handler for it. You can get rid of the `Page_Load` block. The starting portion of `Default.aspx.cs` with which we shall begin work is shown in the following screenshot:

```
1 //using is a directive
2 //System is a name space
3 //name space is a collection of features that our needs to run
4 using System;
5 //public means accessible anywhere
6 //partial means this class is split over multiple files
7
8
9 public partial class _Default : System.Web.UI.Page
10 {
11     protected void Button1_Click(object sender, EventArgs e)
12     {
13
14     }
15 }
16
```

Figure 6.14.5: The beginning snippet of Default.aspx.cs

# Working with lists

The first thing we are going to work with is lists. Start by entering the following under `using System`:

```
using System.Collections.Generic;
```

As you can see, a list is super useful; it's practically one of the most useful things that you can find.

Now, let's take a look at the code. First, so that we don't accumulate the output on the screen, we want to clear the `Label` value every time, between button clicks. For this, enter the following below the open curly brace under the line that begins with `protected void Button1_Click...`:

```
sampLabel.Text = "";
```

So, you set `sampLabel.Text` equal to nothing, which empties the label and readies it for the next click.

Next, make a new list of books, as follows:

```
List<Book> bookList = new List<Book>();
```

In the next stage, we're going to fill this list of books. So enter the following line after we have created the `bookList` object:

```
bookList.Add(new Book(title: "Moby Dick", publicationDate: 1851));
```

Here, we first use the concept of a *named argument*. So we type `title` and then stick in a `title` variable, for example, `"Moby Dick"`, a popular book. For `publicationDate`, type `1851`. Notice that here we are specifying `title` and `publicationDate`. This is because in `Book.cs`, the type of book, whether it's traditional or electronic, is optional, you don't have to type anything after the year, `1851`. It will be assigned a default value, which is the optional value of a traditional book.

Now let's repeat this. We have to show enough variety in order to drive home the point. So, let's do another one as follows:

```
bookList.Add(new Book("13 Steps To Riches", DateTime.Now.Year, "eBook"));
```

For a book that was published a long time ago, you can say `DateTime.Now.Year-50`. Perhaps you can do this for an updated version of a book. For now, just say `"eBook"`.

One more thing. Notice that in this case, `eBook` will override the default value, which is the value of a traditional book.

Let's just drive home the point of named parameters by adding one more book to the list. Next type the following:

```
bookList.Add(new Book(publicationDate: 1937, title: "Think And Grow
Rich"));
```

Take a look. Note that you can switch the code around. For example, if you want `publicationDate` to come first, you can do that. This will be a new book publication date, say, `1937`. Then, change the `title` string here to something like this: `"Think and Grow Rich"`. We'll keep the default value of the traditional book. (Actually, *Think and Grow Rich* by *Napoleon Hill* is a great book!)

# Searching a list

Now imagine that you want to be able to search this list. To do so, enter the following as the next line:

```
List<Book> searchResults = bookList.FindAll(book =>
book.Title.ToLower().Contains (TextBox1.Text.ToLower()));
```

After `List<Book>`, type `searchResults`, which is a really nice feature. To get the results, type `bookList.FindAll`. Now we're going to do some fancy stuff. The `=>` symbol after the book means to apply this to every single book in the list. Then, type `book.Title`, which is the property, then . (dot) `ToLower`. Because people type stuff in uppercase, lowercase, and a mixture of cases, you always want to do everything on an equal footing, so you should convert everything either to uppercase or lowercase. Next, type . (dot) `Contains`. The text to be contained is the one from the `TextBox` control, so type `TextBox1.Text.ToLower()`. Everything is always on an equal footing; that is, the text entered is always compared as lowercase.

Now, hover your mouse over `FindAll`. In the pop-up tip, you can see what the return type is. It says `List<Book>`, so `FindAll` will get your list of books. Alright, nice feature!

# Displaying the results

Now, to display the results, which is the last move here, enter the following:

```
searchResults.ForEach(book => sampLabel.Text += book.ToString());
```

Remember, the `=>` symbol after the book indicates an action to be taken on each book, which is just called `sampLabel.Text`. You finish by typing the name of the `book` and then . (dot) `ToString` to convert it to display form.

# Lesson review

For review, the complete version of `Default.aspx.cs` for this lesson, including comments, is displayed in the following code block:

```
//using is a directive
//System is a name space
//name space is a collection of features that our needs to run
using System;
using System.Collections.Generic;
//public means accessible anywhere
```

```
//partial means this class is split over multiple files
//class is a keyword and think of it as the outermost level of grouping
//:System.Web.UI.Page means our page inherits the features of a Page
public partial class _Default : System.Web.UI.Page
{
    protected void Button1_Click(object sender, EventArgs e)
    {
        sampLabel.Text = "";//clear label every time
        List<Book> bookList = new List<Book>();//make list books
                        //fill list of books using named paramters
        bookList.Add(new Book(title: "Moby Dick", publicationDate:
        1851));
        bookList.Add(new Book("13 Steps To Riches", DateTime.Now.Year,
        "eBook"));
        bookList.Add(new Book(publicationDate: 1937, title: "Think And
        Grow Rich"));
        //line below searches for all matching books based on what's
        entered in the text box
        List<Book> searchResults = bookList.FindAll(book =>
        book.Title.ToLower().Contains (TextBox1.Text.ToLower()));
        //line below prints each book by calling ToString() on each
        //book
        searchResults.ForEach(book => sampLabel.Text +=
        book.ToString());
    }
}
```

Alright, so that's the basic logic. This is a nice application we've built here. Bring it up in your browser. Now if you enter something like mo in the search field and hit the Search button, you will see the results shown in *Figure 6.14.7*. There you go! So, it's working as expected. Exit the screen:

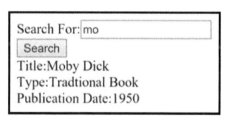

Figure 6.14.7: The final interface we built in this lesson in action

So these are the basics. Remember, we have a class and we have an automatic property whose value is set inside the constructor. We've overridden `ToString` to make the display more professional and useful. Further, when we made the books, we used named parameters or arguments--we also used optional ones--so that if I typed `13` and hit the `Search` button, for example, you would see the results shown in *Figure 6.14.8*. Note that `Type` is `eBook`, so it overrides the default value. Alright, close this and that's it:

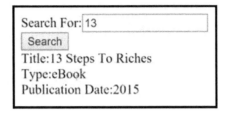

Figure 6.14.8: Search results

# Summary

In this lesson, you learned about several concepts. You built a little application that let you perform a search, as if you were searching Amazon or some other site. You set up a `Book` class, worked with automatic properties, optional parameters, and named arguments. You built the code required to search a list and displayed the results.

In the next lesson, you are going to learn about the null coalescing operator. This is a nice little operator because it helps us write stabler applications that don't crash.

# 48

# Using the Null Coalescing Operator to Write Stabler Applications

In this lesson, you are going to learn about the *null coalescing operator*. This is a nice little operator because it helps us write stabler applications that don't crash and, for example, when an object reference has not been set. Let's take a look at this in action; otherwise, it's going to seem very abstract.

## Setting up the basic HTML for this project

The basic HTML for this project is shown in the following screenshot:

```
1  <%@ Page Language="C#" AutoEventWireup="true" CodeFile="Default.aspx.cs" Inherits="_Default" %>
2
3  <!DOCTYPE html>
4
5  <html xmlns="http://www.w3.org/1999/xhtml">
6  <head runat="server">
7      <title>Our First Page</title>
8  </head>
9  <body>
10     <form id="form1" runat="server">
11
12         <asp:Label ID="sampLabel" runat="server"></asp:Label>
13
14     </form>
15 </body>
16 </html>
```

Figure 6.15.1: The starting HTML for our project in this lesson

# Creating the Car class

The first step is to make a class file. Go to **Solution Explorer** as usual, right-click on the name of the website, select **Add**, and click on **Class**. Name the class `Car` and click on **OK**. When the Visual Studio message comes up, click on **Yes**.

There it is! The section of the `Car` class where we'll begin our work looks like the following screenshot:

```
 9 public class Car
10 {
11
12     {
13
14     }
15 }
```

Figure 6.15.2: Relevant starting section of the Car class

As in the previous lesson, we will make a relatively simple class called `Car` using automatic properties to save time. So, enter the following lines under the open curly brace below the `public` class, namely `Car`:

```
public string MakeModel { get; set; }
public string PreviousOwner { get; set; }
```

To set the values of these automatic properties inside the constructor, add a parameter. So enter the following as the next line:

```
public Car(string makeModel, string prevOwner)
```

Within a set of curly braces within the `public Car` function line, enter the following:

```
MakeModel = makeModel;
```

In other words, in this line, the property is set equal to the parameter value.

Last, enter the following directly below the preceding line:

```
PreviousOwner = prevOwner;
```

That's it! That's our whole class, as shown in *Figure 6.15.3*. So it's a really easy class. Notice again that no backing fields for the properties are required because they are automatic; the values are set to the parameters directly inside the constructor.

```
1 public class Car
2 {
3     public string MakeModel { get; set; }//auto property
4     public string PreviousOwner { get; set; }//auto property
5     public Car(string makeModel, string prevOwner)
6     {
7         //set values of properties inside constructor
8         MakeModel = makeModel;
9         PreviousOwner = prevOwner;
10     }
11 }
```

Figure 6.15.3: The complete Car class code for this lesson

# Searching a database

So that's the whole code. Now, go to `Default.aspx` and write some code that's similar to what you've written before, but more sophisticated. You can search for cars, for example, just as you did before.

Go to **Toolbox** and drag a `Button` control below the line that begins with `<form id...`, as follows:

```
<asp:Button ID="Button1" runat="server" Text="Get Inventory" /><br />
```

Change the `Text` property on the `Button` control to say `"Get Inventory"`, as if you're getting this information from a database--that's the experience we're simulating here. (You can delete the div lines; we don't need them.)

If you go to the **Design** view, you will see a simple button:

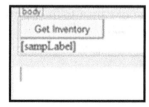

Figure 6.15.4: Our interface includes a simple button

Now left double-click on the **Get Inventory** button, which will bring up the event handler for it. (You can get rid of the `Page_Load` block.) The starting portion of `Default.aspx.cs` with which we shall begin work is shown in the following screenshot:

```
 1 //using is a directive
 2 //System is a name space
 3 //name space is a collection of features that our needs to run
 4 using System;
 5 //public means accessible anywhere
 6 //partial means this class is split over multiple files
 7 //class is a keyword and think of it as the outermost level of grouping
 8 //:System.Web.UI.Page means our page inherits the features of a Page
 9 public partial class _Default : System.Web.UI.Page
10 {
11     protected void Button1_Click(object sender, EventArgs e)
12     {
13
14     }
15 }
```

Figure 6.15.5: The beginning of the snippet of Default.aspx.cs

# Making a list of cars

The first thing to do is make a list of cars so that you can search for them. Under `using System`, enter the following:

```
using System.Collections.Generic;
```

Now, let's go through the process. For the first stage, let's make a list of cars. Start by entering the following within curly braces under the line that begins with `protected void Button1_Click...`:

```
List<Car> carList = new List<Car>();
```

Here, `carList` is the name of the list of cars. On the right-hand side, you reserve memory with `new List<Cars>`, then you add cars.

# The null coalescing operation

To simulate the process of the *null coalescing operation*, you'll need a variety of data types. Enter the following beneath this line:

```
carList.Add(new Car("Honda,Accord", null));
```

First add `"Honda,Accord"`, and then imagine that the previous owner is `null`. That's a possible value. Here, the code works.

Let's do one more. Next we type the following:

```
carList.Add(new Car(null, "Mary Jenkins"));
```

Imagine that the first `MakeModel` business is `null`, and the previous owner is `Mary Jenkins`, for example. Maybe we have `Mary Jenkins` as the previous owner, but nobody ever put down the name of her `MakeModel`.

Let's take a look at another example, as follows:

```
carList.Add(new Car("Jeep,Cherokee", "Bob Jones"));
```

Let's do one that's complete--one that's perfectly complete. Here we put `Jeep Cherokee` and then say that the owner was `Bob Jones`.

Now, enter a final function as follows:

```
carList.Add(null);
```

Remember, this is coming from a database, and a common value in a database might be `null`, meaning that the information is missing. Thus, you can just put in a `null` value here. So, we're simulating a variety of possible problems.

# Displaying the search results

Now, in the next stage of the process, what you want to do is to display the search results. Next start by entering the following:

```
foreach(Car c in carList)
```

You're going to iterate over each car inside a list. That's why we have `Car` after the open parenthesis in this line.

In the next line, you're going to get the `Make` value of the car. But first, let's set this up in the following way, just to show you the errors, and then we will correct them:

```
sampLabel.Text += $"<br>Make:{c.MakeModel.Split(new char[] { ',' })[0]}";
```

With the preceding line, you're going to get the make of the car. To get `Make`, do the following:

- If you enter `{c.MakeModel.Split}`, you can do this because `MakeModel` is `string` and strings can be split. So, c is the car; it has a property called `MakeModel`, and you can split the copy into `(new char[] { ',' })[0]}"`. This means to split the value of `MakeModel` with commas.

In the next stage, `MakeModel` is actually split into an array of strings, so the value that interests us, `Make`, is at index 0, so you're going to put 0 after that. Believe it or not, if you hover your mouse over `Split`, the pop-up tip shown in the following screenshot tells you that it returns a string array:

```
string[] string.Split(params char[] separator) (+ 5 overloads)
Returns a string array that contains the substrings in this instance that are delimited by elements of a specified Unicode character array.
```

Figure 6.14.6: Message displayed when hovering your mouse over Split in the above line

That's why I can have all of `c.MakeModel.Split(new char[] { ',' })` as an array of strings. It looks fancy, but it's still just the name of an array of strings. That's why I can put 0 at the end. Close this with a semicolon.

Imagine that this is the only code there is, just to begin somewhere. Take a look. Crank it up in your browser. Click on the **Get Inventory** button and notice that you get an error, as shown in *Figure 6.15.7*. It says **Object reference not set to an instance of an object**.

Figure 6.14.7: Error message displayed when running the program containing the preceding line

# Debugging your program

Let's start correcting our program. To get the `Make` value properly, enter the following between a set of curly braces under the `foreach`:

```
sampLabel.Text += $"<br>Make:{c?.MakeModel?.Split(new char[] { ',' })[0]}";
```

First, insert a question mark symbol after `c`, and also insert one after `MakeModel`. This is the null coalescing operator, and it helps us ensure, before you make use of anything, that it exists, that it's not null.

So, when you run the code this way and click on the `Get Inventory` button, you will see the screen shown in the following screenshot:

Figure 6.14.8: The application now runs correctly with modifications in the preceding line

Now the application is stabler, correct? It's not crashing anymore and giving us the kind of nonsense that you see in the server application error.

Of course, what we're going to do is extend this. So, in the next stage, imagine that you only want to get the `Model` information. To do this, you can copy (*Ctrl+C*) and paste (*Ctrl+D*) it directly below the `SamLabel.Text += $"<br>Model:....` statement and change where it says `Make` to `Model.`:

```
sampLabel.Text += $"<br>Model:{c?.MakeModel?.Split(new char[] { ','
})[1]}";
```

Alright, so basically, we keep the same things, the only other difference is to change this to index 1. Again, remember that `Split` returns an array of strings, which means that with index 1, you have the `Model` value.

It doesn't matter how fancy it looks; it's still just an array.

Now, the last bit. What if no value for the model or the make is given? We can handle such situations as well. This is what you can do: You can write a double question mark symbol after the index counter, and then put some default text to be displayed. So, for example, you can say `"Make Not Known"`:

```
sampLabel.Text += $"<br>Make:{c?.MakeModel?.Split(new char[] { ',' })[0] ??
"Make Not Known"}";
```

Now, let's repeat this for the next one. Again, imagine that no model is given; this time you will say `"Model Not Known"`. This is the default value to be shown in case no model is available:

```
sampLabel.Text += $"<br>Model:{c?.MakeModel?.Split(new char[] { ',' })[1]
?? "Model Not Known"}";
```

Now, let's do this for the previous owner as well. So, you can enter the following, changing `Model` to `Previous Owner`. This will work fine, but if the previous owner is not known, put a double question mark and then specify `"No Owner Known"`. It looks like this:

```
sampLabel.Text += $"<br>Previous Owner:{c?.PreviousOwner ?? "No Owner
Known"}";
sampLabel.Text +="<br>
```

Remember, with this, we can basically check that `c` exists, then you can check that `MakeModel` exists, and so on. So, it helps to get rid of unstable applications that crash when something does not exist, but you try to make use of it.

# Running the debugged program

Open your browser again and click on the **Get Inventory** button. The results are shown in the following screenshot:

```
Get Inventory

Make:Honda
Model:Accord
Previous Owner:No Owner Known
Make:Make Not Known
Model:Model Not Known
Previous Owner:Mary Jenkins
Make:Jeep
Model:Cherokee
Previous Owner:Bob Jones
Make:Make Not Known
Model:Model Not Known
Previous Owner:No Owner Known
```

Figure 6.15.9: The revised results of running our program after entering the preceding code

# One more fix

Now you have a nice stable application. However, not all the results are being accumulated, so let's fix that quickly.

Enter the following beneath the open curly brace under the line that begins with `protected void Button1_Click...`:

```
sampLabel.Text = "";
```

Type one more thing after the last of the `sampLabel.Text +=` lines you entered, as shown in the following code, to separate the results:

```
sampLabel.Text +=
"<br>-----------------------------------------------------------
---- "
```

You always need `<br>`. It helps to break the output onto different lines. Now when you launch it in your browser and click on the `Get Inventory` button, it looks like the screen shown in *Figure 6.15.10*. Now, it's nice and clean; everything is separated and the application is stable. These are the fundamentals of this concept:

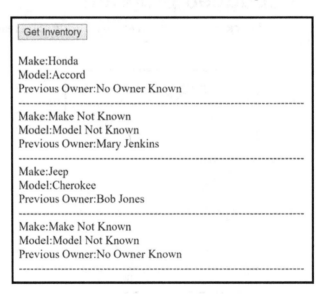

Figure 6.15.10: The results of our nice, clean, and stable application

# Lesson review

For review, the complete version of `Default.aspx.cs` for this lesson, including comments, is displayed in the following code block:

```
//using is a directive
//System is a name space
//name space is a collection of features that our needs to run
using System;
using System.Collections.Generic;
//public means accessible anywhere
//partial means this class is split over multiple files
//class is a keyword and think of it as the outermost level of grouping
//:System.Web.UI.Page means our page inherits the features of a Page
public partial class _Default : System.Web.UI.Page
{
    protected void Button1_Click(object sender, EventArgs e)
    {
        sampLabel.Text = "";//clear label
        List<Car> carList = new List<Car>();//make list of cars
        carList.Add(new Car("Honda,Accord", null));//fill list with new
        //cars
        carList.Add(new Car(null, "Mary Jenkins"));
        carList.Add(new Car("Jeep,Cherokee", "Bob Jones"));
        carList.Add(null);//this one is null, so no car is stored
                //iterate over the cars inside the list
        foreach (Car c in carList)
        {
          //the operator ?. helps to ensure that nothing is null
          //before it's
          //used
          //the operator ?? allows us to include a default value that
          //shows when
          //things are null
          //in lines below, Split returns a string array, so it's
          //allowed to
          //write [0] to get the
          //value at index 0, and likewise for the value at index 1
          sampLabel.Text += $"<br>Make:{c.MakeModel?.Split(new char[]
        { ',' }) [0] ?? "Make Not Known"}";
          sampLabel.Text += $"<br>Model:{c.MakeModel?.Split(new
          char[] { ',' }) [1] ?? "Model Not Known"}";
          sampLabel.Text += $"<br>Previous Owner:{c?.PreviousOwner ??
          "No Owner Known"}";
```

```
            sampLabel.Text +="<br>----------------------------------------
            ----------------------------------- ";
        }
    }
}
```

# Summary

In this lesson, you learned about the `null` coalescing operator. This is a nice little operator because it helps us write stabler applications that don't crash and for example, an object reference has not been set. You created the `Car` class, again using automatic properties and parameters, and set up the code to search a small database of a list of cars. You also introduced some errors and fixed them.

In the next lesson, you are going to learn about overloading operators.

# 49

# Overloading Operators to Perform Custom Operations

In this lesson, you are going to learn about the overloading operators.

## Creating a Vector class

Now create a project as we created earlier, go to **Solution Explorer**, right-click on the name of the website, select **Add**, and click on **Class**. Name the class `Vector` and click on **OK**. When the Visual Studio message comes up, click on **Yes**.

Now, `Vector` is just a collection of numerical values for our purposes, so we have to define what it means to add them. The section of the `Vector` class where we'll begin our work looks like the following screenshot:

```
1
2 public class Vector
3 {
4     public Vector(double x, double y)
5     {
6
7     }
8 }
```

Figure 6.16.1: The relevant starting section of the Vector class

You know because somebody told you when you were very young that the number 2 followed by a plus symbol and 4 is 6. Enter the following at the very top of the `Vector` class:

```
//2+4=6
```

You also know that in the context of C#, something like `"Hello"+" World"` yields a new string that says `"Hello World"`. Enter this line next:

```
//"Hello"+" World"="Hello World"
```

# Overloading a mathematical operator

Alright, so you understand that the + symbol can operate with numerical values, but it's also overloaded--assigned a new meaning as well--so that it can operate on strings.

So the same principle applies here. `Vector`, for our purposes, is like two numbers, separated by commas, between a less-than and greater-than symbol, like the following:

```
//<1,2>+<2,4>=<3,6>
```

# Determining the sum of the vectors

Use the + symbol to add the two vectors as shown. To sum the vectors, add the first number in each vector together, then add the second number in each vector together. In this case, add 1+2=3 and 2+4=6; thus, the sum of the vectors is <3, 6>.

To make this happen, first we need to define the things that make up a vector. Here we're going to deal with all those automatic property settings as efficiently as possible. So, `XCoord` will stand for the x coordinate and `YCoord` will stand for the y coordinate. Then, you will turn these into properties. So enter the following below the open curly brace under `public class Vector`:

```
public double XCoord { get; set; }
public double YCoord { get; set; }
```

Now you can set the values of these properties inside the constructor automatically, so enter the following below the preceding lines:

```
public Vector(double x, double y)
```

The x coordinate represents the first value in the vector, and the y coordinate represents the second value in the Vector method.

Enter the following between a set of curly braces below the preceding line:

```
XCoord = x; YCoord = y;
```

Next, we are going to define what it means to add two vectors, so you're going to type the following below the closed curly brace under the preceding line:

```
public static Vector operator + (Vector vec1, Vector vec2)
```

This will be accessible anywhere--public static means the class level. Of course, Vector is what it returns. Here, operator is a keyword and the addition operator is a specific operator.

In the next stage, what we're going to do is return a new Vector object and add two vectors to it. Remember, in the following comment //<1,2>+<2,4>=<3,6> we took the x coordinate of <1,2> and added that to the x coordinate of the <4,2> and so on. So, you repeat this in the following code. Enter the following between a set of curly braces beneath the preceding line:

```
return new Vector(vec1.XCoord + vec2.XCoord, vec1.YCoord + vec2.YCoord);
```

This is how you override, overload, basically; see the + symbol in the public static Vector operator + line. This will be meaningful when you apply vectors to it.

Also, let's override this line. Enter the following beneath the closed curly brace under the preceding line:

```
public override string ToString()
```

This will automatically generate the following line between a set of curly braces, as shown here:

```
    {
        return base. ToString();
    }
}
```

Remember, ToString is defined inside the base root class called Object. So, in our case, we want to return a nicer representation of a vector that looks more like a mathematical version, so edit this line to read as follows:

```
return $"<{ XCoord},{YCoord}>";
```

That's it! This is our basic `Vector` class. We've got two automatic properties. Set them inside the constructor and now we have an overloaded + symbol. So, the + symbol becomes more meaningful in the context of vectors. Now we also have two strings overridden; this will display the vector so that it looks the way that it would in a textbook.

This is the form of a vector: `<3, 6>`. It has a less-than symbol, two numbers separated by a comma, and a greater-than symbol.

# Adding vectors

Go to `Default.aspx`, which currently looks alike the following screenshot:

```
1 <%@ Page Language="C#" AutoEventWireup="true" CodeFile="Default.aspx.cs" Inherits="_Default" %>
2
3 <!DOCTYPE html>
4
5 <html xmlns="http://www.w3.org/1999/xhtml">
6 <head runat="server">
7     <title>Our First Page</title>
8 </head>
9 <body>
10     <form id="form1" runat="server">
11
12
13         <asp:Label ID="sampLabel" runat="server"></asp:Label>
14
15
16     </form>
17 </body>
18 </html>
19
```

Figure 6.16.2: The starting HTML for this project

What we are going to do is add some vectors together. For our purposes, to keep things efficient, we're going to place a `Button` control in the form, as follows:

```
<asp:Button ID="Button1" runat="server" Text="Add" /><br />
```

We're not going to read the vectors from the user; we could, of course, do this in a real application. For our purposes, all we will have is a `Button` control that says "Add". (Delete the `<div>` tag lines as you won't be needing them.)

Now go to the **Design** view. Our very simple interface is shown in the following screenshot:

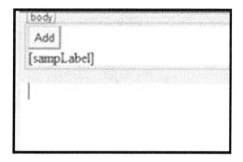

Figure 6.16.3: Our very simple interface in the Design view

Left double-click on the **Add** button. Delete the **Page_Load** block. The section of `Default.aspx.cs` with which we shall begin work is shown in the following screenshot:

```
 5 //public means accessible anywhere
 6 //partial means this class is split over multiple files
 7 //class is a keyword and think of it as the outermost level of grouping
 8 //:System.Web.UI.Page means our page inherits the features of a Page
 9 public partial class _Default : System.Web.UI.Page
10 {
11     protected void Button1_Click(object sender, EventArgs e)
12     {
13
14     }
15 }
```

Figure 6.16.5: The beginning part of the snippet of Default.aspx.cs

# Making vectors

Now we're going to make some vectors. Every time somebody clicks on the `Button` control, you get to make a vector. So, between a set of curly braces under the line that begins with `protected void Button1_Click...`, enter the following:

```
Vector vec1 = new Vector(1, 2);
```

So (1, 2) refers to the x and y coordinates of the vector. Repeat this a couple of times as follows, renaming the vector vec2, vec3, and so on. Also, change the x and y coordinates as shown here so that they're not all the same; otherwise, it's going to get confusing:

```
Vector vec2 = new Vector(3, 4);
Vector vec3 = new Vector(5, 6);
```

Imagine that you want to add these vectors together. For example, you want to add the first vector to the second vector and then the third vector individually. Then, you want to add the second vector to the first vector individually. Finally, you want to add the second vector to the third vector individually.

You will do just this and learn something new along the way. For the first stage, enter the following:

```
foreach (Vector v1 in vecs)
```

We now need to make an array of vectors to accomplish this. Enter the following before the foreach (Vector v1 in vecs) line:

```
Vector[] vecs = new Vector[] { vec1, vec2, vec3 };
```

Now you've made an array of vectors, our own custom-made array of vectors.

Next, between a set of curly braces below the foreach statement, enter the following:

```
foreach (Vector v2 in vecs)
```

Here, we are using nested foreach loops for the following reason: first, the outer loop foreach (Vector v1 in vecs) will fix vec1, then vec2 will be added to vec1, and finally, vec3 will be added to vec1.

# Displaying the results

To display the results and make use of the overloaded + operator, one that's meaningful in the context of vectors, enter the following within a set of curly braces below the foreach statement directly :

```
sampLabel.Text += $"<br>{v1.ToString()}+{v2.ToString()}={(v1 +
v2).ToString()}";
```

First, you want to give a nicely formatted presentation of v1 and v2. For this, do (v1 + v2). If you hover your mouse over the + symbol, it says a vector is returned by this operation, as shown in the following screenshot:

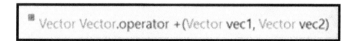

Figure 6.16.6: Pop-up tip showing that a vector is returned by this operation

So, the + symbol in (v1 + v2) returns a vector because we defined it to do so.

Remember, in this context, if it's brown (Windows) or orange (Mac), it will display directly on the screen as is. On the other hand, if it's black, then it's first converted. Also, v1 is the first vector, v2 is the second vector, and so on.

# Running the program

Let's crank this up in your browser and quickly take a look at the results. If you click on the **Add** button, you will see that the vectors have all been added, as shown in the following screenshot:

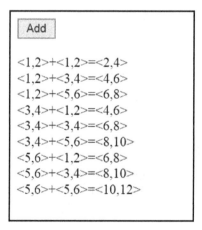

Figure 6.16.7: The vectors are all added

Refer to <1,2>+<1,2>=<2,4>, <1,2>+<3,4>=<4,8>, <1,2>+<5,6>=<6,8>. The first vector is added with the other two, correct? Then, the next block shows that the second vector is added to each of the other two, then with itself. The third vector is added to each of the other two, including itself, and so forth.

Alright, it's working as expected. Remember that the big idea here is that we have made a custom type. It may be necessary to overload or redefine the meaning of some of the basic arithmetic operations, such as addition, subtraction, multiplication, and so on, because this context may dictate it to do so in the way it does here.

# Lesson review

For review, the complete version of the `Default.aspx.cs` file for this lesson, including comments, is displayed in the following code block:

```
//using is a directive
//System is a name space
//name space is a collection of features that our needs to run
using System;
//public means accessible anywhere
//partial means this class is split over multiple files
//class is a keyword and think of it as the outermost level of grouping
//:System.Web.UI.Page means our page inherits the features of a Page
public partial class _Default : System.Web.UI.Page
{
    protected void Button1_Click(object sender, EventArgs e)
    {
        Vector vec1 = new Vector(1, 2);//define three new vector
        Vector vec2 = new Vector(3, 4);
        Vector vec3 = new Vector(5, 6);
        Vector[] vecs = new Vector[] { vec1, vec2, vec3 };//make an
        //array of vectors
        foreach (Vector v1 in vecs)//this loop fixes each vector
        {
            foreach (Vector v2 in vecs)//this one adds the other two,
            //one by one, to the fixed one
            {
                //this line displays the vectors, and the sum of the
                vectors
                sampLabel.Text += $"<br>{v1.ToString()}+
                {v2.ToString()}={(v1 + v2).ToString()}";
            }
        }
    }
}
```

# Summary

In this lesson, you learned about overloading operators. You created a `Vector` class, overloaded a mathematical operator, and found the sum of multiple vectors.

In the next lesson, you are going to learn about **enumerations or lists of named constants**.

# 50
# Using Enumerations to Represent Named Constants

In this lesson, you are going to learn about enumerations or lists of named constants. We use them because it's easier to talk about, for example, Monday, Tuesday, and Wednesday than it is to talk about 1, 2, or 3, correct? If somebody comes to you and says, "Today is 1," you'll say, "Today is 1 what?" But if somebody comes to you and says, "Today is Monday," that you understand, right? That's what we mean by a named constant--it's just more meaningful.

## Setting up a drop-down list

Our starting HTML page for this project is shown in the following screenshot:

```
1 <%@ Page Language="C#" AutoEventWireup="true" CodeFile="Default.aspx.cs" Inherits="_Default" %>
2
3 <!DOCTYPE html>
4
5 <html xmlns="http://www.w3.org/1999/xhtml">
6 <head runat="server">
7     <title>Our First Page</title>
8 </head>
9 <body>
10     <form id="form1" runat="server">
11
12     <div style="text-align:center;">
13         <asp:Label ID="sampLabel" runat="server"></asp:Label>
14     </div>
15
16     </form>
17 </body>
18 </html>
19
```

Figure 6.17.1: The starting HTML page for this project

Now go to **Toolbox** and place a `DropDownList` control below the line that begins with `<form id...`, as follows:

```
<asp:DropDownList ID="DropDownList1" runat="server"></ asp:DropDownList>
```

We're going to be adding some items to this control. First, go to the **Design** view. Click on the drop-down arrow to the right of **Unbound**. Click on **Enable AutoPostBack** so that it refreshes the server every time you submit it. Then, click on the **Edit** item and click on **Add**.

So, for the first one, enter `Monday` and click on **Add**. For the second, enter `Tuesday` and click on **Add**. Finally, enter `Wednesday` and click on **OK**. That's it! Your screen should look like the one shown in the following screenshot:

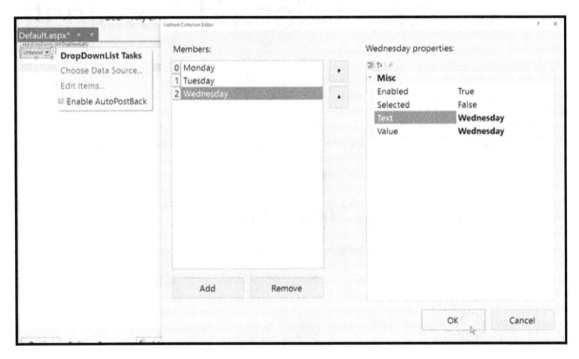

Figure 6.17.2: Enabling AutoPostBack and adding items to the list

If you switch to the **Source** View, you can see that this action has added some items to the **Source** View. The following list of items has been added to the `DropDownList` control. This is the construct now:

```
<asp:DropDownList ID="DropDownList1" runat="server" AutoPostBack="True">
    <asp:ListItem>Monday</asp:ListItem>
    <asp:ListItem>Tuesday</asp:ListItem>
    <asp:ListItem>Wednesday</asp:ListItem>
</asp:DropDownList>
```

Let's take a look at this in the **Design** view, as shown in the following screenshot:

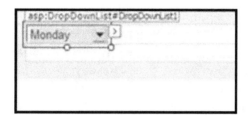

Figure 6.17.3: The current interface in Design view

Left double-click on the button that says **Monday** and bring up the Event Handler for `SelectedIndexChanged`. (Delete `Page_Load block`.) The section of `Default.aspx.cs` with which we shall begin work is shown in the following screenshot:

```
1 //using is a directive
2 //System is a name space
3 //name space is a collection of features that our needs to run
4 using System;
5 //public means accessible anywhere
6 //partial means this class is split over multiple files
7 //class is a keyword and think of it as the outermost level of grouping
8 //:System.Web.UI.Page means our page inherits the features of a Page
9 public partial class _Default : System.Web.UI.Page
10 {
11     protected void DropDownList1_SelectedIndexChanged(object sender, EventArgs e)
12     {
13
14     }
15 }
```

Figure 6.17.4: The beginning part of the snippet of Default.aspx.cs

# Creating the enumeration for this project

Above the line that begins with `public partial class...`, insert the following line:

```
public enum Days { Monday = 1, Tuesday, Wednesday };
```

The `enum` keyword stands for enumeration. Next, you're going to give it a name: `Days`, in this case. Post this, specify the named constants within a set of curly braces and name them. So, you can say `Monday=1` and then `Tuesday`, `Wednesday`, and so on. Close with a semicolon.

In this context, enumerations are usually meant to be accessible everywhere, so you put them outside in your classes; put them at the level of our namespace, for example.

Alright, as you can see, we can use `Monday` now. Because `Monday` is set equal to 1 in the preceding line, if you hover your mouse over **Tuesday**, you will see that `Tuesday` is implied to be 2 and `Wednesday` is implied to be 3. If you set `Monday=0`, `Tuesday` will be implied to be equal to 1 and `Wednesday` will be implied to be 2. So, the numbering is determined by the value that's assigned to `Monday`. Alright, the numbering of the other entries in the list is based on what is assigned to `Monday`.

In the next stage, within the `DropDownList1_SelectedIndexChanged` Event Handler, enter the following between curly braces:

```
switch (DropDownList1.SelectedValue)
```

Now if you hover your mouse over `SelectedValue`, you will be able to see that it's a string.

Alright, we can check the return type, for example, `SelectedItem`. If you hover your mouse over this, things get a little more interesting. It's more complex; it doesn't return just a simple `string` return type, as you can see in the following screenshot:

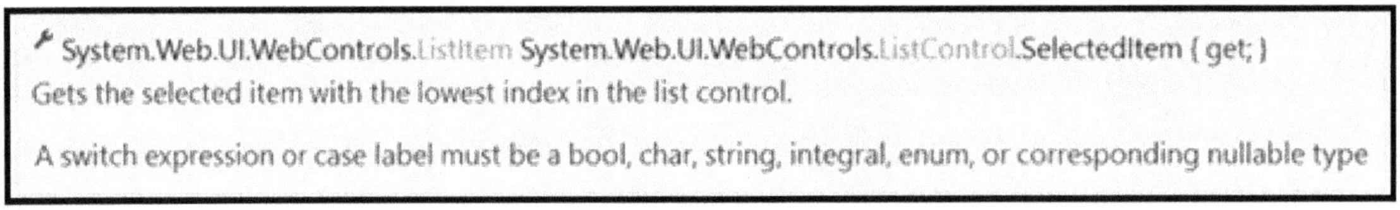

> *System.Web.UI.WebControls.ListItem System.Web.UI.WebControls.ListControl.SelectedItem { get; }
> Gets the selected item with the lowest index in the list control.
>
> A switch expression or case label must be a bool, char, string, integral, enum, or corresponding nullable type

Figure 6.17.5: Pop-up tip for SelectedItem

This is how you can check what is returned: just hover your mouse over it and it will give you some information.

Here, let's go with `SelectedValue`, or if you want, there's also `Selected Item`. Enter the following between a set of curly braces beneath the preceding line:

```
case "Monday" :
```

If somebody selects `Monday`, the selected value is `Monday`. In that case, you can type `{(int)` `Days.Monday}` following between curly braces line:

```
sampLabel.Text = $"{Days.Monday} is day number {(int) Days.Monday}";
```

So, we want the numerical value of `Monday`.

Notice we need one more thing. We need to type a `break;` keyword, correct? So type `break;` on a separate line underneath the preceding line. That's in regard to `Monday`.

Now select this code, press *Ctrl + C* to copy it, and then *Ctrl + V* to paste it on a new line after `break;`. Then, just change `Monday` to `Tuesday`, wherever it appears in this line. Your code should then appear as follows:

```
case "Tuesday" :
sampLabel.Text = $"{Days.Tuesday} is day number {(int) Days.Tuesday}";
break;

case "Wednesday":
sampLabel.Text = $"{Days.Wednesday} is day number {(int) Days.Wednesday}";
break;
```

As you can see, it's easy to work with `Monday`, `Tuesday`, and `Wednesday` rather than the numbers, correct? Numbers are not very meaningful. Numbers have to be given a special meaning as per the context. Whereas with `Monday`, `Tuesday`, and `Wednesday`, we know what they mean.

Notice that in `{Days.Wednesday}`, because we want the day, we leave it as is. However, in `{(int) Days.Tuesday}`, we want the number, so we put the `(int)` data type in front of it to get the number. So you cast it to a numerical value. You change the form to show the numerical value.

# Running the program

Open your browser and your ouput will be, as shown in the following screenshot:

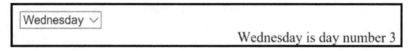

Figure 6.17.6: The results of running the program for our lesson on enumerations

So, `Monday` is day number 1, `Tuesday` is day number 2, and `Wednesday` is day number 3. It's working as expected.

Remember, the big idea with enumerations is to work with a list of named constants. It is named usually for the simple reason: it's easier to deal with intuitive names than with some arbitrary-sounding values, such as 1 or 2.

With Monday, you know what it means. It's the same thing, for example, if you were working with the enumeration of months. You'd do the same thing. You know what January is, right? If somebody asks what month it is and you say "1" (ah! you still know that). However, imagine somebody says it's month "7," then you have to think about that one a little more.

# Lesson review

For review, the complete version of the `Default.aspx.cs` file for this lesson, including comments, is displayed in the following code block:

```
//using is a directive
//System is a name space
//name space is a collection of features that our needs to run
using System;
//public means accessible anywhere
//partial means this class is split over multiple files
//class is a keyword and think of it as the outermost level of grouping
//:System.Web.UI.Page means our page inherits the features of a Page
public enum Days { Monday = 1, Tuesday, Wednesday }; //declare and create
an //enumeration

public partial class _Default : System.Web.UI.Page
{
    protected void DropDownList1_SelectedIndexChanged(object sender,
    EventArgs e)
    {
```

```
switch (DropDownList1.SelectedValue) //switch on the selected
value
{
    case "Monday": //Days.Monday gets Monday, and
    (int)Days.Monday gets
    "1", likewise below
    sampLabel.Text = $"{Days.Monday} is day number {(int)
    Days.Monday}";
    break;
    case "Tuesday":
    sampLabel.Text = $"{Days.Tuesday} is day number {(int)
    Days.Tuesday}";
    break;
    case "Wednesday":
    sampLabel.Text = $"{Days.Wednesday} is day number {(int)
    Days.Wednesday}";
    break;
}
}
}
```

# Summary

In this lesson, you learned about enumerations or lists of named constants. You set up a drop-down list and constructed the enumeration for this project.

In the next lesson, you are going to learn about **namespaces**, which are basically used to construct logical hierarchies.

# 51
# Creating and Using Namespaces

In this lesson, you are going to learn about namespaces. These are basically used to construct logical hierarchies.

## Creating a new project with a new namespace

Let's create a new project. This time, however, click on Visual Studio to make the project. So, select **File** > **New** and choose **Project**, not **Web Site**. In the dialog box that appears, select **Visual C#**. Rename the default Class Library to MathLibrary and then click on **OK**.

Your screen should look like the following screenshot:

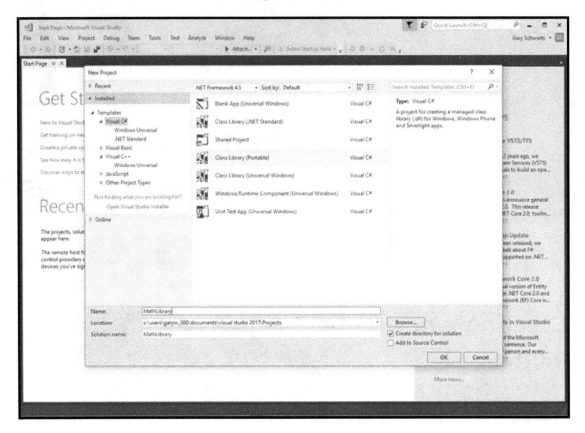

6.18.1: Making a new Visual C# Class Library project in Visual Studio

So this is our namespace, as shown in *Figure 6.18.2*. As you can see, it's called MathLibrary, which, of course, is collapsible. Within it, we have a public class called Class1:

```
7 namespace MathLibrary //define a namespace
8 {
9      public class Class1
10     {
11          {
12          }
13     }
```

Figure 6.18.2: The start of our namespace for this project

# Making new public classes

Let's rename this class from `Class1` to `BasicMath`, as follows:

```
public static class BasicMath
```

We'll make this simple. Within the `BasicMath` class, place one function. So, between a set of curly braces under `public static class BasicMath`, enter the following:

```
public static double Add(double x, double y)
```

Then, within a set of curly braces beneath the preceding line, enter this:

```
return x + y;
```

# Calculating interest

That's it! Just below the open curly brace under the `public static class FinancialMath` class, enter the following:

```
public static double GetInterest(double prin, double rate);
```

Interest is usually calculated on some amount of money, so we'll say `double prin` for principle and `double rate` for the interest rate.

We'll define interest as follows within a set of curly braces below this line:

```
return prin * rate;
```

This is how you get the interest.

Here we have a namespace, `MathLibrary`, as shown in the following screenshot. Within the `MathLibrary` namespace, we have two `Math` classes: `BasicMath` and `FinancialMath`. Each of these stores a function. Everything else that we've learned previously could be put inside these classes. This is the basic hierarchy:

```
namespace MathLibrary //define namespace
{
    public static class BasicMath //define a basic math class
    {
        public static double Add(double x, double y) //define a basic function like Add
        {
            return x + y;
        }
    }
    //code below is as above, just for a financial math class
    public static class FinancialMath
    {
        public static double GetInterest(double prin, double rate)
        {
            return prin * rate;
        }
    }
}
```

Figure 6.18.3: Our complete Class1.cs namespace

Remember we made a class library? So, if you expand `Class1.cs`, as shown in *Figure 6.18.4*, you will see that there are two different classes in there, and the methods available inside each class are shown as well as the signatures of the methods.

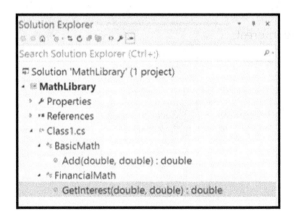

Figure 6.18.4: The classes within Class1.cs, and the methods available inside each class

# Working with dynamic link libraries

When you build the code by selecting **Build** > **Build Solution** or *Ctrl + Shift + B*, notice that it generates the following; observe the highlighted portion done by the cursor, as shown in the following screenshot:

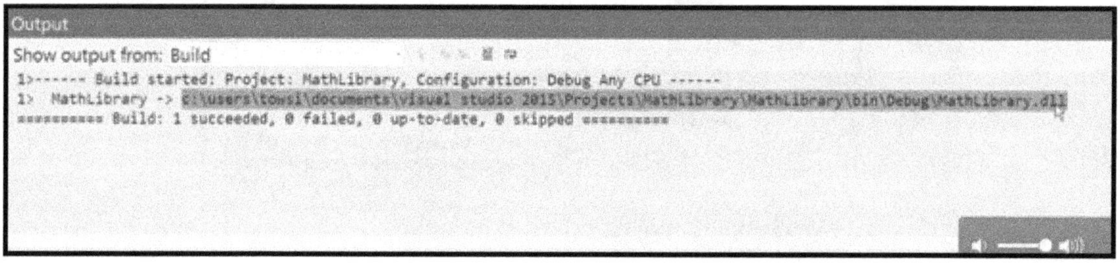

Figure 6.18.5: The dynamic link library built when you build the solution for GetInterest

At the end of the line, it says `dll`. This generates a dynamic link library, which is basically a collection of classes inside a namespace. To make use of it, right-click on and copy the path for `GetInterest`. The `public double GetInterest` block has already been built, so now we have it. Next, select **File** > **Close Solution**.

# Creating a new website from a template

Let's go to **File** > **New** > **Web Site**, as before. Next, choose a template and click on **OK**, as shown in the following screenshot:

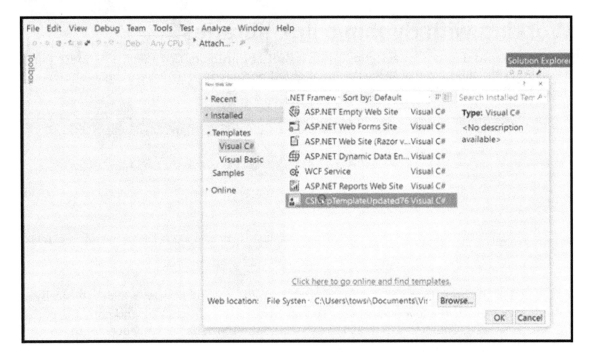

Figure 6.18.6: Starting a new Web Site

In **Solution Explorer**, open `Default.aspx`, which starts out as shown in the following screenshot:

```
1  <%@ Page Language="C#" AutoEventWireup="true" CodeFile="Default.aspx.cs" Inherits="_Default" %>
2
3  <!DOCTYPE html>
4
5  <html xmlns="http://www.w3.org/1999/xhtml">
6  <head runat="server">
7      <title>Our First Page</title>
8  </head>
9  <body>
10     <form id="form1" runat="server">
11
12     <div style="text-align:center;">
13         <asp:Button ID="Button1" runat="server" Text="Add" /><br />
14     <div=v>
15
16     </form>
17 </body>
18 </html>
19
```

Figure 6.18.7 Our starting HTML for this project

Now let's place two `TextBox` controllers within the form so that you can add some numbers, as follows:

```
<asp:TextBox ID="TextBox1" runat="server"></asp:TextBox><br />
<asp:TextBox ID="TextBox2" runat="server"></asp:TextBox><br />
```

So, in the **Design** view, we have two plain boxes. Let's name them `Value 1` and `Value 2`, as follows:

```
Value 1:<asp:TextBox ID="TextBox1" runat="server"></asp:TextBox><br />
Value 2:<asp:TextBox ID="TextBox2" runat="server"></asp:TextBox><br />
```

Next, let's add a `Button` control directly beneath these lines, which will actually find the sum. You can delete the `<div>` tag lines, as you won't be needing them:

```
<asp:Button ID="Button1" runat="server" Text="Button" /><br />
```

We're working with a simple interface as usual (see *Figure 6.18.8*):

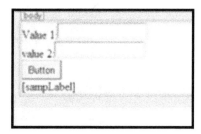

Figure 6.18.8: Our simple interface in Design view

Now, change the `Button` control `Text` property to `Add` so that it's more meaningful.

# Determining the amount of interest

Because we want to make use of both the values, say that we want to find the interest, we'll add one more box below, just to see that we can. So, place a `TextBox` control below the `Button` control indicating the principle to be invested, as follows:

```
Principle: <asp:TextBox ID="TextBox3" runat="server"></asp:TextBox><br />
```

Right below this, put your `TextBox` control for the rate of investment, as follows:

```
Rate: <asp:TextBox ID="TextBox4" runat="server"></asp:TextBox><br />
```

Now we need a new `Button` control to find the interest, so we rename the `textbox1` to
`Find Interest.`:

```
<asp:Button ID="Button2" runat="server" Text="Find Interest" /><br />
```

For review, the complete `Default.aspx` file for this lesson is shown in the following code
block:

```
<%@ Page Language="C#" AutoEventWireup="true" CodeFile="Default.aspx.cs"
Inherits="_Default" %>

<!DOCTYPE html>

<html xmlns="http://www.w3.org/1999/xhtml">
<head runat="server">
    <title>Our First Page</title>
</head>
<body>
    <form id="form1" runat="server">
        Value 1:<asp:TextBox ID="TextBox1" runat="server"></asp:TextBox>
        <br />
        Value 2:<asp:TextBox ID="TextBox2" runat="server"></asp:TextBox>
        <br />
                <asp:Button ID="Button1" runat="server" Text="Add"/>
        <br />
        Principle: <asp:TextBox ID="TextBox3" runat="server">
                </asp:TextBox><br />
        Rate:<asp:TextBox ID="TextBox4" runat="server"></asp:TextBox><br />
            <asp:Button ID="Button2" runat="server" Text="Find
            Interest" /><br />
            <asp:Label ID="sampLabel" runat="server"></asp:Label>
    </form>
</body>
</html>
```

Again, in the **Design** view, we have an **Add** button and a **Find Interest** button, as shown in the following screenshot:

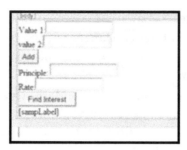

Figure 6.18.10: Our updated interface in Design view

Left double-click the **Add** button. The section of `Default.aspx.cs` with which we shall begin work is shown in the following screenshot:

```
1 //using is a directive
2 //System is a name space
3 //name space is a collection of features that our needs to run
4 using System;
5 //public means accessible anywhere
6 //partial means this class is split over multiple files
7 //class is a keyword and think of it as the outermost level of grouping
8 //:System.Web.UI.Page means our page inherits the features of a Page
9 public partial class _Default : System.Web.UI.Page
10 {
11     protected void Button1_Click(object sender, EventArgs e)
12     {
13
14     }
15 }
```

Figure 6.18.11: Beginning snippet of Default.aspx.cs

# Making a library accessible

This is what we are going to do. First of all, we don't need `Page_Load`; delete that block. Do you see where it says `using System`? Below that, enter `using MathLibrary`. It doesn't work. It's not accessible.

To make it accessible, go to **Solution Explorer** and follow these steps:

1. Right-click on `Bin`.
2. Select **Add Reference**.
3. Select **Browse** in the **Reference Manager** dialog box that appears.
4. Copy the path to the top of the **Select the files to reference...** box. (You can delete the `.dll` file if you want.)
5. Click on **Enter**, and now you see there's **MathLibrary.dll** listed in the **Reference Manager** dialog box.
6. Make sure that **MathLibrary.dll** is selected in the dialog box and click on **OK**. This adds the library, as shown in the following screenshot:

Figure 6.18.12: The MathLibrary has been added and is now accessible

Now you can make use of it as follows. So, below `using System`, enter the following line:

```
using MathLibrary;
```

`MathLibrary` is the namespace. Now it's accessible. Also, remember that `Button1` is the **Add** button that we left double-clicked. So, enter the following within curly braces under the line that begins with `protected void Button1_Click...`:

```
sampLabel.Text = BasicMath.Add(double.Parse(TextBox1.Text),
double.Parse(TextBox2.Text)).ToString();
```

Notice that `BasicMath` shows up as a function from the `MathLibrary` namespace.

# Summing the values

You want to find the sum of two values; we can now do this as usual. Notice that `Add` shows up as a function on the `BasicMath` object, with a tip saying `double BasicMath.Add(double x, double y)`. Alright, close all of that and you should have a parenthesis match; close this with a semicolon at the end. This will display the sum of those two values from `MathLibrary, BasicMath`.

Now, go back to the **Design** view and left double-click on the **Find Interest** button. Of course, there's pretty much the same logic here. So, we'll just take this code (*Ctrl + C*) and paste it (*Ctrl + V*) below the line that begins with `protected void Button2_Click...`, as follows:

```
protected void Button2_Click(object sender, EventArgs e)
{
    sampLabel.Text = FinancialMath.GetInterest(double.Parse(TextBox3.Text),
double.Parse(TextBox4.Text)).ToString();
}
```

Rename `BasicMath` to `FinancialMath`, of course. We'll make a new `FinancialMath` object. Of course, these methods could also be `static` methods so you could type `FinancialMath.GetInterest` or something like that. That's another option.

Next, make `GetInterest` as the function. The interest will be on the principle, so we'll get that from `TextBox3`. We apply the rates to it, which is in `TextBox4`. And that's it!

# Running the program

OK, so these are the basics. Let's open this in your browser. The results of running this program are shown in *Figure 6.18.13*. If you enter 1 in the `Value 1` box, 2 in the `Value 2` box, and hit the **Add** button, it says 3, as you might expect.

If you enter 456 in the **Principle:** box, 0.085 in the **Rate:** box, and click on the **Find Interest** button, it says 38.76. So, this too is working as expected.

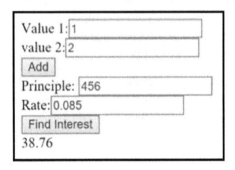

Figure 6.18.13: The MathLibrary has been added and is now accessible

Remember, the big idea here is that namespace groups are related functionality. Inside a namespace, you can even place other namespaces if you want.

 Also, remember when we worked with **using System.Collections.Generic**, `System` was the namespace, followed by `Collections` and then `Generic`. So, you can even nest these.

# Lesson review

For review, the complete version of `Default.aspx.cs` for this lesson, including comments, is displayed in the following code block:

```
//using is a directive
//System is a name space
//name space is a collection of features that our needs to run
using System;
using MathLibrary;//import features from our Math Library
          //public means accessible anywhere
          //partial means this class is split over multiple files
          //class is a keyword and think of it as the outermost level
          of grouping
          //:System.Web.UI.Page means our page inherits the features of
          a Page
public partial class _Default : System.Web.UI.Page
{
    protected void Button1_Click(object sender, EventArgs e)
    {
        //read values
        //convert values to numerical form if possible
        //add them using class library Add method
        //show results back to user
        sampLabel.Text = BasicMath.Add(double.Parse(TextBox1.Text),
double.Parse(TextBox2.Text)).ToString();
    }
    protected void Button2_Click(object sender, EventArgs e)
    {
        sampLabel.Text =
FinancialMath.GetInterest(double.Parse(TextBox3.Text),
double.Parse(TextBox4.Text)).ToString();
    }
}
```

# Summary

In this lesson, you learned about namespaces that are used to construct logical hierarchies. You created a new project with a new namespace, made new public classes, calculated interest, worked with dynamic link libraries, created a new website from a template, and made a library accessible.

In the next lesson, you are going to learn about structs. Structs are usually used to represent simple composite objects, such as a point, where you basically have x and y coordinates, and the idea of structs is that these are value types, not reference types.

# 52

# Structs, Random Points, and Sleeping Threads

In this chapter, you are going to learn about `structs`, which are typically used to represent simple composite objects, such as a point, where you basically have x and y coordinates. The idea behind `structs` is that these are value types, not reference types.

Alright, ready to get started?

## Adding a SimpleStruct class file

Let's make a project, as shown in the following screenshot (I have eliminated the `<div>` tag lines as we won't be needing them):

```
1  <%@ Page Language="C#" AutoEventWireup="true" CodeFile="Default.aspx.cs" Inherits="_Default" %>
2
3  <!DOCTYPE html>
4
5  <html xmlns="http://www.w3.org/1999/xhtml">
6  <head runat="server">
7      <title>Our First Page</title>
8  </head>
9  <body>
10      <form id="form1" runat="server">
11
12      <asp:Label ID="sampLabel" runat="server"></asp:Label>
13
14      </form>
15  </body>
16  </html>
17
```

Figure 6.19.1: The starting HTML for our project

Once you have the project, add a class file and put the struct inside this class file. Go to **Solution Explorer**, right-click on the name of the website, select **Add**, and then click on **Class**. Name the class `SimpleStruct` and click on **OK**. When the Visual Studio message comes up, click on **Yes**.

# Coding the struct

Let's begin by deleting all of the default code and comments in the class you have created. We're going to make a really simple struct called `Point`. Enter the following, starting from the very top:

```
public struct Point
```

You can still define a couple of variables to represent `Point` and properties. So, for example, enter the following below the `public struct Point` line:

```
public double X { get; set; }
public double Y { get; set; }
```

You can also initialize them and you can still have a constructor. So, type the following below the preceding lines:

```
public Point(double x, double y)
```

Then, you can set the values inside the constructor of the properties. Enter the following within a set of curly braces below this line:

```
X = x; Y = y;
```

So, `X` equals `x` and `Y` equals `y`, as we have here.

This is the basic `struct` example, as shown in *Figure 6.19.2*. Remember, it looks superficially similar to a `class`, but internally, it behaves differently because when you make copies it's a *by value* kind of object, not a reference object like a class.

```
1 public struct Point //struct declaration
2 {
3     public double X { get; set; } //auto properties
4     public double Y { get; set; }
5     public Point(double x, double y)
6     {
7         X = x; Y = y; //set values of auto properties through constructor
8     }
9 }
```

Figure 6.19.2: The complete simple struct class

# Modifying the HTML to make use of the struct

Next, we're going to make use of it. Go to `Default.aspx` and place a `Button` control in the form. Change the `Text` property on the `Button` control to something different. So, for example, let's change it to `Make And Show Points` because we're going to make and show some points. Your `Default.aspx` code should look like the one shown in the following screenshot:

```
1 <%@ Page Language="C#" AutoEventWireup="true" CodeFile="Default.aspx.cs" Inherits="_Default" %>
2
3 <!DOCTYPE html>
4
5 <html xmlns="http://www.w3.org/1999/xhtml">
6 <head runat="server">
7     <title>Our First Page</title>
8 </head>
9 <body>
10     <form id="form1" runat="server">
11         <asp:Button ID="Button1" runat="server" Text="Make And Show Points" /><br />
12
13     <asp:Label ID="sampLabel" runat="server"></asp:Label>
14
15     </form>
16 </body>
17 </html>
18
```

Figure 6.19.3: The complete HTML for this project

So, it's really simple: here we have just one `Button` and a `Label` control. If you switch to the **Design** view, the interface looks like the one shown in the following screenshot:

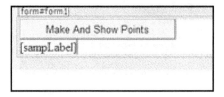

Figure 6.19.4: The simple interface for this project in Design view

So here we have one `Button` control and a `Label` control.

# Making an array of points

Now, left double-click on the `Make and Show Points` button.

Start by deleting the `Page_Load` block in the Event Handler. Your starting `Default.aspx.cs` file should look like the one shown in the following screenshot:

```
10 public partial class _Default : System.Web.UI.Page
11 {
12     protected void Button1_Click(object sender, EventArgs e)
13     {
14
15     }
16 }
```

Figure 6.19.5: Beginning snippet of Default.aspx.cs

Now we are going to make an array of points. So, enter the following between curly braces under the line that begins with `protected void Button1_Click...`:

```
Point[] points = new Point[10];
```

`Point` is the `struct` array that we have made, and `points` is the name of the array. Let's specify the length as `[10]` in this example.

Now, you want to fill in the x and y coordinates of each `Point` type array, so enter the following below the `Point[] points = new point[10];` line:

```
for (int i = 0; i < points.Length; i++)
//Filling the Array with New Points Whose x and y Coordinates Are Random
```

In the next stage, enter the following within a set of curly braces below the preceding line:

```
points[i] = new Point(new Random().Next(-10, 10), new
Random().Next(-10, 10));
```

You need to initialize the x and y variables, and you also want to make them random. You can do this with `Random()`. When you type `Next`, if you hover your mouse over it, you'll notice that the pop-up tip has several versions. One of them is `integer minimum (int minValue) value, max value (int maxValue)`. So here we enter from –10 to 10 and repeat the same for the next one.

# Displaying the results

We'll take a look at whether this works momentarily. So, with the code in place, once we have them generated, of course, we can display them. Enter the following below the closing curly braces below the `foreach` loop:

```
foreach (Point p in points)
```

Now enter the following within a set of curly braces below the `foreach` line. After typing `sampLabel.Text`, you want to make use of the properties that you have, so you're going to show `Point` as you would see it in a book, using parentheses. Also, when you type p. (dot), notice the property shows up in a pop-up list; select X:

```
sampLabel.Text += $"({p.X},{p.Y})";
```

# Running the program

Let's take a look at the effects, to see whether this is what we really want. So, crank it up in your browser. A new `Random` class makes an object, the `Next` function gets a number, and that's how you can initialize x and y coordinates at each .

Alright, hit the `Make` and `Show Points` buttons, and there's an obvious problem, as shown in the following screenshot:

| Make And Show Points |
|---|
| (-4,-4)(-4,-4)(-4,-4)(-4,-4)(-4,-4)(-4,-4)(-4,-4)(-4,-4)(-4,-4)(-4,-4) |

Figure 6.19.6: The results of running the program as currently written are not very random

# Debugging the program

Notice that all of them are the same, right? That's not very random, is it? So, we have to fix this. The way to do this is to go back to the `Default.aspx.cs` file and imagine that you put the following directly below the `using System` namespace line:

```
using System.Threading;
```

Now, as the loop runs, to ensure that there's a bit of space between the time the points are made, we can say something like the following directly below the line that begins with `points[i] = new Point...`:

```
Thread.Sleep(1000);
```

The amount of time specified is in milliseconds. So, for example, 1000 milliseconds equals 1 second. So, it will sleep and then resume.

Let's look at it again in your browser. Click on the `Make` and `Show Points` button controls. The results will appear as shown in *Figure 6.19.7*.

This may take a little bit of time now because as it runs, it sleeps a little every loop, and you'll see whether this is sufficient or not.

| Make And Show Points |
|---|
| (-2,-2)(7,7)(-5,-5)(4,4)(-8,-8)(1,1)(9,9)(-2,-2)(6,6)(-5,-5) |

Figure 6.19.7: The results of running are now random

Now, as you can see, the points are a little more random. And that's what you want. This is the basic code. Again, remember, the SimpleStruct class has a struct keyword. You can still use properties, for example, with get and set, which are daughter properties. You can still write a constructor, like the one we created for the SimpleStruct struct. You can make an array of points, as you did in Default.aspx.cs. You also learned how to make a new Random object, how to generate a value between –10 and 10, and how to ensure that they're not all the same by putting something like Thread.Sleep for 1000 milliseconds, which means 1 second. This allows enough time for the numbers generated to be unique. This is what you witnessed when you ran the revised code. Again, you can still use a foreach loop to access the x and y coordinates of each point and then display them.

# Lesson review

For review, the complete version of Default.aspx.cs for this lesson, including comments, is displayed in the following code block:

```
//using is a directive
//System is a name space
//name space is a collection of features that our needs to run
using System;
using System.Threading;
//public means accessible anywhere
//partial means this class is split over multiple files
//class is a keyword and think of it as the outermost level of grouping
//:System.Web.UI.Page means our page inherits the features of a page
public partial class _Default : System.Web.UI.Page
{
    Proctected void Button1_Click(object sender, EventArgs e)
    {
        Point[] points = new Point[10];//array of points
        for(int i = 0; < points.length; i++ )
        {
            //line below fills array with new points whose x and y co
ordinates are
            //random
            points[i] = new Point(new Random().Next(-10,10), new
Random().Next(-10,
            10));
            //use thread sleeping to ensure the x and y coordinates are not
at all
            //the same
            Thread.sleep(1000);
        }
        //iterate over array of points to show the x and y coordinates
```

```
foreach(Point p in Points)
{
    sampLabel.Text += $"({p.X},{p.Y})";
}
}
}
```

# Summary

In this lesson, you learned about structs, which are ordinarily used to represent simple composite objects, such as a point, where you basically have x and y coordinates. The idea behind structs is that these are value types, not reference types. You added a SimpleStruct struct, coded the struct, modified the HTML to make use of the struct, made an array of points, and filled the array with new points whose x and y coordinates were random. We also ran and debugged the program.

In the next lesson, you are going to learn about delegates. You can think of delegates as function wrappers. Basically, delegates are a way of representing functions and then stacking function calls together.

# 53

# Declaring, Creating, and Using Delegates

In this chapter, you are going to learn about delegates. You can think of delegates as function wrappers. Basically, delegates are a way of representing functions and then stacking function calls together.

## Setting up the HTML for this project

Create a project as shown in *Figure 6.20.1* (I have eliminated the `<div>` tag lines, as we won't be needing them):

```
 1 <%@ Page Language="C#" AutoEventWireup="true" CodeFile="Default.aspx.cs" Inherits="_Default" %>
 2
 3 <!DOCTYPE html>
 4
 5 <html xmlns="http://www.w3.org/1999/xhtml">
 6 <head runat="server">
 7     <title>Our First Page</title>
 8 </head>
 9 <body>
10     <form id="form1" runat="server">
11
12         <asp:Label ID="sampLabel" runat="server"></asp:Label>
13
14     </form>
15 </body>
16 </html>
17
```

Figure 6.20.1: The starting HTML for our project

First, let's put a `Button` control into the project form, as follows:

```
<asp:Button ID="Button1" runat="server" Text="Update Labels" /><br />
```

Next, change the `Text` property in the `Button` markup to read `Update Labels`. Post this, put `Label` controls under this `Button` control. You can keep the one that's there already, but we'll add a couple of other ones. So, change the `ID` property on the existing `Label` markup to say `mainLabel`, as follows:

```
asp:Label ID="mainLabel" runat="server"></asp:Label>
```

Now, before this line, create more `Label` control. Drag in another label; we'll call this `labelOne`, as follows:

```
<asp:Label ID="labelOne" runat="server" ></asp:Label><br />
```

Now let's create one more `Label` control. Take the `labelOne` line and copy (*Ctrl+C*) and paste (*Ctrl+V*) the new label below the preceding line. Let's rename this one `labelTwo`, as follows:

```
<asp:Label ID="labelTwo" runat="server" ></asp:Label><br />
```

# Checking out the interface

In the **Design** view, all that we have is shown in the following screenshot:

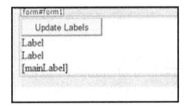

Figure 6.20.2: A simple interface for this project in Design view

Again, if you want, you can also get rid of where it says `Text=Label` since nothing shows up by default when you launch the page. Then, in the **Design** view, it will look like the following screenshot:

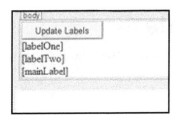

Figure 6.20.3: The interface in Design view when you delete Text=Label"

Your `Default.aspx` file should look like the one shown in the following code block:

```
<%@ Page Language="C#" AutoEventWireup="true" CodeFile="Default.aspx.cs"
Inherits="_Default" %>

<!DOCTYPE html>

<html xmlns="http://www.w3.org/1999/xhtml">
<head runat="server">
    <title>Our First Page</title>
</head>
<body>
    <form id="form1" runat="server">
        <asp:Button ID="Button1" runat="server" Text="Update Labels" /><br
/>
        <asp:Label ID="labelOne" runat="server" ></asp:Label><br />
        <asp:Label ID="labelTwo" runat="server" ></asp:Label><br />
        <asp:Label ID="mainLabel" runat="server"></asp:Label>
    </form>
</body>
</html>
```

Now left double-click on the `Update Labels` button. Start by deleting the `Page_Load` Event Handler. Your starting `Default.aspx.cs` file should look like the one shown in the following screenshot:

```
 9 public partial class _Default : System.Web.UI.Page
10 {
11
12     protected void Button1_Click(object sender, EventArgs e)
13     {
14
15
16     }
17 }
```

Figure 6.20.5: Beginning snippet of Default.aspx.cs

# Making a delegate

To make a delegate, we're going to write the following above the line that begins with `public partial class...`:

```
public delegate void LabelUpdater();
```

This is a delegate. It's `public`, meaning that it is accessible from anywhere. Notice that it's a keyword--it's blue (Windows) or teal (Mac). Then, `void` is a return type and `LabelUpdater` is what we named it. This line will basically be used to represent several different functions. So, in our case now, specifically under the `Button1_Click` event, we're going to write some code.

As our first step, go outside the set of curly braces under the line that begins with `protected void Button1_Click...` and enter the following under closed curly braces:

```
public void UpdateLabelOne()
```

You say `void` because the methods that are called through the delegates have to have that same `void` return type as we have in the declaration of the delegate.

Now, within a set of curly braces below this line, enter the following:

```
labelOne.Text = $"{DateTime.Now}";
```

Update `labelOne.Text` with the current time. That's all.

Then, to see the effects of everything more clearly, let's make the `UpdateLabelOne` function sleep so that things slow down for us. So, under `using System` at the top, enter the following:

```
using System.Threading;
```

Next, under the line that you entered in the beginning with `labelOne.Text...`, enter the following:

```
Thread.Sleep(5000);
```

The time interval of `5000` means 5 seconds: *5000 milliseconds=5 seconds*.

Now, you can repeat this a couple of times for other `Label` controls. So copy the block that begins with `public void UpdateLabelOne()...` and paste it below the `UpdateLabelOne` block. Change this one, of course, to say `UpdateLabelTwo`. Also, change the `Text` property to read `Label2.Text`. The rest of it is the same.

Let's do this one more time. Again, copy the block that begins with `public void UpdateLabelTwo()` . . . and paste it below the `UpdatelabelTwo` block. Now change this one to say `UpdateMainLabel`. Also, change the `Text` property to read `mainLabel.Text`.

Now, within a set of curly braces under `public void UpdateMainLabel()`, enter the following:

```
mainLabel.Text = $"Labels finished updating at:{DateTime.Now}";
```

Remember, in this context, `Thread.Sleep` is only there to exaggerate the effect of time so that the results are more visible.

Now to call `UpdateLabelOne`, `UpdateLabelTwo`, and `UpdateMainLabel`, we can do the following to the delegate; you can make a delegate within curly braces inside the `Button1_Click` event:

```
LabelUpdater lu = UpdateLabelOne;
```

We call it `lu`; next, in order to assign something meaningful to this, you can just write the name of a function, such as `UpdateLabelOne`. Further, you can type the following directly below this line:

```
lu += UpdateLabelTwo;
```

You can stack the function calls together so that they're executed sequentially, after only one button click. Another way of doing this, instead of just writing the function name, is to write a new `LabelUpdater` method and specify the function that this is to wrap, as follows:

```
lu += new LabelUpdater(UpdateMainLabel);
```

If you hover your mouse over `LabelUpdater`, you'll notice where the tip says **LabelUpdate (void () target)**, so you can select `UpdateMainLabel` from the list of functions that appear.

Now, at the end, to make the new `lu` object work, what you can do is the following:

```
lu.Invoke();
```

So, you invoke `delegate` to make it work. Alright, our code is shown in the following code block:

```
//using is a directive
//System is a name space
//name space is a collection of features that our needs to run
using System;
using System.Threading;
//public means accessible anywhere
```

```
//partial means this class is split over multiple files
//class is a keyword and think of it as the outermost level of grouping
//:System.Web.UI.Page means our page inherits the features of a Page
public delegate void LabelUpdater();//declare delegate
public partial class _Default : System.Web.UI.Page
{
    protected void Button1_Click(object sender, EventArgs e)
    {
        LabelUpdater lu = UpdateLabelOne; //make delegate and assign
        //function
        lu += UpdateLabelTwo;//assign another function
        lu += new LabelUpdater(UpdateMainLabel);//assign another
        //function
        lu.Invoke();//invoke delegate
    }
    //this function is called first
    public void UpdateLabelOne()
    {
        labelOne.Text = $"{DateTime.Now}";
        Thread.Sleep(5000);
    }
    //this function is called second
    public void UpdateLabelTwo()
    {
        labelTwo.Text = $"{DateTime.Now}";
        Thread.Sleep(5000);
    }
    //this function is called third
    public void UpdateMainLabel()
    {
        mainLabel.Text = $"Labels finished updating at:{DateTime.Now}";
    }
}
```

# Running the program

Alright, crank this program up in your browser now. Click on the Update Labels button. Remember, this requires a little bit of patience because of how we specified the time intervals, or sleeping times, to exaggerate the effects of time a bit. *Figure 6.20.7* shows that the labels have finished updating and when:

Figure 6.20.7: The results of running the program show that the labels have finished updating and when

Clearly, because of the sleeping times we entered, you can see that this run was updated first at 5:11:47 PM, then at 5:11:52 PM, and finally at 5:11:57 PM, all on 10/16/2015, of course.

These are the basics. Remember the idea here, so you don't forget that the main point is that you have a `delegate` construct, such as `public delegate void LabelUpdater`, and you can make an object of that type, as you can see the type in `LabelUpdater lu`. You can assign different functions to it, and you can stack the function calls together and then `lu.Invoke` will call the functions for you one by one--all the functions that begin with `public void Update...` in our example. That's how you can chain function calls together through delegates. Delegates are used heavily in Windows Event programming. That's it for this lesson.

# Summary

In this lesson, you learned about `delegates`. You should think of `delegates` as function wrappers.

In the next chapter, we'll turn our attention to some of the new features in C# 7, and take a look at using `switch` blocks with the `when` clause.

# 54
# Switch Blocks with when in C# 7.0

In this chapter, we are going to learn how to use `switch` blocks with the `when` clause.

## Creating the classes

Lets start by creating a C# console app and clearing out all of the existing template code. Next, we type the first line of our code:

```
using static System.Console;
```

As usual, we need this so that we can use `WriteLine`. Next, create an `abstract` class to work with. For this, type the following:

```
abstract class Shape
{
}
```

This class here is needed so that we can switch between objects of the type `Shape`. People sometimes do something similar with interfaces. Well, I'm using an `abstract` class for the following reason: classes are used to essentially express the "is a" type of relationship, while interfaces are used to express the "can be used as" type of relationship. Let's take a look and see why I chose to go with a class. Underneath the closing brace of our `Shape` class, start a new line and type the following:

```
class Rectangle:Shape
{
}
```

We've created a new `Rectangle` class with a parent class of `Shape`. Let's examine our logic and see why I chose to use a class rather than an interface system. Well, it's certainly the case that a rectangle *is a* kind of shape. So, `Shape` is the parent class. I wouldn't say that a rectangle *can be used as* a shape. A rectangle is in its essence a shape. If you say that a rectangle can be used as a shape, then perhaps you're implying that it could be used as other things as well; however, I'm not sure what these other things would be. With this decided, let's go ahead and create another class underneath our `Rectangle` class. For this, type the following:

```
class Circle:Shape
{
}
```

Circles are another kind of shape, so `Shape` is the parent class. We'll define the logic of the bodies in a minute. First, let's go ahead and create our `Main` program function. Underneath `Circle`, type the following:

```
class Program
{
    static void Main()
    {

    }
}
```

Now we have a complete skeleton framework for our program. It's time to go ahead and fill in the details. Let's begin with defining our rectangle. Within the `Rectangle` curly braces, type the following:

```
private double width, height;
```

These are the backing fields or instance variables. Remember, we call them that because each instance of the `Rectangle` class has its own values, usually for the `width` and `height` values. Next, let's make a constructor. On the next line, type the following:

```
public Rectangle(double w, double h)
{

}
```

Then, I'll set the values of the instance variables inside the body of the constructor. So, we'll say the following:

```
width = w; height = h;
```

Nothing new here. Next, we are going to code our properties to access the `width` and `height` fields. Add a new line underneath our `Rectangle` constructor and type the following:

```
public double Width { get => width; }
```

This is a new kind of notation that you may not have seen before. What we are saying is that the `Width` function is basically an expression-bodied member. So, properties like this can be expression-bodied members, and you essentially indicate this by using `get =>`. It's the same as in lambda expressions, if you're familiar with them. Remember, the purpose of having our property like this is that the `Width` property gets the value of the `width` backing field. Then, we can repeat this for the `Height` property. The simplest way is to just copy and paste this line and change the names from `width` to `height`:

```
public double Height { get => height; }
```

So remember, fields are usually `private`, which is what we have in our `Rectangle` class definition. Properties give controlled access to fields. In this way, we can make use of the value and calculations we'll discuss inside `Main`.

Now let's move on to the `Circle` class. For circles, there's only one piece of information that's important: `radius`. Inside our `Circle` class, we are going to say the following:

```
private double radius;
```

The radius is the distance from the center to a point on the circumference. Once you know the radius of a circle, you can use it to determine the circumference, the distance around a circle, the area, or the amount of flat space occupied. In other words, knowing the radius is the single most important piece of information that can be used to find other information about circles. Again, it's a `private` value, so it's hidden. `Double` is a data type remember, so you can have radii such as 2.598 and so on.

On the next line, we are going to do something a little different:

```
public Circle(double r) => radius = r;
```

You can also use expression-bodied members when you make a constructor, as we've demonstrated here. This sets the value of the `radius` instance variable right there in the definition. As before, we want to be able to read the `radius` value so we can make use of it in calculations. To do this, say the following:

```
public double Radius { get => radius; }
```

We're using another expression-bodied member to get the value of the `radius` field through the `Radius` property. As you can see, expression-bodied members allow you to write very streamlined code that's neater and more compact. I like them.

# Writing the Main function code

That's that for our class definitions. Let's move on and get into the body of `Main` to create our main program. Type the following within the `Main` method:

```
Shape shape = new Rectangle(4, 5);
```

On the left-hand side, we have `Shape` because both `Circle` and `Rectangle` derive from `Shape`. We don't have any code in the `Shape` class to define shapes. We are using it simply so that we can write `Shape` on the left-hand side to create new objects from that parent class. We're creating a rectangle, so we need to define the dimensions as 4 by 5.

Next, we come to the subject of this chapter: our `switch` block. On the next line, type the following:

```
switch(shape)
{

}
```

This is a new feature of C# 7.0. It is possible to switch between different data types, such as `Shape`, for example. Inside the curly braces of the `switch` block, type the following:

```
case Rectangle r when (r.Width == r.Height):
```

We're doing some really simple math here to check whether a rectangle is actually a square. We're switching our `Rectangle` object and using the `when` keyword to check whether `Width` is equal to (using a `double` equals comparison) `Height`. That's how you would interpret that.

In the next couple of lines, type the following:

```
WriteLine($"Perimeter={4 * r.Width}: Square");
break;
```

So we're using `WriteLine` to print to the screen, then we have the `$` symbol for string interpolation. We also have a simple formula for calculating the perimeter of a square. You could have used width or height here, as they're equal. Terminate with a semicolon, and then as usual, type `break`. The `when` clause allows you to make logical comparisons like this one. This is a new feature of `switch` blocks that I love to use.

That's our math for squares done; let's move on to rectangles. We start in exactly the same way. So, on a new line, type the following:

```
case Rectangle r:
```

We used the `when` keyword for our special case with squares, so there's no need for it in the more general case of a rectangle. We can move straight to the next line and add our math for a general rectangle. When the width and height are different, we have what we might call a more general kind of a rectangle. Now we type the following:

```
WriteLine($"Perimeter={2 * r.Width + 2 * r.Height}: Rectangle");
break;
```

The perimeter is calculated as twice the width plus twice the height. Again, that's pretty simple math. So both of our rectangle possibilities are done. Let's move on to circles now.

On a new line in our `switch` block, below the rectangles, type the following:

```
case Circle c:
    WriteLine($"Circumference:{2 * 3.1459 * c.Radius}: Circle");
    break;
```

If you want, you can read the value of Pi with more accuracy, using the `Math` class. For our purposes, it doesn't really matter. Remember that the circumference of a circle is *2 \* pi \* radius*. So, in our case, it means `2 * 3.1459 * c.Radius`. Read the value of the backing field using the `Radius` property. That's it!

# Running the program

Let's give this a build. So, go to **Build > Build Solution** or use the *Ctrl + Shift + B* key combo, if you like. I do, but not when there are many keys, though. Two keys are okay. I don't like when there are three or four keys you have to press. Once it builds without any issues, go to **Debug > Start Without Debugging** or use *Ctrl + F5*. That's easy. You should see the following:

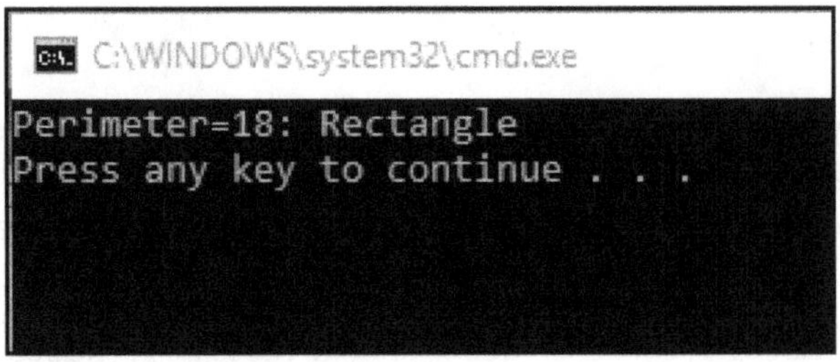

Figure 6.1: Debugging the program

So you have **Perimeter=18**, and it's `Rectangle`. That's correct. Let's check this calculation by hand, just to be sure. We're creating a rectangle with dimensions set to 4 by 5. They're not the same, so it's not a square. Therefore, we go through to the next statement. 2 times 4 is 8. 2 times 5 is 10. 10 plus 8 is 18. It's working! At this simple kind of a level, you should be able to check everything by doing hand calculations or using a calculator.

Let's change this so that the second dimension of our rectangle is also `4`:

```
Shape shape = new Rectangle(4, 4);
```

This should correspond to the case of a square because the height and width are equal. We will calculate the perimeter according to this basic rule: four times the width or the height. Let's take a look at the output, We start by clicking **Debug > Start Without Debugging**:

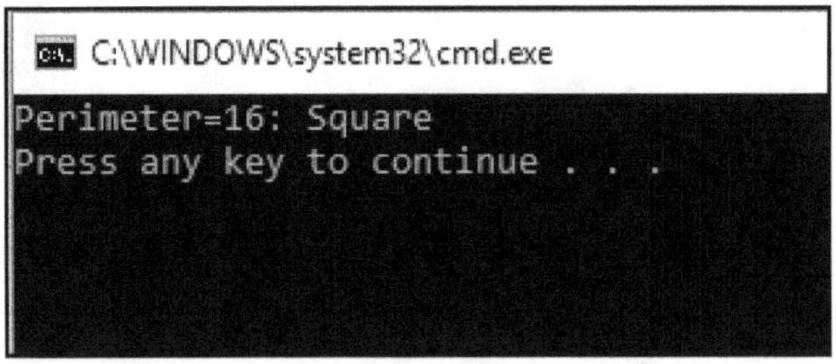

Figure 6.2: Debug the square program

Now you have `Perimeter=16` and it's `Square`. Alright, now let's change this to a circle to check our final case:

```
Shape shape = new Circle(5);
```

Again, run the code with **Debug > Start Without Debugging**. You should see the following:

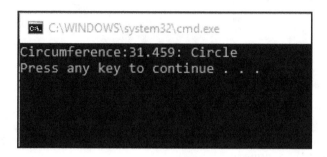

Figure 6.3: Debug the Circumference

Now, `Circumference` is `31.459` (I'll leave you to check that) and it's `Circle`. So everything is working as expected.

Here's the code listing for this chapter in full:

```
using static System.Console; //needed for using WriteLine
abstract class Shape
{
    //is needed so that we can switch on objects of type Shape
    //classes are used to express "is a" type of relationship
    //interfaces are used to express "can be used as" type of relationship
}
class Rectangle:Shape //rectangle is a kind of shape, so Shape if the
parent class
{
    private double width, height; //instance variables
    public Rectangle(double w, double h)
    {
        width = w; height = h; //set values of instance variables
    }
    //properties can be expression-bodied members
    public double Width { get => width; } //Width property gets the
    //value of the width backing field
    public double Height { get => height; } //Height property gets the
    //value of the height backing field
}
class Circle:Shape //circles are kinds of shapes, so Shape is the parent
class
```

```
    {
        private double radius; //radius is the distance from center to a
        //point on the circumference
        public Circle(double r) => radius = r; //set value of radius
        //instance variable
        public double Radius { get => radius; } //Get value of radius field
        //through Radius property
    }
    class Program
    {
        static void Main()
        {
            Shape shape = new Circle(5);
            switch(shape)//it's possible to switch on different data types
            {
                //if a rectangle has width=height, it's really a square
                case Rectangle r when (r.Width == r.Height)://check whether
                //it's a square
                    WriteLine($"Perimeter={4 * r.Width}: Square");
                    break;
                case Rectangle r://when width and height are different,
                //P=2width+2height
                    WriteLine($"Perimeter={2 * r.Width + 2 * r.Height}:
                    Rectangle");
                    break;
                case Circle c://circumference of circle is 2 * pi * radius
                    WriteLine($"Circumference:{2 * 3.1459 * c.Radius}:
                    Circle");
                    break;
            }
        }
    }
```

# Summary

I hope this code has shown you some of the power of the switch block, with expression-bodied members now being used with properties and even constructors. Remember, this means that the following line is an expression-bodied member with a constructor:

```
public Circle(double r) => radius = r;
```

On the other hand, consider this line:

```
public double Radius { get => radius; }
```

This is an expression-bodied member with a property. We also looked at when you should use `class` and when you should use `interface`. Classes express the *is a* type of relationship, while interfaces are usually used to express the *can be used as* type of relationship. Hence, in the code, I have a `Rectangle` class because it *is a* kind of shape and `Circle` because it *is also a* kind of shape. I hope all of this makes sense to you.

In the next chapter, we'll expand our knowledge of `switch` blocks by looking at how C#7 enables us to use `switch` blocks with objects.

# 55

# Switch Blocks with Objects in C# 7.0

In this chapter, you are going to learn how to use `switch` blocks with C# 7.0. The `switch` blocks have been made more powerful because now you can switch objects and not just basic data types, such as integers.

## Creating the interface

Let's take a look at `switch` blocks in action. Create a new C# console app, clear out the existing code, and start typing this:

```
using static System.Console;
```

We need this line, of course, so that we can use `WriteLine`. Next, we're going to make an interface that we'll call `Movable`:

```
interface Movable
{
    void Move();
}
```

This interface only has one method, called `Move`. Remember, the purpose of an interface is to bind a variety of different, essentially unrelated, class types together. What does this mean? It's basically a contract on the functionality, in other words, interfaces allow grouping objects by their behaviors. Let's take a look at this in action by implementing the interface.

# Implementing the interface

On a new line underneath the closing curly brace of our interface, type this:

```
class Human:Movable
{

}
```

We have created a new class called `Human`, and it's going to implement `Movable`. Remember, what this is saying essentially in simple English is: `Human` is a type of `Movable` object. So, in other words, humans can move. Okay, now we actually need to implement the interface. To do this, click on `Movable` and you should see a light bulb appear on the left-hand side. Click on it, then click on the `Implement` interface:

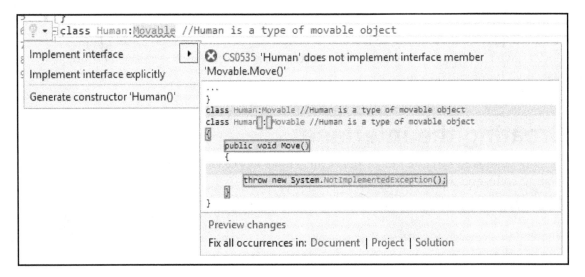

Figure 5.1: Selecting the Implement interface

This will automatically expand your code to the following:

```
class Human : Movable
{
    public void Move()
    {
        throw new System.NotImplementedException();
    }
}
```

Inside `public void Move()`, we're going to define what it means for a human being to move. So, remove the `throw new exception` line and replace it with the following:

```
WriteLine("I move by moving two legs.");
```

This is what it means, for our purposes, for a person to move. There you go! We now have our implementation of human movement. Our `Move` method has to be implemented by classes that implement the `Movable` interface, and this is our first example.

 Remember, we're talking about interfaces. We are not talking about inheritance. We are talking about a contract and functionality, and the benefit is that multiple classes can implement a single interface, and a single class can implement multiple interfaces.

Let's go ahead and create a new class at the bottom of our code:

```
class Fish:Movable
{

}
```

We could use Visual Studio to automatically expand our class, but as it's a pretty simple one, let's just go ahead and write it ourselves. Within our `Fish` class, write the following:

```
public void Move()
{
    WriteLine("I move by flapping my fins.");
}
```

We've now defined what it means for a fish to move. Here, you wouldn't put `Fish` and `Human` as derivatives of some parent class because humans and fish are quite different. The purpose here is that you have an interface named `Movable` and both `Human` and `Fish` are a kind of movable object. This is what binds `Human` and `Fish` together, not the data that they possess, perhaps their behaviors. They're both Movable.

# Creating the Main() program

The next stage here is to create our main program to use these classes. At the bottom of your code, create a new line and type the following:

```
class Program
{

}
```

This will be our main program code and its entry points. Within this, write the following:

```
static void Main()
{

}
```

This is our basic `Main` function setup. Now we are going to make a `Movable` object. Type the following within curly braces:

```
Movable movableObject = new Fish();
```

On the left-hand side of the statement, we have `Movable` as the data type, and we're calling it `movableObject`. On the right-hand side, because we already have our two classes implementing `Movable`, I can put either a new `Human` object or a new `Fish` object. I'm going to use `Fish` for now.

We are going to use this with a `switch` block in a way that has not been possible until now. On the next line, type the following:

```
switch(movableObject)
{
}
```

Unlike before, we can switch an entire object. Now we can decide what we're going to do with it, so within the `switch` block, type the following:

```
case Fish f:
```

Here, we have the data type `Fish`. We give it a name, `f`, in our example. Now `f` is a local variable that's scoped to the `case` block. When we match the case of `Fish`, we should move like a fish. Therefore, on the next line, we'll say this:

```
f.Move();
```

Once we've matched `Fish` and moved, we need to escape from the case. So on the next line, type the following:

```
break;
```

It wasn't possible before to have an object used in a `switch` statement, so we're breaking new ground here.

We created two objects earlier, so let's start a new line and add the other possibility to the `switch` block:

```
case Human h:
    h.Move();
    break;
```

That's exactly the same code we used for our `Fish` object. We've just switched our `Human` object and created a new local variable, namely `h`. So, `h.Move` will call the `Move` method for human beings. And, `f.Move` will call the `Move` method for a fish. As I said, it wasn't possible before to take and switch an object.

# Running the program

Let's go ahead and run this. Go to **Debug > Start Without Debugging** or use *Ctrl + F5*. You should see the following:

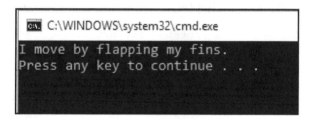

Figure 5.2: The Debug screen

It should say `I move by flapping my fins.`, which is correct. Now, let's head back to our code and change it so that we create a `Human` object, rather than `Fish`. The changed line should read as follows:

```
Movable movableObject = new Human();
```

All we've done here is replace Fish with Human; we're creating a different type of object. Let's go ahead and run this new code. Go to **Debug > Start Without Debugging** and you should see the following:

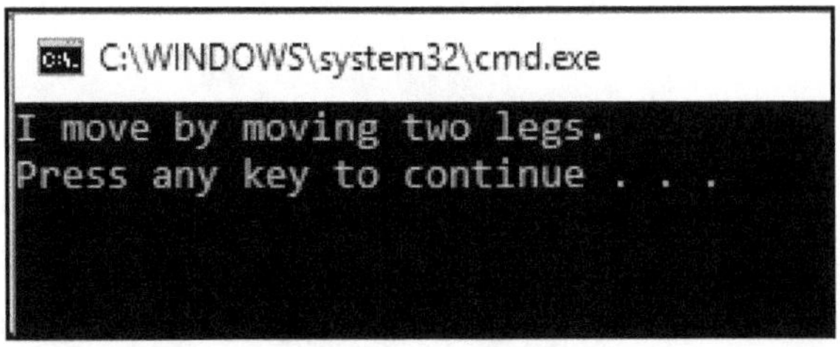

Figure 5.3: The Debug screen

The preceding example uses polymorphism because human and fish are treated as Movable objects, and when the Move method is called on each one, the correct, derived class version of Move is invoked.

Here's the complete code from this chapter:

```csharp
using static System.Console; //needed for WriteLine
interface Movable
{
    void Move(); //this method has to be implemented by classes that implement the
    //interface Movable
}
class Human : Movable //Human is a type of movable object
{
    public void Move()
    {
        WriteLine("I move by moving two legs.");
    }
}
class Fish:Movable //Fish is also a kind of movable object
{
    public void Move()
    {
        WriteLine("I move by flapping my fins.");
    }
}
class Program
{
    static void Main()
    {
        Movable movableObject = new Human();
```

```
switch(movableObject)
{
    case Fish f: //case label is Fish, f is a local variable
        f.Move();
        break;
    case Human h: //case label for a Human type of object, h is a
local
    //variable
        h.Move();
        break;
}
```

# Summary

This chapter has illustrated the new power of switch blocks in C# 7. You can now pass in a whole object unlike before. In the next chapter, we'll look at a handy data structure called tuples, and the new features that C# 7 brings to them.

# 56

# Tuples in C# 7.0

In this chapter, we are going to learn about something called tuples. A simple definition of a tuple is as follows: it is a way of grouping items together. How is it useful? Well, with C# 7.0, what we can do is essentially return multiple values from a function call. Let's take a look.

## Creating the tuple function

Start a new Visual C# console app and simplify the template back to our standard opening code:

```
using static System.Console;

class Program
{
    static void Main()
    {

    }
}
```

Create a new function that will return a tuple. Underneath the opening curly brace of our Program class, type the following:

```
static (double sum, double average) Summarize(double[] arr)
{

}
```

Here, I'm defining the return type of the function, which in this case is a tuple. We're returning two values here and defining each of their data types. That's the unique benefit of tuples: being able to return two values from a single function call. We're calling it `Summarize`, and it will accept an argument called `arr` of type `double array`--so an array of doubles. It's going to return a tuple, which specifically means two values.

With this in place, let's define the body. The body of this function is pretty much the same as the one we used for our `out` keyword example, but we need to do something special here. In order to use tuples, you need to first add the `Tuple` package to your project. In the **Solution Explorer** panel, right-click on **References** and select **Manage NuGet Packages** from the menu that appears:

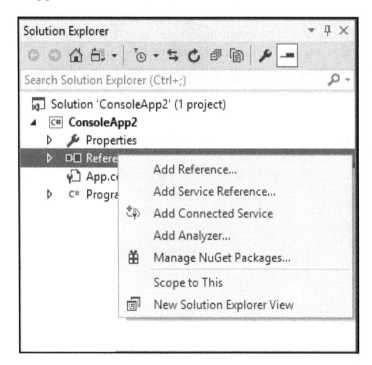

Figure 4.1: Managing Nuget Packages

This will open up the NuGet package manager. From here, click on **Browse** at the top, then in the search box type `valuetuple`. This should narrow down the list, and at the top you should see **System.ValueTuple** provided by Microsoft:

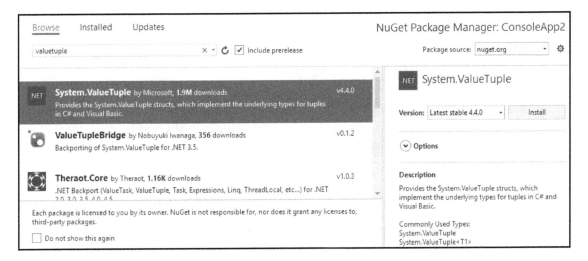

Figure 4.2: The ValueTuple Package

Select it, then on the right-hand side click on **Install** to add it to your project. Accept the agreement that comes up, then you can close the package manager window and return to `Program.cs`.

So how do we make use of this? Well, let's begin at the end so you can see how we can return tuple values. Inside our new `Summarize` function, add the following:

```
return (sum, average);
```

We'll just return those two things at the end of the function instead of one.

Normally, we can return only one value using the `return` keyword, but now we are making a more flexible function using tuples that allows us to return multiple values.

Next, we have to actually create those two values, so how do we go about it? We started at the end of our function so we could see the return values. Let's go back to the beginning to start writing our function in earnest. On a new line underneath the opening curly brace of our function, type the following:

```
double sum = 0, average = 0;
```

Here, we just zero out `average` and `sum` again, exactly as we did in the `out` example. We'll continue with pretty much the same code as before:

```
foreach (var d in arr)
    sum += d;
```

The explanation is the same as before. Grab each value inside the array, then += adds that value to the `sum` variable. Once we have the sum generated, we can find the average. Underneath that, type the following:

```
average = sum / arr.Length;
```

As before, this is the usual definition of an average: the sum of the values divided by the total number of values. That's never been different. Then, at the bottom, we already have our code to return the tuple to the calling code using the `return` syntax with two values.

# Writing the Main() code

How do you make use of this? Well, let's go into the `Main()` code block and type the following:

```
var (sum, average) = Summarize(new double[] { 1, 4, 5, 3, 6 });
```

If you hover over `Summarize` and look at the tooltip, you'll observe that it says **double sum, double average**:

```
var (sum, average) = Summarize(new double[] { 1, 4, 5, 3, 6 });
            (double sum, double average) Program.Summarize(double[] arr)
```

Figure 4.3: Mouse hover tooltip

This confirms that our function is capable of returning two values, not only one value, so it's already more flexible and powerful. We then just send our `Summarize` function a new array containing some random values that we'll use for testing. So, `Summarize` takes an array and finds the sum and average. These values are returned as a tuple, then saved to the `sum`, `average` variable below. After that, they're accessible; you can make use of them. Let's do this now by printing the result. On the next line, type the following:

```
WriteLine($"Sum={sum} \nAverage={average}");
```

As before, we have `using static System.Console` at the top so that we can use `WriteLine`. Of course, this will simply print the values of the sum and average. It speaks for itself really.

# Running the program

With all of this in place, let's give this a go. Click on **Debug > Start Without Debugging** or *Ctrl + F5* key combination. If all goes well, you should see the following result:

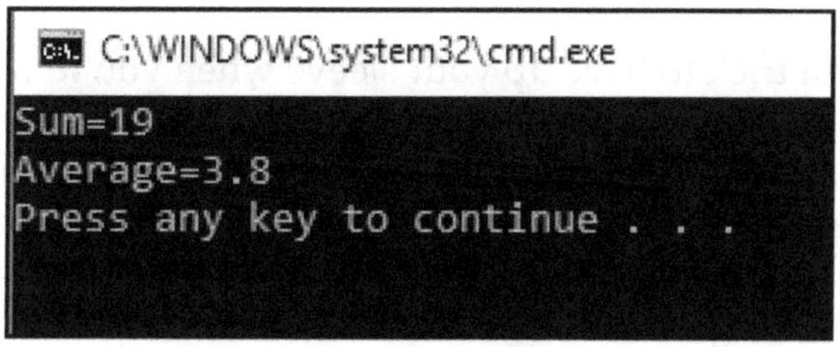

```
C:\WINDOWS\system32\cmd.exe

Sum=19
Average=3.8
Press any key to continue . . .
```

Figure 4.4: The Debug window

Okay, so we have `Sum=19` and `Average=3.8`. It's working as expected, and we returned two values as a tuple.

Here's the final `Default.aspx.cs` code for this chapter:

```
using static System.Console;
//tuple: a way of grouping items together
class Program
{
    static (double sum, double average) Summarize(double[] arr)
    {
        double sum = 0, average = 0; //set to 0 so the sum and averages
        //are not distorted

        foreach (var d in arr) //grab each value in array
            sum += d; //sums up values as loop operates

        average = sum / arr.Length; //sum of values divided by total
        //number of values

        return (sum, average); //return the tuple to the calling code
    }
    static void Main()
    {
        //Summarize takes an array
```

```
//find the sum and average
//those values are returned as a tuple
//then saved to the sum, average below
var (sum, average) = Summarize(new double[] { 1, 4, 5, 3, 6 });
WriteLine($"Sum={sum} \nAverage={average}"); //prints values of
//sum and average
        }
    }
```

# Summary

Tuples are a really useful trick to have up your sleeve when you're working with two linked data points, for example, the first name and the last name or some other piece of information about a person. I like the example that we used int his chapter because, to me, sum and average are two important characteristics of a set of data. That's the basics of tuples covered; we'll take a more detailed look at them in the final chapter of the book. First, though, let's switch to looking at local functions, and see what's new for them in C# 7.

# 57

# Local functions in C# 7.0

In this chapter, we are going to take a look at how to use local functions in C# 7.0.

## Creating the application and core functions

First of all, open a blank console project and begin with the standard starting template. So type the following:

```
using static System.Console;
class Program
{
    static void Main()
    {

    }
}
```

Here, we've created our entry point to the program. What we are going to do is create a function that compares two values. So below the closing curly brace of our `Main` function, type the following:

```
private static double FindBiggestValue(double x, double y, double z)
{

}
```

Remember that `private` means that it is accessible only from here, and `static` means you can call it directly by writing its name. Next, let's pass the three values we're going to compare to our new function.

# Creating the local function

There are a variety of approaches you can take to do this. In this case, on a new line within our new function, type the following:

```
double c = CompareFirstTwo(x, y);
```

Here, we are creating a variable by calling a new function, so let's go ahead and create this function. Start a new line underneath the preceding statement and type the following:

```
double CompareFirstTwo(double a, double b)
{

}
```

With this, we've created a local function inside `FindBiggestValue`. The use of our `CompareFirstTwo` function is highly restricted to finding the biggest value. It doesn't really serve much of a purpose outside that, which is why I'm using it as a local function. Inside our new local function, type the following:

```
return (a > b) ? a : b;
```

So, we are using the ternary operator to compare the two values. If a is greater than b, return a. Otherwise, return b. If you want to, of course, you could actually just have a sequence of these ternary operators inside the main `FindBiggestValue` function, but `CompareFirstTwo` to me is a good name that speaks for itself. That's why I have it inside this local function. `CompareFirstTwo` compares the values of a and b, which are equivalent to the values of x and y. So what this will do essentially is feed three values into `FindBiggestValue`: x, y, and z. You're going to compare x and y using the local function `CompareFirstTwo`. This local function is going to give you back the value of c.

The final thing that we need to do in our function is compare our last value, z, with the result of our local function, that is, c. Create a new line underneath the closing curly brace of our `CompareFirstTwo` function and type the following:

```
return (z > c) ? z : c;
```

This is the ternary operator again, performing exactly the same job as before, but comparing two different values.

The subject of this chapter is local functions, and that's what we have with `CompareFirstTwo`. It is restricted to being used within `FindBiggestValue`. You wouldn't necessarily use it outside this function because it wouldn't have any purpose. That's why I've created it as a local function.

# Running the code

How do you make use of the local function? Let's add a line to our `Main` function. Type the following:

```
WriteLine(FindBiggestValue(10, 5, 6));
```

According to the code we've created, the preceding code should return the biggest value, which is 10 here. Let's go ahead and check that. Go to **Debug > Start without debugging**. You should see the following:

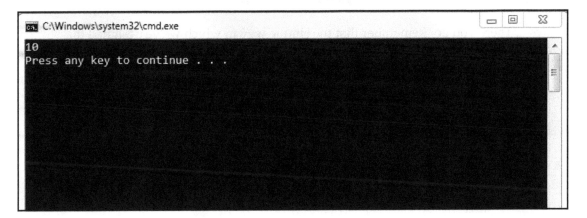

Figure 7.1: The Debug for the Biggest value function

As you can see, 10 really is the biggest value. That's good. Just to test it, let's change those values to 1, 6, and -3. It should return 6. Let's take a look at the result. Go to **Debug > Start Without Debugging**:

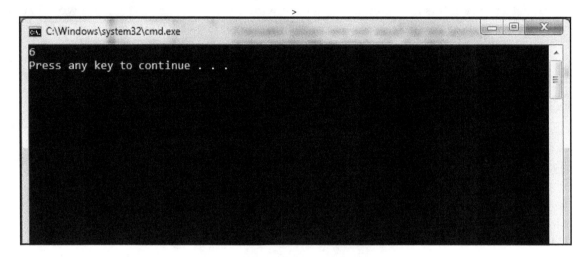

Figure 7.2: Reiterating the Debug process

It says 6. There you go. Remember that the simple way in which we've designed this assumes that the values you're entering here are not equal to one another. If you want to try and alter it so that it could detect equal values, go ahead.

Here's the complete code for this chapter:

```
using static System.Console;
class Program
{
    static void Main()//entry point into program
    {
        //assumes values are not equal to one another
        WriteLine(FindBiggestValue(1, 6, -3));
    }
    private static double FindBiggestValue(double x, double y, double
    z)
    {
        double c = CompareFirstTwo(x, y);

        double CompareFirstTwo(double a, double b)
        {
            //if a is bigger than be, return a
            //if a is not bigger than b, return b
```

```
            return (a > b) ? a : b;
        }
        //line below returns the bigger of z and c
        return (z > c) ? z : c;
    }
}
```

# Summary

Okay, that wraps up our example of using local functions in C# 7, and I hope you've seen how useful they can be. In the next chapter, we'll look at the new abilities that C# 7 has brought to throwing exceptions, and how you can manage them from different parts of your code.

# 58
# Throwing Exceptions in C# 7.0

In this chapter, we are going to learn how to throw exceptions from different parts of our code.

## Creating the main code

Start with a blank C# console app, and on the first line type the following:

```
using System;
```

We need this for exceptions. Remember, exceptions are usually predictable error situations that can occur in your code, and you should be able to handle them. That's why, for example, the .NET framework that Microsoft has created contains a collection of libraries or classes to handle various types of predictable errors well.

We'll begin by creating our standard program entry point; for this, type the following:

```
class Program
{
    static void Main()
    {

    }
}
```

What we are going to do is read two values and try to divide them. So, inside our `Main` function block, type the following:

```
double x = 5, y = 0;
```

These are the values we will try to divide, and we'll do it in this order: $x/y$. So, you can probably see what kind of error we're going to experience. Underneath this, we'll set up our `try`/`catch` block:

```
try
{
}
catch()
{
}
```

# Throwing an exception

We're going to try to divide by zero, but this might generate errors because division by zero is not allowed. Within the `try` block, type the following:

```
var result = (y != 0) ? $"{x / y}" : throw new DivideByZeroException();
```

What is this saying? Well, we're saying if `y` does not equal `0`, then you can do the division. Then, the division is perfectly legitimate. So we have `?` and `$` for string interpolation. After this, within curly braces, we do the division. Remember, this is a logical condition: if `y` does not equal `0`, then this chunk of code runs. The result of this is a string that is stored in the `result` variable. However, if `y` is equal to `0`, then we will use the new `DivideByZeroException` class and terminate the block.

If you're going to throw an exception, then you need to catch it somewhere. First, though, let's quickly add a line that will print the result of our formula if it doesn't contain a zero. On the next line, type the following:

```
Console.WriteLine(result);
```

Nothing special here. We're simply using `WriteLine` to log our `result` variable to the console window.

# Catching an exception

Okay, let's catch the exception! Change the first line of our `catch` block to the following:

```
catch(DivideByZeroException ex)
```

Remember that `DivideByZeroException` is a class, and here we are creating an object from this class, called `ex`. This is the usual name for an exception object. This object carries information, so let's take a look at how we can access it. Within the `catch` block, type the following:

```
Console.WriteLine(ex.Message + "\n" + ex.StackTrace);
```

Here, we're using `WriteLine` to print our error message to the screen; then, on a new line, we're printing `StackTrace`. The good thing about these kinds of errors is that `ex` is an object of the type `DivideByZeroException`, and it carries this useful information. So, `Message` contains the type of error that has occurred, and `StackTrace` enables you to look at what the source of the error is, among other things.

# Running the program

So the coding is done; let's give it a build. Go to **Build** | **Build Solution** or use the *Ctrl+Shift+B* key combo and then select **Debug** | **Start Without Debugging**. You should see the following screen:

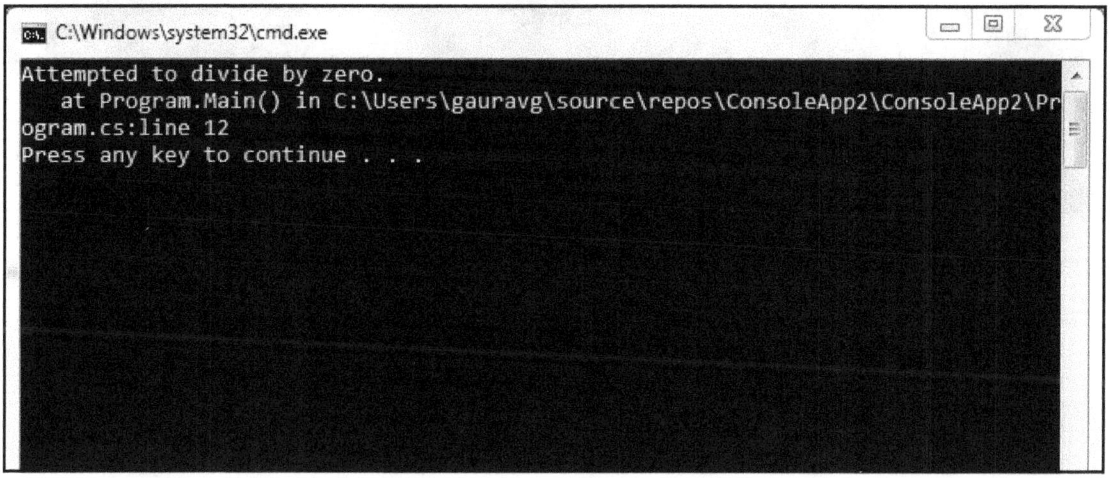

Figure 8.1: Debugging the program entered

It says `Attempted to divide by zero`, which is our message. The next line says
`Program.Main()` was the source of the error. This is our `StackTrace` method. It also gives
you the file it happened in and the line number. So, line 11 was where the error occurred. If
you close this window and look at your code, you'll see that the line it's referring to is our
`var result` line within our `try` block. That's where the exception was thrown from, so
that's correct. Note that I have some extra comments in my code, so your line number might
be slightly different. It should point to the same code, though.

Just as a test, let's change our `y` value to something else, say `5.3`:

```
double x = 5, y = 5.3;
```

Now if you run this with **Debug | Start Without Debugging**, it just gives you the result of
the division as it should:

Figure 8.2: Debugging the program again.

It's not a round number or anything, but it worked, so that's good.

For review, a complete version of the code file for this chapter is displayed in the following
code block:

```csharp
using System; //needed for exceptions
class Program
{
    static void Main()
    {
        double x = 5, y = 0; //these are the values we will try to
        //divide: x/y
        try
        {
            //if y is not zero, do x/y and save to result variable
```

```
        //if y is zero, throw the new divide by zero exception
        var result = (y != 0) ? $"{x / y}" : throw new
        DivideByZeroException();
        Console.WriteLine(result); //displays result of division
    }
    catch(DivideByZeroException ex)
    {
        //displays message when y=0 or the division is not
        //successful
        Console.WriteLine(ex.Message + "\n" + ex.StackTrace);
    }
  }
}
```

# Summary

In C# 7, they've expanded the range of places that you can throw errors from, and the types of errors with useful objects like this one that you can catch. If you were to open this code inside of an older version of Visual Studio, then it wouldn't build at all. So this is a great new feature to have. In the next, and final, chapter of the book we'll return to tuples and take a deeper dive into how they work and some more advanced things you can do with them.

# 59

# Tuples in C# 7.0, Part 2

In this chapter, we are going to take a more detailed look at tuples. We are going to use tuples in a few different ways so that you really get the hang of using them.

## Creating the constructor

Let's begin by creating a new C# console app and removing all of the template code within it. We'll then type:

```
using static System.Console;
```

Nothing special there, just our usual code to enable us to use `WriteLine` without a prefix. Then, on the next line, type:

```
public class Troll
{
}
```

We are going to make a Troll class, so this is a template for stamping out individual troll objects. Between the curly braces, type:

```
private (string firstname, string lastName, int? age) fullNameAge;
```

Remember that fields, or instance variables, are usually declared private so they cannot be modified directly by code from other programs, for example. Now we are going to make use of a tuple in the declaration, so we'll enclose the body of the tuple between brackets. We have two basic strings, `firstName` and `lastName`. This is followed by an integer called `age`. Notice that we have a `?` after `int`, which indicates that the field is nullable. In other words, a value does not have to be specified.

Note that if you try nullable with a `string` datatype you'll get an error. It'll say that the type string must be a non nullable value. So, it's not allowed. Integers are fine, though.

We then provide the name of our tuple, which is `fullNameAge`. In other words, instead of writing out each of these as individual items, we are making this into a tuple, you see? They're being taken together as a unit essentially and the whole unit is named `fullNameAge`. So here we understand that this is a tuple.

If you're getting error messages when you define your tuple, then what you want to do is this: Right-click on **References** in your **Solution Explorer** and then go to **Manage NuGet Packages**:

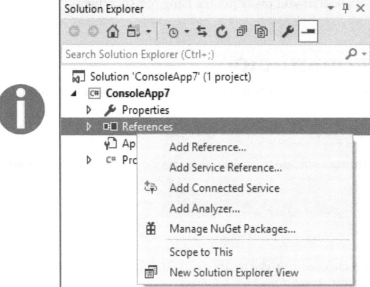

Click on **Browse** in the window that opens, and then type `valuetuple` into the search box. The first result in the list should be **System.ValueTuple**, by Microsoft:

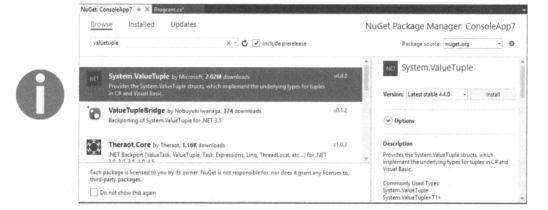

Select that top value, and then click on **Install** on the right. Once that's done, you can close the NuGet window and return to Program.cs.

We now have a tuple to represent a `Troll` object like that. Now that we have that in place, we can start to use it. Type the following on the next line:

```
public Troll((string, string, int?) firstLastAge)
{
}
```

This here is a sequence of data types and these data types correspond to the ones above it in our tuple. Note that we don't have to specify names for each of those values. It also isn't strictly necessary to add the `?` signifying that our `int` is nullable, but I added it there as a reminder. The important thing is that we specify the datatypes and the name. Within those curly braces for `firstLastAge`, type the following:

```
fullNameAge = firstLastAge;
```

This sets the value of the tuple. Remember, in this particular case you can imagine this `fullNameAge` tuple to be the instance variable. So, each `Troll` object that you make will possess a `firstName`, a `lastName`, and an `age`, and the name of that tuple is `fullNameAge`. So the constructor, which is the `firstLastAge` code that we've just been typing, sets the value of the tuple. With that in place, let's take a look at a couple of properties.

# Setting the properties

On a new line below the closing curly brace of our constructor, type the following:

```
public (string, string, int?) FullNameAge
{

}
```

This is a property and it's publicly accessible anywhere, and notice that again it gives back a tuple. So, we have the datatypes and the name of the property. Now let's go ahead and add some code within our new property:

```
get => fullNameAge;
```

So, this simply gets the value of the tuple back to the calling code. Remember that the `=>` means that this is an expression bodied member. It's the same as in a lambda expression, if you've used those before. Okay, next, what if you want to set the value of the tuple again using the property? You can type the following on the next line:

```
set => fullNameAge = value;
```

Notice that we're using exactly the same expression bodied member syntax here. This line sets the value of the tuple for each troll object, so in other words it's going to set the `firstName`, the `lastName` and the `age` all in one go. That's why I like these things, because before you would have to obviously have individual items. Now you can just set them all in one line, so you can write more compact and efficient code.

Let us do one more thing. What if you want to get at the individual components of a tuple? One thing that you can do is this. We'll create a new property under the previous one, and type the following:

```
public int Age
{
    set => fullNameAge.age = value;
}
```

So, this is a property that sets only the `age` component of the tuple.

# Writing the Main function

Okay, with all of that in place, we can start to make use of this code. Right at the bottom, underneath the closing brace of the Troll class, let's add in our standard main program code:

```
class Program
{
    static void Main()
    {

    }
}
```

With that done, let's dive straight into the Main code block and create a new `Troll` object. Type the following:

```
Troll tr = newTroll(("Bob", "Jones", 45));
```

Notice that we have the nested brackets here because we're specifying a tuple. If you wanted to, you could more specifically call it a triple because it has three entries, but in general we call these things tuples. So, it could be one or two or three or four values, however many you need. So how do you make use of all of this code that we have created? Well one thing that you can do is this. On the next line, type the following:

```
WriteLine(tr.FullNameAge);
```

Note that as you type, IntelliSense shows all the features that are available for `Troll` objects:

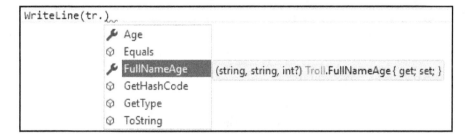

One of them is `FullNameAge`, which holds the value of that property. So, we're going to write the value of that property to the screen. Let's run the code and see what happens when we do that.

# Running the code

Go to **Debug >Start Without Debugging**, or *Ctrl+F5*. Give it a second to load, and you should see the following:

It says Bob, Jones, 45. So that is a triple. It's three items. Note also that our reported value includes the parentheses around the three items.

Alright, what if you want to change something? Well, let's take a look. On the next line, type:

```
tr.FullNameAge = ("Bobby", tr.FullNameAge.Item2, null);
```

There are a lot of things going on here. We're setting all of the `FullNameAge` property values of our `Troll` object at once. Firstly, we're changing the first name to "Bobby". That's simple enough. Next, we want to keep the same last name as our original object. One way of doing that is as we've done here, using the `Item` values within the property. So, `Item1` corresponds to the first name, `Item2` to the last name, `Item3` to the age, and so on if we had more items in our tuple. Lastly, let's say we don't know what this troll's age is, so we can set the third value to just be `null`. Remember, we can do that because up in the class definition we have `int?`. If you were to remove that `?` then you'd see all kinds of errors pop up. Okay, on the next line, let's just print everything again. You can just copy and paste our line from earlier:

```
WriteLine(tr.FullNameAge);
```

Now, run the program with **Debug> Start Without Debugging**, or *Ctrl+F5*, and you should see the following:

Bobby, Jones, and then nothing. That's good, that's exactly what we wanted to see. Now, what if you wanted to get just the age and change it? Let's take a look at how to do that. Back to the code, and on the next couple of lines, type:

```
tr.Age = 56;
WriteLine(tr.FullNameAge);
```

Remember that earlier on, we created a property named Age with the explicit purpose of setting the value of only the age component of the tuple. Using that value keyword, which is a built-in feature of properties in C#, we can very easily give our property a new value. We then copy and paste the same WriteLine command, and if you run that again, you should see the following:

And there we go, it says Bobby Jones and the age of 56 has been updated, so it's working. Close that. You've now seen how to work with tuples in more detail.

Here's the full code for this chapter:

```
using static System.Console; //needed for WriteLine
public class Troll
{
    //tuple to represent a troll object
    private (string firstname, string lastName, int? age) fullNameAge;
    public Troll((string, string, int?) firstLastAge)
    {
```

```
            fullNameAge = firstLastAge; //this sets the value of the tuple
    }
    public (string, string, int?) FullNameAge
    {
        get => fullNameAge; //gets value of tuple back to calling code
        set => fullNameAge = value; //sets value of tuple for each troll
object
    }
    public int Age
    {
        set => fullNameAge.age = value; //sets only the age component of
the tuple
    }
}
class Program
{
    static void Main()
    {
        Troll tr = new Troll(("Bob", "Jones", 45)); //make sure this line
has the
        //tuple
        WriteLine(tr.FullNameAge); //write value of property to screen
        //change the first name, it's going to keep the last name using
Item2
        //age will be set to nothing using the null keyword
        tr.FullNameAge = ("Bobby", tr.FullNameAge.Item2, null);
        WriteLine(tr.FullNameAge); //write value of property to screen
        tr.Age = 56;
        WriteLine(tr.FullNameAge);
    }
}
```

# Summary

Congratulations for reaching the end of the book. We've taken a close look at some of the core features available in Visual Studio and C# 7.0, and also some of the new improvements that Microsoft have introduced. You should be able to use this knowledge to create simple applications, and it will be a strong foundation to build more complex applications upon. You can also use this book as a reference to easily flip back and practice any of the individual elements that you need a reminder on.

# Index

# W

www.ingramcontent.com/pod-product-compliance
Lightning Source LLC
Chambersburg PA
CBHW060637060326
40690CB00020B/4426